FLIGHTPATH

The International Journal of Commercial Aviation

AIRtime Publishing

United Kingdom • United States of America

FLIGHTPATH
The International Journal of Commercial Aviation

Published quarterly by AIRtime Publishing Inc.
UK office: CAB International Centre, Nosworthy Way, Wallingford, Oxfordshire, OX10 8DE
US office: 120 East Avenue, Norwalk, CT 06851

Softbound Edition ISSN 1740-3979 / ISBN 1-880588-65-X
Hardcover Deluxe Casebound Edition ISBN 1-880588-66-8

Publisher
Mel Williams

Editor
Daniel J. March e-mail: airpower@btinternet.com

Deputy Editor
John Heathcott

Sub Editor
Karen Leverington

Editorial Director
David Donald

Russia/CIS Desk
Piotr Butowski, Zaur Eylanbekov e-mail: zaur@airtimepublishing.com

Europe and Rest of World Desk
Jon Lake, Mike Stroud

Correspondents
Argentina: Santiago Rivas
Australia: Nigel Pittaway
Balkans: Vlatko Ilievski, Igor Salinger
Brazil: Claudio Lucchesi
Bulgaria: Alexander Mladenov
Canada: Terry Panapolis
Chile: Alvaro Romero
France: Henri-Pierre Grolleau
Israel: Shlomo Aloni
Japan: Yoshitomo Aoki
Netherlands: Michel van Der Vourt
Peru: Lewis Mejia Prada
Romania: Danut Vlad
Spain: Salvador Mafé Huertas
Switzerland: Moritz Herrmann
Uruguay: Gabriel Llado

Artists
Mike Badrocke, Chris Davey, Zaur Eylanbekov, John Weal

Designer
Zaur Eylanbekov

Controller
Linda DeAngelis

Origination by Chroma Graphics, Singapore
Printed in Singapore by KHL Printing

Flightpath is published quarterly in two editions (Softbound and Deluxe Casebound) and is available by subscription or as single volumes. Please see details opposite.

Acknowledgments
We wish to thank the following for their kind help with the preparation of this issue:

Hayden Biggs, DNRE
David Charlton
Leszek Chorewski, LOT Polish Airlines
Debbie Heathers, Boeing Company
Dennis Hubbard, Ericson Air-crane
Mike Vines
San Francisco Airport Museum

The editors welcome photographs for possible publication but can accept no responsibility for loss or damage to unsolicited material.

Subscriptions & Back Volumes

Readers in the UK & Europe please write to:
AIRtime Publishing, RAFBFE, P.O. Box 1940,
RAF Fairford, Gloucestershire GL7 4NA, England
Tel +44 (0)1285 713456 • Fax +44 (0)1285 713999

Readers in the USA, Canada, Central/South America and the rest of the world please write to:
AIRtime Publishing, P.O. Box 5074, Westport, CT 06881, USA
Tel (203) 838-7979 • Fax (203) 838-7344
Toll free 1 800 359-3003
e-mail: airpower@airtimepublishing.com

One-year subscription rates (4 quarterly volumes), inclusive of shipping & handling/postage and packing:

Softbound Edition
UK £48, USA $59.95, Europe EUR 88, Canada Cdn $99,
Rest of World US $79 (surface) or US $99 (air)

Deluxe Casebound Edition
UK £68, USA $79.95, Europe EUR 120, Canada Cdn $132,
Rest of World US $99 (surface) or US $119 (air)

Two-year subscription rates (8 quarterly volumes), inclusive of shipping & handling/postage and packing:

Softbound Edition
UK £92, USA $112, Europe EUR 169, Canada Cdn $187,
Rest of World US $148 (surface) or US $188 (air)

Deluxe Casebound Edition
UK £130, USA $149, Europe EUR 232, Canada Cdn $246,
Rest of World US $187 (surface) or US $227 (air)

Single-volume/Back Volume Rates by Mail:

Softbound Edition
UK £10.95, US $16, Europe EUR 18.50, Cdn $25.50 (plus s&h/p&p)

Deluxe Casebound Edition
UK £13.50, US $20, Europe EUR 22, Cdn $31 (plus s&h/p&p)

All prices are subject to change without notice.
Canadian residents please add GST. Connecticut residents please add sales tax.

Shipping and handling (postage and packing) rates for back volume/non-subscription orders are as follows:

	USA	*UK*	*Europe*	*Canada*	*ROW (surface)*	*ROW (air)*
1 item	$4.50	£4	EUR 8	Cdn $7.50	US $8	US $16
2 items	$6.50	£6	EUR 11.50	Cdn $11	US $12	US $27
3 items	$8.50	£8	EUR 14.50	Cdn $14	US $16	US $36
4 items	$10	£10	EUR 17.50	Cdn $16.50	US $19	US $46
5 items	$11.50	£12	EUR 20.50	Cdn $19	US $23	US $52
6 or more	$13	£13	EUR 23.50	Cdn $21.50	US $25	US $59

Volume One
Summer 2003

CONTENTS

Major Features planned for Volume Two

Classic Airliner: Boeing 777, **Airline Focus:** Braniff International, **Variant File:** Dassault Falcon family, **Regional Airline Fleets:** Australia's airlines, **Airport Profile:** Amsterdam-Schiphol, **Type Analysis:** Bristol Britannia, **Special Operations:** BETA Air Cargo, **Air Transport Intelligence:** Airbus A380, **Technical Debrief:** TCAS

First flight of 777-300ER

On 24 February 2003 Boeing's latest incarnation of its successful 777 widebody twin-jet family took to the air for the first time from Paine Field, Everett, Washington, for an event-free three-hour flight to Boeing Field Seattle, Wash., in the hands of Capts Frank Santoni and John Cashman. In a pre-planned back and forth pattern between Port Angeles, Wash., and Astoria, Oregon, the aircraft reached 15,270 ft (4654 m) and a speed of Mach 0.5. Testing of the stickshaker (without entering a stall), extension/retraction of the landing gear using both electrical and hydraulic systems, and engine relight procedures were carried out.

The pilots remarked on the obvious increase in power from the aircraft's 115,000-lb (511.7-kN) General Electric GE90-115B engines, which were derated by 10 per cent for this first flight, due to the low take-off weight for the maiden flight. Onboard, the aircraft was loaded with empty water barrels for future centre-of-gravity load-shift tests, which also have a secondary use as heat sinks for the surplus electric power generated by the engines that will be utilised by inflight entertainment systems and cabin lighting on in-service aircraft.

This first test aircraft has been allocated the identity WD-501 and will be heavily involved in the 1,600-hour flight test programme, which is expected to conclude with full FAA certification in early 2004. The test programme will include at least one extended range flight with a duration of some 19 hours. The second and final test aircraft (WD-502) made its maiden flight on 6 April 2003 and will be used for engine, systems, noise pollution, stability and control testing.

WD-501 is finished in Boeing's new corporate livery with the familiar model number displayed on the tail fin (above). The aircraft is powered by the world's most powerful aircraft engine – the GE90-115B – which incorporates a 128.2-in (325.6-cm) diameter fan, the scale of which is evident (right). Launch company ILFC and its customer Air France are due to receive their first example in April 2004.

Industry Update

North American airline crisis

Following a sustained period of falling revenues and mounting costs, the US airline industry suffered further economic set-backs following the launch of Operation Iraqi Freedom and the outbreak of the SARS virus, the latter particularly affecting flights to and from Asia. This, combined with an envisaged increased threat of global terrorism, has reduced demand for seats by as much as 25 per cent. On 9 December 2002 troubled US carrier United Airlines filed for bankruptcy in a US court, after attempts to secure an emergency loan from the US government fell through. The world's second largest carrier had faced severe financial problems that commenced following the downturn passenger numbers in the wake of the 11 September 2001 terrorist attack in the USA. Under Chapter 11 of the US Bankruptcy Code the airline will be able to continue operations while a restructuring plan is put into place. Having already enforced some 20,000 redundancies, the company is likely to programme further job cuts, along with across-the-board pay cuts. In addition, flight frequencies will be altered and unprofitable routes dropped. United chairman Glenn F. Tilton has indicated that the airline could remain under Chaper 11 protection for at least 18 months. Following United Airlines into Chapter 11 bankruptcy protection on 21 March 2003 was Hawaiian Airlines, which had been unable to renegotiate the terms of its leasing contracts to reduce costs.

US giant American Airlines has concluded deals with its three major unions, helping to ease its mounting overheads by introducing pay cuts and productivity improvements, which are envisioned to provide an additional $1.8 billion annually. In addition, international flights have been cut by 6 per cent, with further cuts likely. Management is hoping that these measures will ensure that the airline completes a restructuring process outside of Chapter 11 protection.

Northwest Airlines reduced its workforce by 4,900 in March 2003 along with a 12 per cent reduction in operations, and Continental Airlines has also cut 1,200 jobs and reduced the frequency of flights to London-Gatwick from its Houston, Newark and Cleveland hubs, in a measure estimated to save $500 million. However, both airlines hope to benefit from the newly-sanctioned addition of Delta Air Lines to the Northwest-Continental code-share agreement.

Dwindling cash reserves by March 2003 forced Air Canada into a major 18-month restructuring programme, under the protection of the Canadian bankruptcy court. Less than a year after being declared North America's most profitable hub-and-spoke operator, airline management has blamed falling seat-demand, skyrocketing fuel prices, the war in Iraq and the outbreak of SARS for its predicament. To emerge from bankruptcy the company states it needs to reduce labour costs by $440 million per year, and intends to cut management staff by 20 per cent and union-affiliated staff by 10 per cent, as well as a fleet restructuring which will withdraw some models, to be replaced by an increasing number of 50- and 90-seat regional jets.The bankruptcy filing also includes Air Canada's low-cost Jazz and Zip Air subsidiaries.

In better news, a smaller and more focused US Airways emerged from Chapter 11 protection on 31 March 2003, as predicted by the airline, following 80.8 per cent of claim holders approving the restructuring plan. It had filed for bankruptcy in August 2002.

VIP A380 plan

Lufthansa Technik is working on plans to convert A380s to VIP configuration, as Airbus weighs up the market potential of such a variant. Currently there are over 20 VIP Boeing 747s in service, dominating the ultra-large VIP market. An A380 version could gain valuable replacement orders as well as attracting lease companies.

Antonov's dream

The world's largest aircraft, the Antonov An-225 Mriya (Dream) entered commercial service in December 2002, on behalf of freight company Chapman Freeborn. Making its maiden flight in December 1988, the six-engined An-225 was originally designed for carrying outsize loads for the Soviet government, and in particular the Soviet space programme – including the Buran space shuttle. The aircraft was largely unused for the majority of the 1990s before refurbishment for use in the commercial sector.

Bombardier's Global 5000 business jet completed its first flight from the Downsview, Ontario, facility on 7 March 2003. During the 3-hour 44-min flight the aircraft reached an indicated airspeed of 340 kt (391 mph; 630 km/h) and a height of 45,000 ft (13716 m).

Modifications included an improved ramp and hydraulic system and an increase in maximum take-off weight from 600 tons to 640 tons. With demand for outsize load-carrying aircraft at an all-time high it is likely that the An-225 will not be short of contracts. If sufficient business is garnered, Antonov may consider completing the second An-225.

Boeing 7E7

Following the demise of Boeing's Sonic Cruiser, the company has announced initial details of its replacement – the Boeing 7E7 – the 'E' presumably standing for 'efficient'. As the 10th new airliner in Boeing history, the eight-abreast widebody is of much more conventional design than the radical Sonic Cruiser, although Boeing maintains that the aircraft will incorporate much of the advanced technology and construction techniques that had been under development. The aircraft was devised following in-depth talks with major airlines, concluding that they are more interested in efficiency than speed. Boeing is considering optional outer wing sections for the 200/250-seat aircraft as a way of satisfying both mid- and long-range markets. Whether Boeing opts for a single-engine provider, as is the strategy for the 777-300ER, has yet to be decided, but the 7E7 must succeed if Boeing is to retain credibility after its failed 747X and Sonic Cruiser concepts.

New markets for BAE

BAE Systems is pushing conversions of its ATP and 146/RJ series of regional aircraft for differing roles. In addition to freighter conversions, both aircraft could be offered as water bomber or pollution control aircraft, and other special mission roles. In addition, the company is examining the possibility of offering a cheaper and more simple freighter conversion of the 146, with cargo to be loaded through the existing passenger doors via trolleys.

777-200LR development

Development of Boeing's 777-200LR (Longer Range) 301-seat variant was resumed in March 2003, and will be marketed as a direct competitor to Airbus's A340-500. Maximum take-off weight has been raised to 766,684 lb (347760 kg), with no structural changes, allowing additional fuel to be carried and increasing the range to a stated 9,170 nm (16983 km). The aircraft will be powered by General Electric GE90-110B turbofans engines. Launch customer is Pakistan International Airlines, with delivery of two examples scheduled for early January 2006. Taiwan's EVA Airways has also ordered three of the variant.

Chinese RJ production

Although China is currently striving to create its own regional jet manufacturing base to produce the proposed ARJ21, in a surprise move Embraer has signed an agreement with Harbin Aircraft Industry to create a full production facility in China. China had earlier blocked a sale of Fairchild Dornier 328JETs to Hainan Airlines by placing a ban on all foreign importation of regional jets. China is seen by both Bombardier and Embraer as a key future market, with airlines likely to procure substantial numbers of both 50-, 70- and 90-seat class regional jets over the next two decades. Seen as an important way in to the market, this is Embraer's first industrial venture outside Brazil. The facility is expected to assemble the entire range of the company's ERJ family dependent on orders from the domestic market.

Antonov An-148 progress report

ANTK, named after O.K. Antonov, is currently working on its An-148 family of twin-engined jet airliners. Intended for the regional market, the aircraft will carry 70-80 passengers on sectors with a high-intensity of daily operations.

The first example is being constructed as a 75-seater with a range of 5100 km (3169 miles), and it is predicted that the aircraft will operate at a cruising speed of 820 km/h (510 mph). Part of the design process involved ensuring that the aircraft was able to operate from "low-strength" concrete airfields with runways as short as 1800 m (5905 ft).

The aircraft is configured with a high-wing layout, incorporating engines mounted on underwing pylons. A powerful auxiliary power unit (APU) will allow the An-148 to operate independently of ground-support equipment. To increase reliability and aid maintenance procedures, an onboard computerised monitoring system will display any faults and the aircraft's general condition.

The An-148 is designed to have modern state-of-the-art equipment, including avionics for bad weather and night operations, and will be certified in accordance with the international rules for noise and emissions. The power will be provided by two Progress/Motor-Sich D436-148 turbofans, with a full engine change able to be accomplished in 2 hours. The manufacturer is targeting a monthly utilisation rate for the aircraft of 300 hours. Currently undergoing construction (below), the first example is planned to be rolled out in late 2003. Concurrent with the test flight programme, production will commence at Kharkov, with first deliveries to airlines slated for late 2005. Following a successful introduction of the initial version, a range of variants is planned including: a 40/55-seater with a range of 6000-7000 km (3728-4350 miles); a VIP 10/30-seater with a range of 8000-10000 km (4971-6214 miles); a combi freight/passenger version; a dedicated cargo variant with a outsize cargo door; a dedicated cargo variant with a rear loading ramp; and a medevac-configured version.

IHI joins GP7200 team

Ishikawajima-Harima Industries (IHI) has been accepted as a team member in the General Electric/Pratt & Whitney Alliance GP7200 engine programme, currently under development for the Airbus A380. The Alliance is competing with Rolls-Royce's Trent 900 series engine, which achieved its first test run in March 2003. Both companies have already notched up notable orders.

UK airport defence

For a period of several days, commencing on 11 February 2002, the British government deployed army units and light armour in and around London-Heathrow airport in response to a "credible terrorist threat". An RAF Nimrod was also utilised during the operation for surveillance purposes.

Embraer 170 testing

Between 27 January and 10 February 2003 Embraer successfully completed the 'extreme cold winter environment' tests of its new ERJ-170 regional jet. The fifth pre-series aircraft (s/n 0005) was submitted to temperatures as low as -23.8°F (-31°C) in both ground cold soak and in-flight tests. The aircraft performed a total of 21 cycles in 44 flight hours, including overnight idle periods of a minimum of eight hours.

Sukhoi wins RRJ tender

The Sukhoi-led Russian Regional Jet (RRJ) consortium, including Boeing, Ilyushin and Yakovlev, was in March 2003 selected to develop Russia's next generation regional jet by Russia's state aerospace agency Rosaviakosmos, beating the rival Tupolev Tu-414 design. The RRJ partners plan to develop three variants configured for 55, 75 and 95 seats. Development costs will be offset by state funding of 1.5 billion roubles between 2006 and 2015. The Siberian-based Novosibirsk Aircraft Production Organisation has been selected as the main production facility, with series production commencing in 2006 followed by first deliveries in 2007.

HUDs for Airbus

Airbus is to offer head-up displays (HUDs) as a standard option across its product range, and current operators will be able to retrofit their aircraft with the system. Thales has been selected as the preferred supplier and Airbus will certify the system on each model as part of the aircraft's type certificate.

MA60 gets new avionics

Xian Aircraft of China is to offer its MA60 turboprop (based on the earlier Y-7 modified version of the Antonov An-24) with improved Rockwell Collins Pro Line 21 cockpit avionics. Five of the 15 aircraft ordered by civilian operators are currently in revenue service.

'Quiet' Tu-154M

NPO Saturn has developed a new hushkit for the Tupolev Tu-154M which will comply with the new 'Chapter 3 minus 5db' rule that some European airports are planning to introduce in late 2003. The kit, comprising a new combustion chamber, will cost around $15,000 per engine.

CRJ700/900 common wing

Bombardier has elected to produce the CRJ700 with the CRJ900 wing from the 120th aircraft onwards, to reduce the lead time and increase commonality between the 70-seat and 86-seat family members. The current differences are confined to different skin, spar and wing plank thicknesses, and wing-fuselage attachments.

PROCUREMENT AND DELIVERIES

NORTH AMERICA

Jet Blue converts options

Expanding New York-based low-fare airline Jet Blue has announced a contract converting two A320 options into firm orders. The airline is now in the top 10 largest A320 operators worldwide, with a total of 78 on order, of which 52 will be in service by late 2003. Both Boeing's and Airbus's order books have been rescued in the last 12 months by orders from the expanding low-cost sector, balancing the falling demand from traditional carriers.

Freighters for Northwest?

Northwest Airlines is in consultation with Boeing over the possibility of becoming the launch customer for the Boeing 747-400 Special Freighter (SF) conversion. The aircraft will join the Boeing 747-200 and 747-300 Special Freighter conversion programmes, which allows operators to convert passenger or combi aircraft to full freighter configuration.

Fresh hope for 717

Boeing is hoping that the introduction into service of Midwest Airlines' first Boeing 717-200s in March 2003 will provide fresh impetus in the drive to improve the aircraft's sales performance. The first example was handed over to the airline on 28 February, coinciding with the date for a change of name from the previous Midwest Express to Midwest Airlines. Previously a strong supporter of McDonnell Douglas products, Midwest ordered a total of 25 717s to replace 20 ageing DC-9s. The aircraft are configured for 88 passengers in Midwest's signature 2+2 leather seats, and incorporate enhanced-security flight deck doors in compliance with new FAA regulations that commenced on 9 April 2003.

Winglets in Mexico

On 5 March 2003 Boeing and Aeromexico jointed announced an order for 15 Boeing 737-700s equipped with 8-ft (2.44-m) winglets. An option on all current 737s, the winglets are stated to reduce fuel consumption by up to 3.5 per cent and increase range, especially from hot and high airports such as Mexico City. Eleven of the aircraft will be delivered on a sale-leaseback arrangement with Boeing, six of the aircraft coming from Lombard Aviation Capitol and five from ILFC. The remaining four aircraft will be leased directly from ILFC. The first aircraft is planned for delivery in October 2003, beginning the retirement of 15 DC-9s in current service.

EUROPE

Aeroflot fleet upgrade

Further 'westernisation' of Aeroflot Russian Airlines' fleet will occur in 2003 with the acquisition of the first of 18 Airbus A320s from leasing company GECAS. Likely to replace ageing and uneconomical Tu-134s and Tu-154s within the inventory, the first example is due to enter revenue service in September, with six more to follow before the end of 2003. In addition, the airline is also to lease a further Boeing 767-300ER, bringing the fleet up to five examples.

Mixed fortunes for A318

Airbus's A318 programme, the smallest member of the A320 family, which has suffered a number of cancellations of orders and options in 2002, was dealt a further blow as British Airways scrapped plans to purchase 12 examples. The airline replaced the order with 10 Airbus A321s as direct replacements for existing Boeing 757s. Meanwhile, in a reverse situation, LanChile has requested to change its remaining undelivered A320s for A318s. The aircraft, of which up to 10 could be acquired, will be operated by the airline's low-cost subsidiary LanExpress.

Cyprus Airbus swap

The first of two Airbus A330-200s has been delivered to Cyprus Airways form lease company ILFC, to replace the final A310s in service. The aircraft are powered by two Rolls-Royce Trent 772B-60 engines and will seat 295 passengers in a two-class layout. Following the final delivery, the airline will operate an all-Airbus fleet comprising eight A320s, two A319s and two A330s.

Ryanair adds to 'giant' order

Irish low-fare airline Ryanair has broken all records by announcing on 31 January 2003 that it was adding to its mammoth January 2002 order with a signature for 22 additional Boeing 737-800s, along with options on a further 78. This brings the total orders for the 737-800 to 125 with 125 options within a calendar year – numerically the largest order for a single commercial jet type within a 12-month period ever.

Above: Air Tahiti Nui has taken delivery of two brand new A340-300s, joining two of the type already in service with the airline. An Airbus A340-200, operated since 1998, has been returned to the lessor. The aircraft will be used on existing tourist routes to the US west coast, Japan and Europe, as well as introducing a new service to Paris via Los Angeles.

Copa Airlines of Panama took delivery of its 11th Boeing 737-700 in late 2002 finished in this special livery commemorating the Centennial celebrations of the foundation of the country. The aircraft is the third of Copa's order delivered with winglets.

Hungarian deliveries

On 29 January 2003 Malev Hungarian Airlines became the first operator in that country to place the Next Generation Boeing 737 into revenue service. The airline is due to receive six 737-700s during 2003, with a further 10 in 2004 and two in 2005. The Malev aircraft are significant as the first to place into service the newly-incorporated Navigation Performance Scales (NPS) equipment, allowing the aircraft to traverse through narrower flight paths with a greater degree of accuracy.

Luxair places order

Luxembourg's flag-carrier Luxair announced on 5 March 2003 its intention to purchase two Boeing winglet-configured Boeing 737-700s, with two options. The aircraft will be utilised on European scheduled services out of Luxembourg with the airline anticipating cost-savings compared to operations with its 737-400s and -500s. On delivery the aircraft are expected to introduce a new livery for the carrier, as well as an all-new interior and audio-visual system.

LOT of ERJs

LOT-Polish Airlines has confirmed its intention to acquire 10 Embraer

On 3 February 2003 Bombardier Aerospace delivered the first CRJ900 to launch customer Mesa Air Group. The airline has ordered 25 of the 90-seat class regional jet (with an option for an additional 20 examples), to be operated under its American West banner. Mesa has long been a supporter of Bombardier's RJ products, having already received eight of 15 CRJ700s ordered, and operating 32 CRJ200s. Both the CRJ700s and 900s are configured in a two-class layout of 64 and 80, respectively. Fleet commonality and same pilot rating with both the CRJ200 and 700 were the major drivers for the order.

Left: Deliveries of Bombardier CRJ700s have commenced to US commuter airline Comair, which will operate the aircraft in Delta Connection colours. Comair has firm orders for 20 CRJ700s, of which around a half had been delivered by spring 2003. The aircraft are configured in a single-class 70-seat arrangement, with completion of the deliveries set for late 2003.

Below: Dutch carrier Martinair became the first operator of brand-new Airbus A320s in that country in late March 2003, following the delivery of its first example on the 28th of that month. Its A320 fleet will be leased from Singapore Aircraft Leasing Enterprise and will immediately be busy flying summer-vacation routes around the Mediterranean and to the Canary Islands.

ERJ-170s for use on scheduled regional services within central Europe in a deal believed to be worth $200 million. The aircraft will be an important asset as the airline, in conjunction with Warsaw-Okecie airport, continues the drive to establish a dominant hub for the region.

Iberia goes for Airbus

Following its 30 January 2003 announcement of the selection of the Airbus A340-600 in preference to the Boeing 777, full details of the carrier's acquisition have emerged. The airline will receive eight examples (with options on a further seven), configured for 10 first-class, 42 business-class and 300 economy-class passengers and powered by Rolls-Royce Trent 500 series engines. The A340-600 has the highest seat capacity of current Airbus products, and will replace six elderly Boeing 747-200s in Iberia's inventory. Boeing was clearly not impressed with losing the hard-fought competition stating: "Given that the major airlines of the world – and their passengers – clearly prefer the Boeing 777 over the A340, it is disappointing that Iberia chose what the world recognises as a less capable airplane than the 777, which has outsold the A340 about two to one".

Asia

Indian competition

Both Boeing and Airbus are in the running to fulfil a recently announced Air India requirement for up to 17 new long-haul aircraft. With the Indian market bucking the trend and continuing to grow, despite the gloomy industry forecasts, Air India intends to study both the A340-300 and the Boeing 777-200ER to fill its needs in the 250- to 300-seat class. Higher-capacity routes will continue to be served by its fleet of six Boeing 747-400s. The airline is also looking at acquiring Boeing A320s or Boeing 737s to meet its growing regional requirements.

New market for A340-600

Cathay Pacific became the first Asian operator of the ultra-long range A340-600 with the delivery in late 2002 of its first of three examples from leasing company ILFC. The aircraft are configured with eight first-class, 60 business-class and 220 economy seats, and will enable the airline to operate non-stop services to the US East Coast from its Hong Kong base.

China Airlines places orders

Taiwan's China Airlines has split its long awaited long-haul aircraft order between Airbus and Boeing, continuing the carrier's trend towards operating products from both companies. Airbus is to supply 12 A330-300s plus six options in a £1.1 billion deal, with deliveries to commence in mid-2004. Boeing will make up the remainder of the order with six Boeing 747-400s and four 747-400F freighters, in a deal worth approximately $2 billon. Both variants are already in service with the airline and this additional order will bring the total 747 fleet to 32, with deliveries set to commence in July 2003.

Malaysia A380 deal

Malaysia Airlines is likely to become the 10th airline to order Airbus A380s following a Memorandum of Understanding (MoU) signed in January 2003 between the airline's parent company Penerbangan Malaysia Berhad and the European manufacturer. Planning to operate the type on its key trunk routes, Malaysia will acquire six A380-800s, with deliveries slated to commence in 2007. An important Airbus customer since 1978, Malaysia is predicting that the 555-seat A380 will help the airline overcome predicted slot restraints at its key destinations. Airbus now has 103 orders and options for the type.

A300s still selling

Despite entering service almost 30 years ago, Airbus is still receiving orders for its A300 widebody twinjet. The latest customer is Air Hong Kong, which, on 4 March 2003 signed a contract for six A300-600F freighters as part of an ongoing fleet expansion programme. The signing marks the first firm order for the new A300-600F 'General Freighter' variant, which differs from the A300F4-600R version by the addition of a large side fuselage door and integrated loading system. With DHL a 30 per cent stake holder in the airline, the order is seen as important in Airbus's future freighter prospects. Cathay Pacific holds the remainder of the stock. The aircraft are due for delivery in 2004 and 2005.

RJs enter Indian market

Although Asia has lagged behind North America and Europe in embracing regional jet operations, this trend looks set to change as the first examples entered service in India in March 2003. Air Sahara has leased a single Bombardier CRJ200 from the manufacturer, followed by four more examples leased from UK-based Flybe. The airline is also looking at adding 70-seat CRJ700s in the future. However, Jet Airways will be the first operator of this class of RJ following its order for 10 Embraer ERJ-175s, with deliveries due to commence in 2004.

Boeing 747-400ERF freighter deliveries

Deliveries of the newest incarnation of Boeing successful 747 freighter family– the 747-400ERF – have commenced. In late 2002 Air France placed the first example into revenue service after delivery in November. The airline has committed to five examples, three to be leased from ILFC and two bought outright by the carrier. The first Air France deliveries were followed in March 2003 by the second customer – KLM Royal Dutch Airlines – which received the first of three examples on the 31st of that month. The new model, however, has not received any orders since 31 December 2001 when an unidentified US customer ordered three examples, bringing the total firm orders to 11. The 747ERF offers an increase in maximum take-off weight of 35,000 lb (15876 kg) over the standard 747-400F freighter, allowing an additional 22,000 lb (9980 kg) of cargo or more fuel for increased range.

On 31 January 2003 Luxembourg-based cargo airline Cargolux ordered an additional 747-400F, bringing its fleet to 13, and increasing the total orders for the variant to 98.

Right: Air France became the first Boeing 747-400ERF operator when F-GIUA was delivered in November 2002. Two further examples have since arrived as the carrier aims to protect its position as the fourth largest freight carrier in the world.

Below: PH-CKA is KLM Cargo's first 747-400ERF and was delivered on 31 March 2003. A second aircraft was added in April with the third and final delivery slated for spring 2004.

Boeing's 737s with winglets in service

A growing number of Boeing 737 Next Generation customers around the world are opting to specify economy-improving winglets in their orders, and the aircraft are becoming a common sight at airports worldwide. Their success led to Boeing introducing the technology on the latest members of its 767 and 777 families.

Right (clockwise): Mongolian Airlines 737-800, leased from GATX; specially-painted Qantas 737-800 named* Yanani Dreaming*; Virgin Blue 737-700; Sobelair's first 737-800 with winglets, delivered in December 2002; Kenya Airways 737-700, leased from GECAS; recently-delivered ATA 737-800; Air Europa 737-800.

United finds Thai buyer

Thai Airways International has plans to purchase seven Boeing 747-400s from ailing Star Alliance partner United Airlines. The deal, which will be concluded subject to government approval, is worth some $330 million and is a considerably cheaper option than acquiring brand-new aircraft from the manufacturer. United had placed 12 of its 44-strong fleet of 747-400s in storage following severe financial difficulties and its entry into Chapter 11 bankruptcy protection.

Double Shanzhen order

Shenzhen Airlines of China is to establish a cargo arm to add to its expanding passenger aircraft fleet. Operated as a separate business, the cargo arm has received approval from the Civil Aviation Administration of China (CAAC) for the wet-lease of two Airbus A300-600 freighters. Once a suitable lessor has been found, the airline's board will give final approval for the freight business, and hopes that operations can commence in July 2003. In a further expansion, this time on the passenger side, Shenzhen is awaiting government approval for the acquisition of 10 new Boeing 737-900s. The airline plans to use the new aircraft to establish an international route network from September 2003, with destinations likely to include Singapore, Bangkok and Vietnam. The airline currently operates eight Boeing 737-700s and six 737-300s on a solely domestic route network.

LOT-Polish Airlines regional subsidiary EuroLot has elected to replaced its fleet of ATR42-300s with a newer variant of the same type. Five ATR-42-500s operate alongside the airline's eight ATR72-200s.

REST OF THE WORLD

BWIA's last MD-83

The final MD-83 was withdrawn from BWIA West Indies Airways service in early 2003, following the arrival of a seventh Boeing 737-800 in December 2002. This is part of the fleet rationalisation plan introduced to reduce the airline's mounting debts. Jet aircraft types operated will have dropped from four to two in 2003 with the retirement of the L-1011 TriStar 500 on the arrival of the airline's second Airbus A340-300.

Ethiopian chooses Boeing

Ethiopian Airlines has ordered three blended winglet Boeing 737-700s and three Boeing 767-300ERs as part of its ongoing fleet renewal and expansion plan. The US company won out against a rival Airbus bid for the A319 and A330-200. The new aircraft will replace existing 737-200s and 767-200ERs.

Boeing Réunion

Réunion-based carrier Air Austral has announced an ambitious route and fleet expansion programme, allowing the airline to break the 0.5 million-annual passenger barrier for the first time. Profits within the last 48 months have provided funding for the acquisition of two new Boeing 777-200ERs, delivered in mid-2003 to serve its new Paris-Réunion route. The aircraft are leased from ILFC and have been delivered in the airline's recently updated livery.

Blue 737s

In an important deal in its battle with Airbus's A320 family, Boeing announced on 16 January 2003 that Australian operator Virgin Blue had placed an order for 10 additional 737-800s plus 40 options. Virgin Blue is currently implementing a 10-year fleet expansion plan, as the low-cost market in the country is predicted to undergo a period of steady growth. The aircraft will be equipped with winglets supplied by Melbourne-based Hawker de Havilland. As with the majority of budget carriers, Virgin Blue has adopted a single-model philosophy and, if all options are converted, its inventory will include 78 'Next Generation' 737s, helping to keep pilot training and maintenance costs to a minimum. The first deliveries are scheduled for August 2003 and the airline has expressed an interest in expanding its route network to include destinations in New Zealand, as well as several of the closer South Pacific Islands.

Above: Eurocypria Airlines, Cyprus's only charter airline, began operations with four recently acquired Boeing 737-800s on 28 February 2003. Leased from ILFC by parent company Cyprus Airways, the 189-seat aircraft will replace four Airbus A320-200s that had been operated from 1992.

Below: Launch customer for the long-range Airbus A319LR, Privatair, will launch its specialist business-class service on behalf of Lufthansa from Dusseldorf to Newark airport, using this aircraft, in May 2003. A second aircraft is due for delivery in June, coinciding with the opening of Dusseldorf-Chicago services.

MEA receives A321s

Lebanon-based Middle East Airlines took delivery of the first of six Airbus A321-200s on 17 February 2003. Configured with 31 business-class and 118 economy-class seats, the aircraft will replace leased Airbuses within the MEA inventory. The aircraft will be used on scheduled services within the Middle East and Europe. An increasingly important Airbus customer, MEA also plans to place three leased A330-200s into service in the second half of 2003.

'Q' for Qantas

A strong customer for Bombardier's turboprop family, Qantas of Australia announced in January 2003 an order for three new Q300 Series turboprops, as well as converting a lease agreement with Bombardier for a single Q200 into an outright purchase. The aircraft will be operated by the carrier's Qantaslink regional partners including Eastern Australia Airlines and Sunstate Airlines. The aircraft are likely to be operated on Qantaslink's short-haul services, where the aircraft has shown it can operate more economically than regional jet competitors.

Aircalin goes all-Airbus

To address increasing trade and tourism prospects, New Caledonia-based airline Aircalin (Air Caledonie International) ordered a single A320 for services to neighbouring Pacific Islands, as well as serving destinations in New Zealand and Australia. Powered by IAE V2500-A5 engines, the aircraft is due for delivery in early 2004, giving the airline an all-Airbus inventory. The airline has already placed its two A330-200s into service, mainly flying longer-haul routes for the burgeoning tourist trade.

Qatar expansion plans

Qatar Airways plans to add 35 new aircraft and increase its network to 50 destinations by early 2005. No major orders have yet been placed, but the airline has signalled its intention to acquire a second A319 Airbus Corporate Jetliner configured for long-range operations.

Summary of orders – 4th quarter 2002

Variant	Operator	Number	Engine choice	Remarks
Widebody				
Airbus A330-200	Qatar Airways	1	GE CF6-80E	announced
Airbus A330-200	KLM	6	–	plus 18 'purchase rights'
Airbus A330-300	Lufthansa	10	R-R Trent 700	involves canc. of four A340s
Airbus A330-300	China Airlines	12	–	plus six options, to replace A300s
Airbus A340-300	Air Tahiti Nui	2	CFM56-5	'whitetails' canc. by GATX/Flightlease
Boeing 747-400	undisc.	1	CF6-80	
Boeing 747-400	undisc.	2		
Boeing 747-400	China Airlines	6	–	
Boeing 747-400F	Japan Air Lines	2	CF6-80C2	to replace 747-200Fs
Boeing 747-400F	China Airlines	6	–	
Boeing 767-300ER	Ethiopian Airlines	3	–	to replace 767-200ERs
Boeing 777-200ER	Pakistan Int. A/L	3	GE90	
Boeing 777-200LR	Pakistan Int, A/L	2	GE90-110B	
Boeing 777-300	Singapore A/L	1	R-R Trent 892	
Boeing 777-300ER	Pakistan Int. A/L	3	GE90-115B	
Boeing 777-300ER	undisc.	8		
Narrowbody				
Airbus A319-100	Silkair	2	IAE V2500	conversion of options
Airbus A319-100	Air China	8	IAE V2500	conv. of A318 orders
Airbus A319-100	ILFC	4	–	conv. of A318 orders
Airbus A319-100	EasyJet	120	CFM56-5	plus 120 options
Airbus A320-200	Iberia	1	CFM56-5B4	unannounced
Airbus A320-200	Silkair	4	IAE V2500	conversion of options
Airbus A320-200	Qatar Airways	1	IAE V2500	
Airbus A320-200	TACA	1	IAE V2500	conv. of A319 order
Airbus A320-200	Boullioun Aviation	1		conv. of A319 order
Airbus A320-200	Spanair	1	IAE V2500	conv. of A321 order
Airbus A320-200	Egyptair	5	IAE V2500	conv. of A318 orders
Airbus A320-200	British Airways	1	IAE V2500	unannounced
Airbus A320-200	CIT Aerospace	2		for leasing out
Airbus A321-200	Vietnam Airlines	5		
Airbus A321-200	British Airways	6	IAE V2500	conv. of six A318 and nine A319 orders
Boeing 737-700	Ethiopian Airlines	3	CFM56-7	to replace 737-200s
Boeing 737-700	undisc.	11	CFM56-7	
Boeing 737 BBJ-1	undisc.	1	CFM56-7	for corporate use
Boeing 737 BBJ-1	undisc.	1	CFM56-7	for corporate use
Boeing 737-800	undisc.	4	CFM56-7	
Boeing 737-800	Virgin Blue	10	CFM56-7	plus 40 options
Boeing 737 BBJ-2	undisc	2	CFM56-7	for corporate use
Boeing 737-900	undisc.	1	CFM56-7	Alaska or Continental ?
Regional Jet				
Bombardier RJ200	Air Wisconsin	6	CF34-3B1	for op. by AirTran JetConnect
Bombardier RJ900	Mesa Airlines	5	CF34-8C5	
Embraer ERJ-145	GECAS	2	AE30007A	canc. by Air Moldova
Turboprop				
Bombardier Q300	Qantas	3	PW123B	for Qantaslink
Bombardier Q300	Petroleum Air	1	PW123B	conv. of option, for corporate use
Bombardier Q400	All Nippon A/W	4	PW150A	for All Nippon Network
EADS/ATR42-500	Mount Cook A/W	1	PW127F	
EADS/ATR42-500	Fr. Polynesian gov't	1	PW124B	non-airline use
EADS/ATR72-500	undisc.	5	PW127F	announced Jan. 2003

Dash 8 makes Russian debut

In January 2003 Sakhalin Air Transport (SAT) placed this single Bombardier Dash 8 Series 100 (RA-67251) into service, becoming the first Western-built regional aircraft of any type to operate on the Russian civil register. The aircraft is operated in support of oil and gas development on the island of Sakhalin for the benefit of Exxon Neftegas Ltd. Tasked with operating from semi-prepared runways in some of the harshest weather conditions found in eastern Russia, the Dash 8 is home-based at Yuzhno-Sakhalin, and is expected to fly close to 85 hours per month. If the Dash 8 proves successful, Bombardier is hoping for further demand for the now-renamed Q-Series aircraft in the region.

Airline News

North America

BA-AA codeshares

British Airways (BA) has applied for the rights to codeshare a number of routes with American Airlines (AA) strengthening the relationship between the two carriers. Allowing shorter connection times and improved scheduling for passengers, BA would place its code on AA services from its US gateways to destinations in continental USA, Central America and the Caribbean. In a reciprocal move, it is likely that AA will opt to place its code on a number of BA domestic services, as well as routes within continental Europe, North Africa, the Middle East and Asia.

Delta goes for a Song

Having announced in late 2002 that it intends to wind up its Delta Express operations in the face of increasing competition from low-cost operators in its vital southeast USA market, Delta Air Lines is intending to create a new low-fare airline to compete with AirTran Airways, JetBlue and Southwest Airlines. The new airline – named Song – is due to commence operations in mid-April 2003 with a service between New York's JFK airport and West Palm Beach, Florida. By October 2003 Delta hopes Song will provide 144 daily flights using a fleet of 36 Boeing 757-200s, seconded from the parent company, including services to all three major New York airports. The 757s will be reconfigured with seat-back personal video monitors incorporating live satellite TV programming, MP3 audio programming, multi-player interactive games and in-seat internet connectivity. Delta claims that the 33-in (84-cm) seat pitch will be the most generous of any low-fare operator in the US. In time, Song will look to replace the 757s with aircraft in the 100-seat class, and is currently in negotiation with manufacturers including Airbus (A318), Boeing (717-200) and Embraer (ERJ190/195).

Hooters for Pace

Hooters restaurant chain in the US has acquired North Carolina-based carrier Pace Airlines and looks likely to adopt the new name Hooters Air. With a fleet of 15 'classic' Boeing 737s and two Boeing 757s, the carrier will fly specialist charter operations, including services for the golf industry to Myrtle Beach, SC. Initially only a single aircraft will be repainted in a new Hooters livery.

US airlines demand help

As war in the Middle East and rising fuel costs hit the troubled US airline sector still further, the industry is demanding increased government aid, claiming that combined losses could total $10 billion in 2003. However, as relationships between the US and France and Germany continue to be strained, the European carriers plan to fight any competitive advantage the US airlines may receive through government handouts.

New US carrier

A new carrier on the US domestic market is due to appear in mid-2003. Republic Airlines will be formed as a sister carrier to Chautauqua Airlines and will be based at Louisville International Airport, after the state of Kentucky offered a $7.8 million tax incentive scheme to use the airport. The airline's owners, Republic Airways Holdings, acquired the rights to the name after a previous carrier named Republic had merged with Northwest Airlines in 1986. The airline hopes to have placed 10 Embraer ERJ-145s in service by the end of 2003 with a further 10 RJs joining the fleet in early 2004. The aircraft will be operated in US Airways Express colours following a franchise agreement with US Airways.

Lufthansa has 'WOW' factor

The worldwide cargo market has suffered less than passenger airlines in the post-11 September 2001 commercial market, but a number of measures have been introduced to increase profitability. Cargo subsidiaries of Lufthansa, Singapore Airlines, Scandinavian Airlines (SAS) and Japan Airlines have formed an alliance to connect their services, and therefore expand global reach. The partnership has been named WOW, and Lufthansa Cargo Boeing 747Fs and MD-11s (above) bear the logo on their fuselage sides.

Europe

JET2 launch

New Leeds-Bradford, UK-based low-cost operator JET2 commenced operations on 12 February 2003 with twice-daily services from its base to Amsterdam. The airline was launched by cargo specialist Channel Express using two Boeing 737-300s. As the airline gears-up, further routes to Alicante, Barcelona, Milan-Bergamo, Malaga and Nice will be added.

The President of Aero Continente, Lupe Zevallos, has presented information denying the Consejo de Defensa del Estado, CDE (State Defence Council) accusation that the Chilean branch of the Peruvian airline was involved in money laundering from drug smuggling. The new information provided by Zevallos implies some members of the CDE and the DEA submitted false witness statements in Peru. The CDE president, Clara Sczaranski, responded on 4 February 2003 that it "isn't part of their attributions to manage money and to pay witnesses", qualifying the accusation of Zevallos as absolutely false, but "expectable". Aero Continente Chile currently operates two Boeing 767-200ERs (left) and two Boeing 737-200s.

Elsewhere in Chile, start-up carrier Alpine Air Express is now operating three Beech 1900s (below left) and deliveries of A320s are continuing to LANChile as part of a 25-aircraft order. CC-COQ (below) is the latest to arrive.

Right: El Al's fourth and final Boeing 777-258ER is now in service, following its arrival in 2002. Delivered in a single tourism-class configuration, the aircraft has been re-configured to include first-class (6 sleep seats), a business class (re-christened as Platinum Class) and tourist class. The $120 million purchase of the 777 was financed by El Al's own financial resources, including the return to Boeing of a 757 and a $102 million loan from City Bank, to be returned over the next 12 years.

Below: South African Airways' first Airbus A340-600 overflies Johannesburg Airport, shortly after its arrival in the country in January 2003. The aircraft entered revenue service in February, and the fleet will be used on routes from South Africa to Frankfurt and Hong Kong. The airline is also the launch customer for the Airbus A340-300 Enhanced, with deliveries of six examples due to commence in 2004.

Ryanair acquires Buzz

In a consolidation move within the European low-cost market, Irish carrier Ryanair announced its intention to purchase its rival London-Stansted-based budget airline Buzz on 29 January 2003. Previously owned by Dutch flag carrier KLM, the cost of acquiring Buzz is believed to be EUR23.9 million. Ryanair management intends to apply its own operating and fares structure, but continue to operate under the Buzz name. The target is to increase passenger number from 2 million to 4 million annually, and eliminate operating losses before a return to profitability. Ryanair believes that economic performance can be improved by dropping a number of Buzz's unprofitable routes and increasing frequencies on more popular routes, with a corresponding drop in standard fares. The airline also intends to replace all of Buzz's BAe 146s with Boeing 737s to introduce commonality with the rest of Ryanair's fleet. The 146s will be returned to KLM by April 2004. Ryanair has already set out its stall by insisting on unpopular changes to Buzz's staff working conditions.

Snowflake launch

Adding to the growing number of European low-cost carriers, Scandinavian Airlines (SAS) launched its own low-cost subsidiary, called Snowflake, on 30 March 2003. Equipped initially with four 150-seat Boeing 737-800s transferred form the parent airline and painted in a new livery, services commenced from Copenhagen to Alicante, Athens, Bologna, Lisbon, Malaga, Palma, Pristina and Sarajevo. Routes from Stockholm and later Oslo are intended once the carrier is established. Pilots and cabin crew are provided by SAS.

Scottish start-up

A new airline has been launched in Scotland, UK, under the name Air Scotland. Funded by Egyptian entrepreneur Dhia Al-Ani, the carrier is based at Glasgow Airport and will serve holiday routes, including Alicante, Barcelona, Fuerteventura, Malaga, Palma and Tenerife.

Final call for Air Lib

In early February 2003 Dutch investment group Imca withdrew its bid to buy Air Lib, after failing to achieve the price it wanted for the purchase of 29 Airbus A320s. The troubled French carrier had debts of EUR120 million, and administrators will now sell the company's assets to repay creditors where possible.

Virgin Express eyes new routes

Facing increasing competition in the low-cost market in northern Europe, Belgium-based no-frills carrier Virgin Express has expressed an interest in acquiring a number of routes from the defunct French carrier Air Lib. Any purchase of the rights would have to be settled with the collapsed carrier's administrator.

Hapag's new hub

A spin-off from parent company Hapag-Lloyd, itself a subsidiary of Preussag, Hapag-Lloyd Express has chosen Hanover as its second German hub. To allow new routes from the airport to destinations such as Rome, Venice and Nice, the airline will double its current fleet of eight Boeing 737-700s.

Iceland Express

The expansion of low-fare airlines has reached Iceland, with the commencement of services of the newly-formed Iceland Express in February 2003. Catering for the tourist market, the new carrier is in direct competition with established flag-carrier Icelandair, offering services between Reykjavik, London-Stansted and Copenhagen.

Volga-Dnepr grows

Successful specialist charter cargo operator Volga-Dnepr Airlines is creating a new division as a way into the lucrative $50 billion per year scheduled cargo market. Two Boeing 747Fs will be acquired as the new venture plans to specialise in scheduled services of oversize freight.

BerlinJet non-starter

Berlin-Schoenefeld airline BerlinJet suspended flights on 19 February 2003 after operating for less than two weeks. The airline had already fallen into debt and had failed to pay overdue landing fees. The airline operates a small fleet of Boeing 737s.

Alitalia for first ERJ-170s

Alitalia may well become the first airline to place Embraer's next-generation regional jet into service, following cancellations and delivery delays to launch customer Swiss' acquisition plans. The Italian flag-carrier is due to receive its first example in late August 2003, with revenue services likely to commence the following month.

UK low-cost market

Yet another low-cost airline is to be launched in the UK, in what is becoming an increasingly overcrowded market. Consolidation looked likely with the acquisition of Go by EasyJet in 2002, but since that time three new carriers have entered the market. Scheduled to commence operations in June 2003, Now will initially operate two Boeing 737-300s on routes from Luton Airport to Hamburg, Ibiza, Jersey, Lisbon, Manchester, Rome and Tenerife. Future plans involve adding a third 737-300, before eventually re-equipping with an all 737-700 fleet.

Italian's change to Airbus

Italy's AzzurraAir has opted to change its fleet of five Boeing 737-700s for six Airbus A320s, leased from GATX. Four Avro RJ70s and three RJ85s will remain with the airline. The decision was driven by major shareholder Air Malta's current plan to rationalise its fleet with all Airbus aircraft.

DHL and AirEx to merge

Brussels-based DHL is intending to merge with fellow package delivery specialist Airborne Express in a move to establish the combined company as a real competitor to UPS and Federal Express in the US express delivery market.

Concorde to retire

Both British Airways and Air France announced in early April 2003 their intention to retire Concorde from service later in the year. Demand for the world's only supersonic jet transport never recovered to previous levels following the July 2001 crash of Air France Concorde F-BTSC, and a downturn in the business traveller market has affected ticket sales further. The aircraft underwent extensive modi-

Following the stabilisation of Afghanistan, Ariana Afghan Airlines has started to re-equip and re-establish services flown prior to the conflict. Airbus A300 YA-BAB was presented as a gift from India and is seen at Sharjah in late 2002.

Boeing's failed concept

Demise of the Sonic Cruiser

Seen initially as a knee-jerk response to Airbus's launch of the A380, many sceptics believed that the Sonic Cruiser would never be built. With the aid of high-tech research in areas such as CFD (computational fluid dynamics) and modern composite structures, Boeing confidently stated that the aircraft would "change the way the world flies", offering shorter flight times and increased levels of comfort. Whether these grand claims would have stood the test of time will never be seen, economic turndown in the industry combined with indifference from prospective customers sealed the fate of the project. However, much of the technology may be implemented in the less ambitious Boeing 7E7.

In the early 1990s Boeing conducted a number of studies focusing on the engineering, technology, materials and processes which could be incorporated into the next generation of commercial aircraft. Computational analysis was also conducted of a wide range of aircraft configurations analysing aerodynamic efficiency, performance and stability. These initial studies were consolidated in 1995 under the umbrella title '20XX', although the project was later to be known within the company as 'Project Glacier'.

In 1999 a team of engineers was established to integrate the data gathered under 20XX and begin the process of formulating a viable design using concepts and technologies developed or under development throughout the entire company, including the military and space divisions. Using advanced computer-aided design, by the final months of 2000 the engineering and design team had formulated a layout which, since that time, differed little in general form.

Configuration

As unveiled on 29 March 2001, the Sonic Cruiser was a notable departure from current large commercial aircraft design. The aircraft featured a constant cross-section cabin of sufficient diameter to incorporate a twin-aisle internal layout. The large-area double or 'cranked' rear-mounted delta wing was of 'gloved' configuration and featured raked wingtips (raked wing tip technology has recently been introduced to the Boeing 767 and 777).

The twin engines were mounted either side of the 'gloved' section of the rear fuselage with a near-vertical tail surface mounted on each of the nacelles. Towards the top of the forward fuselage, behind the cockpit section, were large canards which, along with elevons on the trailing edge of the 'gloved' section, would have provided pitch control and longitudinal balance for the rear-mounted wing. Roll control would presumably have been effected by wing-mounted ailerons augmented by asymmetric elevator control, asymmetric canard control and wing-mounted lift-dumpers or spoilers.

To enable operations in the high subsonic/transonic range, the wing was sharply swept on the inboard section, but less so on the outboard section to ensure that sufficient lift was created to prevent a prohibitively high rotation speed and its associated long take-off run.

The cranked delta wing was defined as the optimum arrangement for transonic speeds. Sonic Cruiser Program Manager Walt Gillette stated that the Sonic Cruiser's shape was "more drawn by evolving up from a subsonic aircraft with a constant cross-section, than coming down from a supersonic design". Gillette insisted that the configuration and design would be tailored for Mach 1 and no faster, stating that "the maturity of the technology is not yet there for a modern Mach 1.4 to Mach 2 SST". The initial Project Glacier findings pinpointed Mach 0.98 to Mach 1.02 as the best range for a transonic design, with drag in this range being kept within workable limits. The studies included research into a faster aircraft, but the company stated that to achieve performance in the Mach 1.2 to 1.6 range would require more powerful engines with much greater fuel burn.

Boeing's CEO Alan Mulally unveiled the detailed model of the Sonic Cruiser at the 2001 Paris Air Show. Its futuristic shape, along with Boeing's claimed time savings the aircraft would have achieved (including 2 hours saving for New York to Tokyo, 2 hours 45 mins for Los Angles to Singapore and 1 hour New York to London), grabbed the public's imagination. Winning over the airlines to place orders proved a more difficult task.

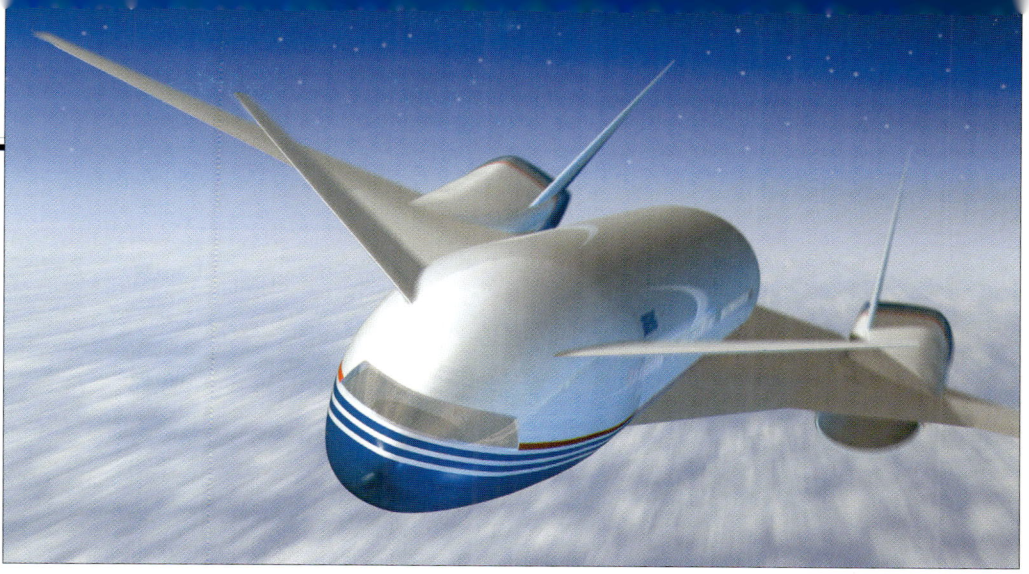

By mid-2002 Boeing was looking at around 60 per cent carbon fibre composite structure by weight for the Sonic Cruiser (compared to 10 per cent for the 777), including the main fuselage, majority of the wing, canards, fins and nacelles. However, the company kept its options open as aluminium companies, threatened by composite technology, strove to produce cheaper, lighter and stronger alloys.

Boeing also investigated the possibility of the aircraft operating in the Mach 1.02-1.05 range, and wind tunnel tests proved that the aircraft had good stability with no indication of 'Mach tuck' or the onset of buffet on passing Mach 1.

The key driver behind defining the Sonic Cruiser's configuration, size and aerodynamic qualities was the use of computational fluid dynamics (CFD).

Largely thanks to CFD work, by July 2002 Boeing had refined the configuration with a new nose section profile, larger zero-dihedral canards, revised engine nacelles incorporating vertical tail fins mounted further aft and elevator control surfaces on the aft deck.

Engines

Taking into account the economy demands of the airlines and practical engineering solutions, the only practical powerplant layout for the Sonic Cruiser was a twin-turbofan design. With a thrust requirement of 90,000-100,000 lb (400.5-445 kN) per engine, Boeing's initial publicity statements alluded to the fact that modified versions of the engines currently available for the company's Model 777 (Rolls-Royce Trent, General Electric GE90 and Pratt & Whitney PW4090) could be developed at relatively low-cost. By the end of 2001, however, results from the initial wind tunnel tests, combined with further CFD analysis, resulted in a rethink with the results pointing to a major change to the existing engines, if not a brand new engine.

The main reason for the dropping of the 777-derivative engine was core size and environmental noise issues. Engine core size is traditionally governed by top-of-climb thrust requirements, and in Sonic Cruiser's case would point to a take-off rating above 100,000 lb (45400 kg).

The most likely solution would probably have emerged by combining the low-pressure spool performance of the most powerful engines, as fitted to the 777-300/300ER, with the cruise performance of the engines fitted to the 777-200 whilst keeping the inlet diameter within the set design limits and the exhaust velocity low enough for noise considerations.

Having signed an exclusivity deal with Boeing to power the new Boeing 777-200LR and -300ER with versions of its GE90, General Electric are looked upon as Boeing's favoured partner, and was the only company to release some details of its proposed powerplant. Known as the 'Gen X' study, the engine was basically an 80 per cent scaled down version of the GE90-115B nine-stage turbofan. The smaller core size resulted in increased fan pressure ratio and therefore increased noise, however, GE believed this would have been overcome by the noise shrouding properties of the aircraft's S-duct nacelle. Boeing was keen to maintain that it wanted to offer the Sonic Cruiser with a choice of engines from all three manufacturers and proposals from both Rolls-Royce, using the basics of the Trent core, and Pratt & Whitney using a derivative of the PW4098, were expected.

Customer requirements

After leaked reports in the winter of 2000-2001 Boeing officially announced its Sonic Cruiser project the following March. Instead of competing with the Airbus A380 for the large-capacity hub and spoke market, the new aircraft was designed to appeal to airlines for different reasons. Key to the concept was reduced flight time on point-to-point routes. Boeing's argument centred on the premise that airlines and their customers place an intrinsic

Above: Boeing claimed that the Sonic Cruiser would climb more steeply, cruise at higher altitudes (42,000-50,000 ft; 12800-15240 m) and descend more steeply, keeping it free of congested airspace both close to the airports and en route.

Below: Boeing stated that no major changes to airport infrastructure were necessary for Sonic Cruiser operations. How the front canards affected the use of airbridges, however, was a question of debate. This image shows the final canard, tail fin and nacelle arrangements, although Boeing admitted some details "may not be entirely accurate" to conceal details from competitors.

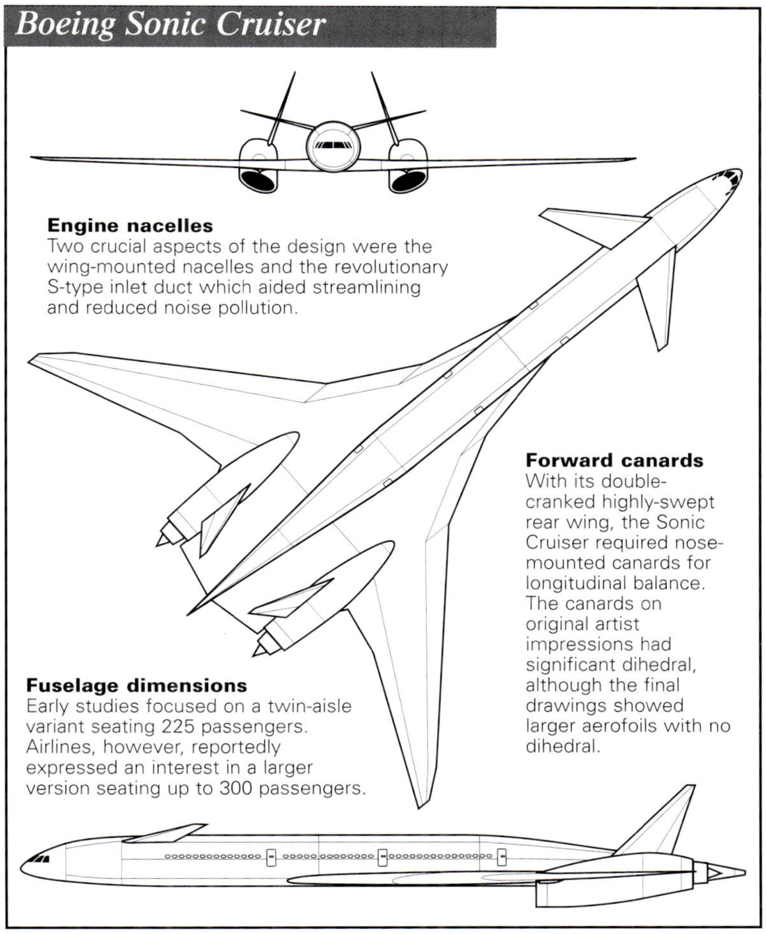

With such a large proportion of the Sonic Cruiser intended to be constructed from composite materials, Boeing conducted structural tests on this sample 75 per cent-scale representative fuselage section. The 20-ft (6-m) section was used to test installation techniques, durability and repairability.

value on time and therefore speed.

Early in the Sonic Cruiser's marketing campaign Boeing insisted that the aircraft would have similar economics to today's airliners and a higher price per seat would not necessarily result. Its argument was based on the fact that the lower capacity (200-250-seats) on an aircraft roughly the size of a Boeing 777 would be compensated for by weight reductions, using a host of new technology and composite construction, and increased utilisation rates (a 15 per cent increase in speed meant an extra 20-30 per cent utilisation rate per year according to Boeing figures).

However, critics pointed out that the higher-cost per unit negated any increased utilisation rates, which themselves were subject to the vagaries of slot availability and night flight limitations. In addition, flight crews may have demanded a pay-premium (such as that offered to Concorde crews) to fly the Sonic Cruiser.

Airline consultation

To protect confidentiality, a 15-strong airline group (believed to include American Airlines, All Nippon Airways, British Airways, Cathay Pacific, Japan Air Lines, United Airlines and Singapore Airlines) was consulted on an individual basis and a number expressed a concern that the time savings may not have been sufficient. In answer to a questionnaire issued by Boeing as part of the initial configuration studies, several airlines expressed a preference for a supersonic capability for overwater operations in the Mach 1.02 to Mach 1.05 range. Boeing hoped to bring together the group of airlines under the 'working together' concept used successfully in the Boeing 777 programme.

A key part of Boeing's strategy for the development of the Sonic Cruiser was the inclusion of a wide range of 'partner companies' to lend their own particular expertise to the research and development phase. By August 2002 eight development partnerships had been formed:

Japan Aircraft Industries:	advanced composites
Alenia:	structural materials
Vought:	advanced materials
Boeing Wichita Division:	structural design
Hawker de Havilland:	advanced composites
FACC:	composite aerostructures
Stork Fokker:	advanced material manufacture
GKN:	transfer moulding

Wind tunnel testing and aerodynamic configuration

Once the data from CFD work had been analysed and the initial configuration confirmed, Boeing commenced a series of wind tunnel tests to prove the CFD data.

The initial series of wind-tunnel tests (right) were conducted in August-September 2001 at the University of Washington's low-speed and Boeing transonic speed facilities. The Washington data, using a 8 x 10 ft tunnel, provided "good aircraft sizing data" according to Walt Gillette, and proved the low-speed stability, take-off and climb and approach characteristics as predicted by initial CFD iterations. The first round of transonic tests at Boeing's facility helped satisfy two major areas of concern: drag rise as the aircraft approached Mach 1 and the aircraft's stability on passing through the sound barrier. Testing produced a linear and stable rise in drag up to acceptable levels at Mach 0.98, and no longitudinal or lateral control problems above this speed where the aircraft's performance was quoted as being "remarkably stable". Basic stability and control characteristics were confirmed up to speeds of Mach 1.08. Walt Gillette said the aircraft's wing-mounted strain gauges "showed no sign of buffet onset" as Mach 1 was reached.

The successful initial tests marked the first stages of the configuration definition phase, which was focused on defining the exact wing-sweep, thickness ratio, canard location and tail location for the aircraft. Three further comprehensive high-speed sessions were planned for the development phase, bringing the total to one more than for the 777 programme. This is unsurprising due to the radical nature of the concept, and three or four more rounds would have been required without the CFD work. Walt Gillette stated the tests "confirmed the basic design and validated that CFD is accurately portraying aerodynamics of the vehicle at Mach 1". This would have allowed Boeing to use CFD as a design tool in refining the configuration and trading various parameters such as cabin cross-section against performance and efficiency.

The end of the road

Intense discussions with chosen airlines failed to convince the carriers that the increase in speed was sufficient to offset a higher seat price. Boeing stated that it and the airlines had yet to truly assess the 'value of speed'. This seems extraordinary given that Boeing's initial research before launching the project must have given indications that high subsonic speeds were sufficient to attract widespread interest in the aircraft. At the end of 2002 Boeing pulled the plug on its ambitious Sonic Cruiser programme, citing as the primary factors insufficient interest from the airlines, the downturn in the global economy, increased threat of terrorism, and mounting fuel and insurance costs.

Boeing 7E7

In anticipation that the Sonic Cruiser could be shelved, the company concurrently quietly progressed with its alternative 'Yellowstone' conventional project. This 757/767-sized aircraft has now been unveiled as the Model 7E7, but does not offer the Sonic Cruiser's speed advantages.

In truth, many observers believed the radical new concept was doomed as soon as the events of 11 September 2001 occurred. With much of the industry suffering financially, the new aircraft, at the airlines' behest, will place emphasis on efficiency rather than speed. After the failed 'new-generation 747' and Sonic Cruiser projects, sceptical airlines need to be convinced that this aircraft will be built and will not be compromised by trying to cover too many bases. Boeing is likely to spend much of 2003 talking to 20-30 major airlines to determine the exact requirements.

Much of the work on the Sonic Cruiser will not, however, go to waste. The advances in CFD techniques will undoubtedly be applied in defining the exact configuration of the new aircraft Designed to 'plug the gap' in the 210- to 250-seat class aircraft, the big three engine makers will use manufacturing, fuel burn and environmental improvements they would have included in the Sonic Cruiser in the quest to power the new aircraft. In addition, many of the development partnerships garnered for Sonic Cruiser will transfer to the new project.

Whether the Sonic Cruiser was the right aircraft at the wrong time, or a failed concept from the beginning is a matter of debate, but what is certain is that a challenger to Concorde for high-speed premium air travel is now not likely to enter service before the latter marks its 50th birthday.

Daniel J. March

Boeing Sonic Cruiser

Computational fluid dynamics

The use of CFD was a vital tool in the evolving Sonic Cruiser design. It is claimed not only to have proved the fundamental viability of the project, but been crucial in formulating the overall initial configuration, as it is seen here, by accurately predicting the interaction of features, such as the engine nacelles and fins, at transonic speeds.

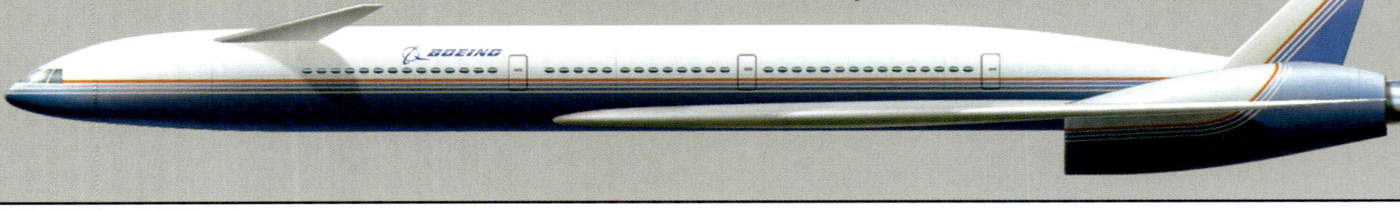

Argentina airline review

Surviving the financial crisis

Devaluation of the currency, severe financial restrictions and the corresponding dramatic fall-off in passenger numbers have pushed the country's already stricken commercial aviation companies to the edge of bankruptcy. Despite drastic reductions in fleet numbers, ticket prices and Draconian cost-cutting measures, the immediate future of several of the better-known carriers is under very real threat.

Above: Named after Southern Winds' main operating base of Córdoba, LV-WPF was the first of six Bombardier RJs delivered to the airline. The type has been used to expand international services from Buenos Aires's domestic airport to neighbouring countries to offset the collapse of the domestic air travel market.

Left: In happier times passengers board one of LAER's two ATR 42-300s for a domestic flight to Parana. The airline ceased operations in May 2002 and is currently up for sale.

Argentina will remember 2001 as the year when the country's economy entered catastrophic meltdown. For several years the country's economy had been in a severe recession and stability had only been maintained by the Peso's valuation link to the US dollar. In 2001 the underperforming Argentinian economy was no longer able to support this link, and the government was forced to set the Peso free to find its own value on the open market. The currency entered freefall, and to protect their monetary reserves both individuals and companies began transferring their holdings abroad. This further exacerbated the devaluation of the Peso, forcing the government to impose financial restrictions on the already-suffering companies.

The events of 11 September 2001 could not have come at a worse time for the airlines as the already faltering international market saw sales drop to a level of unsustainability. With the busy summer period of 2001/2002 approaching it was clear that the airlines were providing far too much capacity in terms of demand.

The financial crisis caused mass postponements and cancellations of holidays, and reservations in the autumn period practically disappeared. The summer season ended before it began and the cost to the airlines was near catastrophe. Ticket sales in 2001 had dropped by 26.8 per cent from 2000 levels (which had already fallen 16 per cent compared to 1999) and in 2002 sales were running at 60 per cent of the previous year. The situation on international routes in 2002 was even worse, with only 20 per cent of the usual tickets sales being recorded by some carriers.

Backed by the Spanish group Marsans, Aerolíneas Argentinas is one of the few airlines to begin emerging from the crisis relatively intact. To remain competitive however, the airline needs to replace its ageing fleet of Boeing 737-200s (right) for domestic and regional services and the long-serving Boeing 747-200s on long-haul routes. Airbus A340-600s are due to replace the latter from 2004, providing commonality with AA's four A340-200s.

The massive devaluation in the Peso hurt the airlines in other ways. With spares, insurance, airport fees, fuel and other running costs being charged in dollars the overheads more than doubled in the space of months. The main carriers began grounding a large proportion of their fleets and the inability to acquire spares resulted in cannibalisation of a number of aircraft to keep the remainder flying.

To make matters worse, the government insisted that domestic air tickets could only be charged in Pesos and, with demand almost non-existent, the Sports and Tourism minister banned any rise in the standard fares. In early 2002,

With too many aircraft for too few passengers, unsurprisingly an ill-afforded price war commenced in October 2001, and by 2002 it had become possible to fly some domestic routes at prices lower than that of bus services.

The airlines emerged from the summer season in a parlous state: below is a resumé of the current situation of the six largest passenger carriers.

Aerolíneas Argentinas

Having recently ended negotiations with creditors, the country's flag-carrier is the only company to show any growth in 2002 but, since early 2001, has suffered some of the worst performance figures in its history. With a large international schedule, the company was able to continue offering dollar rates for these flights as the Peso devalued. This protected income has been vital in maintaining its routes, and the airline has had the full backing of its owners – the Spanish Marsans Group. With an ageing fleet, Aerolíneas has announced major re-equipment plans, replacing its 26 Boeing 737-200s and six MD-83/-88s with Airbus A321s and Boeing 737-300s, the first delivery due in 2003. In 2004/05 six Airbus A340-600s are due to replace the elderly Boeing 747s, giving the company one of the most modern fleets in South America.

Further steps to solidify the company have included the integration of Austral (which itself was in a dire financial position), with the aircraft carrying the titles of both companies until a definitive logo is defined. In June 2002 a new hub was established at Madrid using two of the company's MD-88s to provide regional services. Additionally, the Marsans Tourist Group, also based at Madrid, has utilised two of the Boeing 747s on charter flights to the Canary Islands.

Aerovip

Commencing operations in 1999 as a feederliner for Aerolíneas Argentinas with six BAe Jetstream 32EPs, Aerovip has had a remarkably turbulent three years of operations. In 2001 the perilous state of Aerolíneas's finances forced the

***Left:* American Falcon has managed to weather the worst of the financial conditions by leasing out its fleet of a single Fokker F28 Mk 1000 and two Boeing 737-200s (left) to Dinar and LAPA. The airline is currently restructuring its services and is planning regular services to Santiago and Puerto Montt in Chile for the summer 2002/03 season, serviced by two additional Boeing 737-200s.**

***Below:* Fitted with 65 seats in a single-class layout, LAER's ex-air force Fokker F28 was only delivered in November 2001. The smart new livery was barely dry before the aircraft was withdrawn from service, prior to LAER ceasing operations in May 2002.**

company to realign itself to LAPA/ARG, with Eurnekian acquiring a majority shareholding. As AIRG itself found itself plunged into financial difficulties the shares were re-acquired by the previous owner and the aircraft have now been repainted again, back into Aerovip colours. However, the leasing contract runs out in March 2003, and the lessor is unwilling to renew it.

LAPA

The problems experienced by Líneas Aéreas Privadas Argentinas stem back to 1999 when the airline suffered the loss of a Boeing 737-200 at Buenos Aires airport in a crash which killed 67. The airline was taken over by the Eurnekian Group, which changed the name to ARG, Línea Privada Argentina. After painting a number of the fleet in the new livery it emerged that Aerolíneas Argentinas had already registered the ARG name and the company was forced into another new identity, this time emerging as AIRG.

The financial crisis has left the company in a perilous state. Negotiations with leasing companies to reduce its rates in the short term have proved unsuccessful, and in May/June 2002 AIRG was forced to return its fleet of eight brand-new Boeing 737-700s to the leasing company. Attempts to replace the aircraft with leased 737-300s from Delta foundered as the US company doubted AIRG's ability to finance the deal. The loss of the 737-700s compounded the earlier return in 2001 of the company's two Boeing 757-200s and single 767-300ER.

A meeting between the President of Argentina Eduardo Duhalde and majority shareholder Eduardo Eurnekian early in 2002 seemed to have secured the airline's future. Eurnekian is also the major stakeholder in the Aeropuertos Argentina 2000 consortium which administers 33 airports within the country, and in return for a reduction in government tariffs applied to these airports Eurnekian promised AIRG's continued operations. However, the deal was never closed and in September the airline was sold to a group headed by Bolivian airline Aerosur, who decided to return to the LAPA name, with a new logo.

Revitalised, LAPA restarted several of its services, and added new destinations such as Santiago, Puerto Montt and Sao Paulo. Most of the passengers come from outside Argentina and are paying in dollars, eager to take advantage of the cheapness of Argentina as a destination.

Dinar

Dinar has been hit as hard as any of the Argentinian carriers. The airline's three DC-9-41s and one MD-81 in service in mid-2001 were returned to the lessor. Pegasus Capital leasing has, since February 2002, been attempting to recover its two DC-9-34s as Dinar, restricted by the ban on transferring money overseas, was unable to pay the lease fee.

Dinar launched an advertising campaign promoting regular services to Brazil, but the financial situation caused the cancellation of these services, along with important routes to Córdoba and Neuquén. Unable to acquire aircraft from foreign sources, Dinar's much reduced network was serviced by two Boeing 737s leased from the Argentinian charter company American Falcon. Dinar was expecting losses of around $170 million in 2002 and therefore it was something of a surprise when, in mid-2002, American Falcon acquired Dinar's remaining interests. Dinar operations ceased and half the workforce was fired. However, this situation was short-lived as American Falcon sold the company to an Argentinian group some days later, which restarted operations with the two DC-9-34s.

Southern Winds

Southern Winds responded to the crisis by suspending a large proportion of its staff, 20 pilots among them. The airline managed to achieve a slightly higher seat occupation rate of 65 per cent in the summer 2001/2002 months, which the company deemed was low, but acceptable.

The fact that the company operated 50-seat Dash 8s and Canadair RJs was a major factor in the airline weathering the storm in a more healthy state than its competitors operating larger, more expensive types.

Before the crisis struck Southern Winds had initiated a forward-looking plan to expand into the international arena. The company signed an agreement to lease two Boeing 767-300ERs to provide services from Córdoba to Miami with the possibility of extending the route to New York. The first 767 arrived at Exeiza international airport on 4 February 2002, followed by the second example on 12 April. Crew training was accomplished in Brazil and Sweden, however, the worsening financial situation allied to trouble

***Below:* Austral's fleet of nine Boeing 737-200(A)s, two MD-81s and two MD-83s are to be integrated into the Aerolíneas Argentinas fleet following their decision to unify in 2002. It is likely that the aircraft will carry joint liveries until the corporate branding of the new company has been derived. LV-ZXV (below), like Austral's other 737s, is leased from Triton Aviation Services and is likely to be returned when the joint airline re-equips with modern A321s/737-300s from 2003.**

***Above:* Southern Winds has ambitious plans to expand into the international market and therefore plans to replace its fleet of six Dash 8-100s with six leased Boeing 737-200s. The Dash 8 and the airline's Bombardier RJs were more suited to adapting to the changes in domestic demand during 2001/02 than its competitors aircraft and utilisation rates remained relatively high, negating the need for substantial price rises following the Peso's devaluation.**

obtaining insurance and registration ensured the 767s remained idle for some while.

With the prospects of a slight improvement in the country's financial situation and the ironing out of the registration difficulties, Southern Winds commenced operations on the Miami route in August 2002, followed by Madrid, Spain in September. The introduction of the 767 was a major risk in the present financial climate and the company has found it difficult to compete with Aerolíneas and other international carriers. The past does not auger well for the enterprise: according to researcher Pablo Potenze, "All the Argentine private companies that tried long-range international flights ended in ruins".

To reinforce its new 'international' status Southern Winds returned its fleet of six Dash 8s and replaced them with second-hand Boeing 737s. The company's RJs have already introduced new routes into Chile, Bolivia, Brazil and Uruguay during the first half of 2002. In an attempt to foster further stability, Southern Winds recently announced a new frequent flyer programme (SW Value Miles) in association with American Airlines.

These changes will determine the future viability of the company, whether the merger with AIRG proceeds or not, but the exodus of aircrew leaving for Malaysia, South Africa, Europe and Chile may be an ominous portent of what will be a difficult few years.

LAER

LAER's 35-year history as an operating airline came to an abrupt halt in May 2002 as the company ceased operations due to financial problems. The company is currently up for sale and has returned three Jetstream 32s and two ATR42-300s to their owners. There is a plan to privatise the company to restart operations.

Above: Dinar is in a perilous financial position. Unable to pay the leasing fees, it has had to return or ground its DC-9 fleet (including DC-9-34 LV-ZXE, above). Remaining services are flown by two Boeing 737-200s leased from American Falcon.

Right: Argentina also has numerous cargo carriers, of which CATA is one of the larger. With a fleet of six F27 Friendships, the carrier is based at Buenos Aires-Aeroparque.

American Falcon

This charter airline started regular flights to Santiago de Chile and some domestic flights during 2002. Performance was generally good, although there were problems when it bought Dinar. The company, flying two Boeing 737-200s and one Fokker F28 Mk 1000, is owned by US investors and has operated charter flights since 1995. Its main business is to lease out aircraft to Dinar, LAPA and Southern Winds.

With Argentina's finances and politics in a state of flux, long-term planning for the remaining carriers is extremely difficult, and with war in the Middle East and the increased threat of terrorism, along with rising insurance costs hitting the industry, further mergers and bankruptcies are likely.

Santiago Rivas and Florencia Lucero Heguy

Argentine airliner fleets

Type	No. in fleet
Aerolíneas Argentinas	
Airbus A340-200	4
Boeing 737-200	19
Boeing 737-200(A)	7
Boeing 747-200	6
McDonnell Douglas MD-83	1
McDonnell Douglas MD-88	5
American Falcon	
Fokker F28-1000 (leased to LAPA)	1
Boeing 737-200(A) (leased to Dinar)	2
American Jet	
Dornier Do 228-200	2
Fairchild SA227DC Metro 23	1
Gates Learjet LR-25D	1
(non-scheduled and cargo operator)	
AeroVip	
BAe Jetstream 32EP	6
Austral Líneas Aéreas	
McDonnell Douglas MD-81	2
McDonnell Douglas MD-83	2
Boeing 737-200	9
(now owned by Aerolíneas Argentinas)	
Baires Fly	
Fairchild SA226TC Metro II	1
Fairchild SA226AC Metro III	4
(cargo only)	
Cardinal Líneas Aéreas	
Boeing 737-200	1
(aircraft leased to LAPA or Dinar)	
Cata Líneas Aéreas	
Fairchild F-27J Friendship	4
Fairchild FH-227B Friendship	2
IAI Arava 102	1
(cargo and non-scheduled operations)	
Dinar Líneas Aéreas	
Douglas DC-9-34	2 (not in service)
Hawk Air	
Fairchild SA226TC Metro II	1
Fairchild SA226AT Metro III	1
(cargo only)	
Helyjet	
Fairchild SA226AC Metro III	2
Gates Learjet LR-25D	2
MBB BO105C	1
(cargo only)	
LADE (Líneas Aéreas del Estado)	
DHC-6 Twin Otter 200	8
Boeing 707-300C	3
Boeing 707-300B (SCD)	1
Fokker F27M Troopship 400	5
Fokker F27 Friendship 600	4
Fokker F28 Fellowship 1000	4
Lockheed L-100-30	1
(operated on behalf of the air force)	
LAER (Líneas Aéreas Entre Ríos)	
Fokker F28 Fellowship 1000	1
(ceased operations May 2002)	
LAPA (ex-ARG and AIRG)	
Boeing 737-200	5
Boeing 737-200C	1 (out of service)
Patria Cargas Aéreas	
North American Sabreliner 60	1
(cargo only)	
Servicios Aéreas Patagónicos	
Fairchild SA227DC Metro 23	1
STAF	
McDonnell Douglas MD-11(CF)	1
(cargo only)	
Southern Winds	
Boeing 737-200	5 (three operating)
Boeing 767-300	2
Transportes Aéreas Petroleros	
Saab SF 340A	1
DHC-6-300 Twin Otter	1
(ceased operations in 2001)	

Formerly AIRG, LAPA has lurched from crisis to crisis in the last 18 months. Firstly the new ARG logo (as on Boeing 737-200(A) LV-YBS; above) had to be changed to AIRG as Aerolíneas Argentina had the licence for the word. Then the financial crisis took effect, ruining the company's plans to modernise the fleet with Boeing 737-700s and resulting in its sale and renaming as LAPA. AeroVip works as a feederline for LAPA with six Jetstream 32EPs incorporating underfuselage cargo pods (left), but following the latter's financial difficulties the aircraft have been repainted in AeroVip colours. The airline is currently assessing its alliances and has established its own booking system.

Airbus Industrie
Airbus Corporate Jetliner

Using its proven A319 airliner airframe as a basis, Airbus has created the Airbus Corporate Jet – ACJ – or A319CJ. Having first entered service in 1999, the aircraft continues to keep Boeing's BBJ marketing team on its toes, thanks to its combination of attractive interior options and operational efficiency. While Airbus has deliberately restricted production, the ACJ continues to find orders and has even broken into the lucrative government and military markets.

Above: Qatar Airways has a single ACJ, with a second remaining on option. The aircraft is flown in a 36-seat configuration, typically with four additional centre fuel tanks in its hold. The airline quotes a range of 4,500 nm (8325 km) with these tanks.

Below: Aero Services Executive flies the ACJ alongside its fleet of Dassault Falcons and Beech King Airs. Aero Services' managing director stated that the ACJ was chosen over the BBJ for the prestige of being the first French operator and because of the company's long-standing relationship with Aérospatiale and Airbus.

The use of commercial airliners as business aircraft pre-dates World War II. In the late 1920s large US corporations such as Continental Oil, Standard Oil, the Texas Company (Texaco), Phillips Petroleum, Bell Telephones, the Royal Typewriter Company, Monarch Foods and Union Electric Light and Power bought Ford Tri-Motors to carry their executives around the country and for product promotion. The Tri-Motor's manufacturer, Ford, itself established one of the earliest (and still surviving) corporate flight departments, using its own products.

Corporations were also early customers for the first 'modern' airliners, the Boeing 247 and Douglas DC-2, when they became available in the 1930s. Among operators were Hoechst Celanese, Phillips Petroleum and Union Electric Company with the Boeing; and Swiftlite Corporation and Standard Oil with the Douglas.

Post-war this trend continued, fuelled by the ready availability of surplus military transports

such as the Douglas C-47 and Lockheed Lodestar, many of which – along with smaller numbers of twin-engined bombers such as the B-25 Mitchell, B-26 Invader and Lockheed Ventura – were converted into luxury executive transports that formed the flagships of the US corporate aviation fleet. Conversions of Convairliners and Martinliners, Fokker/Fairchild F27/F-27 Friendships and Vickers Viscounts also found favour among major business operators. It was not until the first dedicated large business aircraft – Grumman's twin Rolls-Royce Dart-powered Gulfstream – came on the scene in 1959 that corporate flight departments had the option to move away from airline equipment if they needed increased speed, large-cabin comfort and range.

Accommodation within the ACJ's main cabin can be varied widely to meet customer requirements. Here the rear cabin of Qatar Airways' machine demonstrates a fairly standard, albeit very luxurious, fit. It is worth remembering that in regular airline service an A319 would be flown with six-abreast seating as standard. An alternative fit on the Qatari aircraft sees two of the aft seats removed to make room for a SERAI EVASAN International Air Medical Unit. This consists of a stretcher, oxygen supply and optional medical equipment according to the needs of the patient.

Designed for VIPs

Although virtually every Western-built turboprop and jet airliner has been adopted for corporate or VIP use at some time, manufacturers of airliners had made little effort specifically to court these markets until the early 1990s, when Bombardier Business Aircraft and Gulfstream Aerospace announced development of ultra-long-range business jets, respectively the Global Express and Gulfstream V (now G500).

Boeing was first to offer an alternative to the two 'global range' bizjet contenders. In July 1996 it announced development of a dedicated corporate/VIP long-range version of its Next-Generation 737 called the Boeing Business Jet (BBJ). A year later, at the Paris Air Show on 15 June 1997, Boeing's arch-rival, the international Airbus Industrie concern, announced that it too had a business jet on the stocks, the Airbus Corporate Jetliner, or ACJ.

Airbus's aim was to develop an aircraft costing about the same as existing top-of-the-line bizjets with intercontinental range, but appealing to a much larger market. It chose to manage the ACJ programme through a dedicated in-house team of about 40 people, using the full resources of the company's sales and marketing, engineering, production and support departments.

From the outset Airbus made a number of strategic decisions that it recognised would be important for the success of the ACJ. It identified the particular needs of the corporate jet market, but at the same time planned to capitalise on its vast expertise in designing, building and supporting airliners.

Unlike Boeing, whose BBJ is a hybrid airframe combining elements of the 737-700 and 737-800 and not directly equivalent to any of the 737NG airliner models, Airbus opted to base the ACJ on the unmodified airframe of the Airbus

Above: The Aero Services Executive ACJ is actually operated by Aero Services Corporate, a sister company which deals with service for more than 20 passengers in a single mission.

Left: DaimlerChrysler began corporate transatlantic flights with a modified A320 in early 1999. The aircraft was soon replaced by the A319CJ illustrated, which, unlike the A320, did not have to stop for fuel in Iceland.

A319. At the time of the ACJ's launch the A319 was the smallest of Airbus's single-aisle A320-derived family, and had just completed its first year in airline operations.

The ACJ (engineering designation A319CJ) therefore retained all standard A319 airframe components, flight systems and avionics, as described below. A choice of engines was offered, between the CFM International CFM56-5B7 and International Aero Engines V2527M-A5, each rated at 26,500 lb st (117.92 kN) take-off thrust. The IAE powerplant, which has been selected by about half the airline operators of the A320, has since been adopted as the 'reference engine' for the ACJ as part of a partnership agreement between Airbus Industrie and IAE.

Also common between the A319 and the ACJ is a standard fuel capacity of 6,303 US gal (23860 litres). But to achieve the ACJ's maximum design range of 6,300 nm (11668 km) and give it true 'global' capability, this can be supplemented by between three and six additional centre tanks (ACTs) in the underfloor cargo hold area. These increase capacity to (with three ACTs) 8,520 US gal (32250 litres), (four ACTs) 9,095 US gal (34430 litres), (five ACTs) 9,899 US gal (37470 litres), and (six ACTs) 10,717 US gal (40570 litres).

Unlike the BBJ, whose three-to-nine PATS Inc-manufactured supplementary underfloor fuel tanks are semi-permanent and require substantial engineering work to install or remove, the ACJ's Airbus-developed ACTs can be fitted or removed at will via the outward-opening cargo door, even during an overnight stop. This enables an aircraft to be precisely configured for any mission, trading range for payload/baggage capacity or vice-versa as required.

Combined with the aircraft's modular cabin

Flying controls and the flight deck

The ACJ has an electronic flight control system (EFCS) featuring five redundant-architecture computers, with digital fly-by-wire (FBW) for all primary and secondary control surfaces via sidestick controllers for pilot and co-pilot. The rudder and tailplane pitch trim are also signalled mechanically, providing a backup mode sufficient to control the aircraft in instrument conditions in the unlikely event of system failure. The FBW system provides protection against excesses of operating limits, stalling, overspeeding or aerodynamic or structural overstressing of the aircraft outside the normal operating envelope; windshear protection; and gust alleviation via aileron and spoiler deflection.

The ACJ flight deck features an ARINC 700 avionics suite that includes a digital automatic flight control system (AFCS) integrating the functions of a SFENA autopilot and Honeywell flight management system (FMS) that incorporates provision for the Future Air Navigation System (FANS).

Instrumentation comprises six CRT screen displays that are fully display/function interchangeable, with electro-mechanical instruments as backup. Four screens, two in front of each pilot, form the electronic flight instrument system (EFIS), while two central screens are the display part of the electronic centralised aircraft monitor (ECAM).

The outboard EFIS screens are primary flight displays (PFDs) that display a range of parameters including speed, altitude, aircraft attitude and heading, and FMS status. The inboard screens are for navigation display, and show data on the aircraft's position and course with selectable modes Arc, Rose ILS, Rose VOR or Plan. The central ECAM screens display information derived from sensors throughout the aircraft that keep systems under constant surveillance and show, both manually and automatically, engine and systems parameters and cautions. Multipurpose control and display units (MCDUs) are located on the central control pedestal. In addition to accessing the FMS, these provide systems maintenance data in the air and on the ground. Failure messages can be printed out for later action or they can be transmitted ahead during flight via an optional aircraft communication addressing and reporting system (ACARS) link to give maintenance providers advance warning of problems. An enhanced ground proximity warning system (EGPWS) and TCAS II traffic collision avoidance system are also standard fit.

The ACJ shares the A319 airliner's Extended-range Twin-engine Operations (ETOPS), Reduced Vertical Separation Minima (RVSM) and Cat IIIB autoland approvals.

Above: Not surprisingly, the ACJ is equipped with the latest in electronic cockpit information systems. The two screens immediately in front of each pilot's position are the primary EFIS display units, but any of the screens can be selected to show any desired set of data.

Right: Drag-reducing winglets are a standard A319 fit. All primary flight controls, such as ailerons and flaps, are hydraulically actuated.

***Right:* 'Green' aircraft leave this Airbus factory at Hamburg for any one of six completion centres around the world. The ACJ's cabin provides interior designers with 6,000 cu ft (170 m³) of space to play with. Airbus also offers its own cabin designers, who are able to work to a client's brief.**

***Below right:* Airbus envisages that many ACJ customers will be trading up from converted ex-airliners. As such, the company is keen to point out the improved operating economics of the A319CJ, as well as its ability to operate from 'secondary and discrete airports with runways that are off limits to aircraft heavier than the A320 family'.**

furnishing system (see below) and its certification as a public transport airliner to European Joint Aviation Authorities JAR-OPS 1 and US Federal Aviation Administration FAR Pt 121 requirements, this will enable a used ACJ to be sold to an airliner operator without major de-modification. Airbus points to the consequently high resale value as a key attribute. It estimates that an ACJ delivered in 2000 will retain 76 per cent of its residual value in 2010 and 53 per cent of its residual value by 2020.

Airframe

The ACJ is based on the airframe of the A319, which is itself a shortened version of Airbus's single-aisle 'core model' A320, with fuselage length reduced by removal of two frames (5 ft 3 in; 1.60 m) forward of the wing and three frames (6.99 ft; 2.13 m) aft of the wing.

The airframe structure is primarily of aluminium alloy, but with extensive use of advanced composites. Aramid fibre-reinforced plastic (AFRP) is used for the underbelly centre-section fairing, glassfibre-reinforced plastic (GFRP) for the fin leading-edge and fin-to-fuselage fairing. The tailplane, elevators, fin, rudder, flaps, flap track fairings, landing gear doors and fairings, cabin floor panels and many access doors are manufactured from carbon fibre-reinforced plastic (CFRP).

As with all Airbuses, manufacturing of compo-

***Below:* Qatar Airways' aircraft was built in December 2000 and carries the registration A7-HHJ. Like all of the ACJs delivered to date, the machine is IAE-powered, in this case by V2527M-A5 turbofans, each rated at 26,500 lb st (117.92 kN). The airline's regular A320s are also IAE-powered.**

Inside the ACJ

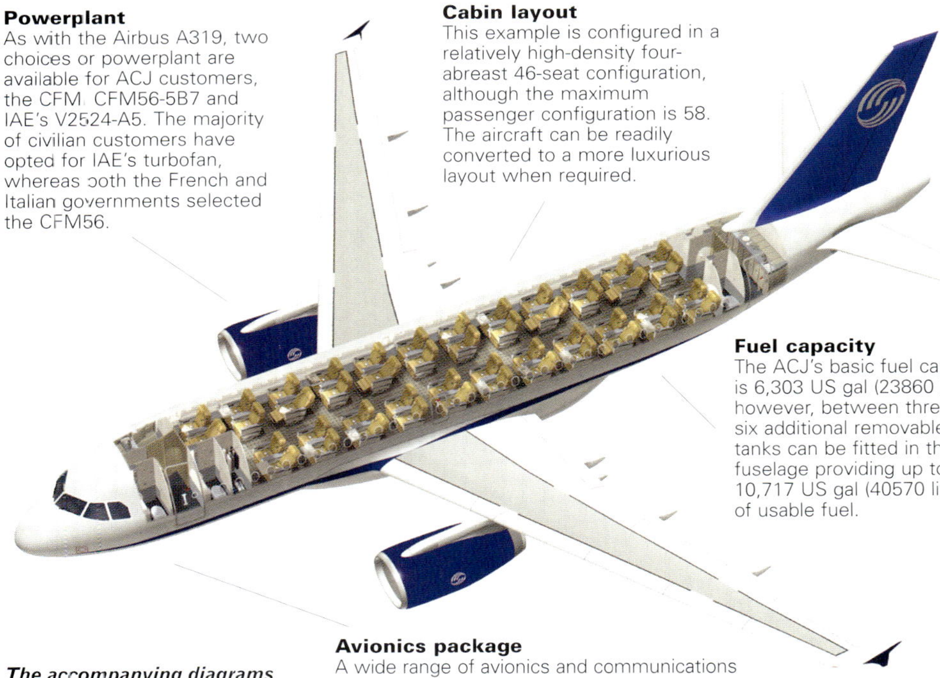

Powerplant
As with the Airbus A319, two choices or powerplant are available for ACJ customers, the CFM CFM56-5B7 and IAE's V2524-A5. The majority of civilian customers have opted for IAE's turbofan, whereas both the French and Italian governments selected the CFM56.

Cabin layout
This example is configured in a relatively high-density four-abreast 46-seat configuration, although the maximum passenger configuration is 58. The aircraft can be readily converted to a more luxurious layout when required.

Fuel capacity
The ACJ's basic fuel capacity is 6,303 US gal (23860 litres), however, between three and six additional removable fuel tanks can be fitted in the fuselage providing up to 10,717 US gal (40570 litres) of usable fuel.

Avionics package
A wide range of avionics and communications equipment is offered to customers, including satcom, CAT IIIB automated landing equipment, ground proximity warning systems, TCAS II and multi-mode receivers

*Below: As with all top-of-the-line business jets, the Airbus **ACJ** is finished internally with the finest materials available. Although **Boeing's BBJ** is the most obvious competitor for the **ACJ**, the aircraft is priced to compete effectively with the more traditional products offered by **Gulfstream** and **Bombardier**. It might be considered that the Airbus and Boeing aircraft lack the 'sexy looks' of the **Gulfstream 500/550** and **Global Express**, but they make up for this by their larger cabin sizes and increased interior flexibility. In addition, the **ACJ's** built-in airstairs and **Honeywell GTCP 36-300** auxiliary power unit (**APU**) provide autonomous operation that is not dependent on airport facilities, further enhancing its capability as an office, conference facility or 'flying hotel room'.*

*The accompanying diagrams give an impression of the flexibility of cabin configuration offered by the **ACJ**. The illustration above shows the machine in a possible 46-seat corporate shuttle configuration, which, by **ACJ** standards, might be considered high density. The upper plan view to the right shows a 10-seat layout similar to that which Airbus considers to be the baseline cabin configuration for a corporate-tasked **ACJ**. It should be noted that the two couches positioned to face inwards in the rear part of the forward cabin are not flight-rated. They are therefore not included in any description of seating capacity. The lower cabin plan illustrates a 41-seat corporate layout which has the increased flexibility of a 'First Class' section when compared to the 46-seat layout above, but for minimum loss of capacity.*

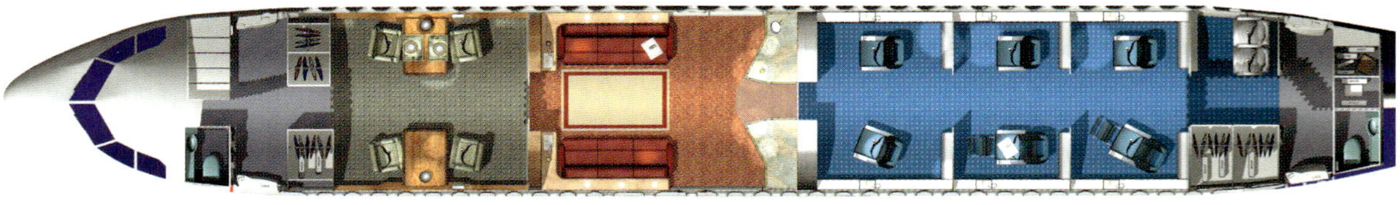

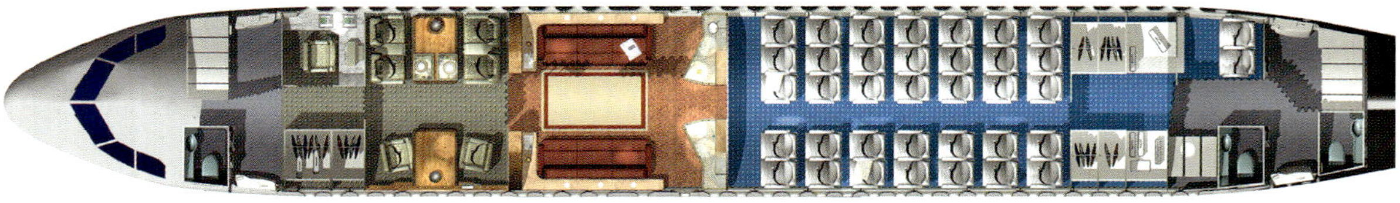

*With the Airbus 'all-in-one' concept, the **ACJ's** modular forward cabin can easily be reconfigured overnight using one of 17 standard modules. Once a **VIP** job has been completed for example, the cabin can swiftly be returned to executive shuttle configuration for its next task. When the lounge/bedroom area is not required, but the mission calls for working meetings with clients during a short daytime flight, the **ACJ** 'all-in-one' concept also allows an intermediate step between the **VIP** and executive shuttle configurations, in which part of the cabin is rearranged with work tables surrounded by blocks of four double-club seats, as illustrated below and below right. Note that different furnishings are available even within a 'double-club four' cabin arrangement (left and below right).*

Cabin arrangements

ACJ cabin interior arrangements are extremely flexible. Airbus offers a choice of six standard cabin layouts that provide accommodation from 10 to 39 seats and weigh some 8,500 to 10,700 lb (3855 to 4853 kg).

In typical Corporate configuration, the ACJ's 78-ft (23.77-m) long, 6,000-cu ft (170-m^3) volume cabin can accommodate a private conference suite with four seats and a three-seat divan and dining/conference table at its forward end, linked by a separate corridor to a communications suite, secretary's station and toilet. Enclosed within this area is a private office furnished with two seats, a work table, three-place divan, shower and toilet. An executive cabin for eight people in double-club configuration with central dining/work tables occupies the mid-section, with a Business Class cabin for 25 passengers in five-abreast layout to the rear, and a crew rest area, galley and toilet in the aftmost position. Thus configured the Corporate ACJ can carry 39 passengers. An alternate Corporate layout caters for just 20 passengers, featuring a forward business centre for two, private suite with full-height shower room, executive cabin for 16 passengers, and closets and galley station at the rear.

Three standard Shuttle configurations are offered. Corporate Shuttle provides fore and aft First Class cabins for 16 and 20 passengers respectively, separated by a secretary's station and toilet, with crew rest areas, toilets and galley facilities at the front and rear of the cabin. Executive Shuttle substitutes a 16-passenger double-club-configured executive suite in the forward cabin. VIP Shuttle features a forward lounge with two seats and a three-place divan, mid-section First Class cabin for eight, and a 20-passenger rear cabin, for a total of 30 passengers accommodated in considerable luxury.

Airbus offers ACJ customers an 'all-in-one' cabin concept that it believes will deliver unmatched space and flexibility, allowing customers to use the same aircraft to fulfil different roles at different times by means of rapid cabin reconfiguration.

It cites as an example an ACJ with a 46-seat cabin, typically used as an executive shuttle. Despite the demands of a busy schedule, there will still be some hours every week when ACJ time is available for other duties. 'What better way than to use them to bring a valued VIP customer to visit?' asks Airbus. 'For this role, a slightly different layout is needed – perhaps a lounge area for business discussions enroute or, if the customers live a long way away, a private bedroom, so that they can fly overnight.'

Satellite-based telephone and fax, a fully-equipped business and communications centre, computer/modem ports at VIP seats, work stations, Video/DVD/Hi-Fi Stereo and Airshow monitors can be part of the ACJ's cabin fit. Airbus has formed a strategic partnership with Tenzing Communications to offer in-flight e-mail and Internet access to airline passengers (known as Airbus in-flight information services – AFIS), in what could be the first widespread operational service of its kind, and this service will also be available to ACJ operators. Tenzing's proprietary software will run on a computer server aboard the aircraft, employing existing L-band air-to-ground satellite links to allow passengers to send and retrieve virtual e-mail via their own laptop computers. Though slow-operating by ground-based standards, and lacking a facility to log-on live to an individual user's regular Internet service provider, Airbus and Tenzing see this as only an interim solution that will evolve to make use of real-time broadband communications once it becomes economically viable through increased airline take-up.

Interchangeable cabin modules allow for quick changes of cabin layout. The majority of configurations allow the inclusion of toilets and galley facilities, while the majority include a bathroom and/or bedroom.

Rotating and reclining seats offer the ultimate in comfort on longer flights. Fully reclined, the seats can be converted into full-length beds as demonstrated above. Note the inclusion of armrest controls for communications and entertainment systems on all the seats illustrated.

The Al Kharafi Group's ACJ is offered for charter on a global basis. The aircraft can be contracted at offices around the world for a variety of transport or special charter missions. As with all ACJs, its ability to operate from relatively austere airports is a boon to any passengers who might be sensitive about attracting publicity – movie and pop stars for example. Nevertheless, the aircraft is also fully equipped to make the most of the latest technologies at the world's leading airports. Capabilities include automatic landings and roll out in CAT IIIB zero visibility conditions.

nents for the A319/A319CJ is shared among programme partners in France, Germany, Spain and the United Kingdom. Final assembly takes place at DaimlerChrysler Aerospace Airbus's plant at Hamburg-Finkenwerder on a common production line with the A318 and A321. ACJs are delivered 'green' to six Airbus-designated completions centres, as described below. Because of the high demand for the Airbus single-aisle range, the number of A319 airframes that can be released to Airbus Corporate Jets is strictly limited, and has been set at four per year until 2003, although ACJ Vice-President, Sales Richard Gaona is pushing for the release of up to eight per year to meet demand and avoid completions and delivery backlogs. Typical 'green' cost of an ACJ prior to outfitting is around $37-$38 million in 2001 US dollars.

Outfitting and support

Airbus Industrie has appointed six approved completion centres/outfitters for the ACJ. They are: Lufthansa Technik at Hamburg, Germany; Jet Aviation at Basle, Switzerland; Ozark Aircraft Systems at Bentonville, Arkansas, USA; Associated Air Center of Dallas, Texas, USA; Air France Industries at Toulouse, France and the latest, appointed in April 2001, EADS Sogerma, with facilities at Toulouse and Lake Charles, Louisiana. The typical outfitting cost of an ACJ is between US$8 million and US$12 million. Average completion time is from four to eight months from delivery in 'green' condition from the Hamburg factory.

For maintenance support Airbus has set up a 'one call handles all' system for ACJ customers that gives clients access to the worldwide Airbus support network, plus other services, via an Airbus-managed single point of contact provided by United Services, a division of United Airlines – one of the world's largest Airbus A319/A320 airline operators.

Though it is well used to dealing with the product support needs of small carriers, since around half of its airliners are flown by airlines with a fleet of four or fewer aircraft, Airbus recognised that a corporate flight department ACJ may be flown and maintained by a team as small as two pilots and a mechanic, and that a more comprehensive and different kind of support is essential. Thus ACJ customers need only call one freecall telephone number, staffed 24 hours, 365 days a year, to receive immediate technical advice, troubleshooting guidance, spares coordination and warranty backup. The support specialist has immediate access to the aircraft's service history, allowing a customised response. ACJ operators also obtain additional services through this 'one call handles all' service via United Services and its Star Alliance partners, including maintenance, spares and engineering support, and crew recurrency training. Air France Industries provides European and Middle East coverage under the scheme, and as a major operator of the A320 family is also able to provide operators with crew training and aircraft maintenance facilities.

Test flying and certification

The first ACJ built was the 913th airframe manufactured in the A320 series. Then registered D-AVYL, it first flew at Hamburg on 12 December 1998. Ultimately destined for the ACJ's launch customer, it was temporarily retained by Airbus for test and demonstration flying. Because ACJ certification was to be on the basis of an amendment to the A319's type certificate, the certification programme was not extensive, focusing on qualification of the six additional fuel tanks (ACTs) and the higher maximum cruising altitude of 41,000 ft (12497 m). The A319 airliner is certificated to 39,000 ft (11887 m).

ACT trials began on 31 May 1999, when the IAE V2527M-powered ACJ took off from Hamburg and flew to Airbus's flight test centre at Toulouse-Blagnac. The flight test installation included six ACTs in the cargo hold, and in the unfurnished cabin 5,511 lb (2500 kg) of test

Above: Operated by Twinjet, the al Kharafi ACJ has been used extensively since its introduction into service in 1999. One of its most meritorious flights so far involved a round-the-world flight which was completed in 144 hours. Twinjet used all of its ACJ-qualified crews to support the aircraft as it left London-Luton at 07:00 on 30 May 2001. The aircraft flew its first sector to Delhi as part of the Airbus marketing strategy for the ACJ, crossing four continents and visiting eight countries during its circumnavigation. The aircraft's payload consisted of 28 members of a government delegation and their baggage. Throughout the journey, the cabin crew served cuisine in keeping with the countries that had been visited.

Left: For corporate customers such as the Volkswagen Group, the ACJ makes for a better buy than a Gulfstream or Global Express when larger numbers of people must be transported on a regular basis. Its ability to be converted to an airliner also makes it a more attractive re-sale prospect.

equipment capable of measuring 2,000 parameters simultaneously, 31 water tanks to simulate payload, and a flight engineer's station. Crewing the flight were the captain, Airbus engineering test pilot Lucien Benard, with François Fabre of the Centre d'Essais en Vol (CEV) as co-pilot, and flight test engineers Jacky Joye and Gerard Desbois of Airbus and Michel Cartier of the CEV. Enroute to Toulouse the ACJ reached Mach 0.80 and attained its maximum operating altitude of 41,000 ft (12497 m).

Just over two weeks later, on 16 June 1999, the ACJ made the type's public debut at the Paris Air Show after a spectacular record-breaking non-stop flight from Santiago, Chile, to Paris-le Bourget, covering the 6,918 nm (12812 km) in 15 hours 13 minutes. Though planned as a show-stopper, the flight was also part of the ACT qualification trials. In command was Airbus's veteran test pilot and V-P of Training Pierre Baud, with engineering test pilot Ed Strongman and the CEV's Didier Poisson as co-pilots, and flight test engineers Jacky Joye and Gerard Desbois. The flight followed a non-stop outbound trip from Toulouse to Buenos Aires, Argentina, three days earlier. It routed over Brazil and across the South Atlantic, off the west coast of Africa and over Portugal and Spain. "We have linked continents with an aircraft whose job originally was to fly within them," commented Baud on arrival at le Bourget.

After completion of further flight trials, European Joint Aviation Authorities certification was granted to the ACJ on 18 August 1999, following which the two aircraft then flying were delivered to Jet Aviation at Basle and Lufthansa Technik at Hamburg for completion.

Mike Jerram

Above: From outside the ACJ is unmistakably an airliner. The same can be said of the BBJ, but less so of the Global Express and particularly the G500/550. In terms of performance the ACJ offers a near identical cruising speed to that of the BBJ at around Mach 0.80 to 0.82. The Global Express also cruises around 0.80 when long range is to be achieved, although Mach 0.85 is more usual. None come close to the G500 which cruises in the high Mach 0.80s and only the Global Express can near it for cruising altitude. Cruising up around 50,000 ft (15240 m), G500 crews have commented that there is little to look out for apart from Concordes and passing U-2s. Conversely, none has ever been able to welcome in excess of 30 passengers on board, safe in the knowledge that they can convey them one third of the way around the world in comfort equal to the best on offer from any manufacturer. Qatar Airways' ACJ is illustrated in its immaculate grey and white corporate colour scheme.

Above: Italy's Aeronautica Militare Italiana (AMI) is an important military customer for the aircraft, ordering three examples. While the first two machines replaced DC-9s, the third has replaced one of two Gulfstream IIIs. The second Gulfstream will be exchanged for a Falcon 900EX. Both Airbus and Dassault took on the GIIIs as part of their deals, although the AMI had hoped to convert them for EW support missions.

Right: L'Armée de l'Air was an early, if somewhat predictable ACJ customer. Further government/ military sales are possible, although potential customer Australia opted for the rival BBJ

Aero Services Executive

Paris-le Bourget-based Aero Services Executive is the first French civilian operator of the ACJ. Its ACJ (F-GSVU) was the first to be outfitted by the EADS Sogerma completion centre and is operated by subsidiary company Aero Services Corporate.

The aircraft is equipped with five ACTs, giving a maximum range of 5,000 to 6,000 nm (8260 to 11112-km) and 12 hours' endurance with reserves.

The cabin is configured in a three-abreast VVIP layout for 29 passengers sitting face-to-face in groups of two and four to facilitate enroute business discussions, plus a forward lounge and separate flight-crew and cabin rest areas. The aircraft entered service in July 2001 and is used mainly on flights to the Middle East, North America and Latin America.

In December 2001 it flew non-stop from Toulouse to New Orleans, Louisiana, to appear at the National Business Aviation Association Convention, and made the A319CJ's public debut in Latin America at the FIDAE 2002 air show at Santiago, Chile, in April 2002. Aero Services has an option on a second ACJ, for which it sees a need in the future for the development of its VIP charter market.

Aero Services Executive has its ACJ laid out in a similar cabin configuration to that of Twinjet, which preceded the French-registered aircraft into service by more than a year. The principle differences between the configurations of the two aircraft lie in the rear cabin, where the Aero Services machine has its seats arranged in a club layout; and in their fuel systems where the French ACJ employs ACTs.

al Kharafi Group/Twinjet Aviation

Launch customer for the Airbus A319CJ Corporate Jet, announced on 18 December 1997, was Mohamed Abdulmohsin al Kharafi/al Kharafi Aviation 2000 Ltd of Kuwait. The al Kharafi Group's ACJ, registered in the UK after completion of certification trials as G-OMAK, entered service on 8 November 1999, and is operated on behalf of the owner and on charters by Twinjet Aircraft based at London-Luton Airport, UK. G-OMAK has only the standard A319 fuel tanks installed, sufficient for an endurance of 8 hours 30 minutes with National Business Aviation Association IFR reserves.

Twinjet Aircraft has obtained 120-minute Extended-range Twin-engine Operations (ETOPS) approval, enabling the ACJ to route at up to 810 nm (1500 km) away from a suitable alternate airport. Its 28-passenger interior features three separate cabins: two lounges in the forward area each equipped with comfortable divans that convert into beds for overnight flights, and two 'master' seats, plus a further 24 First Class, 60°-reclinable seats in the main cabin. As configured, the Al Kharafi/Twinjet ACJ has underfloor cargo capacity of five tonnes – a necessity for some operations: one charter customer arrived for check-in with no fewer than 200 individual pieces of baggage!

In its first two years of service G-OMAK logged more than 900 hours in 350 flights, mostly in Europe and to the Middle East and North America, but including a round-the-world trip, carrying a variety of customers (at around US$9,000 per flight hour) ranging from heads of state and senior company executives to pop stars to journalists attending new car launches and Airbus press conferences.

The aircraft has a non-standard pwerplant of two IAE V2524-A5 turbofans in place of the more usual V2527-A5s.

Twinjet's A319CJ is made available for private charter with itineraries and operating locations chosen to suit the client. It is also available through specialist travel operator Goodwood Travel, which employs the machine on its 'Flights of Fantasy' tour programme. Packages offered include trips to the Monaco Grand Prix and various world tours.

DaimlerChrysler Aviation

When two long-established automotive manufactures – Chrysler in the US and Daimler-Benz in Germany – merged in 1998, there was an immediate need to set up a regular air link for executives travelling between the two corporate headquarters. DaimlerChrysler therefore set up DaimlerChrysler Aviation GmbH, which continues to work its single ACJ very hard in 2003.

Formed in 1998 DaimlerChrysler Aviation, a subsidiary of the parent DaimlerChrysler company, was another early customer. Its ACJ, D-AVYE, first flew on 6 May 2000. It was outfitted by Jet Aviation at Basle. The completed aircraft was handed over to operator DaimlerChrysler Aviation GmbH on 13 November 2000. Named *Transatlantic Star*, it replaced a converted A320 airliner with a similar name and is used as a corporate shuttle to reduce executive travel costs, typically making four round trips per week between its base in Stuttgart, Germany, to the company's American headquarters at Auburn Hills, Michigan, and four trips per week to its facility in Vittoria, Spain.

Transatlantic Star, configured to carry up to 44 executives in first-class seats, and certified for 120-minute ETOPs, began operations in January 2000. By the end of 2001 it had made over 300 transatlantic round trips with an average daily utilisation of around 11 hours – higher than the A320 airliner family's fleet daily average of 8 hours 28 minutes. On a round trip between Europe and the USA the aircraft can be in the air 18 hours out of 24.

With an average load of 20 executives on each flight, DaimlerChrysler says its transatlantic travel costs are less than for Business Class tickets on commercial carriers. Company executives also benefit from the convenient timings of the non-stop flights to Michigan, and the greater security, comfort and confidentiality on board. Airbus ACJ spokesman Richard Gaona has stated that "DaimlerChrysler is an excellent example of how a company can save money by operating a dedicated corporate shuttle with the ACJ".

Qatar Airways/Amiri Flight

Although the ACJ is targeted at international corporations, governments, heads of state, VVIPs and high net-worth individuals, Airbus has courted commercial operators in niche markets. The first airline customer for the aircraft was Qatar Airways, which ordered one ACJ, plus one option, in October 2000. Dubbed *The New Orient Express*, the first aircraft entered service in the summer of 2001. Opulently outfitted for 36 passengers in luxurious sleeperette seats, it is used for private charters and scheduled services from its base at Doha to destinations such as London and Singapore.

Under the guidance of its new CEO Akbar al Baker, who took charge in 1996, Qatar Airways has expanded in many regions and set up its Amiri Flight based at the company's headquarters at Doha airport.

Volkswagen Group

The Volkswagen Group has similar corporate transport requirements to DaimlerChrysler, with plants across Europe and in South America. Volkswagen Air Services operates a single ACJ, in addition to two Dassualt Falcon 2000s and two Falcon 900s, to support these needs.

Volkswagen's A319CJ, VP-CVX, was delivered on 13 November 2000. The company has, however, revealed little about its ACJ operations.

French government/Armée de l'Air

In November 1999 Airbus Industrie confirmed its success in winning an order for two CFM56-5B7/P-powered A319-115(X)CJs from the French government for VVIP/VIP operation by the Armée de l'Air.

The first aircraft, D-AVYV, made its maiden flight on 2 May 2001 and (as F-BXFA) was ferried to Chateauroux for completion eight days later. It was formally delivered to the Armée de l'Air as 1485/F-RBFA on 13 February 2002. The second French Government ACJ flew as D-AVYI on 9 August 2001, and (as F-GXFB) was ferried to Chateauroux on 3 September. It entered service as 1556/F-RBFB in spring 2002. The aircraft are painted in a white, red and blue livery with 'Republique Française' titles.

The Armée de l'Air ACJs are configured for up to 50 passengers, and have a range of 5,400 nm (10000 km), facilitating direct flights to Africa, India and French overseas territories in the Caribbean.

Italian government/Aeronautica Militare Italiana

Italy and France have taken the lead in European military ACJ orders, with planned fleets of three and two aircraft, respectively. MM62173 of 306° Gruppo is seen here at Sydney's Kingsford-Smith airport during a visit to Australia in February 2002.

Airbus Industrie has achieved some success in marketing the ACJ to governments for head of state and VVIP transport. First disclosed customer in this category was the Italian Ministry of Defence, which ordered two ACJs, with a third order recently confirmed, for operation by the Italian Air Force's 31° Stormo/93° Gruppo at Rome-Ciampino, replacing a pair of veteran McDonnell Douglas DC-9-32s. The first AMI ACJ, serialled MM62173, was outfitted by Lufthansa Technik and delivered to Rome on 24 May 2000, where it was accepted by then Italian Prime Minister Dr Massimo D'Alema and Italian air force Chief of Staff General Mario Arpino.

The second AMI aircraft, MM62174, was delivered on 15 September 2000. Powered by CFM56-5B7s for commonality with Italian state airline and AMI ACJ maintenance provider Alitalia's A320 fleet, they are configured (with seats by Italy's Avio International) for 40-50 passengers, providing sufficient full-cabin range to fly Rome-Washington, DC or Rome-Ottawa nonstop, or with a smaller payload, Rome-Johannesburg. Formal permission for the purchase of Italy's third ACJ was granted early in 2002, with the aim of having the machine in service by year end. The aircraft is configured in a VIP layout for 31° Stormo service, and replaces a Gulfstream GIII. Airbus is hopeful of orders from other European government or military agencies and there has been talk of possible British, German and Spanish procurement interest.

Sharjah Ruler's Flight

The ruler of Sharjah, H. H. Sheikh Dr Sultan Ben Mohammed al Qasimi has the use of A319-133(X)(CJ) A6-ESH as the sole asset of the Sharjah Ruler's Flight, which was formed in 1985. Used as a state transport aircraft, it replaced the previous VIP-configured Boeing 737-2WD. In common with the majority of ACJs delivered so far, the aircraft is powered by IAE V2527M-A5 turbofans offering a maximum take-off weight of 75500 kg (166,450 lb). The aircraft completed its maiden flight on 25 May 1999 and was delivered on 29 March 2000. Airbus, however, lost out in neighbouring Dubai, whose Air Wing operates two Boeing BBJs.

The ACJ of the Sharjah Ruler's Flight is finished in this simple colour scheme featuring an all-white airframe with red trim and cheatline.

Venezuelan government

The third disclosed military customer for the A319CJ, and the first sales success for the aircraft in Latin America, is the Venezuelan Government. Following its first flight on 2 May 2001, the single example was delivered as FAV-0001 on 30 July 2001, for operation by the Grupo Aéreo de Transport 4/Escuadrón Presidential, Fuerza Aérea Venezolana, as a head of state and VVIP transport.

Undisclosed/prospective operators

Airbus Corporate Jet has hopes of securing further government orders for the ACJ. Announcing the French Government contract in November 2000, ACJ's Richard Gaona said that he expected to sell the aircraft to the German and Spanish governments. The ACJ has also been mooted as a possible replacement for the BAe 146s operated by the Royal Air Force's No. 32 (The Royal) Squadron based at RAF Northolt. Following the collapse of the order for up to 15 ACJs by the United Airlines-funded Avolar fractional ownership company, Airbus hopes to sell directly into the important US market. As of late 2002 16 ACJ's had been delivered (including several for undisclosed customers) and a further 15 were on order. These include two examples for SAPO who plan to offer VIP charter flights from 2003.

LOT Polish Airlines

One of the oldest airlines in existence, LOT-Polish Airlines (Polskie Linie Lotnicze) has endured a roller-coaster ride since its formation in 1929. Through the decimation of its fleet during the German Blitzkrieg of 1939, the imposition of communist rule and Soviet-built fleets from 1950-1990 and the failure of the Qualiflyer Group alliance in 2001, LOT has remained an integral part of Poland's transport network. As the first Soviet bloc country to order contemporary western airliners, LOT remains at the vanguard of modernisation in eastern Europe and, with its recent entry into the Star Alliance and the growth of its Eurolot subsidiary, the company can look forward to the future with justifiable optimism.

Main picture: The Boeing 767 holds an important place in LOT's history as the first western-built jet airliner to enter service. Today, the original pair of 767-200ERs has been supplemented by three 767-300ERs, which are the largest aircraft in LOT's inventory. Capable of operating direct services to the lucrative US market, the 767s are likely to remain an important component of the airline's overall business strategy for many years.

Inset: Two of LOT's most important Cold War-era types stand side-by-side on the apron in front of Warsaw-Okecie's control tower in 1966. The Antonov An-24V (foreground) took over the domestic and shorter-range regional services from the Ilyushin Il-14 (rear), which had become uneconomical to operate after over a decade in service.

Below: Flying as a civilian was still very much a novelty in Poland in the mid-1920s. Perceived as fashionable and glamourous, air travel was also beyond the financial reach of much of the populace and deemed inherently dangerous (despite the excellent safety records of both Aerolot and Aero). Aero produced this poster of a Farman F.70 flying in a patriotically-coloured sky to help boost sales, however, it is a fact that the company would not have existed without large government subsidies.

LOT's forerunners

Reg.	Type	C/n	Del.	Name	Fate
Polska Linia Lotnicza – Aerolloyd, 1922-25					
P-PALA	Junkers F 13	580	8/22	*Adam*	to AL
P-PALB	Junkers F 13	589	8/22	*Bronek*	to AL
P-PALC	Junkers F 13	627	8/22	*Cezar*	to AL
P-PALD	Junkers F 13	582	-/22	*Daniel*	to AL
P-PALE	Junkers F 13	640	-/22	*Edward*	to AL
P-PALF	Junkers F 13	776	-/22	*Franek*	to AL
P-PALG	Junkers F 13	533	-/23	*Gustaw*	to AL
P-PALH	Junkers F 13	755	-/23	*Henryk*	to AL
P-PALK	Junkers F 13	735	-/23	*Karol*	to AL
P-PALL	Junkers F 13	745	4/25	*Ludwik*	to AL
P-PALM	Junkers F 13	754	4/25	*Mietek*	to AL
P-PALN	Junkers F 13	683	4/25	*Nasiek*	to AL
Polska Linia Lotnicza – Aerolot, 1925-29					
P-PALA	Junkers F 13	580	5/25	*Adam*	to LOT
P-PALB	Junkers F 13	589	5/25	*Bronek*	to LOT
P-PALC	Junkers F 13	627	5/25	*Cezar*	to LOT
P-PALD	Junkers F 13	582	5/25	*Daniel*	to LOT
P-PALE	Junkers F 13	640	5/25	*Edward*	to LOT
P-PALF	Junkers F 13	776	5/25	*Franek*	to LOT
P-PALG	Junkers F 13	533	5/25	*Gustaw*	to LOT
P-PALH	Junkers F 13	755	5/25	*Henryk*	to LOT
P-PALK	Junkers F 13	735	5/25	*Karol*	to LOT
P-PALL	Junkers F 13	745	5/25	*Ludwik*	to LOT
P-PALM	Junkers F 13	754	5/25	*Mietek*	to LOT
P-PALN	Junkers F 13	683	5/25	*Nasiek*	to LOT
P-PALO	Junkers F 13	731	8/25	*Olek*	to LOT
P-PALP	Junkers F 13	680	8/25	*Pawel*	–
P-PALR	Junkers F 13	732	8/25	*Roman*	to LOT
P-PALS	Junkers F 13	686	8/25	*Stefan*	w/o -/25
P-PAWA	Junkers G 23W	841	8/25		to DLH
Aero – Komunikacja Powietrzna, 1925-29					
P-POZA	Farman F.70	15	5/25		wfu -/29
P-POZB	Farman F.70	14	5/25		wfu -/29
P-POZC	Farman F.70		10/25		wfu -/29
P-POZD	Farman F.70		10/25		wfu -/29
P-POZE	Farman F.70		10/25		wfu -/29
P-POZM	Fokker F.VIIa	5062	11/28		to LOT
P-POZN	Fokker F.VIIa	5089	11/28		to LOT
P-POZO	Fokker F.VIIa	5090	12/28		to LOT
P-POZP	Fokker F.VIIa	5091	12/28		to LOT
P-POZR	Fokker F.V Ia	5092	12/28		to LOT
P-POZS	Fokker F.V Ia	5093	12/28		to LOT

Aerolloyd Junkers F 13 **P-PALC** *Cezar awaits its complement of passengers and mail outside the first airport terminal at Krakow-Rakowice airfield in 1924. Note the early-style triangular tail fin and rudder, which was replaced by a more conventional unit on later models.*

It was during the latter part of the first decade of the 20th Century that fixed-wing aviation really began to flourish in western Europe. By 1909 the first tentative steps towards establishing aviation in Poland had commenced with the designation of four small aerodromes at Warsaw, Krakow, Poznan and Lvov. However, development of any practical use for aircraft was negligible until the outbreak of World War I. The dynamic evolution in design and construction techniques that occurred in the war years, along with the training of numerous pilots and aircrew – Poles included – allowed for the massive expansion of commercial aviation in the post-war era.

Having regained its independence in November 1918, the Polish government expressed an immediate desire to establish a dedicated Polish air transport system. Lacking expertise, infrastructure and trained aircrew, the government concluded that the logical first step was to employ the services of a foreign company to help establish international routes from Warsaw. In July 1920 an agreement was signed between the government and French/Romanian carrier CFRNA to establish a regular service from Warsaw to Paris via Prague. Due to the time taken to establish the facilities, it was not until April 1921 that the first flight on the route was actually flown.

By this time preparations were well underway for the opening of the prestigious Poznan Fair and, to facilitate transport links, a group of enterprising Polish businessmen leased six Junkers F 13s from Gdansk-based German air mail company Danziger Luftpost. The opening of the fair on 28 May 1921 marked the establishment of their fledgling airline AeroTarg – the first Polish-owned passenger transport company. Always intended only to be in existence for the duration of the fair, AeroTarg completed 88 flights in nine days carrying 100 passengers and 3000 kg of mail on its Warsaw-Poznan and Gdansk-Poznan routes.

Establishing Aerolloyd

Although in existence for one of the shortest periods of time of any airline in history, AeroTarg's success paved the way in 1922 for the establishment of a publicly limited company named Polska Linia Lotnicza-Aerolloyd. Backed by the Austrian Fanto Oil Company, Polish business and the government, and loosely connected to the large German Lloyd group, Aerolloyd commenced scheduled operations on 5 September 1922 flying the Gdansk-Warsaw-Lvov route. Its fleet at this time comprised three Junkers F 13s acquired with the assistance of Danziger Luftpost and Danziger Luft Reederei and fitted with a four-passenger interior.

Aerolloyd's initial success prompted the opening of a new route between Warsaw and Krakow on 18 July 1923, by which time the fleet had grown to eight Junkers F 13s.

An event-free period of service followed until, on 27 April 1925, Aerolloyd established its first international route extending the Warsaw-Krakow route onto Vienna. A few days later, on 9 May, the foreign interest in the company was removed and the airline became a joint-stock company under a new name – Polska Linia Lotnicza-Aerolot – inheriting Aerolloyd's fleet of 12 F 13s. A month later the operating base was moved to a new facility at Mokotow airport, Warsaw. Known as 'the Aerolot yard', the base was the first in Poland capable of overhauling and servicing contemporary metal aircraft. Aerolot soon established an excellent reputation for reliability. The Viennese coined the expression 'Polish weather' to describe conditions so bad that only Aerolot pilots dared fly.

Expansion of the routes within Poland progressed slowly. Lvov-Krakow was established in 1925 and a service to Vienna, via Brno in Czechoslovakia, was added in 1927. In addition, a single Junkers G 23W floatplane was used on the short-lived and unsuccessful service between Puck (near Gdansk) and Copenhagen in 1925.

By 1929 Aerolot's fleet had grown to 16 Junkers F 13s and it (and its predecessor Aerolloyd) had carried 27,533 passengers, 724422 kg of luggage/freight and 52045 kg of mail in 12,234 flights. Given the rudimentary nature of

In 1929 the Polish civil registration prefix was changed from P- to SP-. Junkers F 13 **SP-AAW** *Walek previously operated with Aerolot as* **P-PALO** *Olek, and was one of 15 inherited by LOT. LOT's famous crane logo was not adopted on the aircraft until 1934.*

Left: Soon after formation a competition was launched for the design of LOT's new emblem. It was won by the young Polish artist Tadeusz Gronowski, who created the stylised crane enclosed within a blue circle, which remains the company's logo today. Gronowski later became famous for his advertising artwork and created LOT's first poster (seen here).

LOT named its aircraft according to the last letter of their registration – Fokker F.VIIa SP-AAO was named Olenka. The six F.VIIs were used on domestic routes and, in 1935, had their original Lorraine-Dietrich engines replaced by Bristol Jupiters.

Below: The introduction of the three-engined 10-seat Fokker F.VIIb/3m created an expansion in passenger numbers and routes. SP-ABA opened a connection to Bucharest on 1 June 1930, commemorated by a plaque just visible beneath the cabin windows.

navigational aids, a lack of night/bad weather instrumentation and the often inclement weather conditions in winter, it is a testament not only to the aircrew but to the durability of the Junkers F 13 that not one aircraft was lost in this period.

New start-up airline

During the 1920s Aerolot was not the only start-up airline to provide services within Poland. In the spring of 1925 Aero Kumunikacja Powietrzna-Poznan (Aero Air Transport-Poznan) was formed by the Poznan branch of the Union of Polish Airman as a joint stock company, with initial capital of 20,000 zlotys. Selection of aircraft type for the new company was the responsibility of managing director Antoni Wroniecki. Having studied the Paris-Strasbourg-Prague-Warsaw operations by Farman F.70s of the French carrier CIDNA, Wroniecki selected the type, with the first two examples arriving in Warsaw on 19 May 1925. With accommodation for four passengers in an enclosed cabin and a pilot situated in an open cockpit, the Farmans never achieved the reliability or comfort levels offered by Aerolot's Junkers F 13s and never posted an operating profit.

Aero received a subsidy from the Polish Ministry for Railways, enabling it to open what was to become its only scheduled route, Warsaw-Poznan via Lodz, on 25 May 1925. Three further F.70s were added in October of that year, all five remaining in service until 1929. Like Aerolot, the airline achieved a 100 per cent safety record in its four years of operations, however, in the latter years engine failures and forced landings became commonplace with passengers continuing their journeys by train.

By the end of the decade the rapid expansion of Warsaw had engulfed the original Mokotow

Desire for indigenous designs

The PWS.24 was not a great success in LOT service. SP-AGR was the first delivered in 1932 and; like several others, was converted for aerial survey following a short period of domestic route service.

Soon after its formation LOT came under increasing pressure from the Polish government to acquire indigenously-designed aircraft types to boost the country's fledgling aircraft industry.

Types evaluated for passenger or postal/cargo services in 1930-35 included the Lublin R-IX, R-XI and R-XVI, the RWD-11, the PWS.20, 21, 24 and 54, and the PZL 27. Much to the government's chagrin the only type purchased by LOT was the four-seat single-engined PWS.24. Six Wright J-5-powered examples, delivered in 1932-33, were followed by five Pratt & Whitney Wasp-powered PWS.24bis in 1934-35.

LOT's fleet acquisitions 1929-35

Reg.	C/n	Del.	Name	Notes
Junkers F 13				
SP-AAA	580	1/29	*Adam*	ex-P-PALA
SP-AAB	589	1/29	*Bronek*	ex-P-PALB
SP-AAC	627	1/29	*Cezar*	ex-P-PALC
SP-AAD	582	1/29	*Daniel*	ex-P-PALD
SP-AAE	640	1/29	*Edward*	ex-P-PALE
SP-AAF[1]	776	1/29	*Franek*	ex-P-PALF
SP-AAG	533	1/29	*Gustaw*	ex-P-PALG
SP-AAH	755	1/29	*Henryk*	ex-P-PALH
SP-AAJ[2]	754	1/29	*Mietek/Janek*	ex-P-PALM
SP-AAK	735	1/29	*Karol*	ex-P-PALK
SP-AAL	745	1/29	*Ludwik*	ex-P-PALL
SP-AAT	683	1/29	*Nasiek/Tadek*	ex-P-PALN
SP-AAU[1]	732	1/29	*Roman/Ursyn*	ex-P-PALR
SP-AAW	731	1/29	*Olek/Walek*	ex-P-PALO
[1]later converted to W 33 standard				
[2]re-registered SP-AGK in 1931 and named *Felek*				
Fokker F.VIIa				
SP-AAM	5062	1/29	*Maryla*	ex-P-POZM
SP-AAN	5089	1/29	*Nina*	ex-P-POZN
SP-AAO	5090	1/29	*Olenka*	ex-P-POZO
SP-AAP	5091	1/29	*Pola*	ex-P-POZP, destroyed at Warsaw 9/39
SP-AAR	5092	1/29	*Rena*	ex-P-POZR
SP-AAS	5093	1/29	*Slawa*	ex-P-POZS
Fokker F.VIIb-3m				
P-PAAA	5057	1/29		w/o Baghdad 7/31
SP-ABA	1	12/29	*Anka*	modified for aerial photography 11/30
SP-ABB	2	12/29	*Basia*	
SP-ABC	3	12/29	*Celina*	sold to SABENA 9/30
SP-ABC	11	1/31	*Celina*	
SP-ABD	4	12/29	*Danusia*	
SP-ABE	5	12/29	*Ewa*	
SP-ABF	6	12/29	*Flora*	
SP-ABG	7	12/29	*Grazyna*	
SP-ABH	8	4/30	*Hela*	
SP-ABI	9	4/30	*Iza*	
SP-ABK	10	4/30	*Krysia*	
SP-AMH[1]	1	8/34		*ex-Polish air force, evac. to Bucharest 9/39*
SP-AMI	2	8/35		*ex-Polish air force, evac. to Bucharest 9/39*
SP-AMK	3	8/35		*ex-Polish air force*
[1]*converted as twin-engined F.VIIb-2m in 1937*				
de Havilland DH.60G Gipsy Moth				
SP-ADX	1109	7/30	*Xawery*	Sold to Warsaw Aeroclub 10/33
Podlaska Wytwornia Samolotow PWS.24				
SP-AGR	1	-/32	*Roman*	conv. for aerial survey
SP-AJF	2	-/33	*Filip*	conv. for aerial survey
SP-AJG	3	-/33	*Genek*	
SP-AJH	4	-/33	*Hipek*	conv. to PWS.24bis as SP-ASY in 1935
SP-AJJ	5	-/33	*Jozek*	conv. for aerial survey
SP-AJK	6	-/33	*Kazik*	
R.W.D.5				
SP-LOT	71	12/33		Sold to B. Herse
Podlaska Wytwornia Samolotow PWS.24bis				
SP-AMN	586	-/34		
SP-AMO	587	-/35		
SP-AMP	588	-/35		conv. for aerial survey
SP-AMR	589	-/35		
SP-AMS	590	-/35		conv. for aerial survey, evac. to Bucharest 9/39

The second half of the 1930s saw a rapid modernisation of the LOT fleet including Ju 52/3m SP-AKX (left) powered by Bristol Pegasus engines, three DC-2s of which SP-ASK (above) was the first delivered in August 1935, and 10 L-14H Super Electras, including SP-BNE (below) which escaped to Bucharest in 1939.

LOT's fleet acquisitions 1935-40

Reg.	C/n	Del.	Notes
Douglas DC-2-115F			
SP-ASJ	1318	2/37	w/o after hitting mountains, Bulgaria, 23/11/37
SP-ASK	1377	8/35	evac. to Estonia, 9/39
SP-ASL	1378	8/35	evac. to Romania 9/39
Lockheed L-10A Electra			
SP-AYA	1045	1/36	w/o at Tomaszow Lubelski, 12/36
SP-AYB	1046	2/36	w/o at Athens, Greece 12/36
SP-AYC	1047	3/36	evac. to Romania 9/39
SP-AYD	1048	2/36	w/o at Piaseczno, Poland 11/37
SP-BGE	1085	3/37	evac. to Romania 9/39
SP-BGF	1086	3/37	evac. to Romania 9/39
SP-BGG	1087	3/37	evac. to Romania 9/39
SP-BGH	1088	3/37	evac. to Romania 9/39
SP-BGJ	1099	5/37	aban'd Wiszenka, Poland 9/39
SP-BGK	1100	5/37	captured and used by Soviet air force from 9/39
Junkers Ju 52/3m			
SP-AKX	5588	9/36	evac. to Romania, 9/39
R.W.D.13			
SP-BFO	168	-/37	w/o at Nowy Sacz, Poland, 6/38
SP-BNU	283	-/38	evac. to Romania 9/39, currently in Krakow museum
Lockheed L-14H Super Electra			
SP-BNE	1420	3/38	evac. to Romania 9/39
SP-BNF	1421	3/38	named *Lowicz,* evac. to England 9/39
SP-BNG	1422	4/38	crashed at Stulpica, Romania 7/38 after lightning strike
SP-BNH	1423	4/38	evac. to Romania 9/39
SP-BNJ	1424	4/38	w/o at Bucharest, Romania 8/38
SP-BNK	1425	5/38	made world's first transoceanic delivery flight, re-reg'd SP-LMK 5/38, evac. to England 9/39
SP-BPK	1492	3/39	evac. to Romania 9/39
SP-BPL	1493	4/39	evac. to Romania 9/39
SP-BPM	1494	5/39	named *Lublin,* evac. to UK 9/39
SP-BPN	1100	5/39	evac. to Estonia 9/39

airport and a brand new facility was planned on the southern border of the city in the Okecie district. Developed as the centre of both civil and military aviation in Poland, the airport boasted a modern steel and glass terminal and good transport links to the city centre. The airport eventually opened in 1933. This investment, along with financial support to the aviation industry offered by the government and investment companies, created a significant tax burden on the general public that was becoming increasingly sceptical that Aerolot and Aero could ever support themselves financially.

Ever-bigger subsidies in 1928 finally prompted action by the Polish government and in the latter months of that year, following the publication of the Presidential Air transport decree, the liquidation of all Polish commercial airlines was enforced.

Formation of LOT

On 1 January 1929 a new state-run airline, Linie Lotnicze-LOT, was formed with a monopoly on all domestic and international revenue services. Taking over the routes, assets, aircraft and staff of both Aero and Aerolot, LOT commenced operations the following day. Early operations were boosted by the introduction into service of six Fokker F.VIIas, originally ordered by Aero to replace its unreliable Farman F.70s. The additional aircraft, added to Aerolot's Junkers F 13s, allowed a rapid expansion of routes, including Warsaw to Katowice and Bydgoszcz and Katowice to Poznan. An aggressive marketing strategy was also launched incorporating the first countrywide poster campaign and promotional low-cost tickets to the all-Poland fair at Poznan in the summer of 1929, at which LOT had a heavy presence.

The formation of LOT gave the Polish aviation scene new impetus and recognition within Europe. In October 1929 Warsaw was chosen as the venue for the first international convention on commercial air travel. LOT representatives were among those from 33 nations, which signed a treaty governing the laws of air travel. Known as the Warsaw Convention, it still holds good

LOT's darkest hour – escape and evacuation

At the time of the German invasion on 1 September 1939 the LOT fleet comprised two Douglas DC-2s, seven Lockheed L-10As, eight Lockheed L-14Hs, a Ju 52 and a handful of Fokker F.VIIb/3ms and PWS.24s, the latter used for aerial survey work, and an RWD-13 – a total of 26 aircraft.

Hours before the invasion any aircraft situated at airfields in the west of Poland were evacuated eastwards to Warsaw and Lvov, and for four days LOT tried to maintain services essential for the defence of the country. Despite the Luftwaffe's almost total air supremacy during this period, not one aircraft was lost. Many of the flights were conducted at altitudes below 250 ft to avoid detection. However, on 5 September the decision was made to evacuate the fleet abroad. Five aircraft (one DC-3 and four L-14Hs) were sent via the Baltic states with the intention of reaching the UK. Of these, the DC-3 was impounded by the Latvian authorities at Riga and one of the L-14s suffered a similar fate in Estonia, however, three of the L-14Hs reached the UK. SP-BNF saw service throughout the war, firstly in Polish markings with Imperial Airways in France and from 1940-45 with BOAC as the transport aircraft for the Secretary of State for Air. SP-BPM was also dispatched to France and served there with BOAC until being destroyed in the evacuation of 1940. SP-LMK was used by Imperial Airways, BOAC and RAF Ferry Command until wfu in 1944.

A total of 16 aircraft (two F.VIIb/3ms, one PWS 24, one DC-2, five Lockheed L-10s, five L-14s, the Ju 52 and the remaining RWD-13) escaped to Romania along with much of LOT's property and many of the staff. LOT hoped to recommence operations from here and planned a further evacuation to the Middle East and France. However, coveting the assets that had literally dropped in their lap and coming under increasing pressure from Nazi Germany, Romania interned the aircraft and equipment and the LOT employees abandoned them in Bucharest. Many of the aircraft were used by Romanian carrier LARES having had camouflage, along with Romanian civilian prefixes added to their registrations.

Of the five aircraft which did not attempt an evacuation due to unservicability or a lack of pilots four (two F.VIIb/3ms, one L-10 and one PWS.24) were destroyed, along with ground installations, vehicles and other equipment, to prevent them falling into enemy hands. One L-10 was captured and used by the Soviet Air Force.

SP-BGF was one of five L-10A Electras which evacuated to Romania. It is seen here in camouflage with the registration YR-BGF in 1942 during its service with LARES. After a decade of further service the aircraft was wfu and broken-up in 1953.

Ex-US Army Air Force C-47As and Soviet-built Lisunov Li-2s were the mainstay of the LOT fleet in the decade following the end of World War II. Despite looking a near identical copy of the Douglas aircraft, the Li-2 actually incorporated 1,293 engineering changes to the original Douglas drawings. SP-LAL** Lucynka **(left) was in the first batch of 20 Li-2Ps delivered in late 1945/early 1946 and served with the airline for almost 15 years, before being written off in a fatal accident near Gdansk during an aerial survey flight. Later in their careers the Li-2Ps were fitted with engine baffles in winter to reduce cooling airflow, as demonstrated by SP-LAA, carrying special markings to celebrate LOT's 30th anniversary in 1959.

Below: LOT was seen as an important asset in the reconstruction of post war Poland. In desperate need of aircraft, LOT purchased nine war surplus C-47As from the US government and hastily converted them for civil airline use. Many operated in military camouflage. Built as a C-47A-70-DL, SP-LCE has received a rudimentary livery but still carries its US military serial (42-100820) on the tail.

today in over 120 countries worldwide.

Major new equipment entered service in 1930 in the form of 10 Fokker F.VIIB/3ms, licence-built by E. Plage and T. Laskiewicz and powered by three 240-hp (179-kW) Wright Whirlwind radial piston engines. The new aircraft enabled LOT's management to start fulfilling its dream of becoming a major international carrier in eastern Europe, by opening the Warsaw-Bucharest route. Within months the company had extended the route to encompass Sofia, Bulgaria, and Thessaloniki, Greece. Marketed as 'the link between the seas' the inauguration flight carried a cup of Baltic water to the Aegean Sea.

By the end of its first year of operations LOT had increased its passenger figures by over 100 per cent and the expansion was not to stop there. By the end of 1935 the airline had extended its route network and was firmly established at its new Okecie headquarters. The link between the seas was extended to include Tallinn, Vilnius and Riga at the northern end, and Warsaw received a connection to Berlin via Poznan. The aircraft fleet also expanded with Fokker F.VIIb/3ms now numbering 18, joining 11 PWS.24s and the surviving Junkers F 13s and Fokker F.VIIas. In addition, a single DH.60G Moth was employed on air taxi, liaison and training duties.

American aircraft arrive

It was in 1935, however, that LOT realised that its fleet was becoming obsolete and the new generation of all-metal low-wing monoplanes were transforming air travel. The management were quick to react, firstly ordering two Douglas DC-2s, followed by four Lockheed L-10A Electras and a Ju 52/3m (which was exchanged with Junkers for the nine remaining F 13s). The first to be delivered were the DC-2s in August 1935, and their success prompted the acquisition of the third in 1937. The first four Electras were delivered early in 1936 and were followed by six more and the Ju 52 in 1937. This significant upgrading of the fleet allowed the airline to position itself as one of Europe's premier carriers. The Baltic-Aegean route was again extended to incorporate Helsinki to the north and Athens, Rhodes and Lydda (Tel Aviv) to the south, thus becoming the longest European north-south service, measuring over 2,675 miles (4300 km).

By the end of 1938 the growth in the route network, the modernisation of the fleet and a return to profitability had cast an all-enveloping glow of optimism over the company. In May/June the first of an eventual 10 Lockheed 14H Super Electras had made a record-breaking delivery flight from Lockheed's factory at Burbank, California, to Warsaw (via Central and South America, the South Atlantic, Africa and the Middle East) under the command of LOT managing director Waclaw Makowski – the first transoceanic delivery flight of

Light utility aircraft 1945-60

Type	Reg.	C/n.	Type	Reg.	C/n
Po-2t	SP-ABN	1213	CSS-13R	SP-ASW	0403
Po-2t	SP-ABZ	9847	CSS-13R	SP-ASX	0407
Po-2t	SP-ACC	2713	CSS-13R	SP-ASY	0409
Po-2t	SP-ACE	7126	CSS-13R	SP-ATA	0408
Po-2t	SP-ADB	2014	CSS-13R	SP-ATB	0410
CSS-13R	SP-ABA	0317	L-4A Cub	SP-AGC	8684
CSS-13R	SP-ABD	0315	L-4J Cub	SP-AGM	12428
CSS-13R	SP-ABF	0335	L-4B Cub	SP-AGW	10347
CSS-13R	SP-ABN	0318	L-4H Cub	SP-AGZ	11136
CSS-13R	SP-ABR	0323	L-4J Cub	SP-AHB	12406
CSS-13R	SP-ABW	0329	L-4J Cub	SP-AHI	12496
CSS-13R	SP-ABZ	0333	L-4H Cub	SP-AHN	11387
CSS-13R	SP-ACN	0319	L-4B Cub	SP-AIE	9989
CSS-13R	SP-ADO	0322	L-4A Cub	SP-AIH	8871
CSS-13R	SP-AEL	0337	L-4J Cub	SP-AIT	12768
CSS-13R	SP-AKZ	48-013	L-4J Cub	SP-AKR	12435
CSS-13R	SP-AMT	49-019	L-4H Cub	SP-AMB	10707
CSS-13R	SP-AOK	49-047	L-4H Cub	SP-ANY	12334
CSS-13R	SP-AOU	49-056	L-4B Cub	SP-ANZ	9831
CSS-13R	SP-APG	49-067	L-4B Cub	SP-AOF	9896

Post-war crop-spraying and agricultural work

With the political situation deteriorating in the late 1940s, LOT was increasingly hemmed into its own backyard. Eight Li-2s, surplus to requirements for passenger carrying, were converted for forest pest spraying duties (particularly against infestations of Colorado Beetles). These operations were conducted between 1948-54. In addition, 20 Polish licence-built versions of the Polikarpov Po-2, designated CSS-13, were acquired between 1948 and 1953 for crop-dusting, along with 15 ex-US military Piper L-4 Cubs.

Above: Both Li-2P and Li-2T versions were used in the pest control role. The highly toxic pesticide was loaded into a tank in the cabin through a hatch in the fuselage roof by ground staff in protective clothing and masks. Towards the end of the flight the pilot's eyes would often be streaming tears and chest complaints were commonplace.

Left: SP-AMT was one of 20 CSS-13Rs procured by LOT for crop spraying. A ram air generator was fitted on the port side of the forward fuselage.

***SP-LDA** was the first of five **SE.161** Languedocs accepted by **LOT** in 1947-48. A huge disappointment, the **SE.161** was quietly withdrawn from service a little over a year later due to the grave inadequacies of the **Gnôme-Rhône** engines. The communist state authorities considered the whole episode to have been sabotage and **LOT's** Executive Director **Wojciech Zielinski** and Technical Director **Eugeniusz Roland** were arrested and convicted in a show trial.*

an airliner in history. The early adventure-seeking customers had given way to a healthy mix of government officials, businessmen and members of the general public, the latter group being attracted by a series of price reductions and promotional tariffs. The arrival of the L-14Hs allowed new routes to be opened to Budapest, Belgrade, Venice and Rome, and preparations were underway for a pioneering transatlantic service to Los Angeles. The airline was also operating a pair of RWD-13s and an RWD-5 for taxi flights and occasional scheduled services.

From the highs of 1938, the following year would become the most turbulent in the company's history. The early months started well with the company continuing the successes of the previous year. The remaining L-14Hs were delivered and new routes were opened to Beirut and Copenhagen. Test flights of a new Polish large transport (the PZL.44 'Wicher') were conducted and LOT and the Polish aviation industry were positioning themselves to be a major player in the future of European air travel.

All these plans came to a swift and brutal end on 1 September 1939 when Hitler launched the devastating Blitzkrieg on Poland. The day before

Post-war re-equipment with Soviet-types began in 1949 with the arrival of five Ilyushin Il-12Bs. Fitted out to carry 32 passengers, the Il-12 was unreliable and unpopular, but soldiered on, mainly servicing domestic routes until the introduction of the Il-14 in 1955. SP-LHA is seen soon after delivery in the summer of 1949.

Poland's ambassador to Germany, Josef Lipski boarded the LOT service from Warsaw to Berlin in a last ditch attempt to prevent the German invasion; he was however to return empty handed that same day.

Invasion and evacuation

After retreating to eastern Poland, LOT's fleet was evacuated to prevent the aircraft falling into German hands. Many of the staff that remained in Poland joined the 'Underground Poland' resistance movement. Many of LOT's pilots managed to escape and joined growing numbers of Polish airman in France and the UK. With the defeat of France, some Polish airmen were concentrated within certain RAF operational squadrons, while others became ferry pilots bringing valuable aircraft and resources from North America.

In the latter half of 1944 civil aviation re-emerged in Poland in the liberated territory called 'Lublin Poland'. With the assistance of Soviet Transport Aviation, the Polish Committee of Nation Liberation (PKWN) commenced vital courier flights using a range of borrowed Soviet types. Mail flights were also re-introduced using Polikarpov Po-2 biplanes.

In early 1945 former LOT staff began rebuilding the civil aviation infrastructure and, boosted by the growing numbers of returning pre-war employees, Polskie Linie Lotnicze was reactivated

Powerplant
The Il-14P was powered by twin Shvetsov ASh-82T piston engines, each producing 1,900 hp (1417 kW). This version of the ASh-82 offered improved fuel consumption compared to the ASh-82FNs fitted to the Il-12.

Licence production
SP-LNH was one of five Il-14Ps acquired by LOT in 1959 that had been built under licence by VEB at Dresden, East Germany. A total of 80 was built by the plant for both civil and military operators.

Anti-icing
The Il-14P introduced an improved thermal anti-icing system (based on that used by Convair on the Cv 240), which demanded less power from the engines. This system provided good adverse weather protection as well as offering a greater margin of safety if an engine was lost.

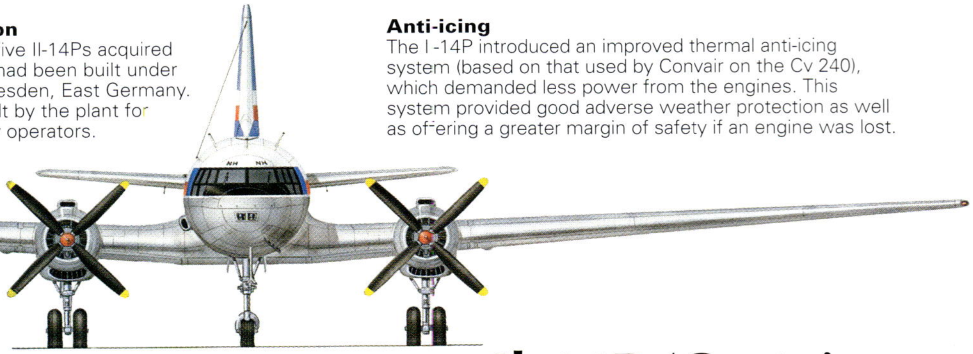

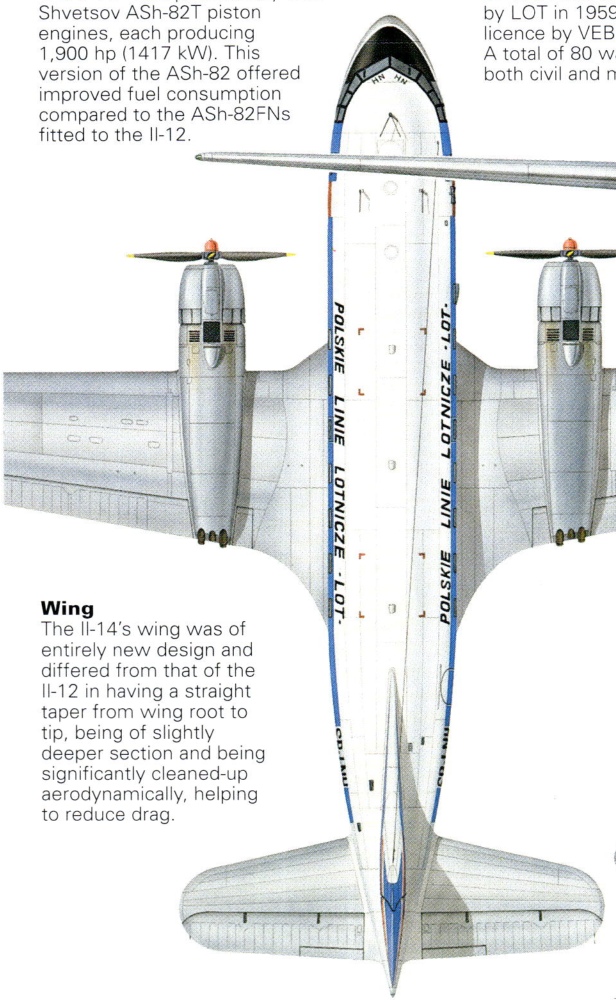

Il-14P 'Crate'

SP-LNH c/n 387
Polskie Linie Lotnicze
Warsaw, 1958

Wing
The Il-14's wing was of entirely new design and differed from that of the Il-12 in having a straight taper from wing root to tip, being of slightly deeper section and being significantly cleaned-up aerodynamically, helping to reduce drag.

Il-14P variant
Designed to rectify the shortcomings of the Il-12, the Il-14 was, in fact almost completely new. The only sections of the Il-12 retained were the fuselage cross-section and the landing gear. The Il-14P was the first production basic 18-seat version with a maximum take-off weight of 17000 kg (37,480 lb). A total of 13 was delivered to LOT from 1955 and they were utilised on domestic and regional services until supplemented and eventually replaced by, firstly, five CV 240s and subsequently by 10 An-24Vs. The aircraft's rugged landing gear allowed operations from a number of Poland's unpaved regional airports.

on 6 March 1945. With a lack of trained personnel the assistance of the Polish military was required. Following a request for help, the Commander of the Polish armed forces issued an order for four units of Lisunov Li-2s and Polikarpov Po-2s to be allocated for civil transport duties.

Post-war revival

Services commenced on 1 April 1945 between Warsaw-Poznan and Warsaw-Szczecin flown by Li-2Ts of the Seventh Independent Civil Aviation Squadron. Before the year's end some 115 air force Po-2s had seen service on LOT's VIP and air mail routes, however, only five of these were officially presented to the airline.

Essentially military aircraft pressed into civil use, the Li-2Ts had metal bench seating parallel to the fuselage sides with no seat belts, and offered none of the comforts associated with civil airline flying. Ten of the military-owned examples were eventually allocated to LOT in December 1945, by which time the airline had received the first 11 of an eventual 29 Lisunov Li-2Ps. With individual furnished seats in a 2+1 abreast layout and featuring a soundproofed interior and overhead storage, the Li-2P was much more suited to flying LOT's fare-paying passengers and helped the route network rapidly expand during 1946.

On 18 July 1945 the airline had been taken fully under governmental control as the State Enterprise Polish Airlines LOT, the pre-war crane was re-adopted as the emblem and uniforms and ranks were allocated to aircrew and ground crew.

With much of the airfield infrastructure back in operating order, 1946 was a crucial year of operations. Keen to re-establish its pre-war international connections the airline commenced the Warsaw-Berlin route with Li-2s on 11 May. By this time the airline had begun to receive ex-USAAF Douglas C-47s to supplement its Li-2 fleet. Despite being a later licence-built version of the DC-3, the Li-2P was found to be inferior in terms of speed, range and durability compared to the war-weary

LOT's fleet acquisitions 1945-55

Reg.	C/n	Del.	Notes
Lisunov Li-2P			
SP-LAA	18422702	12/45	
SP-LAB	18422703	10/45	named *Baska*
SP-LAC	18422704	10/45	
SP-LAD	18422705	10/45	named *Duska*
SP-LAE	18424001	11/45	named *Ela*, w/o at Katowice 4/55
SP-LAF	18424004	11/45	named *Fela*
SP-LAG	18423202	12/45	named *Gabrysia*
SP-LAH	18422703	12/45	named *Hela*, hit mountains near Limanova 3/54
SP-LAJ	18424005	12/45	named *Jasiek*
SP-LAK	18424002	12/45	named *Krysia*
SP-LAL	18424008	12/45	named *Lucynka*, w/o near Gdansk 8/60 on aerial survey flight
SP-LAM	18422610	12/45	
SP-LAN	18424006	1/46	named *Nelli*
SP-LAO	18424007	1/46	named *Olenka*, w/o 10/52
SP-LAP	18423204	1/46	named *Piotrus*
SP-LAR	18424003	2/46	named *Rena*
SP-LAS	18423203	2/46	named *Stasiek*
SP-LAT	18423205	2/46	named *Tomek*
SP-LAU	18423206	3/46	named *Urszulka*
SP-LAW	18424009	3/46	named *Wojciech*
SP-LKA	18438505	-/51	w/o 11/51
SP-LKB	18438504	-/51	
SP-LKC	23441010	-/52	
SP-LKD	23441501	-/52	
SP-LKE	23442002	-/52	
SP-LKF	33444510	-/53	
SP-LKG	33444801	-/53	
SP-LKH	33444507	-/53	
SP-LKI	33444804	-/53	
Lisunov Li-2T			
SP-LBA	18422009	12/45	named *Antos*, w/o 3/50
SP-LBB	18419802	12/45	
SP-LBC	18419010	12/45	w/o 5/48
SP-LBD	18419804	12/45	w/o 5/52
SP-LBE	18420203	12/45	
SP-LBF	18420205	12/45	
SP-LBG	18418308	12/45	
SP-LBH	18419602	12/45	
SP-LBI	18419704	12/45	
Douglas C-47A (DC-3)			
SP-LCA	7367	-/46	SP-LCA is a C-47
SP-LCB	-	-/46	w/o at Stokholm 5/48
SP-LCB	12704	-	replacement a/c
SP-LCC	9903	-/46	w/o 3/50
SP-LCC	13348	-	replacement a/c
SP-LCD	19499	-/46	
SP-LCE	19289	-/46	
SP-LCF	9938	-/46	
SP-LCG	9165	-/46	w/o 11/51
SP-LCG	-	-	replacement a/c
SP-LCH	9106	-/46	w/o Katowice 12/53
SP-LCH	13552	-	replacement a/c
SP-LCI	9801	-/46	
Cessna UC-78 Bobcat			
SP-LEA	4332097	12/46	
SP-LEB	4332078	12/46	
SP-LEC	437847	12/46	
SP-LED	4331812	12/46	
SP-LEE	4331813	12/46	
SP-LEF	112688	12/46	
SP-LEG	112567	12/46	
SP-LEH	112864	12/46	
SP-LEI	111823	12/46	
SP-LEK	112578	12/46	
SP-LEL	-	12/46	
SP-LEM	112793	12/46	
SP-LEN	111901	12/46	
SP-LEO	-	12/46	
NC-701 (Siebel Si 204D)			
SP-LFA	185	5/47	aerial survey, later to army
SP-LFB	227	5/47	aerial survey, later to army
SP-LFC	228	5/47	aerial survey, later to army
SP-LFD	230	5/47	aerial survey, later to army
SP-LFE	231	5/47	aerial survey, later to army
SP-LFF	232	5/47	aerial survey, later to army
SNCASE SE.161 Languedoc			
SP-LDA	21	7/47	w/o Reims, France 5/48
SP-LDB	22	7/47	
SP-LDC	18	10/47	
SP-LDD	15	7/47	
SP-LDE	44	-/48	
SP-LFF	232	5/47	
Ilyushin Il-12B			
SP-LHA	93013501	7/49	cancelled 11/59
SP-LHB	93013502	8/49	cancelled 11/59
SP-LHC	93013506	12/49	w/o Warsaw, Poland 7/52
SP-LHD	93013504	11/49	cancelled 11/59
SP-LHE	93013505	11/49	caught fire on start-up -/50
SP-LHF	93013515	7/52	leased from CSA until 11/52
Aero Ae-45			
SP-LLA	50140	1/52	
SP-LLB	50141	1/52	w/o 4/53
SP-LLC	50142	1/52	

The late 1950s saw LOT desperately attempting to expand its route network to western Europe. The unpressurised Il-14s lacked the sophistication to attract western customers and alternatives were sought. Remedy arrived in October 1957 in the shape of three second-hand Convair CV 240s, purchased from the Belgian state airline SABENA. SP-LPA (left) had previously served with SABENA as OO-AWP from March 1949 and remained in service with LOT until 1966. The CV 240 was used on LOT's most prestigious routes to London, Zurich and Athens (below). Two further CV 240s were acquired in May 1959 from Iran Air and KLM, and registered SP-LPD and -LPE, respectively, the latter remaining in service in the USA, following disposal by LOT in 1966, well into the 1990s.

Delivered in a plain bare-metal finish, with the legend Polskie Linie Lotnicze LOT on the upper fuselage, the Il-12B fleet received this smart blue cheat line and red tail markings in the early 1950s as part of a fleet-wide standardisation of the livery. SP-LHB served LOT for a decade from August 1949.

C-47s and, once fitted with airline interiors and re-designated as DC-3s, it was the latter aircraft that were to lead further expansion, being utilised to open routes to Paris and Stockholm.

To fulfil the growing need for air crew a dedicated initial training base was established at Radom airfield, near Jedlinsk. Ground mechanics, flight engineers and radio operators were also trained at Radom. Today the airfield is the home of the Polish Airlines Aero Club, which trains the majority of contemporary LOT pilots.

International expansion

By early 1947, with the Li-2s concentrating on domestic routes and the hard-pressed DC-3s flying the majority of the international routes, it became obvious that LOT required new equipment to continue its international expansion. After a brief assessment of the options, the LOT management concluded that the only brand-new aircraft available almost immediately at a reasonable cost was the SNCASE SE.161 Languedoc. Five were ordered and deliveries took place between July 1947 and February 1948.

As the first four-engined type to be operated in Poland, the Languedoc was intended to be the symbol of LOT's re-emergence as one of Europe's foremost airlines. Fitted with 33 luxurious seats the aircraft would open new services to Bucharest, Budapest, Copenhagen and Brussels. Open these new services the Languedoc most certainly did, however, almost immediately major problems began to manifest themselves. Like many of the contemporary French designs the engines were unreliable and unsuitable for the task. LOT's SE.161s were fitted with four Gnôme-Rhône 14N 68/69s, which had already developed an unenviable reputation. After numerous in-flight failures and insurmountable maintenance problems for the ground engineers, the Languedocs

Prop and turboprop fleet 1955-90

Reg.	C/n	Del.	Notes
Antonov An-2			
SP-LMA	13047305	5/55	operated until 12/55 on loan from Aeroflot
Ilyushin Il-14P			
SP-LNA	4340607	6/55	
SP-LNB	4340510	6/55	later conv. for aerial survey
SP-LNC	4340509	6/55	
SP-LND	6341404	-/56	
SP-LNE	6341602	-/56	later conv. for aerial survey
SP-LNF	6341607	-/56	w/o Moscow 6/57
SP-LNG	14803010	-/57	built by VEB, later conv. for aerial survey
SP-LNH	14803012	-/57	built by VEB
SP-LNI	14803013	-/57	built by VEB
SP-LNK	14803014	-/57	built by VEB
SP-LNL	14803017	-/57	built by VEB
SP-LNM	14803018	-/57	built by VEB
SP-LNN	703108	-/57	built by Avia
SP-LNO	14803065	-/63	leased in 1963 and 1964
SP-LNP	14803069	-/63	leased in 1963 and 1964
SP-LNR	14803055	-/63	leased in 1963 and 1964
SP-LNS	14803073	-/66	leased during 1966
SP-LNU	14803069	-/66	leased in 1966 and 1968
Convair CV 240			
SP-LPA	153	10/57	CV 240-12 from SABENA
SP-LPB	155	10/57	CV 240-12 from SABENA, w/o during training flight Warsaw 4/58
SP-LPC	156	10/57	CV 240-12 from SABENA
SP-LPD	9	5/59	CV 240-2 from Iran Air
SP-LPE	143	5/59	CV 240-4 from KLM
Ilyushin Il-18			
SP-LSA	180002403	3/61	Il-18V, conv. to cargo config. 4/76, wfu 10/88
SP-LSB	180002404	3/61	Il-18V, wfu 11/88
SP-LSC	181002805	3/61	Il-18V, conv. to cargo config. 2/76, sold Balkan 6/88
SP-LSD	184007102	4/64	Il-18V, preserved in old PLL LOT colours 1/91, now used as a restaurant
SP-LSE	181002504	9/65	Il-18V acquired from Polish air force, sold 11/90
SP-LSF	185008601	11/65	Il-18E, sold Balkan 7/91
SP-LSG	185008603	12/65	Il-18E, conv. to cargo config. 4/89, sold Balkan 7/91
SP-LSH	181002701	6/66	Il-18V acquired from Polish air force, sold 4/89
SP-LSI	185008905	3/75	Il-18E acquired from Polish air force, conv. to cargo config. 12/89, sold Balkan 7/91
SP-LSK	185008503	1/88	Il-18E acquired from Polish air force, sold -/93
OKL MD-12P			
SP-PBD	003	8/61	
Vickers V.804 Viscount			
SP-LVA	248	11/62	w/o St Trond, Belg. 8/65
SP-LVB	249	11/62	w/o Warsaw, Pol. 12/62
SP-LVC	395	12/62	sold to NZNAC 1/67
Antonov An-24V			
SP-LTA	57302203	3/66	derelict behind cargo terminal, Warsaw
SP-LTB	57302205	3/66	sold to Air Ukraine 2/92
SP-LTC	57302208	4/66	wfu -/87?
SP-LTD	57302209	4/66	force-landed in field, Poland 11/88
SP-LTE	67302405	4/66	w/o Wroclaw, Poland 1/69
SP-LTF	67302406	4/66	w/o Zawoja, Poland 4/69
SP-LTG	67302504	6/66	sold to Air Ukraine, 2/92
SP-LTH	67302505	6/66	sold to Air Ukraine, 2/92
SP-LTI	67302506	6/66	sold to Air Ukraine, 1/92
SP-LTK	67302507	6/66	sold to Air Ukraine, 2/92
SP-LTL	77302905	11/67	sold to Balkan, 12/87
SP-LTM	87304406	7/68	sold to Balkan, 11/87
SP-LTN	97305005	3/69	wfu 6/78
SP-LTO	67302801	5/69	from Polish air force (ex-011), sold Air Ukraine 2/92
SP-LTP	67302802	5/69	from Polish air force (ex-012), sold Air Ukraine 1/92
SP-LTR	97306006	5/70	sold to Balkan 12/87
SP-LTS	97307903	7/72	sold to Balkan 11/87
SP-LTT	97305701	9/73	from Polish air force (ex-013), sold Air Ukraine 2/92
SP-LTU	97306007	6/74	from Polish air force (ex-015), w/o 3/81
SP-LTZ	87304504	1/77	from Polish air force (ex-014), sold Donbass A/L -/92
Antonov An-12BP			
SP-LZA	6344307	6/67	cargo operations for gov't, w/o Beriut, Lebanon 5/77
SP-LZB	6344308	10/68	cargo operations for gov't, sold Air Sofia 3/95
SP-LZC	-	6/69	leased for cargo operations for gov't, 1969

A second western airline type joined LOT in 1962 with the acquisition of three second-hand Vickers V.804 Viscounts from British United Airways. The aircraft had a chequered career with the airline, SP-LVA and -LVB being lost in fatal accidents in 1965 and 1962, respectively. SP-LVC (right) soldiered on until 1967, before being replaced by the first tranche of Antonov An-24Vs which included SP-LTH (below).

Following on from the tradition of designer Tadeuz Gronowski, LOT employed a number of innovative artists to produce distinctive advertising posters. These included Janusz Grabianski who composed many superb works in the 1960s, such as this image of happy passengers disembarking from an Il-18.

*The longest serving of all **LOT** types in its 74-year history is the **Il-18**, and **SP-LSB** (seen here at London-Heathrow in the mid-1960s) was the longest serving of the Il-18s (March 1961 until November 1988). Four of the eventual 10 Il-18s were converted to freighters in the 1970-80s for **LOT**'s burgeoning cargo operation.*

***LOT** refined its livery in the early 1960s with a darker blue cheat line, silver/bare metal lower surfaces and a white upper surface, as demonstrated by both the Il-18 (above) and Il-14 (below). In addition, the tail was now largely blue with the crane logo appearing within a white circle on the upper portion.*

were withdrawn from service after little over a year and returned to France in 1949 to be re-fitted with Pratt & Whitney R-1830s.

Communist clampdown

The Languedocs were destined never to return, as in the wake of the Berlin Airlift and the start of the Cold War the communist authorities now perceived western European countries as the enemy. The early 1950s were a dark period in LOT's history as pilots and employees who had spent the war years in the UK fighting the Germans were deemed as 'likely traitors' and were fired. Many of the LOT employees who remained in Poland as resistance fighters were similarly treated. Instead of fostering communications and expanding its route network, the authorities forced the company to abandon its routes to many of its west European destinations and was restricted almost entirely to its own domestic market.

Aircraft acquisitions were allowed only from communist countries and the first to arrive were five Ilyushin Il-12Bs in 1949 as replacements for the Languedocs. Almost as unsuitable, the Il-12s were placed into service on the growing domestic network, but suffered from reliability problems. Many of the Li-2s and DC-3s were surplus to requirements and began to be placed into storage. This situation was to rapidly change as the country was blighted by a massive infestation of the Colorado beetle. A number of the Li-2s and DC-3s were hastily converted as crop-sprayers and flew in this role, alongside similarly converted CSS-13Rs and Piper Cubs, until 1954.

With no international connections, only a small but growing number of domestic routes and strict governmental control, LOT reached the nadir of its operations in 1950-53. However, in an attempt to increase its route network and profile, LOT was one of the initiators of the 'Pool of Six', a group of eastern European airlines established to provide air links between the capital cities of socialist countries. The agreement resulted in the opening of the Warsaw-Sofia service in 1953 and two years later by the prestigious Warsaw-Moscow route.

The political thaw

The latter service was possible thanks to the arrival of the first three of an eventual 13 Il-14Ps. The Il-14 was a great improvement on the disliked Il-12 and quickly replaced the latter on the more important routes. In the summer of 1955 the Moscow route was extended to Vilnius, and a thawing in the political atmosphere allowed the airline to open up its first western European service – to Vienna.

It was the Hungarian uprising of 1956 that

Ilyushin Il-18 liveries (1961-1991)

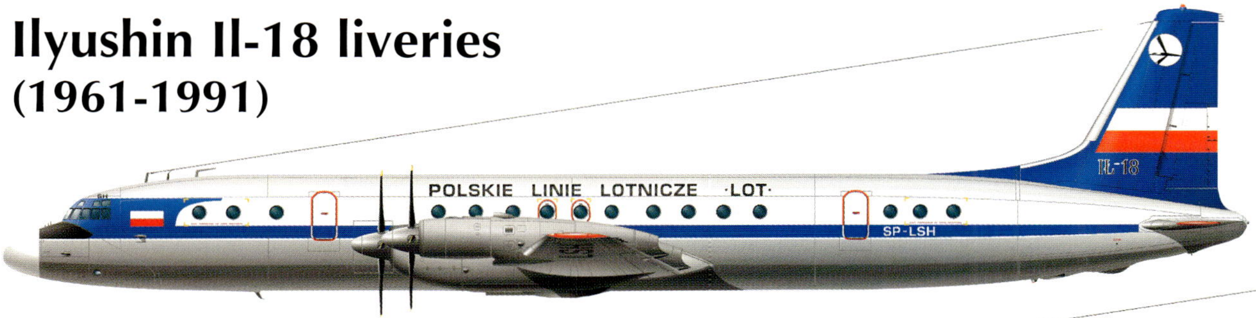

SP-LSH was acquired from the Polish air force in June 1966 and adopted the standard livery of the period. The Il-18 was regarded as the best of the Soviet aircraft acquired – not a single aircraft was lost over a service period of 30 years.

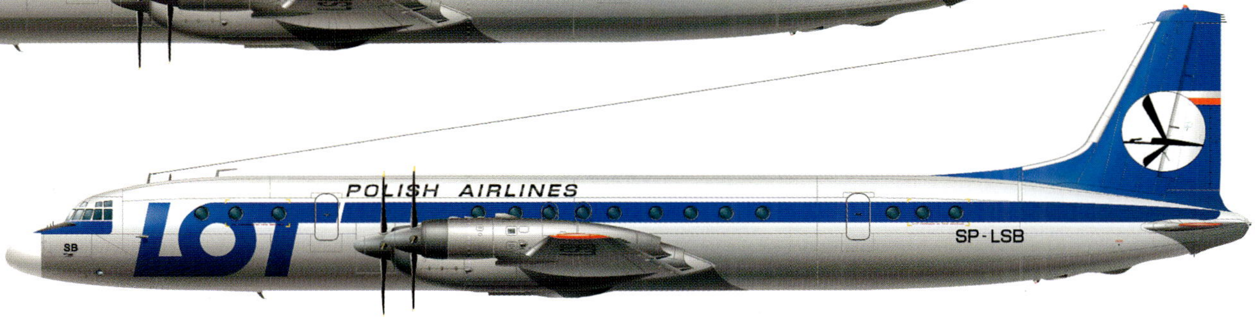

***LOT** adopted its current livery in the mid-1970s. The scheme was deemed a radical departure from contemporary designs, with the **LOT** trademark taking up much of the forward fuselage. Not only the aircraft but all ground vehicles adopted the scheme.*

LOT's first jet aircraft was the Tu-134, of which five were delivered between November 1968 and May 1969, the last being SP-LGE (above). Ideally suited to Scandinavian routes, the Tu-134 also allowed the opening of new routes to western Europe and the Middle East. Commencing in March 1973 with SP-LHA (left), the fleet was augmented by seven Tu-134As, incorporating a fuselage stretch of 2.10 m (83 in) allowing capacity to be increased to 76. Of the five original Tu-134s, SP-LGB was written off at Warsaw in January 1980, with the remaining four being sold to Aeroflot in June 1982.

provided the spark which brought about the end of almost a decade of stagnation. Hungary's appeal for help created a groundswell of sympathy and increasing resentment of Soviet interference. A large proportion of LOT's Il-14s and remaining Li-2s were used to transport medicine, clothing and food to Budapest. Fearful of further unrest in their own country, Poland's leaders relaxed the travel and trade restrictions imposed on its people and businesses.

LOT responded quickly to this new opportunity opening a route to Athens in the spring of 1957 (with seasonal stop-offs at Belgrade and Tirana in the summer months). However, to continue expansion the airline desperately needed new aircraft. With Soviet aircraft production running at almost full capacity to fulfil its military needs, deliveries of civilian airlines were lagging well behind, the aircraft that were built invariably going to Aeroflot. To help relieve the situation VEB of East Germany and Avia of Czechoslovakia had been granted permission to licence-build the Il-14, and it was from these sources that LOT received a further seven Il-14Ps in 1957 (six and one, respectively). In addition, LOT had applied for permission to acquire the first western aircraft since the communist clampdown of 1949. This manifested itself in October of 1957 with the arrival of three second-hand Convair CV 240s. Able to seat 40 passengers in a pressurised cabin, the CV 240s were used to launch two prestigious routes to London and Zurich. Two further CV 240s were added in 1959, along with services to Amsterdam and Rome, although one of the original trio had by then had crashed during a training flight at Warsaw-Okecie in April 1958.

By the end of the 1950s many of the world's major airlines had successfully introduced turboprop aircraft into their fleets. The Soviet aviation industry lagged someway behind the West in the development of practical turboprop airliners with the civil version of the Tu-95 'Bear' bomber, the Tu-114, being the only aircraft available. Aeroflot and the eastern bloc carriers waited anxiously for the design bureaux to produce competitors to the Vickers Viscount, Bristol Britannia, Fokker F27 and Lockheed Electra.

Turboprop era

The first truly successful Soviet turboprop airliner – the Ilyushin Il-18 – emerged in 1958. LOT was anxious to acquire the type and after the initial Aeroflot demands had been met, LOT was granted permission to place an order for an initial three aircraft. The introduction of the Il-18 into service on 24 May 1961 allowed the airline to begin the long-awaited process of retiring its older piston-engined aircraft. With over three times the range and twice the speed of its predecessors, the Il-18 rapidly established an excellent reputation among both aircrew and passengers – a reputation that would endure for three decades.

With no modern equipment available from the Soviet Union for shorter routes requiring less capacity than that offered by the Il-18, LOT enquired about the possibility of acquiring three Vickers Viscounts for use on its regional services. Although, this deal was much to the displeasure of the Soviet leaders, the increasing amount of autonomy, allowed in the wake of the 1956 Hungarian uprising, allowed the deal to go through. In November/December 1962 the airline received its three examples, becoming one of the very few eastern bloc carriers to re-equip with a western type in the 1960s.

The integration of the Il-18 and Viscount allowed the expansion of international routes, new services being provided to Zagreb, Helsinki and Milan. By 1967 Frankfurt, Beirut and Shannon, Ireland, had been added and a further five Il-18s had been added to the fleet. The increase in capacity provided by the Il-18s was tempered by the loss of two of the three Viscounts (one during crew training at Warsaw soon after delivery in December 1962 and a second at St Trond in 1965).

Regional upgrade

Having upgraded its fleet on the prestigious international routes, the next stage in LOT's ambitious development was to address the ageing domestic and regional fleet. In 1965 these services were still being fulfilled by the tired, slow, piston-engined Il-14s and CV 240s, along with the even more obsolete Li-2s. However, the arrival of 10 brand-new Antonov An-24Vs the following year helped transform the frequency, speed and comfort of short and medium-haul services. The Li-2s, Il-14s and CV 240s, as well as the remaining Viscount, were withdrawn from use over the remainder of the decade as a further six An-24Vs were acquired. The consolidation of the fleet to just two main types (An-24s and Il-18s) by 1968 helped to massively boost the airline's profitability by reducing maintenance costs and the expenses of acquiring spares for a wide range of types. This money would become crucial in the next stage of

SP-LAB was the second Il-62 delivered to LOT, arriving at Warsaw in April 1972. It took an immense amount of negotiations and effort for LOT to secure Il-62 procurement in the face of great reluctance from both the USSR and the USA. Eventually, however, LOT could begin its much longed for and prestigious services to New York and Chicago.

Left: In their original livery, LOT's Il-62s carried a portrait of the subject after which each aircraft was named, exemplified by SP-LAA **Mikolaj Kopernik** *seen here at Heathrow in late 1972.*

Below: Il-62Ms were acquired as a direct replacement for the Il-62s and were operated in the new livery. SP-LBE was delivered in April 1981.

Despite their Soviet origins, the Ilyushin Il-62s were much-loved in LOT service and featured on many of the contemporary adverts and posters as the pinnacle of LOT's international services.

development – entering the jet age.

Annual growth for the company in the late 1960s was a respectable 10-12 per cent and additional connections to Leningrad and Kiev had consolidated the airline's position as an important carrier in eastern Europe. To continue its expansion, LOT needed to catch-up with the majority of major carriers, which by then had equipped with first- and second-generation jet transports. Restricted to Soviet bloc-designed aircraft, LOT's Executive Director finally placed an order for five Tupolev Tu-134s. For the first time, interior layout and equipment levels were integrated as specified by LOT, and the 72-seat arrangement was more luxurious than found on standard Tu-134 interiors. Ideally suited for LOT's Scandinavian and other medium-range European routes, the first two Tu-134s arrived at Warsaw in November 1968, entering service that same month. This watershed event not only involved the retraining of the flight crew for jet operations, but extensive new maintenance and technical techniques for airframe and powerplant engineers.

Benefits of jet power

The Tu-134s helped LOT expand its route network in Europe and the Middle East (adding new services to Istanbul and Nicosia) and helping to increase international travel in the early 1970s by 30 per cent.

With LOT's international expansion gathering pace, the Soviet Union became increasingly uneasy with Poland's connections to the West. LOT's management was desperate to acquire the Ilyushin Il-62, which would enable routes to the large Polish communities in North America to be established. Political apprehensions and centrally-planned economic considerations caused the Soviets to block the sale time and again. Instead, LOT was urged to purchase medium-range Tupolev Tu-154s and increase its operations to 'Soviet friendly' destinations. However, LOT management persisted and eventually, in 1970, was granted permission to purchase three Il-62s configured to carry 168 passengers.

With the Il-62 acquired to explore new horizons it was entirely appropriate that the first example (SP-LAA) was named in honour of Poland's famous 15th Century astronomer Mikolaj Kopernik on its arrival in Warsaw in March 1972.

The troubles in establishing services to the US were, however, far from over. US airlines, which had the market exclusively to themselves, objected to LOT 'muscling in' on their customers. In addition, to meet US air traffic and FAA regulations, the Il-62s had the almost insurmountable problem of being fitted with western radio and navigation equipment, as the sales of such materials to Eastern bloc countries was under strict embargo. While these problems were addressed, the three Il-62s entered service on the Moscow, Paris, London and Milan routes.

After lengthy procedures, Ilyushin granted its

Communist-era jet acquisitions

Reg.	C/n	Del.	Notes
Tupolev Tu-134			
SP-LGA	8350602	11/68	sold to Aeroflot 6/82
SP-LGB	8350603	11/68	w/o Warsaw 1/80
SP-LGC	9350804	4/69	sold to Aeroflot 6/82
SP-LGD	9350805	5/69	sold to Aeroflot 6/82
SP-LGE	9350806	5/69	sold to Aeroflot 6/82
Tuplolev Tu-134A			
SP-LHA	3351808	3/73	wfu 6/93
SP-LHB	3351809	4/73	wfu 6/92, to Polish aviation museum, Krakow
SP-LHC	3351810	4/73	wfu 3/93
SP-LHD	48400	6/76	wfu 7/94, to tech. school, Wroclaw
SP-LHE	48405	6/76	wfu 11/93, to museum
SP-LHF	3352005	8/77	from Polish air force (ex-101), wfu 6/94
SP-LHG	3352008	9/78	from Polish air force (ex-102), wfu 3/94
Ilyushin Il-62			
SP-LAA	11004	3/72	named *Mikolaj Kopernik*, w/o Warsaw 3/80
SP-LAB	21105	4/72	named *Tadeusz Kosciuszko*, sold to USSR 11/82
SP-LAC	31401	3/73	named *Fryderyk Chopin*, sold to USSR 6/82
SP-LAD	41604	4/74	named *Kazimierz Pulaski*, sold to USSR 4/83
SP-LAE	41802	12/74	named *Henryk Sienklewicz*, sold to USSR 9/83
SP-LAF	62204	5/76	named *Adam Micklewicz*, sold USSR 5/83
SP-LAG	2725456	5/77	named *Maria Curie-Skiodowska*, sold to USSR 6/82
CCCP-86450	52104	4/80	leased from Aeroflot 4/80 to 10/80
CCCP-86610	41801	3/85	leased from Aeroflot 3/85 to 10/85
CCCP-86611	41803	5/84	leased from Aeroflot 5/84 to 11/84 and 3/85 to 9/85
CCCP-86663	50103	5/78	leased from Aeroflot 5/78 to 10/78 and 5/79 to 9/79
Ilyushin Il-62M			
SP-LBA	2932526	4/79	named *Janusz Kusocinski*, sold to Air Ukraine 1/92
SP-LBB	1034152	2/80	named *Ignacy Paderewski*, sold to Air Ukraine 1/92
SP-LBC	3036253	10/80	named *Joseph Conrad-Korzeniowski*, sold to Air Ukraine 1/92
SP-LBD	1138234	3/81	named *Gen. Wladyslaw E. Sikorski*, sold to Air Ukraine 1/92
SP-LBE	1138546	4/81	named *Stanislaw Monluazko*, sold to Air Ukraine 2/92
SP-LBF	2343554	7/83	named *Fryderyk Chopin*, sold to Air Ukraine 2/92
SP-LBG	3344942	4/84	named *Tadeusz Kosciuszko*, w/o at Warsaw 5/87
SP-LBH	1748445	7/87	sold to Air Ukraine 2/92
SP-LBI	4831739	6/87	leased from Aeroflot 6-87 to 6/88
SP-LBR	4727546	5/86	leased from Tarom 5/86 to 4/87
YR-IRE	4831628	5/84	leased from Tarom 5/84 to 11/84 and 12/84 to 12/85
Yakovlev Yak-40			
SP-GEA	9230224	8/81	loan from Aviation Institute
SP-LEA	9021660	-	loan from 36. SPLT, Polish AF
SP-LEB	9541843	-	loan from 36. SPLT, Polish AF
SP-LEC	9541943	-	loan from 36. SPLT, Polish AF
SP-LED	9542043	-	loan from 36. SPLT, Polish AF
SP-LEE	9021560	-	loan from 36. SPLT, Polish AF
Tupolev Tu-154B-2			
CCCP-85331	331	5/85	leased from Aeroflot 5/85 to 9/89
CCCP-85334	334	5/86	leased from Aeroflot 5/86 to 6/86
CCCP-85455	455	5/85	leased from Aeroflot 5/85 to 10/88
Tupolev Tu-154M			
SP-LCA	727	5/86	sold to Turan Air 7/95
SP-LCB	733	8/86	sold to Turan Air 7/95
SP-LCC	745	3/87	sold to Buryatia A/L 12/96
SP-LCD	755	8/87	sold to Buryatia A/L 8/97
SP-LCE	769	3/88	sold to Bashkirian A/L 12/95
SP-LCF	774	5/88	sold to Bashkirian A/L 4/97
SP-LCG	775	6/88	sold to Samara A/L 11/95
SP-LCH	776	6/88	sold to Bashkirian A/L 1/96
SP-LCI	805	6/89	sold to Samara A/L 7/95
SP-LCK	806	6/89	sold to Samara A/L 9/95
SP-LCL	812	8/89	sold to Bashkirian A/L 5/96
SP-LCM	824	1/90	sold to Aeroflot 8/94
SP-LCN	831	3/90	sold to Aeroflot 8/94
SP-LCO	862	1/91	sold to Polish AF 9/94

The late 1990s/early 2000s was a period of sustained growth for LOT in terms of both passengers and (with the exception of 2001) economic performance. 2001 saw over 3 million passengers flying with LOT for the first time in the airline's history, thanks to its route network expansion programme and the fruit borne by entry into the Qualiflyer Group alliance. The current flight network embraces 12 domestic and 49 international destinations. The airline also boasts one of the youngest fleets in the region, comprising 51 aircraft (5 767s, 19 737s, 8 ATR 72s, 5 ATR 42s, 14 ERJ-145s).

The collapse of the QFG alliance in 2001 led to a substantial loss in that year and led to the Change Program LOT 2001, introducing a corrective route network plan, suspending certain connections and downgrading the frequency of some operations. The operating results of 2000-2002 are shown below:

	2000	2001	2002
Passengers (million)			
total	**2.79**	**3.22**	**3.39**
international	**1.99**	**2.16**	**2.30**
domestic	**0.45**	**0.64**	**0.71**
charter	**0.34**	**0.42**	**0.37**
Cargo (tons)	**22,400**	**21,100**	**20,500**
Profit/loss (mil. Zl)	**33.7**	**-639.1**	**109.3**
Seat load factor	**65%**	**61.8%**	**69.6%**

The increase in core business for LOT in 2002, in the face of a world recession in the industry, justified these measures and, with LOT now a member of Star Alliance, new routes, code-sharing strategies and cost-reduction schemes are again being refined.

Code-sharing has been an important part of LOT's strategy since the mid-1990s. Since 1996 an agreement with American Airlines has given LOT customers access throughout continental USA from New York and Chicago. A code-sharing agreement with British Airways also brought great dividends. However, integration into the Star Alliance (rival to the British Airways-led One World alliance) led to its discontinuation from 30 March 2003. This has been replaced by a code-share agreement with Lufthansa for all 15 route connections between the two countries. Since September 2001 new code-share agreements have also been established with Aeroflot, Austrian Airlines and Cyprus Airlines.

New services to existing routes and an expansion of destinations is also underway with direct services to Bratislava, Odessa and Kaliningrad having been introduced within the last two years. This expansion will be further accelerated by the introduction of the eagerly-awaited EMBRAER ERJ-170 regional jets.

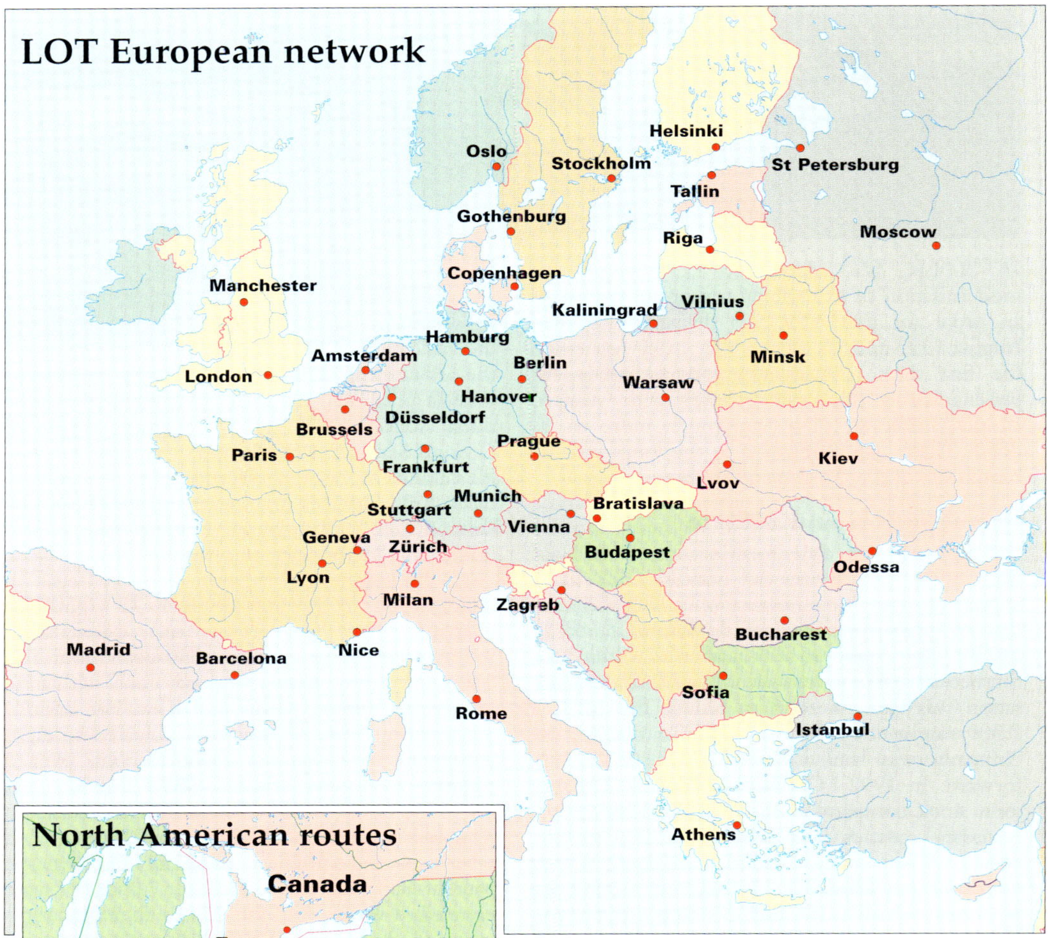

***LOT** has established an extensive European network encompassing many destinations in eastern and western Europe, as well as maintaining long-established routes to Scandinavia and the Baltic. North American destinations comprise New York and Chicago as well as ski holiday charter flights to Edmonton in Canada.*

Boeing 767

LOT's first western-built jet aircraft purchase, the Boeing 767 remains today the sole type used on the prestigious long-haul routes to North America. The first 767-200ER arrived in April 1989 and a further example a month later. Additionally, an Air New Zealand 767-200 was leased for the summer seasons of 1992-94. The higher capacity 767-300ER arrived in 1990 and three are currently operated. From 1996-97 an additional aircraft was leased from Gulf Air. The 767 fleet also plays a major role in LOT's cargo operations, which distribute over 20,000 tons of freight annually. A single 767 is also used by the holiday charter arm of the company, flying twice-weekly services to Tenerife and Las Palmas, as well as other holiday routes when demand is in excess of the capacity of the Boeing 737.

Reg.	C/n	Delivered	Notes
Boeing 767-25DER			
SP-LOA	24733	4/89	named *Gniezno*, ex-N6046P
SP-LOB	24734	5/89	named *Krakow*
Boeing 767-204			
ZK-NBJ	23250	-	leased from Air NZ 5/92-9/92, 3/93-10/93, 5/94-11/94
Boeing 767-35DER			
SP-LPA	24865	8/90	named *Warszawa*, leased to Air NZ 11/95-4/96, 11/99-4/00 and Air Europe 11/96-4/97
SP-LPB	27902	5/95	named *Gdansk*, leased to Universal A/L 12/01
SP-LPC	28656	5/97	named *Poznan*
Boeing 767-3P6ER			
A40-GH	24484	-	leased from Gulf Air 6/96-11/97

Above: SP-LOA** Gniezno **was the first of five Boeing 767s acquired by LOT. The two 767-200ERs are configured to carry 202 passengers (12 business class in 2+2+2 seat layout and 190 in 2+3+2 economy class). Economy seat pitch is around the industry norm of 32 in (81 cm) with seat width at 17 in (43 cm). The larger 767-300ERs seat 18 in business class and 225 in economy using a similar layout. Both versions are powered by twin General Electric CF6-80 turbofans.

Right: Like all Boeing 767s, LOT's examples are capable of carrying LD-2 cargo containers in the lower fuselage. Cargo revenue is a vital component of LOT's profitability, especially on the important North American routes. LOT has its own cargo hub at Warsaw for processing the freight.

***Right:** Once the baton had been passed from the Il-62 to the Boeing 767, **LOT** had a truly modern aircraft with which it could compete with western airlines. **SP-LPC** Poznan was the last of three 767-300ERs, arriving at Warsaw in May 1997.*

***LOT** has never been adverse to leasing aircraft to meet short term demands. Air New Zealand's **ZK-NBJ** operated in **LOT** titles in the mid-1990s.*

Boeing 737

Reg.	C/n	Delivered	Notes
Boeing 737-300			
SP-LMB	23535	-	737-3Q8 leased from ILFC 5/96-8/97
SP-LMC	28668	7/97	737-36N
SP-LMD	28669	7/97	737-36N sub-leased to Olympic A/W 2/98-5/98
ZK-NGD	28732	-	737-3U3 leased from Air NZ 3/99-10/99
Boeing 737-400			
SP-LLA	27131	4/93	737-45D
SP-LLB	27156	6/93	737-45D
SP-LLC	27157	7/93	737-45D
SP-LLD	27256	3/94	737-45D
SP-LLE	27914	7/96	737-45D, ex-N1786B
SP-LLF	28752	4/97	737-45D
SP-LLG	28753	6/97	737-45D
SP-LLH	25594	-	leased from Indigo 4/00-10/00
Boeing 737-500			
SP-LKA	27416	12/92	737-55D
SP-LKB	27417	12/92	737-55D
SP-LKC	27418	12/92	737-55D
SP-LKD	27419	12/92	737-55D
SP-LKE	27130	3/93	737-55D
SP-LKF	27368	4/95	737-55D
SP-LKG	24825	10/00	737-53C, ex-F-GHOL
SP-LKH	24826	12/00	737-53C, ex-F-GHUL
SP-LKI	24827	11/00	737-53C, ex-F-GINL
SP-LKK	28996	3/01	737-5L9, ex-OY-APL
SE-DNI	26419	-	737-59D, leased from Linjeflyg 4/92-3/93
SE-DNK	26421	-	737-59D, leased from Linjeflyg 5/92-4/93
Boeing 737-800			
SP-		-/03	737-85D, on order
SP-		-/03	737-85D, on order

The most numerically important aircraft in LOT's inventory, the Boeing 737 became the second acquisition from the manufacturer in the early 1990s, as the airline strived to modernise its fleet following the end of the Cold War. The deal for initially six Boeing 737-500s was signed in 1990, with the first four examples entering service in December 1992. The aircraft were employed on LOT's more prestigious connections to western Europe with the Tu-154M fleet continuing to serve the routes to east European cities, southern Europe and the Middle East. Prior to the delivery of the final two 737-500s from the batch of six, LOT leased two similar aircraft from Swedish airline Linjeflyg.

The 737-500s were joined between April 1993 and June 1997 by seven higher capacity 737-400s, their arrival allowing the retirement of the austere and expensive to operate Tu-154Ms. From May 1996 a third variant of Boeing's 'Baby Jet' was added in the shape of the 737-300. Destined for operations to the Mediterranean and other holiday routes, initially a single example was taken on short-term lease from ILFC, before two more permanent lease aircraft arrived from GECAS in July 1997, both of which are still in LOT service today. An additional 737-300 was leased from Air New Zealand for the summer season of 1999.

A further four second-hand 737-500s were added to the fleet in 2000-01, bringing the total of 737s operated up to today's inventory of 19.

Playing a major role in LOT's successful expansion and rise to profitability in the 1990s, the 737 is likely to remain a key component of LOT's long-term strategy for many years. This has been reinforced by an order for two new-generation 165-seat 737-800s placed in October 1996. Initially intended to enter service in 1998, the aircraft are now due for delivery in 2003. LOT's entire fleet of 737s are arranged in a 3+3 configuration with seat pitch and width matching the 767 standard of 32 in (81 cm) and 17 in (43 cm), respectively. The smaller 737-500s seat 108 passengers, with 72 in economy and 16 in business. The stretched 737-400s increase capacity to 147 with 99 economy and 48 business class seats. The 737-300s, as is the way with most charter operations, have a single economy-class layout accommodating a maximum of 145 passengers.

***SP-LMC** is one of the two 737-300s leased for charter operations. Charter levels peaked in 2001 at 415,000 passengers, but a downturn in the Polish economy and worries following the September 2001 terrorist attack in New York reduced 2002 figures to 372,000.*

***LOT**'s Boeing 737-400 fleet is utilised on the higher-density European routes. In addition, two of the seven aircraft are used for charter flights as the need arises. **SP-LLE** (right) was delivered to the airline in July 1996, two weeks after its first flight. The Boeing 737 fleet carries the majority of the 2.3 million passengers that travel annually on **LOT**'s international scheduled flights. All of **LOT**'s current 737s are powered by **CFM56-3C1** engines (below). The 737-800s will be powered by **CFM56-7B26s**.*

Russia's trijet workhorse

Tupolev Tu-154s in Russian service

For almost 70 years commercial aviation in the Soviet Union was dominated by the all-encompassing state-owned airline Aeroflot. By 1990, fulfiling scheduled, charter, cargo and military needs, the giant company had over 550 Tu-154s, connecting centres of population within that vast country as well as routes into eastern and western Europe, and the Middle East. The break-up of the Soviet Union in the early 1990s and the subsequent de-regulation of commercial aviation encouraged a plethora of fledgling airlines to form, some from the former Aeroflot directorates and many more from scratch. Of these, a large percentage were to survive only a few short years or even months, but the survivors have been steadily consolidating and expanding their routes and services, in many cases thanks to the availability of the 'Tushka' in large numbers and at knockdown prices.

***Main picture:** Still the most important medium-range passenger transport type in Russia, the Tu-154, especially in its M variant, will continue to litter the aprons of Russia's commercial airports for years to come. New noise regulations have restricted its use in western Europe, but its low unit-cost and availability are an attractive proposition to many of the cash-strapped carriers. Here two Siberian Airlines examples (Tu-154B-2 and Tu-154B) line-up next to a pair of Tyumenaviatrans Tu-154Ms at Moscow-Vnukovo.*

***Below left:** Ural Airlines Tu-154B-2 RA-85193, a converted Tu-154B-1, is seen landing at its home airport (Ekaterinburg-Koltsovo) in May 2000.*

AEROBRATSK

Formed as joint stock company Bratsk Air Enterprise in 1995 from the remnants of Aeroflot's Bratsk division, the carrier was renamed Aerobratsk in 2001. The airline currently has a single Tu-154B-2 and two Tu-154Ms on its books, all configured in a single-class 164-seat layout. The former may now have been withdrawn from use and the latter pair is currently leased out to Aviaekspresskruiz and East Line Airlines, respectively.

AEROFLOT-DON

In 1993 Donavia Airlines (Donskie Avialinii) was formed from Yug Avia, itself a product of Aeroflot's Rostov-on-Don division. The airline operated a large fleet (including many Tu-154Bs) under this name until Aeroflot Russian Airlines acquired a controlling (51 per cent) interest in 2000. Flying internal and international charter and scheduled routes, the carrier has been renamed Aeroflot-Don and its current fleet includes a single Tu-154B-1, six Tu-154B-2s and two leased Tu-154Ms, most of which, such as Tu-154B-2 RA-85435 (below), still carry Donavia titles.

AEROFLOT RUSSIAN AIRLINES

Formerly Russia's International directorate, Aeroflot Russian Airlines is the largest of around 300 companies which were created following the privatisation of Aeroflot. Known as Aeroflot Russian International Airlines from 1992-2000, the carrier currently has some 22 Tu-154Ms in its fleet, which are used to connect cities within Russia and the CIS, as well as flying routes to the Middle East, Asia, and eastern and western Europe.

AEROKUZBASS

Based at Novokuznetsk, Aerokuzbass previously operated as Aerokuznetsk between 1992-99 having originally been formed as Aeroflot's Novokuznetsk division. Today it owns two Tu-154B-2s and three Tu-154Ms, two of the latter being leased out to Iran Air Tours. Aerokuzbass also owns three Mi-8s and an An-24RV.

AIRLINES 400

Airlines 400 takes its name from Aircraft Repair Plant 400 based at Moscow-Vnukovo, whose management formed the airline in 1999. Along with a fleet of three Il-76 freighters, A400 operates three Tu-154Ms on charter and some scheduled routes in a single-class 164-seat layout. Wearing the company's smart blue and white livery, RA-85847 is seen at Tivat, Montenegro, in August 2001.

AJT Air International

Formed in 1992, AJT Air International, operating out of Moscow-Sheremetyevo, currently flies a single Tu-154M (above right) in addition to its fleet of up to eight Ilyushin Il-86s, the majority of which are leased. Three further Tu-154s (one S and two Ms) are currently with the airline on short-term leases, which may be extended. The airline operates scheduled services and, since its take-over by Natalie tours in 2001, an increasing number of charter flights to Europe, Asia and Africa.

Aviaekspresskruiz

Based at Moscow-Vnukovo, Aviaekspresskruiz was established in 1993 as an *ad hoc* charter outfit. Along with its fleet of six Yak-40s, the airline leases variants of the Tu-154 according to demand. The company has varied between a minimum of two and maximum of four aircraft in recent years.

Alrosa Mirny Air Enterprise

Originally formed as Aeroflot's Mirny division, the company operated as the transport wing of the diamond producing company Almazy Rossii Sakha between 1995 and 2000. Based at Mirny airport, the company was renamed Alrosa in 2000. Its current fleet includes four Tu-154Ms (including RA-85684; left) which are used to support the parent company's mining and trading activities, as well as offering scheduled passenger services.

Aviaenergo

A subsidiary of the United Energy System of Russia, Aviaenergo was established in 1994 to fulfil the company's air logistic needs and is based at Moscow-Sheremetyevo. The company currently has two Tu-154Ms on its books, configured with a three-class interior, complementing its two Ilyushin Il-62s (one in VIP layout) and a single Ilyushin Il-76, currently on loan to East Line Airlines.

Avial NV

Avial NV is a Moscow-Domodedovo-based cargo airline with a single passenger-configured Tu-154B-2, which is used in support of its fleet of Antonov An-12 and An-26 freighters.

AVL (Arkhangelskie Vozdushnye Linii)

Formed as Aeroflot's Arkhangelsk directorate, AVL (Arkhangelsk Airlines) can trace its own identity back to 1961. Having operated a large fleet of Tu-154s from its Arkhangelsk base in the 1980s, only four Tu-154B-2s now remain on the books, of which two are currently leased out. One of the remaining B-2s is configured in a very high-density 180-seat passenger configuration.

Baikal Airlines

When formed from Aeroflot's Irkutsk division in 1992, Baikal Airlines had one of the largest fleets of the newly formed airlines, including some 25 Tu-154s. Economic realities have resulted in a drastic reduction of the fleet and, accordingly, only four Tu-154B-2s and four Tu-154Ms remain, of which three of the former and all of the latter are currently leased out, including RA-85690 (right) currently with Sibir Airlines. The remaining Tu-154B-2 operates scheduled services from Irkutsk International in a single-class 164-seat layout.

(BAL) – Bashkirskie Avialinii (Bashkirian Airlines)

Operating from 1933 as part of Aeroflot's Bashkirian directorate, BAL emerged in its present form in 1994 and currently has some 10 Tu-154Ms in its fleet. Several of these are regularly leased out, including RA-85773 (left) seen here with Karachi-based carrier Shaheen Air International in late 2001 and now back serving with BAL.

Blagoveshchensk Airlines

Recent start-up carrier Blagoveshchensk Airlines commenced operations in 2001 and has recently received three Tu-154Ms in a single-class 164-seat layout. In addition, for its low-density short-haul operations the airline operates three Yak-40s.

CHERNOMOR-AVIA

Named Chernomorskie Airlines from its inception in 1994 until 1997, Chernomor-Avia is based at the Black Sea port of Sochi. Its Tu-154 fleet comprises a single B-1, seen below in the newly applied green livery at Sharjah in March 2002, and two B-2s, one of which (RA-85332; right) is shown prior to repainting in the house colour scheme.

CHITAAVIA

Originally Aeroflot's Chita division, ChitaAvia was established in its present form in 1991 and, apart from a single Polish-built Antonov An-2, the only aircraft operated from its Chita-Kadala base are two Tu-154B-2s and a single Tu-154M.

CONTINENTAL AIRWAYS

Operating out of Moscow-Sheremetyevo, Continental Airways fly three Tu-154Ms (one leased and two under a lease-to-purchase arrangement), mainly on charter flights. The airline began operations in 1995 with two leased Ilyushin Il-86s.

DAGHESTAN AIRLINES (AVIALINII DAGESTANA)

Unofficially the national airline of the autonomous Republic of Daghestan, Daghestan Airlines was formed originally as Makhachkala Air Enterprise in 1994 from Aeroflot's Makhachkala division. Today the airline operates two Tu-154Ms, of which RA-85840 (below) is the sole example to wear the airline's impressively colourful livery.

DALAVIA

Known from 1953-1995 as Far East Avia and from 1995-1998 as Khabarovsk Aviation Enterprise, Dalavia operates a fleet of six Tu-154B-1s, six Tu-154B-2s and a single Tu-154M from its Khabarovsk-Central base on scheduled passenger-carrying routes within Russia and the CIS.

EAST LINE AIRLINES

Operating scheduled, charter and cargo flights in Russia, east Asia, the Middle East and Europe, East Line Airlines was founded in 1995 by the East Line Group, which also has the controlling interest of Moscow-Domodedovo airport. The airline owns one Tu-154M outright, but has long- and short-term leases for additional Tu-154B-1s, Tu-154B-2s and Tu-154Ms, varying between 5-11 in number, according to demand. A number of the aircraft wear original Aeroflot colours or the livery of the owner, however, sister-ship RA-85829 (below), on a long-term lease from Enkor, has been repainted in standard East Line colours.

ENKOR (FORMERLY CHELYABINSK AE)

Emerging from Chelyabinsk Air Enterprise in 2000, Enkor adopted the former's fleet of Tu-154s. Many were still in Aeroflot colours at this time, but are being repainted as they reach major overhaul. All but one of the Tu-154B/B-1/B-2s have now been sold, although at least four Tu-154Ms have been retained, including RA-85754 (below) which is configured with a two-class 128-seat layout.

EURASIA AIR COMPANY (YEVRAZIA ROSSIA)

Operating since 1997 from Moscow-Bykovo, Eurasia Air Company is believed to operate a single Tu-154B-2 in single-class 150-seat configuration. Other assets include two leased Yak-40s, two Antonov An-12 freighters and an Ilyushin Il-86.

GAZPROMAVIA

Gazprom is the world's largest gas company, which accounts for 94% of Russia's gas production (some 23% of world output). With interests throughout Russia and the CIS, the company maintains a fleet of over 100 aircraft operated by Gazpromavia, the majority of which are helicopters and cargo aircraft used to support the company's operations. Gazpromavia does, however, operate a fleet of passenger transports, including five Tu-154Ms in a 166-seat layout. Gazpromavia has major bases at Moscow-Ostafyevo and Vnukovo and sub-bases at Kaluga, Perm, Samara-Smyshlaevka, Sochi, Ukhta, Yamburg and Yugorsk.

IDF – IRON DRAGONFLY

Republic of Tatarstan charter airline Iron Dragonfly was formed in 1993 and operates from Kazan-International. The airline operates a single Tu-154B-2 (seen below with IDF Tatarstan titles) and two Tu-154Ms. The company's cargo operations are fulfilled by a fleet of leased Ilyushin Il-76s, and a single Antonov An-12 and An-26.

G-BOAF

Aérospatiale/BAC

Concorde

Concorde was the perfect child of the 'love-hate' Anglo-French relationship. National pride on both sides of the English Channel/La Manche ensured that the very best was brought out of the engineers who worked on the programme. In spite of – and arguably because of – the tension which existed between the two partners, certainly at cultural and political levels, the result was the most beautiful and capable aircraft ever built, which ushered in an entirely new means of spanning the world's oceans. However, a global fuel crisis, hostile US industrialists, meddling politicians, and a concerted and lifelong crusade against it by environmental lobbyists conspired to rob Concorde of the true commercial success it so richly deserved, while in recent times the world's most publicised commercial aircraft tragedy cast further doubts on its viability in an air transport world obsessed with seat-mile costs. The Concorde community recovered briefly from the crash, but terrorist attacks in the US, a global economic down-turn, and a war in the Middle East combined to provide the final blows to Concorde's questionable profitability, and both Air France and British Airways announced that they would cease operations in 2003. Yet, through it all, Concorde emerged as one of the handful of true technological marvels of the 20th Century, with capabilities as yet unmatched in the 21st, and which may not be achieved again for decades – if at all.

"Soon there will be only two kinds of airlines: those with Concorde and those which take twice as long." That was how the Aérospatiale/BAC team advertised the Concorde to the world in its formative years. Nearly forty years on the statement is still essentially true (provided one is flying between New York and London or Paris), but the supersonic revolution in air transport envisaged by the airlines, manufacturers and politicians failed to materialise. Nothing, however, should be taken away from the huge technological achievement of the Concorde programme.

At a time when most airliners look so alike that even dedicated plane-spotters find some of them hard to tell apart in a single glance, one aircraft stands out from the crowd. Although most commercial aircraft share the same configuration – a blunt and relatively fat fuselage, a modestly swept high-aspect ratio wing, underslung podded engines and a conventional tail unit – Concorde is unique: a needle-nosed tailless delta, with paired engines in nacelles mounted directly under the centre section. It is instantly recognisable to most of the population, and is even widely regarded as a thing of beauty.

Concorde is not just unique in appearance. While other modern airliners cross the Atlantic in seven hours, Concorde can fly the route in less than half that time, cruising at up to 60,000 ft (18288 m), high above other airline traffic scuttling along at 35,000 ft (10668 m) – this is more than 10 miles (16 km) high, where the sky is a deep dark blue and the earth's curvature is clearly apparent. Concorde's speed is particularly awe-inspiring, since the aircraft zips along at more than 20 miles (32 km) per minute, or 1,350 mph (2173 km/h) – equivalent to the speed of a 0.303-in rifle bullet – and sustains this speed for hours on end! Military aircraft can reach these speeds and heights, of course, but usually only briefly, and with their aircrew carefully insulated from the environment in bone-domes, partial pressure suits and the like, whereas Concorde has done it routinely, every day, its crew in shirt-sleeves, drinking coffee, eating a normal meal, sometimes stretching their legs by walking back into the cabin, perhaps occasionally chatting with the passengers.

"Stewards will have no trouble serving martinis and meals. Passengers will find no difficulty consuming them. They will just have to drink a little faster – New York will be only a few hours away," said one analyst. Concorde has made supersonic flight almost boringly dull.

Almost, but not quite, because flying on Concorde is still a rare experience, available to only a select few. Few of even its most regular passengers do not cast a glance at the Machmeter in the cabin as the aircraft accelerates smoothly through the sound barrier and then on past Mach 2, and the aircraft retains a mystique and charisma even among its pilots. When Concorde first entered service, many of its pilots had a military background, and they, in particular, appreciated Concorde's crisply responsive flying controls, its stability, and the enormous reserves of power available.

Everything happens more quickly in Concorde, but the aircraft is in many ways easy to fly, with handling characteristics that flatter the pilot. With its massive high-lift delta wing, auto-stabilisation and precise auto-throttles, the aircraft is particularly easy to land; it can literally 'land itself', with the two autopilots taking the aircraft safely down (by ILS) to where Concorde's wheels are only 15 ft (4.5 m) above the runway. At this point, the pilot must decide whether he has sufficient visibility to complete the roll-out (200 m/656 ft is the 'magic figure') and take over (and possibly overshoot), or let the aircraft complete its landing.

Concorde's performance was more than just a 'pilot pleaser', however. Speed has always been of critical importance in transport, and has always been able to attract the payment of premium rate fares, from mail coaches to express trains and from fast sailing clippers to the first steamships. In interwar commercial aviation, lumbering biplane airliners rapidly gave way to faster, sleeker monoplanes like the Douglas DC-3.

The demands of war drove up the performance of military aircraft between 1939 and 1945, stimulating the development of aero engines, airframes and aerodynamics. By the end of the war, jet- and rocket-powered fighters with lightweight airframes and swept-back wings were in front-line service. It was always inevitable that some of these advances would subsequently filter through into the development of new, faster airliners. The first generation of jet airliners marked a relatively small improvement over their piston-engined predecessors, with modest wing sweep and early-generation centrifugal flow turbojet engines. Nonetheless, even aircraft like the de Havilland Comet and Sud Caravelle were significantly faster than the propliners they replaced, and transported their passengers in greater comfort at higher altitude.

Accent on economy

While the Cold War stimulated higher and higher performance in military aircraft (including supersonic speed capability), airliner performance did not increase as rapidly, with development instead being concentrated on making aircraft more reliable and economic to operate. Thus, the Boeing 707 was only marginally faster than the Comet, though it had a longer range and higher capacity. The overpowered VC10 was significantly faster and capable of using shorter, more primitive runways, but was not a major sales success.

The development of supersonic bombers like the Convair B-58 led some observers to expect similar performance in commercial transport aircraft. A B-58 Hustler crossed the Atlantic to participate in the 1961 Paris Air Salon in only

Many observers predicted that the tragedy at Gonesse on 25 July 2000 might have ended Concorde operations for good, but following over a year on the ground, the aircraft returned to work. Here F-BTSD flies Air France's first post-crash service.

In recent years British Airways operated a larger Concorde fleet than Air France, with five aircraft in use to guarantee a daily New York service plus capacity for a seasonal Caribbean Concorde service (once a week) to Barbados, serving the luxury holiday market. Initial plans called for all seven aircraft to be brought back into service after modification to allow a twice-daily New York service.

Above: Assembly of the prototype, 001, began at Toulouse in April 1966. This view from October shows the fuselage and main wing section virtually complete, with the forward fuselage about to be mated.

Right: Six forward fuselage sub-assemblies are constructed at Weybridge. The central fuselage (designed by BAC at Filton) and wings were built in France, including outer wing panels by Dassault.

Below: F-WTSC, the second French production aircraft, takes shape on the Toulouse line as the first, F-WTSB, has the finishing touches applied in the foreground. Each line built one prototype, one pre-production and eight production Concordes.

Some of the differences were cultural, as many French programme insiders found the British informal and casual, especially in their easy use of first names. This was reportedly highlighted at the end of one particularly complicated and controversial meeting at which agreement had finally been reached on a difficult point. The British engineer had a suggestion for his French opposite number, saying, "Jean, just so that both sides are clear on what has been agreed, why not get Honorine in so that you can dictate a note on this into the record?"

The puzzled Frenchman supposedly replied, "D'accord, mais qui est Honorine?" ["OK, but who is Honorine?"] Honorine was his own secretary, whom he knew only as 'Mademoiselle Dupont'.

Co-operation between these two countries thus was not always easy, and the relationship sometimes showed considerable strains, but it did result in a generation of superb aircraft, all of which became leaders in their respective categories.

The French short-range SST model was finally dropped in May 1964, upon French recognition that only a transatlantic SST would be viable. The longer-range version was redesigned and increased in size, with a 14-ft (4.26-m) fuselage stretch, 15 per cent more wing area, and a higher gross weight of 367,000 lb (166470 kg), together with more powerful Olympus 593 engines. This aircraft quickly attracted the interest of Pan Am, whose chairman, Juan Trippe, signed options for six of them on 3 June 1963.

Competition from the US

The US had already made tentative steps towards developing its own SST, but when the XB-70 bomber programme fell by the wayside, so, too, did the original American SST. Pan Am was the nearest thing the US had to a flag-carrying national airline, and its order for the European SST provided enough of a shock to relaunch a US SST programme. President John F. Kennedy (who also promised to put an American on the moon before the decade was out) threw his weight behind the project, calling for state and private investment to create "a commercially successful supersonic transport superior to that being built in any other country in the world".

Congress allocated $100 million to the SST programme in the FY 1964 budget, while TWA and Pan Am put in $2.1 million in October 1963, outlining their requirement for a total fleet of at least 21 SSTs. Boeing and Lockheed produced competing designs, the latter being much like a scaled-up Concorde in configuration, albeit with improved materials promising much higher cruising speeds.

Congress finally gave Boeing funding for the manufacture of a first Model 2707 prototype in late 1965, but this put the US SST programme years behind the European and Soviet SSTs. The programme was delayed further when it became clear that the original variable-geometry 'swing-wing' design would be unworkable (even with canard foreplanes, added to produce the 2707-200). The redesigned 2707-300 switched to a tailed delta configuration, with podded engines hung from close to the trailing edge of the wing.

Boeing decided that the best way to recapture any market share lost to the European Concorde would be to build a bigger, faster, and more efficient design, taking advantage of the US's greater financial muscle to effectively skip a generation. Crucially, Boeing opted to produce an aircraft that would cruise at Mach 2.7 while carrying 234 passengers. This dictated the use of exotic titanium alloys and inferred an all-up weight of about 1 million lb (454000 kg). This was too ambitious for the technology then available and made it inevitable that the programme would fail – and in doing so, it consumed huge amounts of government funding and generated considerable opposition. Had the aircraft entered service, its speed would have given little advantage over Concorde, since even a Mach 3 cruise would have shaved only about half an hour off Concorde's journey time. The US SST also sparked an environmental backlash, and the Coalition Against the SST ran a memorable full-page advertisement that read "SST Airplane of Tomorrow. Breaks windows, cracks walls, stampedes cattle and will hasten the end of the American Wilderness".

By 1968, Boeing had received 122 options for its SST, while BAC and Aérospatiale could count 78 options. Crucially, while Concorde was then expected to be certificated in 1972, no-one expected the US SST to enter service before 1978, leaving a six-year gap during which more Concordes were likely to be sold, giving a predicted production total of 240 Concordes.

On 18 May 1971, the US Senate finally voted to end funding in a 58-37 vote, after far more money had been spent than was ever spent on the Concorde programme. Cancellation effectively left Concorde as the 'only supersonic game in town' for US airlines.

Continued development

In 1965 an additional 6 ft 6 in (1.98 m) was added to Concorde's fuselage and the aircraft became a 140-seater, with new engines each producing 40,000 lb st (177.89 kN). Quite apart from Concorde's promised performance, the aircraft was said to be a generation ahead of any other civil transport aircraft programme, thanks not only to its advanced configuration and supersonic aerodynamics but also to its highly advanced and sophisticated flight controls, propulsion and auxiliary systems.

Harold Wilson's incoming Labour government (which supposedly supported and embraced what it called the "white-hot technological revolution") announced Britain's withdrawal from the Concorde programme on 19 November 1964, prompted mainly by US pressure. Britain's economy was in difficulties and relied heavily on US co-operation, and the US had made no secret of the fact that it felt that in pursuing such a high-cost prestige project as Concorde, the British were attempting to 'box above their weight' and thus could not be expected to be bailed out. The British government soon became aware that the November 1962 agreement would completely prevent unilateral withdrawal, unless massive penalty fees were to be paid. Instead, the Wilson

Above: British Concordes were assembled in the 'Brabazon' hangar at BAC Filton, originally built to produce the airliner of the same name. In this view the first UK production aircraft G-BBDG is virtually complete in the background, while two more take shape. Most of Concorde's UK airframe content (forward and rear fuselage, fin) was built at Weybridge. BAC Filton was responsible for the engine nacelles and intakes.

Above left: In the late 1960s Air France flew a Breguet Br.763 'Deux Ponts' service between Paris-Orly and Bristol-Lulsgate, initially weekly but later increased to thrice-weekly. As well as carrying passengers, the 'Deux Ponts' transported engines and engine parts between the Bristol Siddeley (later Rolls-Royce) Patchway plant (part of the Filton complex) and SNECMA's facility at Melun-Villaroche.

Olympus testbed

Its load-carrying capability, good range, outstanding altitude performance and adequate ground clearance made the Vulcan the only candidate to provide a testbed for the Olympus 593. Having earlier been involved in Blue Steel missile trials, XA903 – a Vulcan B.Mk 1 – was bailed to Bristol Siddeley in January 1964 and was fitted with an Olympus in a nacelle under the fuselage. It was modified to house a crew of seven and carry over 11 tons of test equipment, which could include an icing rig (left, over Weston-super Mare in 1971). In its new guise it flew again on 9 September 1966. From April 1973 it flew with the Tornado's RB.199 engine, and made the last flight of a Vulcan B.Mk 1 on 22 February 1979 before being scrapped in 1984.

Concorde 001 was formally rolled out at Toulouse-Blagnac on 11 December 1967, the date on which the UK officially accepted the French spelling of the aircraft's name. Up to this point BAC had been more than happy with the 'e' spelling, and its publicity material reflected that. However, the UK government had steadfastly called the aircraft 'Concord' up to Anthony Wedgwood-Benn's famous blessing for the French spelling.

Above right: At the time of its roll-out Sud was maintaining the February 1968 first flight date for 001, although this was obviously not going to happen. A two-month factory strike by Sud workers in early 1968 further held up the programme. Here the aircraft utilises its brake chute during the long series of taxi tests which culminated in 120-kt runs.

Top right: In August 1968 001 was used to test the emergency runway barrier at Toulouse, installed at the end of the newly-constructed 13,000-ft (3962-m) Runway 33. Thankfully this equipment was not needed at any time during Concorde development.

government cancelled a plethora of military aircraft programmes – initially the HS.681 STOL transport and the RN/RAF P.1154 V/STOL strike fighter, and later the BAC TSR.2 as well, replacing all of them with off-the-shelf US aircraft.

On 20 January 1965 it was quietly (but nonetheless humiliatingly) announced that Britain would not, after all, withdraw from the Concorde programme. In terms of Britain's relations with France, however, the damage had been done, and UK aspirations to join the Common Market were dealt a heavy blow. The first metal was cut for the first prototype in April 1965.

Workshare on Concorde was evenly divided, with each country making different sub-assemblies for the two national final assembly lines. In France, Concorde work was divided between four main Sud-Aviation factories (at Bouguenais, Marignane, St Martin/Toulouse and St Nazaire), and Dassault at Bourges provided outer wings, Hispano Suiza the main landing gear and Messier the nose gear. The forward fuselage, nose, rear fuselage, fin and rudder were built by BAC at Weybridge, while BAC was also responsible for the fuel, electrical, oxygen, air-conditioning and fire protection systems. BAC Filton designed the nose (built at Weybridge) and the mid fuselage (built in France), and built the engine bays and intakes.

Remarkably, these nationally produced sub-assemblies were normally transported inside the cavernous hold of a Super Guppy freighter (so that parts of every Concorde built – like every early Airbus – made their first flight carried aloft by Boeing-built wings). The assemblies fitted together with exemplary precision, leading one distinguished author to describe the Concorde final assembly as being like "watch-making in a hangar". Work on the engine continued in parallel, though Bristol Siddeley by then had been absorbed by Rolls-Royce.

Structural tests

In March 1966 the first centre fuselage and inner wing section (weighing some 16 tonnes) was delivered to the Centre des Essais Aéronautiques de Toulouse (CEAT) (Aeronautical Testing Centre) for static and thermal testing. A 70-ft (21-m) fuselage and nose section was delivered to the Royal Aircraft Establishment at Farnborough for static fatigue testing in December 1970. The facilities at CEAT were impressive: it could record and process 8,000 data points every two seconds, test loads were applied via 80 servo-controlled hydraulic jacks, 35,000 infra-red lamps provided kinetic heating, and 70000 litres (15,400 Imp gal) of liquid nitrogen were available for cooling, capable of reducing skin temperature from +120°C to -10°C (248°F to 14°F) within 15 minutes. The Farnborough fatigue specimen had simulated flight loads applied by 100 servo-controlled hydraulic jacks, with accurate simulation of cabin pressurisation, air conditioning and fuel movement, as well. The Farnborough airframe was encased in an outer 'glove', through which hot and cold air was pumped (driven by 2,300-hp/1716-kW fans) to simulate the flight temperature cycle. Final assembly of the first flying prototype (001) began at Toulouse in April 1966, while assembly of the British prototype 002 began at Filton in August.

Individual systems were tested in various rigs. A hydraulics rig that completely replicated the flying control system with its associated hydraulic and electrical systems (incorporating the undercarriage functioning system) was installed at Aérospatiale's Blagnac facility. The fuel systems test rig at Filton consisted of a complete reproduction of the aircraft's fuel tank system mounted on a movable platform which could change position to simulate the attitudes and accelerations that the real system would experience in flight, and could accurately simulate real-world fuel temperatures and pressures. Simulators were used for the investigation of flying characteristics and for studies of control-system response, and two full-scale electrical systems rigs were also built.

001 first flight

Commanded by André Turcat, with Michel Rétif, Henri Perrier and Jacques Guignard on the flight deck, and Claude Durand and Jean Belon in the instrument-packed cabin, F-WTSS lifted off from Toulouse-Blagnac's Runway 33 at 1538 local time on 2 March 1969. Take-off weight was 116 tonnes, of which 28 tonnes was fuel. After 42 minutes, during which the undercarriage remained down and locked, the aircraft made a downwind landing, requiring the brake chute to be deployed. Throughout the flight 001 was accompanied by a Meteor NF.Mk 11 from the CEV flown by Gilbert Defer, and an MS.760 flown by Jean Dabos and with a Sud-Aviation photographer on board. An Alouette III was airborne to provide emergency fire/rescue cover. A second flight was performed on 8 March, during which the undercarriage was retracted.

An Olympus 593B engine was run 'on the bench' at Filton in November 1965, and a complete engine with its SNECMA variable-geometry exhaust assembly was test-run at Melun-Villaroche, France in June 1966. Following this, engine testing began at the NGTE (National Gas Turbine Establishment) at Pyestock on the periphery of the RAE airfield at Farnborough. Meanwhile, the Olympus 593 engine on test at Filton achieved 35,190 lb (156.50 kN) of thrust, which exceeded the engine's Stage 1 brochure requirements, setting the scene for further testing.

Olympus 593 takes flight

On 9 September flight testing of a Rolls-Royce/ SNECMA Olympus 593 engine began, the engine being mounted in a dummy nacelle and intake under the belly of a Vulcan B.Mk 1 (XA903). The Vulcan's performance limitations meant that the tests were restricted to a maximum speed of Mach 0.98, but proposals that a TSR.2 should be used for high-speed testing were rejected. The TSR.2 prototype had been flown with Olympus 22R (Mk 320) engines, which were the first supersonic Olympus engines, using the same materials as the Concorde engines and having dimensions similar to those of Concorde's 593s. The Olympus-Vulcan testbed had logged 100 flying hours by January 1968, and it, and the variable-geometry exhaust assembly (tested at Melun-Villaroche), were finally cleared for flight in the Concorde prototypes. From April 1967 simulated high-altitude testing began in the high-altitude chamber at Saclay. This was a crucial area, since the production Concorde was expected to cruise at great height, above the tropopause, in the stable and cloudless air of the stratosphere, where very low temperatures would significantly increase the engines' thrust – which is limited by operating temperature. This is naturally reduced by lower temperature air entering the intake.

Fortunately, the Olympus 593 was destined to be a superb engine, reliable and fulfilling all expectations of its performance, while development was also generally trouble-free. For example, in February 1970 the engine ran continuously for 300 hours, equivalent to nearly 100 non-stop transatlantic flights. Such progress was achieved even while minor refinements were made to the engine design. In July 1969 an annular combustion system, designed to reduce exhaust smoke, was specified for the engines fitted to the pre-production and production aircraft, and in May 1970 a new low-noise, lower-weight, aerodynamically refined Thrust Reverser Aft (TRA) was added.

Pan Am's interest in Concorde was soon echoed by other airlines, and by May 1967 Concorde sales options had reached a total of 74 aircraft for 16 customer airlines, thanks partly to a full-scale Concorde interior mock-up presented to potential customer airlines at Filton from February 1967.

In August, Concorde 001, the first French prototype, underwent resonance testing at Toulouse. Its ceremonial roll-out came on 11 December 1967 in front of 1,100 VIP guests. The roll-out was marked by a series of PR photographs, one of which included a stewardess from each of the 15 airlines which by then had committed to the

Above: Having been beaten into the air by the Tupolev Tu-144 (first flight 31 December 1968), the Anglo-French consortium was eager to get Concorde flying. Bad weather delayed the first flight until the late afternoon of 2 March. This is the memorable moment when 'TSS lifted off from Runway 33 at Toulouse.

Left: Salut! The crew of 001's 45th flight – (from left) Henri Perrier, Jean Pinet, Michel Rétif and captain André Turcat – celebrate Concorde's first supersonic flight (9 minutes at up to Mach 1.05) on 1 October 1969. Turcat subsequently took 002 to Mach 2 on 4 November 1970.

The second prototype, 002/G-BSST, nears completion in 1968, alongside the central wing/fuselage structure for the first pre-production airframe.

G-BSST was formally rolled out at Filton, incomplete, in September 1968. However, it had already begun taxi trials the previous month. Both prototypes lacked certain systems at the time of their maiden flights, these being added in subsequent lay-up periods as the envelope expanded. At one point it was thought that the UK prototype would be ready first, although parts priority was given to 001.

Above: G-BSST runs its engines at Filton. A similar facility existed at Toulouse for the French aircraft. During runs the aircraft was restrained by track-mounted metal structures.

aircraft. Britain's Minister of Technology, Anthony Wedgwood Benn, announced at Toulouse that from then on the British aircraft would also be called Concorde. "Concorde has an e for excellence, England, Europe and entente," he affirmed. Behind the scenes, Benn did more than make speeches, and in February the British government made available a £125 million loan to launch Concorde production. It is interesting to note that while the UK government had hitherto refused to use the French spelling for Concorde, BAC had been using the 'e' in its publicity material for years.

As preparations for the first flight progressed, Concorde 001 underwent preliminary engine testing at Toulouse in March 1968 and began taxi trials in August. Concorde 002 (G-BSST, the first aircraft assembled in Britain) was rolled out from the Brabazon hangar at Filton on 19 September 1968.

002 first flight

BAC's Chief Test Pilot, Brian Trubshaw, commanded G-BSST on its first flight, assisted by John Cochrane (seen at left with Trubshaw in the cockpit of the aircraft preparing for its 9 April 1969 maiden flight) and Flight Engineer Brian Watts. To prepare for the occasion, Trubshaw had flown the Vulcan Olympus testbed, another Vulcan, a Lightning, the HP.115 and BAC 221, Mirage III, Mirage IV and the B-58 Hustler. He also flew alongside Turcat on 001's fifth flight. With a Canberra flying chase, G-BSST took off from Filton (below) but landed at RAF Fairford.

Soviet SST

Before the Concorde prototypes could take to the air, the USSR stole a march on the West by flying the first prototype of its Tu-144 supersonic airliner on 31 December, thereby gaining the honour of flying the world's first SST. The Tu-144 flew from the LII test airfield at Zhukovskiy, accompanied by a MiG-21 testbed converted with a similar ogee wing, the A-144 Analog.

The Tu-144 bore a passing resemblance to the Anglo-French Concorde, and there were suggestions that the Soviet Union had mounted a major intelligence effort to uncover Concorde's secrets. There was certainly evidence of espionage, but the Tu-144 differed from the Anglo-French SST in a number of key respects, including its closely grouped engines, its semi-oval fuselage cross-section and forward-located engine nozzles, as well as a simpler wing without camber, a twin rudder, and a simpler flying control layout.

Due to its resemblance to Concorde it was nicknamed 'Concordski' by Western media. NATO's Air Standards Co-ordinating Committee allocated the less judgmental reporting name of 'Charger'.

The Tu-144 was a simpler, cruder aircraft than Concorde, and was never expected to operate as efficiently as its Anglo-French counterpart. Intended to be a symbol of national prestige and to fly VIPs, scientists, bureaucrats and military personnel across the vast distances of the USSR's expansive interior, the Tu-144's operating costs were of secondary importance. When Tupolev told Premier Khrushchev that an SST would be extremely expensive to operate, and fuel thirsty, he was sharply reminded that there was "plenty of kerosene" but that national pride dictated that the USSR should show itself capable of building an SST, and was instructed to beat the US and Anglo-French SSTs into the air.

The production Tu-144 was enlarged and extensively redesigned, with a straight-edged double-delta wing, canard foreplanes, a redesigned undercarriage and Concorde-type engine intakes, but this was not enough to bring the aircraft into Concorde's class. Its operational life was brief and limited.

Maiden flight

The first Concorde (packed with 10 tonnes of test instrumentation) finally flew on 2 March 1969, from Toulouse-Blagnac, delayed for several days by bad weather. The aircraft was flown by an all-French crew captained by chief test pilot André Turcat and was accompanied by a Meteor NF.Mk 11 chase aircraft and a photo-chase MS.760 Paris. The

Concorde took off after 4,700 ft (1433 m) of runway, rotating at a speed of 205 kt (380 km/h). Turcat left the landing gear down throughout the flight and the 'droop-snoot' nose was also left lowered.

Inside Concorde's cramped cockpit, instrumentation was of conventional analog type, though the prototype had panel space left for a moving map display. Avionics were similarly conventional, albeit cleared for operation over the full range of temperatures encountered in supersonic flight, and the aircraft's navigation equipment was much the same as that being fitted to contemporary airliners such as the Boeing 747, with three INS systems and DME. The prototypes had an even more confined flight deck, because they carried a dedicated navigator as part of the crew. The pilots controlled the aircraft using conventional rudder pedals and unusual M-shaped open 'ram's horns' rather than the more usual half-wheel yokes used in most airliners. The ram's horns were similar to those fitted to the Bristol Britannia, and were more natural to use one-handed than a yoke, while giving minimum obstruction of the instrument panel and good clearance from the pilots' legs.

Controlling Concorde

The Concorde's control surfaces consisted of a two-part rudder on the trailing edge of the tailfin and three-section elevons on the trailing edge of each wing. These could never have been moved by muscle power alone, and instead were actuated by individual hydraulic power flying control units (PFCUs), pressurised to 4,000 psi by engine-driven pumps. Two separate hydraulic systems power the PFCUs (a third provides redundancy), with two separate electrical channels (main and standby) signalling the control actuators; an emergency mechanical system links the control column directly to the PFCUs via hydraulic relay jacks and rods. In the unlikely event of the control column or rudder pedals jamming, strain gauges can measure the force being applied by the pilot and send the appropriate signals to the control surfaces.

This was one of the first uses of fly-by-wire control technology in a civil aircraft and allowed the incorporation of auto-stabilisation, including the automatic application of rudder in the event of an engine failure, and a safety flight system that provided protection against exceeding angle of attack limits. The latter first gently opposed the pilot's demand for increased pitch, then applied a stick-shaker, and then automatically deployed all the elevons to force the nose downwards. A similar system was used to link the pilots' toe brakes with the brakes themselves (providing what has been referred to as 'brake by wire') and incorporated an electrically signalled anti-skid system.

The control surfaces have a limited trimming function, but for countering more major trim changes (including the rearward shift of the centre of lift during acceleration to Mach 2) Concorde uses movement of fuel to change weight distribution. Without this, Concorde would have to make a major upward deflection of the elevons, with a massive increase in drag.

On take-off, the centre of gravity is deliberately moved farther aft to put the aircraft slightly out of trim. The elevons move down to counteract this, thereby increasing camber and producing increased lift.

Concorde's cabin was as conventional and cramped as its cockpit, and rapidly became quite old-fashioned in appearance as wide-bodied jetliners were introduced. When BA introduced Concorde, the airline was worried that passengers might be apprehensive at the thought of supersonic flight, and deliberately opted for a cabin interior that was undramatic and as similar as possible to the interiors of other aircraft. The cabin was also quite dark, with portholes that were noticeably smaller than those on other aircraft. This was necessary because the failure of a conventionally-sized window at Concorde's operating height would be catastrophic, and the pressurisation system would not be able to maintain an adequate cabin pressure while the pilot descended to lower altitude.

During the same month in which the prototype made its maiden flight, the shape of the Concorde test programme was finally determined. UK government authority was received for the production of nine Concorde airframes, adding two static test airframes, two pre-production (01 and 02) and three production type aircraft (201, 202, and 203) to the two prototypes. In December, government authority was given for the construction of three more production aircraft (204, 205, 206), and in April 1971 for another four (207, 208, 209,

Top: Among the early tasks for G-BSST were engine relights, engine(s)-out go-rounds and general handling. Later, in 1973, it was used for icing trials, flying behind a USAF KC-135 or, as here, a converted Canberra B(I).Mk 8 spray aircraft.

Above: With its chase Canberra in the background, G-BSST is seconds away from its first landing at Fairford. This airfield, which was home to the Hercules of Nos 30 and 47 Squadrons, was chosen for Concorde testing in preference to Filton because its runway was longer and in better condition. An earlier plan to use A&AEE Boscombe Down had been rejected. For the first flights, the nose could be drooped by 17.5° for landing, although early experience and a lack of visual reference for the pilot led to this being revised to 12.5°.

Paris 1969

Both prototypes made a dramatic world debut at the 1969 Salon de l'Aérospace at Paris-le Bourget. On its 14th flight on 29 May, F-WTSS flew from Toulouse to le Bourget, overflying the centre of Paris on its approach (left). It remained at the show site for the duration, flying several times on demonstration sorties. G-BSST, meanwhile, was operating from its Fairford test base. On 7 and 8 June it flew from Fairford to Paris, and joined its French counterpart in an unrehearsed co-ordinated display that thrilled the large crowd (right). Londoners got their chance to see the Concorde soon after, during the Queen's Birthday Flypast, in which G-BSST overflew Buckingham Palace.

When G-AXDN, the first pre-production aircraft, was rolled out at Filton on 20 September 1971 it exhibited the revised, production-standard nose/visor installation which offered the pilots a much better forward view at supersonic speeds and greatly improved the aircraft's looks.

After an initial test phase, 'XDN returned to Filton for fitment of the digital air intake control system, and it became the main vehicle for tests of this system. Most of these tests were conducted at Tangier in Morocco (later Casablanca), routing down the coast of West Africa where very cold ambient temperatures could be found at altitude.

and 210). Government authority for another six production type aircraft (211, 212, 213, 214, 215, and 216, destined to be the final Concorde aircraft built) was given on 13 April 1972. Approval for the procurement of advance (long lead time) materials for six more production aircraft (217, 218, 219, 220, 221, and 222) was received on 14 September 1972, although, in the event, they remained unbuilt.

Five weeks after 001's maiden flight, on 9 April 1969, Brian Trubshaw took the second prototype on its first flight from Filton, chased by a Canberra and a Lightning. Trubshaw landed at RAF Fairford, which was destined to be the aircraft's home for its initial flight test phase. Fairford was an ex-US Strategic Air Command deployment base and at this time it was in use by the RAF as a base for Hercules transports, but was about to be vacated and downgraded to reserve status; it enjoyed a superb long and even runway. Filton, by contrast, was busy, and its runway had undesirable slope and unacceptable 'sterile areas'. A DC-3 was specially purchased to act as a staff ferry between Filton and Fairford, augmenting BAC's existing Herons and Beagle 206s.

Trubshaw made an impeccable landing on this flight, despite the loss of both radar altimeters. Sitting 35 ft (10.6 m) above (and far in front of) the nosewheels, he was presumably glad for the time he'd spent in the Concorde flight simulator at Toulouse, which had been commissioned in June 1966, and for Turcat's generosity in allowing him to fly 001 on its fifth flight. Trubshaw was a long-serving Vickers test pilot, having flown the Viscount, Vanguard, Valiant and VC10, as well as the BAC One-Eleven, and had prepared himself for Concorde by flying the Lightning, Mirage and Vulcan, and even the USAF's Convair B-58.

Long legs and tail bumper

The Concorde's very tall undercarriage was necessitated by the nose-high pitch angle required on landing, which brought the engine nozzles perilously close to the runway on touch-down. This danger also led to the provision of a pair of retractable tailwheels whose function was principally to act as tail bumpers if the touchdown angle was too steep. The high angle of attack flown at low speed (in the circuit and on approach), coupled with Concorde's long nose, gave the pilots a very poor view forward over the nose – this was the reason for the aircraft's innovative hinged nose cone and retractable visor.

At speeds above 250 kt (463 km/h), Concorde flies with its nose and visor raised, giving the pilots a relatively restricted forward view (especially in the prototypes with their solid visor), limited to about 5° downwards. Below this speed, with an angle of attack at about 7°, the visor is lowered

These dramatic shots capture G-AXDN undergoing wet runway water ingestion trials. These were among the aircraft's first phase of trials tasks, which also included flutter, handling and performance tests. For the first nine months of its career 'XDN was not fitted with an air intake control system, and was restricted to Mach 1.5 before it was modified. It was also fitted with the original engine nozzles throughout.

Once fitted with the new AICS, G-AXDN proved to be the fastest of the Concordes, achieving Mach 2.23 on one flight. A series of supersonic test tracks was established which could accessed by both Toulouse- and Fairford-based aircraft. French-operated tracks were in Secteur A over the Bay of Biscay or Secteur M over the Mediterranean, while the UK-run test areas were E.1 (Bay of Biscay/ Southwest Approaches), E.2 (North Sea) and E.3 ('Boom Alley'). The latter was the longest straight-line track available, running from a point to the north of Scotland, down the Irish Sea to a point in the Bay of Biscay, with radar and SAR cover provided all the way.

by 5° (giving a 10° view over the nose), and when the undercarriage is lowered the nose is drooped to its full extent, about 12.5°. The prototypes originally had a lower maximum droop position of about 17.5° but this made pilots feel as though they were looking over a precipice, and also reduced directional stability.

On approach, with the nose high and the gear down, Concorde is in an extremely high-drag configuration and rapid throttle responses may be required to counter gusts or other airspeed changes. Similarly rapid responses may be required during other phases of flight – for example, during supersonic cruise if the temperature changes and the aircraft exceeds its Mach 2.04 limiting speed. For this reason, the aircraft is fitted with a sophisticated auto-throttle system, whose longitudinal accelerometers can detect the slightest change in the aircraft's forward speed and compensate with immediate but tiny throttle adjustments.

Public debut

Both Concordes were publicly unveiled at the 1969 Paris Air Salon at Le Bourget, and the French prototype (F-WTSS) first made a low-level flight over the city on 29 May. With 002 operating from Fairford, the two aircraft even managed to fly a co-ordinated flying display, and many VIPs (especially chairmen of potential customer airlines) were flown aboard 001.

Following the show, the flight test programme continued in earnest, and the two aircraft began to record a succession of important milestones. On 1 October F-WTSS exceeded Mach 1 for the first time, during its 45th test flight, briefly reaching and sustaining a speed of Mach 1.05 at an altitude of 36,000 ft (10973 m). The British prototype exceeded Mach 1 for the first time on 25 March 1970. Much supersonic testing was carried out in a corridor over the Irish Sea, nicknamed 'Boom Alley', calibration of which was the task of a specially instrumented Gloster Javelin (the last airworthy example of the breed).

Concorde made its first night landing on 12 November 1969. During 1970, both aircraft reached Mach 2 (separately, on 4 and 12 November). 002 (G-BSST) participated in the Farnborough SBAC show and then, on 13 September, finally visited London's Heathrow Airport, generating a number of noise complaints from local residents – although there were strong suspicions that these were carefully orchestrated by anti-Concorde groups, since the aircraft was little noisier than many of the types that routinely used Heathrow. This, in itself, was remarkable, since the aircraft was diverting after a Farnborough appearance so was at maximum landing weight and flying an entirely unrepresentative 'development type' constant-speed approach that made it much noisier than it would be in service.

Concorde 001 (F-WTSS) was kept busy during 1971, when it made the type's first automatic landing on 13 May 1971, before participating in the Paris air show and then flying on to Dakar, Senegal, completing this 2,500-mile (4023-km) journey in only two hours and seven minutes. The aircraft was then used for a two-week tour of South America, making its first transatlantic flight to Rio de Janeiro, routeing via the Cape Verde islands, Cayenne and São Paulo, arriving back at Toulouse on 18 September 1971.

Left: 01 floats across the threshold at Fairford. The aircraft survived at least one attempt to ground it prematurely, and it became a vital stepping-stone between the prototypes and service aircraft.

BAC rolled out the first pre-production aircraft at Filton on 20 September. This aircraft incorporated a number of modifications by comparison with the prototype aircraft, including twist and camber on the wing leading edge and a revised 'droop-snoot' nose with a fully transparent visor. This was developed by Triplex after the US Federal Aviation Authority made it clear that the original metal visor would never be certificated, although many insist that the early metal visor was only ever intended as an interim fit. The aircraft's fuselage was also stretched from the original 184 ft to 193 ft (56.08 m to 58.83 m), although production Concordes would be stretched even farther, to 204 ft (62.18 m). G-AXDN made its maiden flight on 17 December, flying from Filton to Fairford.

A routine publicity photograph has been the posing of Concorde with the national aerobatic teams ('Red Arrows' and 'Patrouille de France'). The first UK incarnation involved G-AXDN partnering the 'Arrows' in their Folland Gnats.

002's Australian adventure

Leaving Fairford on 2 June 1972, 002 embarked on a major sales tour to Australia and the Far East. The tour routed through Athens, Tehran, Bahrain, Bombay, Bangkok, Singapore, Manila, Tokyo, Manila, Darwin, Sydney, Melbourne, Darwin, Singapore, Bangkok, Bombay, Dhahran, Beirut, Toulouse, London-Heathrow and arrived back at Fairford on 4 July. A total of 32 flights was undertaken (with demo flights in Tehran, Singapore, Tokyo, Sydney, Melbourne, Dhahran and Beirut), covering around 46,000 miles (74000 km). Accompanying Concorde was a VC10 and Belfast from the RAF, the latter carrying a spares pack which included an engine.

G-BSST *is seen over Sydney Harbour (above), and at Bombay (right). On the return leg to the UK, Brian Trubshaw accomplished a very tricky landing at Bombay in monsoon conditions. The next day's planned demo flight was the only one of the tour to be cancelled: all others met their pre-planned schedule.*

Singapore was one of the few cities to receive a Concorde service – albeit briefly – and featured prominently in sales tours. It was visited twice during G-BSST's marathon journey, and is seen here over the waterfront by what is now the main financial district, and at top taxiing in at Paya Lebar airport (now an air force base since Changi opened). From Singapore 002 routed north to Japan, and then headed south to Manila and on to Australia. The Darwin-Sydney sector was Concorde's first sustained overland supersonic flight.

1972 and 1973 saw 002 assume an increasing share of the flight test burden. The British prototype (flying with the production type undercarriage from 7 February) attended the Hanover Air Show in April, and on 2 June began a 45,000-mile (72420-km) sales tour of the Far East and Australia (supported by an RAF VC10 and with an RAF Belfast carrying a spare engine), visiting 12 countries and returning to Heathrow on 1 July. In Iran, the Shah (a keen and proficient pilot) flew the aircraft from the left-hand seat, immediately promising that Iran Air would order three aircraft, a promise that was soon fulfilled. At Bombay, Concorde landed in heavy rain, and the 707 that followed it ran off the end of the runway. By this time, the first three Concordes had amassed more than 1,000 flying hours (this milestone having been reached on 18 May), while the test engine had reached 5,000 equivalent flying hours. G-BSST then went on to star in the Farnborough flying display and made a number of 'show the people' flights to different regions of the UK.

The first pre-production Concorde (01 G-AXDN) was 'laid up' for the end of 1972 and the beginning of 1973, returning to Filton where it was converted to near production standard, including the installation of the production-standard Olympus 593 Mk 602 engines. The aircraft flew to Filton on 10 August, finally returning to Fairford on 15 March.

While 'XDN underwent modifications at Filton, the French pre-production aircraft (Concorde 02, F-WTSA) was rolled out on 28 September and made its maiden flight on 10 January. Among its first major achievements was a 3,728-mile (6000-km) non-stop return flight from Toulouse to Iceland, achieved in three hours and 27 minutes (including two hours and nine minutes at Mach 2). This flight, undertaken on 23 February, was broadly equivalent to a Paris-New York journey. On 3 March the same aircraft made a 3,900-mile (6276-km) return flight from Toulouse to West Africa in three hours and 38 minutes, a flight that Concorde's marketeers presented as being directly equivalent to the journey between Frankfurt and New York.

First in the United States

After all its 'equivalent transatlantic' flights, it was perhaps appropriate that Concorde 02 should become the first to actually visit the US. The aircraft left Paris on 18 September and flew to the opening ceremony of Dallas-Fort Worth Airport on 20 September, routeing via Las Palmas and Caracas. Fitted with clean, smokeless new versions of the Olympus engine, 02 was a great success, and contrasted with the unduly smoky first and second prototypes. At last, BAC and Aérospatiale had a Concorde that looked environmentally friendly and could land at an airport without leaving thick smoke trails. On its return flight (on 26 September) F-WTSA shattered the Washington-Paris record by completing the flight in three hours and 33 minutes, landing at Orly in front of a huge crowd of interested spectators both at the airport and in their cars outside the airport, on roads rendered stationary by 10-mile (16-km) traffic jams.

Above: Concorde 02 (F-WTSA) was the first with a lengthened tail. This increased the fineness ratio (length: maximum diameter) which is a crucial factor in supersonic performance. The Pyrenees, close to the Toulouse test centre, form an impressive backdrop.

Above left: After a first overseas trip to Dakar in May 1971, and a South American tour in September, 001's next trip – and Concorde's first real tasking – was to take Président Georges Pompidou to the Azores for a meeting with President Richard Nixon on 12 December 1971. Here it is seen arriving at Orly the day prior to the journey.

The British Concorde prototype was equally busy, setting off for Jan Smuts Airport at Johannesburg, South Africa for 'hot and high' airfield performance trials on 22 January, before joining 001 for a series of high-altitude sampling flights in support of an international research programme during June. On 30 June, 001 carried scientists from Britain, France and the US on a flight from Las Palmas, Canaries to Fort Lamy, Chad to observe a solar eclipse (predicted to be the longest for 1,000 years), its speed making the eclipse continuously visible to the scientists for 80 minutes. Concorde 002 flew to Torrejon, near Madrid, on 9 July to conduct temperature and altitude accountability trials.

The Concorde flight test fleet was briefly reduced to three aircraft when 001 (F-WTSS) was retired to the French Air Museum at Le Bourget Airport on 19 October. On retirement, the first prototype had logged 812 flying hours (255 of them at supersonic speed) during the course of 397 flights.

First production aircraft

The development fleet was soon restored to four aircraft by the addition of Concorde 201 (F-WTSB), the first production aircraft, which made its first flight from Toulouse on 6 December, and was further reinforced when Concorde 202 (G-BBDG), the second production aircraft, made its first flight from Filton to Fairford on 13 February 1974.

French Concordes grabbed most of the headlines during the first half of 1974. In early February, Concorde 02 (F-WTSA) flew to Fairbanks, Alaska where it undertook 'cold soak' tests at low temperatures, then in June it made a 12,000-mile (19310-km) return trip from Paris to Rio de Janeiro in 12 hours and 47 minutes. From 20 to 28 October the same aircraft undertook a tour that encompassed London, Gander, Mexico City, San Francisco, Anchorage, Los Angeles, Lima, Bogota, Caracas and Las Palmas, before returning to Paris. The airport authorities in both San Francisco and Los Angeles went out of their way to welcome Concorde, and officially praised the aircraft's noise levels and environmental performance.

On 17 June the Concorde team mounted an extraordinary demonstration of the potential impact of the aircraft's phenomenal speed. At 08:22 (Eastern Standard Time) an Air France Concorde left Boston's Logan Airport for Paris, just as an Air France 747 took off from Paris-Orly en route to Boston. The Concorde landed at Paris-Orly and spent 68 minutes on the ground, then departed back for Boston to arrive there 11 minutes ahead of the 747.

Decades before, in 1946, Britain had effectively resigned its technological lead in high-speed flight by cancelling its Miles M.52 research aircraft. This allowed the US, with the Bell X-1, to gain the honour of breaking the sound barrier, and handed America a useful lead. Some British aircraft did briefly set new world speed records, but there was no doubt that the US was at the forefront of high-speed flight, especially with the debuts of the F-104 Starfighter, the B-58 Hustler supersonic bomber and the Mach 3 SR-71 'Blackbird'. With the introduction of Concorde, however, the lead was seen to have passed back to the Europeans, and it was soon being said that the tiny fleet of British and French airliners had accumulated more supersonic flight time than all of the world's air forces put together.

Above: Between 26 May and 4 June 1973 F-WTSA was at le Bourget for the Salon de l'Aérospace, where it made its public debut. During the course of the show the aircraft made nine demonstration flights, each carrying 32 passengers and involving a Mach 2 sector over the Atlantic. The aircraft had a sumptuously appointed rear cabin and became the main vehicle for demonstration rides.

Left: Wearing British Airways colours to starboard and Air France to port, F-WTSA made the first visit to the United States, flying from Orly on 18 September 1973 to Dallas-Fort Worth via Las Palmas and Caracas. The occasion was the opening of the new DFW airport.

Above: Large crowds greeted F-WTSA on its return to Orly from Concorde's first US visit. After leaving Dallas, 02 stopped at Washington-Dulles, and then flew the Atlantic in a record-breaking 3 hours 33 minutes.

Above, far right: F-WTSA visited the US again in February (Fairbanks and Anchorage in Alaska: demo rides and cold weather trials) and June 1974 (demos in Boston and Miami). In October it departed London for another major sales tour which took in Anchorage, Los Angeles (illustrated), San Francisco, Mexico City, Acapulco, Caracas, Bogotá and Lima, with en route stops at Gander and Las Palmas.

Above right: This view of a development aircraft taking off underlined the environmental fears – particularly in the US – over pollution. F-WTSA was the first to introduce the smokeless engines.

On 7 August 1974, BAC's Concorde 202 (G-BBDG) visited Teheran, continuing on to Bahrain for hot weather testing and then on to Abu Dhabi, Qatar, Kuwait, Muscat and Dubai for a sales tour. On 3 September the aircraft flew on to Singapore for runway response trials. Later that year, from 28 October, Concorde 202 was based at Casablanca, Morocco, for certification testing, where Concorde 201 (F-WTSB) was also temporarily based for intake control work.

Even with the increasing availability of production standard aircraft, the pre-production examples continued to play a vital part in the flight test programme. On 7 November Concorde 01 flew to Grant County Airport at Moses Lake, Washington, via Bangor, Maine, to carry out natural de-icing trials. In doing so, it made the fastest ever civil crossing of the North Atlantic. The aircraft had previously flown behind the A&AEE's converted Canberra spray rig, and a modified USAF KC-135. On 26 February 1975 the same aircraft flew out to Nairobi, Kenya for tropical icing trials, and 02 (F-WTSA) started flooded runway tests on 3 March.

Concordes 203 and 204 (F-WTSC and G-BOAC) joined the fleet in February 1975, and during the same month 202 (G-BBDG) started certification trials at Madrid, with runway, take-off, climb, and landing performance trials. As the countdown towards service entry continued, Air France started a two-week flight crew training programme in April, using the airport at Dakar in Senegal, and finalised an agreement allowing its Concordes to land in Brazil on scheduled flights the following month.

Preparing for service

Concorde 203 (F-WTSC) was awarded a special category Certificate of Airworthiness on 28 May, when its registration was changed to F-BTSC. The aircraft then started endurance flying trials, between Paris and Dakar, Paris and Gander, Paris to Rio via Dakar and Paris to Caracas via Lisbon. The aircraft was augmented by Concorde 201, which flew to Bodo, Dakar, Keflavik, Shannon and Tangier, and on subsonic flights within France. On 4 October pre-production Concorde 02 (F-WTSA) flew from Paris to Montreal for the opening of that city's new Mirabel International Airport, routeing via London and Ottawa. Five days later, on 9 October, the type received its French Certificate of Airworthiness.

Although Air France had started crew training in April, it was not until 19 June that the new British Airways (Britain's new state airline, formed by a merger of BOAC and BEA) began Concorde flight training at Fairford. Eleven days later, on 30 June, the British CAA awarded Concorde 204 (G-BOAC) its special category Certificate of Airworthiness, allowing this aircraft to commence endurance flying on 7 July, with flights to Bahrain, Beirut, Bombay, Damascus, Gander, Kuala Lumpur, Melbourne, and Singapore. This included a unique pair of return flights to Gander on 1 September – the first time any aircraft had made four Atlantic crossings in a single day.

Concorde's auto-throttle would not intervene automatically to limit speed to below Mach 2, so the aircraft could theoretically over-speed in certain circumstances (temperature shear) and reach speeds of Mach 2.1 (which was outside the certificated flight envelope). The remedy was simple and merely required the pilot to ease back the throttles, but BA insisted that this was unacceptable and Flight Manager Brian

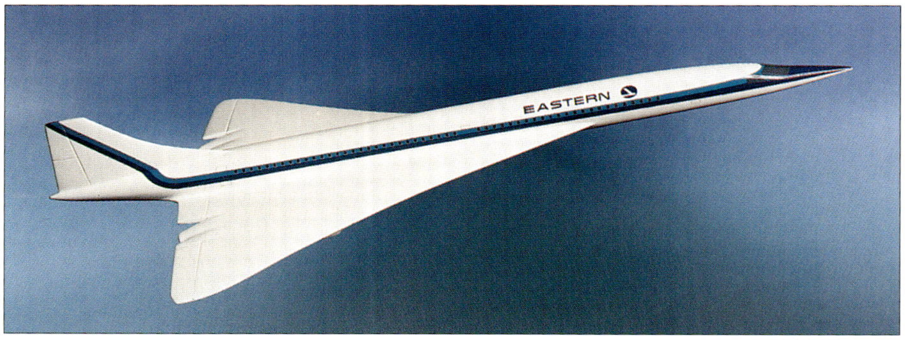

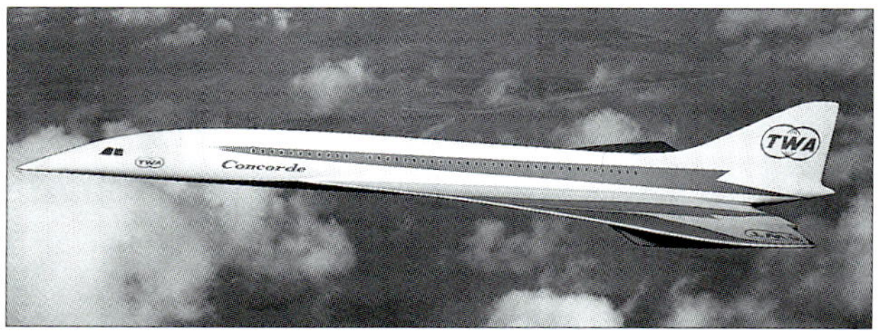

Sixteen airlines held options for Concorde, including six of the US 'giants' (American, Braniff, Continental, Eastern, Pan Am, TWA and United). In the event, only Braniff was to operate the type, but then only briefly and on a subsonic route.

Calvert formally objected to the granting of a C of A. The Air Registration Board's response was to insist that a BAC test pilot should captain every route-proving flight (from the jumpseat if required), Trubshaw and John Cochrane being appointed as CAA Flight Inspectors for the purpose.

Finally, on 5 December, the CAA awarded Concorde its full British Certificate of Airworthiness, opening the way for the aircraft to enter airline service. Flight testing continued for some time, though G-BSST was finally retired on 4 March 1976, and the BAC flight test team moved back to Filton from Fairford on 30 November 1976.

Export orders and cancellations

By 1969, the Concorde partners had orders or options for 94 aircraft from 16 airlines. Pan Am's stated requirement stood at eight aircraft, BOAC had 14, Air France eight, TWA 10, Continental three, American 10, United six, Sabena two, Qantas eight (two more options having been cancelled in 1966), MEA two, Lufthansa three, JAL three, Eastern eight, Braniff three, Air India two, and Air Canada four. Pilots from BOAC, Air France, Pan Am and TWA took turns at the controls of Concorde 001 (F-WTSS) on 8 November 1969, each flying the aircraft for some two hours and experiencing simulated emergencies of their own choice. All expressed themselves to be delighted with the aircraft's handling and none had any reservations about training young and relatively inexperienced crews to operate the aircraft. Pan Am was particularly enthusiastic about the aircraft, and following the type's first flight had taken out full-page newspaper adverts shouting "Welcome to tomorrow!"

The interest of US airlines in Concorde was further stimulated on 24 March 1971 when the US Congress announced that it had formally abandoned the US supersonic transport programme, and by the FAA's 14 December announcement that Concorde was within American airport noise limits.

With hindsight, it's easy to see that Concorde's high fuel consumption would limit its usefulness in the world after the oil crisis of the 1970s, but when the aircraft was taking shape no one could foresee this. Oil was cheap and apparently almost limitless, so when Boeing started designing its leviathan, the Model 747 (immortalised as the 'Jumbo Jet'), it was clear from the start that it would have to be capable of adaptation to the freight-carrying role because the life of any subsonic airliner was thought to be limited once the supersonic era had dawned. Even the most optimistic marketeers at Boeing expected the 747 to have a 10-year life, at most, in the passenger transport role, before the airframes would be replaced by SSTs.

Interest in Concorde was equally strong elsewhere in the world, and on 24 July 1971 China signed a preliminary agreement to purchase two Concordes (adding a third aircraft on 28 August). BOAC, which had announced its intention to order five aircraft on 25 May, finally signed up on 28 July, when Air France also ordered four Concordes.

This underlined the fact that throughout its gestation and development, Concorde actually had no firm orders, and lack of customer input did lead to mistakes and flaws – including the original intention to provide an entirely unnecessary moving map display, calibration of the hydraulic instrumentation in bars, and the selection of new avionics items (including the over-sensitive Ferranti-SAGEM inertial navigation system), although potential customers preferred proven, in-service items. Getting an order from BOAC was never straightforward, the airline having exercised a pro-Boeing and anti-British bias for some years (perhaps since the trauma of the Comet I crashes). Although nationalised (i.e., owned by the state), BOAC saw itself as being obliged to operate under normal commercial and financial principles (when this suited the management) and always resisted home-grown aircraft as a matter of principle. BOAC had even had to be forced into procuring the excellent VC10, for example, and had operated a split fleet (with 707s) when an all-VC10 fleet would have reduced operating costs and given much greater profits. Within BOAC there was a great deal of scepticism about Concorde, the company's technical director having described it as "the largest, most expensive and most dubious project ever undertaken in the development of civil aircraft". In contrast, BEA, the short-haul nationalised airline,

F-WTSA taxis during its first US visit. On the ground, at least, Concorde was welcomed by huge crowds and airport officials.

Far left: It was common practice during sales tours to fly the local flag on arrival, as displayed here in the United States. During a trip to Africa for demonstrations and hot-and-high trials by 002 in early 1973, the crew arrived at Luanda in Angola unwittingly flying the opposition's rebel flag, as provided by the Sales Department, much to the consternation of the welcoming party.

Another high-profile transatlantic trip by F-WTSA took Concorde 02 to Canada for the opening of Montréal's Mirabel airport in October 1975. Before flying to Montréal it also visited CFB Ottawa-South, where it is seen on 4 October. Air Canada (four aircraft) was among the 16 airlines with Concorde orders/options, to which can be added CAAC of China and Iran Air with intents to purchase.

Above: F-BTSA shows off its 'BA' side during a visit to Caracas (the other side wore Air France colours). This city became Concorde's third scheduled destination, when Air France opened a service on 9 April 1976. This routed via Santa Maria in the Azores.

Below: BAC's first production Concorde (c/n 202) was G-BBDG. Shortly before its retirement in 1983, and wearing 'Aérospatiale – British Aerospace' titles to reflect the amalgamation of the UK industry after 1977, the aircraft posed with the 'Red Arrows', by then flying Hawks.

had a much better record of supporting indigenous aircraft.

On 5 October 1972 Iran Air signed a preliminary purchase agreement for two aircraft (with an option on a third). This was destined to be the last bit of good news for the Concorde marketeers, as a recession gathered, Concorde's Certificate of Airworthiness was delayed and another Arab-Israeli war was about to break out (triggering a massive oil crisis and a dramatic hike in the cost of oil).

United leads the retreat

Three weeks later, on 26 October, United Air Lines opted not to take up the options it had for six aircraft (these were due to expire in February 1973), and TWA and Pan Am followed suit on 31 January 1973. Continental Airlines decided not to take up its options for three aircraft on 29 March, and, slowly but steadily, Concorde's order book emptied, until the very future of the programme was in real doubt. It has been suggested that some of the US airline options never represented serious intentions to order, but senior programme insiders dispute this vehemently. Whatever the case, customers did lose confidence in Concorde and finally, on 19 July 1974, British Prime Minister Harold Wilson and French President Valery Giscard d'Estaing agreed to cap production at 16 aircraft, though they did also agree to continue the Concorde programme.

Even then, there were efforts to find overseas buyers for the five unsold production Concordes, since BA had ordered only five aircraft and Air France four. At one stage it appeared as though Singapore Airlines might wet-lease or even buy all five, as described earlier, and efforts were also made to sell the aircraft in the Philippines and in Korea.

In 1981-82 a major feasibility study was carried out to determine the practicality of converting one or more aircraft into high-speed freighters for Federal Express, which was interested in leasing three aircraft from BA and others from Air France for a minimum period of 10 years (later revised to seven years for the Air France aircraft). Neither Britain nor France was then prepared to commit to more than five years, and the deal foundered.

Concorde finally entered service as scheduled on 21 January 1976, with G-BOAA opening the British Airways service between London-Heathrow and Bahrain, and F-BVFA beginning the Air France service between Paris and Rio, via Dakar. (Reservations for these services had opened on 14 October.) In the face of US obstruction, BA and Air France had been forced to turn to other destinations and, although loudly trumpeted, these services were always regarded as something of a compromise. The Rio route was potentially profitable and proved politically straightforward,

Below: Although built as a full production aircraft, G-BBDG was retained by BAC for test work, and it became the principal post-certification powerplant trials airframe, with an emphasis on engine surge tests. Headquarters for the BAC test team moved back to Filton, where 'BDG was based, but much of the test work was accomplished at Casablanca in Morocco.

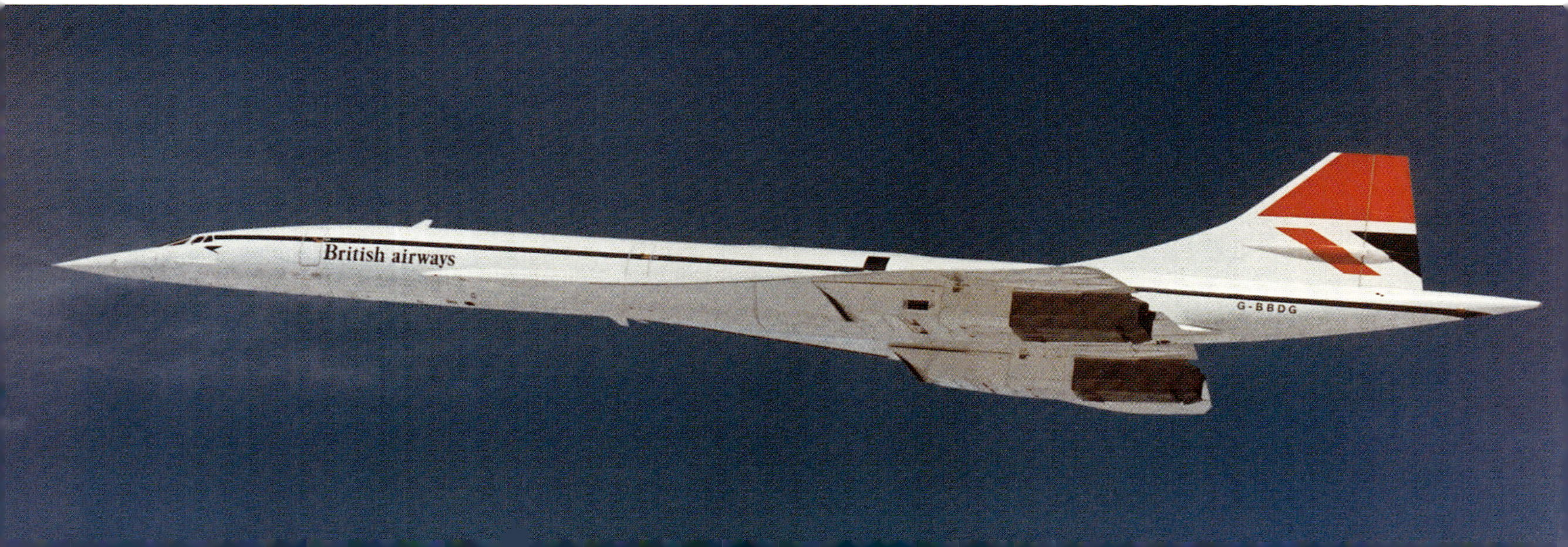

and BA's Bahrain service held the intriguing possibility of being the first stop on a route to Singapore and Australia. Both British Airways and Air France regarded transatlantic services across the North Atlantic, to the US itself, as being Concorde's natural forte, and were eager to begin them; tentative plans were to fly six times per day to New York-John F. Kennedy Airport and to Washington-Dulles.

Extending the routes

In the absence of services to the US, both Air France and British Airways extended their initial routes. On 9 April Air France opened a weekly Concorde service to Caracas, Venezuela, with a technical/refuelling stop in the Azores at Santa Maria Airport. Similarly, on 9 December, British Airways and Singapore Airlines began a London to Singapore service (via Bahrain) that operated three times per week. The runway at Singapore had been relaid at British government expense to permit Concorde to operate there, giving an illustration of the importance attached to this route.

At one time, it appeared likely that Singapore Airlines might buy the five unsold Concordes (203, 213, 214, 215 and 216) and negotiations for a wet lease reached an advanced stage, only to founder over the provision of flight crews for

F-BTSC was the second French production aircraft, although it, like G-BBDG and F-WTSB, was built as a Model 100 with higher structural weight. After conversion to the full production Model 1010 standard, it entered full airline service in 1980.

First commercial services

Nearly seven years after the type's first flight, Concorde inaugurated scheduled services on 21 January 1976, with the simultaneous launch of British Airways flights to Bahrain and Air France services to Rio de Janeiro. At exactly 1140Z both G-BOAA and F-BVFA began their take-off runs, from Heathrow's Runway 28L and Paris-Charles de Gaulle. The BA aircraft (flight BA300) was under the command of Captain Norman Todd, with Brian Calvert and John Lidiard. The aircraft flew subsonically across France before a supersonic run to Bahrain, landing after 3 hours 40 minutes. The Air France (flight AF025) aircraft was crewed by Pierre Chanoine, Pierre Dudal and André Blanc and flew supersonically to Dakar in 2 hours 44 minutes. After a 91-minute turnround, the aircraft departed for Rio, arriving there 3 hours 20 minutes later, a delay of six minutes caused by a minor problem with the secondary air inlet on climb-out from Dakar.

Above: F-BVFA was used for the first Air France scheduled service to Rio on 21 January 1976, and is seen at the Brazilian destination in June 1978. The Rio flight fuel-stopped at Dakar in Senegal before making the crossing to Rio.

Left: G-BOAA lifts off on its maiden scheduled voyage. Among the passengers on board the BA aircraft were HRH The Duke of Kent, Sir George Edwards (BAC chairman) and Sir Stanley Hooker (Rolls-Royce engine 'guru'). The aircraft and some of its passengers were greeted by the Amir of Bahrain.

Above: F-BTSC had a checkered career before its tragic loss at Gonesse. It was used for endurance tests before being leased to Air France for much of 1976, employed on sales tours, route-proving and training duties. In November it embarked on a major Far East tour, during the course of which it visited Singapore (illustrated). After this it was returned to Aérospatiale, to become one of the five unsold Concordes which Air France and British Airways had not originally purchased from the authorised 16-aircraft production run. In 1980, after conversion to full Model 101 standard, it was bought by Air France, along with F-WJAM and F-WJAN, for the nominal sum of 1 Franc each.

Above right: The Middle East was seen as potential market for Concorde, and there were several sales visits. The first was undertaken by G-BBDG in August/September 1974, taking in Abu Dhabi, Bahrain, Doha, Dubai, Kuwait City, Muscat and Tehran. Hot weather trials were undertaken at Bahrain during this tour, including a take-off at 47°C (117°F). Here the aircraft is seen at Dubai, still wearing its photo-calibration mark on the fuselage.

the four-year period required by the Singapore-based carrier. This proposal was superseded by the agreement to operate joint services with BA, which saw one aircraft painted with Singapore Airlines livery on one side.

The Singapore service was short-lived, however, and was suspended after one week and three return flights. This was the result of the Malaysian government banning Concorde from its airspace on 13 December 1977. The service eventually resumed just over one year later, on 24 January 1979, but was finally discontinued on 1 November 1980, along with the service to Bahrain, by which time Boeing 747s were in widespread service. These aircraft could fly to Singapore directly and took only four hours more than the 'stopping' Concorde service.

The planned Concorde service to Australia never reached maturity, either, even though a supersonic overland route to Sydney was found, proved and cleared for the aircraft. In the event, Concorde's Australian destination was switched to Melbourne due to difficulties in increasing Qantas 747 services to London from Sydney, and this entailed only subsonic overland flying.

British Airways initially was unable to agree new rates of pay for cabin crew on the new aircraft type, and in the absence of agreement had used cabin crew from Air India, Gulf Air and Singapore Airlines, supervised by senior BA cabin staff during route-proving flights. Agreement was reached for proper services, and the foreign cabin crew were replaced by BA's finest. On the first service, they had a full complement of VIP guests to look after, including former BAC (and Vickers) Chairman Sir George Edwards, CAA head Lord Boyd-Carpenter, and Leonard Cheshire, VC, as well as the Minister for Trade and Industry, Peter Shore, and HRH the Duke of Kent. One eccentric passenger arrived in a purple and white cape and head-dress, with his face painted silver. This, he explained, was a "futuristic outfit for a futuristic aeroplane".

From the very beginning, Concorde enjoyed enormous glamour and a highly exclusive image, which was only reinforced when Britain's queen and her consort, HM Queen Elizabeth II and HRH Prince Philip, chose Concorde for their return from a silver jubilee tour of Barbados on 2 November 1977. The royal couple flew aboard Concorde again on 12 February 1979, using the aircraft to get to Kuwait for a three-week tour of the Middle East.

US resistance

Once the US's own SST programme had died, an alliance of environmentalists, anti-Europeans and protectionist interests banded together in an attempt to deny Concorde access to the United States.

Environmental objections to Concorde took a number of forms. Much attention was focused on the supposed ill effects of the sonic boom. Any aircraft causes a shock wave as it flies through the air: it spreads outwards like a ripple, albeit at the speed of sound, moving air molecules in front of the aircraft out of the way. If the aircraft is moving faster than the speed of sound, air molecules cannot move out of the way and build up in front of the aircraft in the form of a conical shock wave, like a three-dimensional bow wave, and trail behind the aircraft. Behind this shock wave, pressure suddenly and sharply increases, causing a booming sound. The strength and intensity of the wave (and the associated boom) decays as it travels out from the aircraft. For example, the shock wave caused by Concorde as it flies at Mach 2 at 50,000 ft (15240 m) increases air pressure on the ground by about 0.01 per cent directly below the aircraft, with the boom reducing to no more than a rumble as little as 25 miles (40 km) from the aircraft's track. Normal atmospheric pressure is in the order of 2,160 lb/sq ft, with a sonic boom adding no more than 3 lb to this figure, which is equivalent to a sudden 30-mph (48-km/h) gust of wind.

There are circumstances in which the boom can be more intense. As the aircraft accelerates, a series of booms can reach the ground at the same point, causing what is known as a focused boom over a very small area. Even this is barely sufficient to cause physical damage on the ground (occasionally, window panes can be broken and plaster cracked), but was found to be sufficient to cause annoyance and disturbance to the population. Some tests were carried out in the US and Britain, in which military aircraft deliberately 'boomed' certain cities. These were well publicised and, unsurprisingly, resulted in complaints and damage claims, though many were for times when the aircraft involved had not actually been flying!

Whatever the rights and wrongs of the sonic boom argument, public concern was sufficient to limit supersonic flying to routes over the oceans and sparsely populated areas, though the anti-Concorde lobby opposed even this, expressing fear that sonic booms would still damage fisheries by affecting reproductive and other behaviour of fish and other marine life.

Environmentalists also made dire forecasts about Concorde's likely effect on the atmosphere. This was focused around the predicted effect of exhaust emissions from very high flying SSTs, operating close to the ozone layer (which protects the earth from ultra-violet light), where chemical reactions are more pronounced. Nitrous oxide (NOx) emissions were predicted to have dire effects on ozone, while water vapour, hydroxyl radicals (OH) and carbon dioxide (CO_2) emissions were expected by some to have a disproportionate effect on climate. It was claimed that a 100-aircraft fleet of supersonic transport aircraft would damage the ozone layer more quickly than the total world-wide output of chlorofluorocarbons (CFCs); interestingly, US environmental groups focused their ire on Concorde alone, and ignored the USAF's much larger fleet of supersonic fighters, reconnaissance aircraft and bombers, which were doing even greater damage.

F-BVFB is seen in the Toulouse paintshop prior to its first flight on 6 March 1976. Although trials aircraft had worn a variation of Air France's existing colour scheme, a bright new livery was introduced by the time services began in January 1976. André Turcat flew his last Concorde flight as captain in this aircraft, on 31 March 1976. Henri Perrier succeeded him as Director of Flight Test.

Singapore service

In December 1977 British Airways and Singapore International Airlines flew three return services to Singapore as an extension of the Bahrain route. The aircraft routed to the south of Sri Lanka, as India withdrew overland supersonic rights. The service was quickly halted after Malaysia denied supersonic flights down the Straits of Malacca, but was reinstated in January 1979 after negoatiations with the government in Kuala Lumpur. One aircraft (G-BOAD) received an SIA paint scheme on its port side. The service was flown by BA flight crew and alternating BA/SIA cabin crews. A global recession caused a considerable downturn in passenger traffic on this service, which was finally abandoned in November 1980.

Right: Apart from the original customers, only SIA and Braniff could claim to have operated the Concorde. This aircraft exhibits evidence of both: the SIA scheme on one side and the hybrid US/UK registration required for Braniff operations.

Top: F-BVFA rests on the flightline at Toulouse, displaying the new Air France colour scheme in which it was rolled out in 1975. At the time Toulouse could claim to be the world's centre of airliner technology: production Concordes were issuing from the assembly line, as were examples of the the ground-breaking Airbus A300.

Above: Air France's first Concorde taxis at Paris-Charles de Gaulle in March 1976, two months after the start of scheduled services.

Below: Initially, Air France flew services to South America. In 1978 the Washington service was extended twice-weekly to Mexico City.

Even as early as January 1975, such fears were found to be ill-founded. A US Department of Transportation Climatic Impact Assessment Program report concluded that even a fairly large (400+) fleet of SSTs would have a negligible effect on ozone, and that water vapour and CO2 emissions would have little greenhouse effect. In fact, it has been shown that the passage of SSTs through the upper atmosphere actually improves air circulation – having what one expert described as a "major cleansing effect" on the atmosphere.

One objection to Concorde was almost irrefutable, and that was on the basis of noise. At a time when most airliners were switching to ever-quieter high bypass turbofan engines, Concorde was undeniably noisy, with a notable low frequency weighting. Low frequency noise penetrates indoors more easily than other types of sound, and Concorde was thus expected to be more annoying than other aircraft. In practice, Concorde certainly attracted noise complaints. Many people, though, regard its noise as not being intrusive, and large numbers of ordinary people actually welcome it, looking up with affection and some pride at the distinctive shape majestically piercing the sky, a reaction that scientists could never have predicted and at which opponents would scoff.

Moreover, by dint of its performance, Concorde can minimise its noise nuisance by climbing out very steeply and very quickly, and manoeuvring to pass over the fewest number of people on the ground. It may also be able to use the least disturbing runway at an airport, if ATC permits, and its high speed tends to make it take off and land at more sociable hours of the day, at least on the Atlantic coast.

Threat to the US aviation industry

The least obvious opposition to Concorde came from US industrial interests, who saw the Anglo-French aircraft as a powerful threat to US aircraft builders and to those airlines that did not operate SSTs. Such interest groups may have had powerful allies. Bill Gunston, then the technical editor of *Flight International* and a distinguished aerospace commentator, observed, "The United States, working quietly through many channels, did all it could to make sure that airlines around the world did not show a positive interest in this pioneer SST."

There are suspicions that some of the British media critics of Concorde were inspired by pro-Americanism, or at least by a contempt for Britain's own aircraft industry and technology base. Others may have sincerely believed that the investment in Concorde represented an unwelcome diversion of money from more socially useful spending. Whatever the motives of the commentators, many of the arguments trotted out by supposedly intelligent people were at best specious and at worst disingenuous, though the roster of Concorde critics looked (at least superficially) respectable enough, including, as it did, *The Economist*'s Mary Goldring and *The Observer*'s Andrew Wilson.

In his book *Disinformation: American Multinationals at War Against Europe* (2001; Algora Publishing; ISBN 1892941503), Rémi Kauffer, a distinguished French writer and investigative journalist, and a teacher at the College for Political Science in Paris, offered intriguing evidence of the existence of an American anti-Concorde task force led by the CIA that operated during the 1960s. Kauffer is an acknowledged expert on government intelligence services and espionage, and on the shadowy world of commercial and economic espionage and warfare.

The power of the anti-Concorde lobby was reflected in the US House of Representatives vote on 18 December, which placed a six-month ban on Concorde landing in the US. The margin against Concorde was tiny (199 votes to 198) and the aircraft did have useful allies, including Ohio Senator Clarence J Brown, who observed that he could see "no reason to oppose the SST just because we were stupid enough to get out of the SST business ourselves".

US go-ahead ... but not to New York

Despite the vote in the House of Representatives, on 4 February 1976 William Coleman, the US Secretary of Transportation, gave his approval to British Airways and Air France to each operate three Concorde services to the US – two each to New York and one each per day to Washington-

routes, to allow them to be operated by US-licensed aircrew. The five British Airways aircraft carried dual British and American registrations, while those from Air France carried only their new US registration numbers. The procedure was for an engineer to remove the letter G from the BA Concordes' tails at Washington, followed by a piece of paper changing hands to confirm the change of ownership. A British Airways aircraft, G-BOAA, flew to Dallas on 10 December for route-proving flights to 16 cities in the southeast and mid-west.

Concorde was awarded a US Certificate of Airworthiness on 9 January. Braniff inaugurated its Concorde service on 12 January, though it lasted only until 1 June 1980, when it was discontinued due to a lack of passengers and an increase in fuel costs – and because Braniff went bust! It had never been likely that Concorde could operate successfully on an entirely subsonic route, except as a novelty. Braniff was unable to gain approval for supersonic services from Washington to Dallas, and went to the wall before supersonic routes to South America could be instituted.

From 20 September 1978 Air France was able to extend its route network from Washington, DC by beginning a twice-weekly Concorde service from Washington to Mexico City.

Concorde under threat

On 16 December 1979 a British Airways Concorde flew from London to New York in under three hours, completing its otherwise routine transatlantic crossing in only two hours 59 minutes and 36 seconds.

While the BA and Air France Concorde services across the Atlantic proved to be a technical success, concerns about the aircraft's running costs plagued the British and French governments, which jointly announced in September 1979 that no more Concorde aircraft would be built and that all unsold aircraft and engines were to be given to British Airways and Air France.

Following its entry into service, Concorde received a number of improvements and modifications, including a thinned and lowered lower intake lip, a sharper extended fin leading edge, and extended sharper control surfaces. Structural weight was increased, the aft centre of gravity limit was relaxed slightly, and fuel tankage was increased. Tyre limiting speed was also increased and take-off thrust ratings were increased by 7.8 per cent. The aircraft's subsonic cruise limit was raised to Mach 0.95.

These improvements were small beer compared to those offered by the so-called 'B Model Concorde'. This was first outlined some four months after the start of scheduled services in 1976, following a proposal from Jacques Mitterrand, the chairman and managing director of Aérospatiale, to M. Cavaille, the French Secretary of State for Transport. An official go-ahead was soon given for an exploratory, FF9 million nine-month study (which was actually already well under way) for an improved version of Concorde.

The Version B was very much a minimum-change derivative of the initial production model (today, it would doubtless have been known as a '-200') and aimed to upgrade and refine the existing Concorde design, and to provide a stepping stone to bridge the gap between Concorde and a genuinely new, second-generation SST, which was expected to emerge (perhaps as a result of collaboration between Europe and the United States) during the 1990s. Aircraft 217 was to have been the first Concorde built to the new standard, and was expected to be ready in 1982.

Developing a B Model Concorde promised to result in an in-service aircraft far more rapidly than would an all-new design, and at much lower cost, building on areas revealed in flight testing of the original model. The new model would involve its operators in a smaller investment in training, maintenance, infrastructure and even spares holdings, yet promised to deliver significant improvements in performance and direct operating costs, and even a reduction in environmental impact.

G-BOAA is serviced at JFK between flights (above), while at left an Air France aircraft settles on to the runway at Roissy (Charles de Gaulle). With the adoption of special routes and noise abatement flight profiles, Concorde became a 'good neighbour' to New Yorkers, and came to be regarded by the city as 'one of its own'. The first revenue services were flown by both airlines on 22 November 1977.

For five days from 10 to 14 December 1978 G-BOAA was flown by Braniff crews on route-proving flights to 16 different US cities, including Las Vegas where the aircraft is seen here. Soon after, Concorde received US certification and on 12 January 1979 Braniff began its subsonic service from Washington to Dallas, as an extension of the BA and Air France services to Washington, where the aircraft were formally handed over to US crews.

In the final government approval for Concorde production, issued in April 1972, 16 production aircraft were authorised (plus long-lead purchases for another six). Although British Airways and Air France had signed up for five and four, respectively, and the manufacturers were to retain one each for trials purposes, at the time there appeared to be little difficulty in selling the remaining five. However, the export options evaporated over the next months, leaving five unsold 'white-tail' aircraft. To avoid any continuing embarassment, the aircraft were sold in 1980 to the national airlines for a nominal sum. G-BFKW entered BA service, but was grounded in April following a Mach 2 intake ramp failure. It is seen here at BA's maintenance facility, awaiting repair. It was then grounded again to serve as a spares 'Christmas tree', before being restored again to service status with the new registration G-BOAG.

As well as the three major special schemes, Air France Concordes have on occasion worn smaller additional markings for special events or sponsorships. Here F-BVFB sports markings for Teleclub.

The incorporation of the modifications proposed for the B model would have been relatively inexpensive, requiring fairly minor changes to the existing production line and allowing the majority of tooling to be maintained. Certification costs were also expected to be very low.

Concorde's manufacturers had hoped to ensure continued growth in the demand for supersonic aircraft, a market in which the Anglo-French Concorde remained the only serious contender, and hoped that working on a B Model Concorde would maintain and expand their knowledge base, experience and technological lead. This would make the partners indispensable participants in any future second-generation SST programme.

Increasing the range

In order to increase the usefulness and sales appeal of the B model, BAC and Aérospatiale aimed to increase the type's range and reduce its noise levels in an attempt to make the aircraft suitable for service over a wider network of routes. The manufacturers hoped to stretch the aircraft's range enough for it to be able to reach US East Coast cities from European cities farther east than Paris and London, or to fly from the United States to Japan in two sectors, or from Europe to Australia in three sectors.

Part of the solution to this lay in increasing internal fuel capacity – and this, in turn, was achieved partly through increasing the size (and volume) of the wings and the associated integral tanks, and by adding a new fuselage tank. The new tanks contained 99790 kg (220,000 lb), compared to 95254 kg (210,000 lb) on the original model.

Rather than simply adding fuel tankage, the manufacturers hoped to reduce fuel consumption, which accounted for about one-third of the aircraft's direct operating costs. Reducing fuel burn was expected to make the aircraft more marketable and so allow operators to reduce ticket prices, as well as increasing range.

Major structural changes were ruled out by the need to reuse manufacturing tools and jigs wherever possible, and changes to the airframe were limited to refinements to the camber and twist of the wing leading edge, extended wingtips, and the addition of droop slats on the leading edges of the wings. These aerodynamic refinements reduced induced drag at supersonic speeds and increased available lift at slower speeds, conferring a 2,392-mile (3850-km) increase in range.

The addition of leading-edge droops allowed the aircraft to fly at lower angles of attack at slow speeds, reducing drag and thereby requiring lower power settings in the circuit, in turn reducing noise. Noise was also cut back by the incorporation of acoustic processing in the air intake and the ejector.

The manufacturers outlined potential engine improvements, reasoning that the addition of an increased-diameter low-pressure compressor and extra low-pressure turbine stages, coupled to a new discharge system, would increase the margin of air flow through the engine by 25 per cent on take-off and 35 per cent during approach. The resulting thrust gains were such that the reheat (afterburner) system could be removed, reducing noise and fuel consumption.

However, BAC and Aérospatiale found it hard enough to sell the five remaining Concordes from the initial 16-aircraft production run, and the B Model thus remained unbuilt. Some observers believe that the additional range and performance offered by the B Model would have resulted in additional sales, but this is no more than speculation.

The Concorde team went on to form the backbone of the team that later built the European Airbus family. With this group of aircraft, Europe finally put an end to the American monopoly in civil aviation manufacturing.

Writing off the costs

During the same year that Concorde production was finally capped at 16 full production aircraft, the British government began to look for a way in which Concorde could continue in service without cost to the taxpayer, supported by BA alone. As an initial step, the government cancelled £160 million of divident capital originally issued to cover the purchase of the aircraft, in return for 80 per cent of any surplus produced from operating the aircraft. (By 1982 BA's Concordes were producing an operating surplus of about £10 million per annum.) This arrangement left support costs in government hands, however, which was unacceptable in the long time.

The British House of Commons Industry and Trade Committee on Concorde published its long-awaited report on 14 April 1982, expressing grave dissatisfaction with the programme's cost figures, and urging greater efforts to ensure that the costs would be shared more equally with France. The government replied to the report with a robust defence of both the programme and its position, but in September commissioned a joint report with the French government into the future of the programme.

Throughout the rest of the year, the British and French governments discussed the future of the Concorde programme, considering complete cancellation, a phased run-down of the programme or indefinite continuation of the project. The British government carefully reviewed Concorde's costs, leading to the August 1982 decision to cease funding the aircraft's support costs. British Airways, which had formed a dedicated Concorde Division in May 1982, soon decided that it would like to keep the aircraft in service, and that it might be possible to fund the aircraft's support costs from revenue – in other words, that the aircraft would be paying for itself and even making an operating

Right: F-BVFF, the last Concorde to be built in France, was one of three 'white-tail' Concordes inherited by Air France, entering service in October 1980 after 22 months in limbo at Toulouse. When Air France dropped all but the New York service in 1982, the fleet's utilisation rate dropped and several aircraft went into storage.

Special schemes

F-BTSD – Pepsi (above and left): in 1996 Pepsi Cola launched a new brand design and logo, and on 2 April F-BTSD was revealed painted in these colours at London's Gatwick airport, accompanied by sundry celebrities and supermodels. The aircraft embarked on a 10-city tour of Europe and the Middle East, before returning to Air France colours after a fortnight.

F-BTSC – movie star (below): in 1978-79 F-BTSC was used in the film *Airport '79: The Concorde*, for which it received this scheme.

F-WTSB – anniversary (bottom): in March 1989, on the 20th anniversary of the Concorde's first flight, the first production aircraft was specially painted by French university students, before being handed over for display outside the Airbus assembly building at Toulouse (restored to Air France colours).

One of British Airways' regular charters is an annual visit to the Royal International Air Tattoo, held at RAF Fairford. The Gloucestershire base was, of course, host to most of the British pre-certification trials campaign.

profit. New chairman Lord King had been charged with preparing BA for privatisation, and took a tough line on reducing costs and increasing revenue, but was predisposed to keeping Concorde, which he saw as being a great advert for the airline, and good for staff morale. He was also optimistic that the aircraft could at least cover its costs. When Lord Marshall joined BA as chief executive in 1983, he was even more enthusiastic about Concorde, retaining the dedicated Concorde Division as what amounted to an airline within an airline.

British Airways finally became fully responsible for funding Concorde's support costs on 31 March 1984, after 18 months of talks and a 12-month extension of state funding. BA paid the government £16.5 million and received spares nominally worth £120 million (actually worth much less), including G-BOAG and the partly cannibalised 202 (G-BBDG). Service support for the first year under the new arrangement cost £7 million, but the airline no longer had to give 80 per cent of its Concorde profits to the government.

British Airways was upbeat about Concorde, and even opened a new service (continuing from Washington to Miami) on 27 March 1984. During 1985 British Airways inaugurated several Concorde services within Europe (mainly to gain publicity, and to fulfil public demand to sample the Concorde experience without paying full fares across the Atlantic). The company also launched Concorde services to a number of destinations across the Atlantic, in association with the Cunard Shipping Line, and mounted an aggressive drive to gain charter work, successfully gaining charter routes to Sydney (establishing a world record time of 17 hours and three minutes on its first Sydney service) and Cape Town (gaining another record with a journey time of only eight hours and eight minutes). A number of novelty charters were also instigated – flying to see Santa in Lapland, Christmas shopping excursions to New York, or even seeing the Bolshoi Ballet in Moscow.

On 15 November 1989 F-BVFF left Paris on Air France's first round-the-world charter tour, organised by American Express. Under various tour operators, including Kuoni and Intrav, at least 29 more such charters were flown up to February 1998, peaking at five a year in 1987 and 1988. Routes varied considerably, but Air France Concordes became almost regular visitors to such unlikely destinations as Oakland, Papeete and Christchurch.

Air France was less optimistic, by contrast, and had closed down its routes to Caracas and Rio on 31 March 1982 and to Washington on 29 October 1982, but spirits were revived somewhat by BA's new optimism and drive. Some British travel agents began chartering Air France Concordes as well as BA aircraft. The aircraft's profile and prestige was enhanced by its increasing use by French presidents and British prime ministers for official visits and summits.

Concorde set free

Concorde celebrated 10 years in commercial service on 21 January 1986, by which time it had accumulated 71,000 supersonic flying hours. The following year, BA carried its 1 millionth scheduled transatlantic Concorde passenger and the aircraft was used to spearhead the advertising campaign that accompanied the privatisation of British Airways.

Charter flying continued to expand, and 1986 saw Concorde making its first charter flight to New Zealand on 5 April (viewing Halley's Comet over the Indian Ocean while en route). Later that year, between 8 and 23 November, Concorde made its first round-the-world charter flight, logging a total flying time of 31 hours and 51 minutes. A second round-the-world trip, organised by Goodwood Travel, departed on 7 March 1987.

More unusual flights and events followed. On 1 September 1990, 15,000 people watched the first landing of a chartered Concorde in Japan at the offshore airport of Omura. It was announced in March 1992 that Concorde was to make a visit to Nigeria and South Africa. 10 October 1993 saw British Airways make a special Concorde flight to Jeddah in Saudi Arabia, and on 3 December that year Concorde took part in the 'fastest show on earth' when the Bee Gees flew around the Bay of Biscay for the charity Children in Need.

BA did not ignore the development and streamlining of its scheduled services during the late 1980s and early 1990s. On 12 December 1987 British Airways started a once-weekly Concorde service to Barbados for the winter season, and inaugurated a twice-weekly Concorde service to Dallas between 15 June and late August 1988.

Routes were lost as well as gained, and on 11 January 1991 it was announced that the Concorde service between Washington and Miami would be discontinued from 31 March. In October 1994 the long-standing British Airways Concorde service to Washington was also discontinued, although an extra British Airways Concorde was based

Right: With the end of regular services to South America and Washington, both fleets have had spare capacity which is used, where possible, for charter work. These range from major world tours and occasional high-profile government charters to more mundane flights within Europe. The latter include Concorde 'experience' flights, providing a luxury day out, and trips to special events such as airshows and sporting occasions. F-BTSD is seen here in the rather unlikely surroundings of RAF Finningley during one such charter in 1992.

F-BVFA rests at Toulouse. This aircraft is the Air France fleet leader, by nearly 4,000 hours over the next aircraft. However, all but one of BA's aircraft have more hours than 'VFA, illustrating the much heavier utilisation by the British airline.

The typical landing approach is flown at an attitude of 11° on a glideslope of 3°, giving an angle of attack of 14°. The nose droops by 12.5° to allow the pilots a good view of the runway ahead. Once the landing run has been completed, the nose is raised to a 5° setting for taxiing. Visible in this view are the prominent bars in front of the mainwheels which reduce the likelihood of foreign objects being thrown forward and up into the engine intakes.

in New York to serve the growing charter market in the US. It briefly looked as though the entrepreneur Richard Branson's Virgin Atlantic airline might begin transatlantic Concorde services, when he announced that his company might lease Concordes and crews from Air France.

In October 1995 it was announced that a programme was underway to investigate extending Concorde's life to 8,500 reference flights, which was expected to allow operation of the oldest of BA's Concordes until about 2007, at then-current utilisation rates.

The original fatigue test specimen had been tested to only 20,000 cycles, which, after a 2/3 scatter factor had been applied, gave a safe life of only 6,700 cycles. G-BOAF was fitted with strain gauges and comprehensive instrumentation, and this confirmed that the structure was in much better shape than might have been expected from the original fatigue tests, clearing the way for a fatigue life extension. Concorde airframes' remarkably good condition prompted British and French airworthiness authorities to rule that no major modifications were required, and mandated only six changes to the aircraft's maintenance schedule.

BA funded studies into the work required to extend the aircraft's life to 10,000 cycles, which would have allowed the oldest of its Concordes to operate until 2013, at current utilisation rates. The studies were dropped in 2003 when the fleet retirement was announced

On 7 February 1996, Captain Les Scott set a new record between New York's John F. Kennedy Airport and London's Heathrow, taking only two hours, 52 minutes and 59 seconds – shaving a full minute off BA's previous best time, and landing G-BOAD some 40 minutes ahead of schedule.

Under threat again

While the story of Concorde during the 1990s was largely one of successful charters, glamorous and famous new passengers, and the apparently effortless solving of minor age-related structural problems, the very future of Concorde was soon to be threatened not once, but twice.

Environmental objections to Concorde had largely been overcome by the tiny size of the Concorde fleet – there is, after all, a limit to the damage that can be done by only 14 active aircraft – and Concorde's noise nuisance was confined to more social times of day and was largely restricted to three airports (Heathrow, Charles de Gaulle and New York's John F. Kennedy) with a relatively small number of movements. It seemed easy to treat Concorde as something of a special case, and to allow it a degree of immunity from some regulations.

All that changed in 1999, when the aircraft became entangled in a row about the continued operation of older-generation jetliners that had been fitted with hush kits. On 10 February, the European Parliament approved a ban on newly hush-kitted aircraft, in a move which it claimed was intended to reduce aircraft noise and the environmental damage caused by older, less fuel-efficient aircraft.

The EU claimed that hush kits incur significant weight and performance penalties, producing 50 per cent higher fuel consumption on take-off, while still being noisier than current technology engines.

Nevertheless, it planned to permit aircraft registered in the EU (or already operating in the EU) before 1 January 1999 to continue to operate unfettered, thereby penalising only airlines based outside Europe. Since many US carriers had turned to hush kits in an effort to comply with International Civil Aviation Organisation noise limits, and all major hush kit manufacturers were US companies, the European move was interpreted as being motivated more by trade than environmental considerations.

The US response was to threaten a ban on Concorde (which did not actually meet the ICAO hush kit standards) by revoking long-standing waivers on the aircraft's operation into US airports. The House of Representatives passed legislation to this effect on 3 March 1999, though it was clear that this would take effect (subject to Congressional approval) only if the EU approved its proposed ban. The crisis was defused before the US ban on Concorde could take effect.

Tragedy at Gonesse

The second threat to Concorde's future emerged following a horrifying and spectacular crash in July 2000. Concorde

British Airways' new 'Landor' scheme was revealed on the restored-to-flight G-BOAG (formerly G-BFKW) on 25 April 1985, and was quickly applied to the rest of the fleet. At the same time the original grey interior and seats was replaced by brown. In 1993 another interior change restored the decor to its original grey. The new livery was adopted to reflect BA's – and Concorde's – refined and businesslike image.

Top: Concorde has made numerous airshow appearances over the years, often in the course of charter work.

Above: In 1998 F-BVFF received markings for the football World Cup, held in France.

Below: Seen in happier times, F-BTSC taxis at Charles de Gaulle. Having just completed its D Check major overhaul, 'TSC was the aircraft which crashed at Gonesse on 25 July 2000 while taking off on a German tour charter.

had suffered a succession of minor accidents and incidents, including 57 tyre bursts and deflations, 12 of which caused puncturing of or damage to the fuel tanks. None of these was serious, however, until an overweight Air France Concorde taking off for New York suffered a similar tyre burst at Charles de Gaulle Airport. The tragedy was caught on video, and footage of F-BTSC trailing an enormous plume of blazing fuel was broadcast across the world. The pilot struggled to maintain control of the stricken aircraft, but with one engine shut down and the undercarriage unretractable, the end was inevitable. A delta-winged aircraft like Concorde does not stall in the conventional sense, but the result was the same: the aircraft pitched up rapidly, departed from controlled flight, and struck the ground near Gonesse almost vertically, tail first, demolishing a small hotel. All 109 people on board lost their lives, along with four on the ground.

Air France immediately grounded its Concorde fleet. British Airways suspended its Concorde operations on 25 July 2000, cancelling two services (BA003 from Heathrow to New York and the returning BA004). BA, however, resumed operations the next day, although it did implement an extensive series of additional checks and procedures, above and beyond the aircraft's already demanding maintenance and inspection schedule.

In the immediate aftermath of the tragedy BA pointed out that there was "no technical, safety or operational evidence to suggest that Concorde should not operate safely into the future", and stated that it had received "no information from Air France or the French or British airworthiness authorities" that would justify grounding its Concorde fleet. Perhaps surprisingly, passenger confidence in Concorde remained unshaken, and services flew with loads that were entirely typical for the time of year.

Nonetheless, British Airways Concorde operations were suspended on 15 August 2000 when it became clear that the CAA would be "minded to accept" a recommendation from the French BEA that the aircraft's Certificate of Airworthiness be suspended.

Return from New York

Air France made what many people expected to be the last-ever Concorde flight on 21 September 2000, returning the single aircraft that had been stranded in New York when the airline suspended its Concorde operations immediately after the crash. This aircraft finally returned to Paris with five crew and no passengers, after the French Civil Aviation Authority (DGAC) granted permission to make the one-off ferry flight.

Some observers doubted that Concorde would ever fly again, while others believed that the chain of events that had led to the crash were unique and made grounding the French aircraft (let alone the BA aircraft) an unnecessary overreaction.

British Airways immediately began looking for ways to resume Concorde operations as quickly as possible, co-operating with airframe and engine manufacturers and the airworthiness authorities in an effort to find a solution that would lead to a rapid restoration of the aircraft's Certificate of Airworthiness.

Right: F-BTSC is seen trailing a plume of fire during its desperate last seconds as its crew attempts to keep the aircraft in the air long enough to put it down on the nearby runway at le Bourget. Just a short distance from potential safety the aircraft departed and fell almost vertically, tail-first, on to a hotel at Gonesse. The immediate grounding which followed the crash stranded F-BVFC in New York until 21 September.

Air France (above left) and BA (above) engineers are seen installing the Kevlar tank liners, while the undercarriage of G-BOAF is seen during its post-mod roll-out, shod with Michelin's new NZG tyres (left). Below a BA Concorde is seen receiving a freshen-up in the paintshop after modification.

Post-crash modifications

The main element of the modification process was the installation of EADS-designed Kevlar tank liners (saturated in Viton waterproof sealant), but changes were made to wiring in key areas and extra protection was added. New tyres, with increased damage tolerance and greater fragmentation qualities, were also incorporated into the upgrade, although these had already been under development before the Gonesse crash.

The safety modifications obviously had to provide real solutions to the 15 possible problems then considered as being possible causes of the catastrophic fire, but also had to be economically viable. This meant that the modifications had to be light enough for Concorde to continue to be able to fly transatlantic services with a commercial load, and to be capable of being incorporated into the aircraft without a complete rebuild.

Fuel tank protection

The chosen solution included the installation of a set of more than 150 tray-like Kevlar/rubber sandwich compound fuel tank liners. They were designed in Toulouse by the European Aeronautic Defence and Space Company (EADS), the former Aérospatiale, to prevent catastrophic losses of fuel, reducing such loss to less than 0.4 litres (0.09 Imp gal) per second even in the case of a major tank penetration. These liners fitted between wing ribs and stringers, mounted on brackets that allowed them to 'float' a few millimetres from the bottom of the tank, with fuel circulating below them to allow the normal vital heat transfer between the wing and the fuel. The liners cost around £17,000 per aircraft set, and imposed a weight penalty of about 400 kg (882 lb).

Access to the fuel tanks was extremely limited, some openings being as small as 12 or 13 in (30 or 33 cm) across. The chief engineer had to put out a call for engineers small enough to fit inside the tanks, and those who answered had to find their own ways of getting into the tanks; one woman climbed in head first before doing a backward roll into the space. BA assigned a team of 270 engineers to the programme, working three round-the-clock shifts.

The modification package also included protection for some critical underwing electrical and hydraulic systems, and provided improved shielding of the fuel tanks from potential sources of electrical arcing. Concorde's normal operating procedures were changed so that the 115V electrical supply to the cooling fans for the carbon brakes were deactivated during the take-off run, because there were suspicions that a spark from this wiring may have ignited the leaking fuel during the Air France accident. It was estimated that the full modification package would cost £17 million for the BA Concorde fleet.

Meanwhile, the airline pressed ahead with an ambitious and long-planned cabin interior upgrade (with new seats, bathrooms, interiors, and tableware), which it undertook while the aircraft were grounded so they could re-enter service in their upgraded form. The new interiors modernised the look and feel of Concorde's narrow-body cabin, making it seem more spacious and luxurious, while using modern materials and technologies to produce a weight saving of 400 kg (882 lb) that offset the additional weight of some of the new safety modifications. Without the new interior, Air France's aircraft are now restricted to a maximum

Apart from cancelling two flights on the day of F-BTSC's tragic loss, British Airways kept its Concorde fleet flying until 15 August following a hasty safety inspection. Initially expecting a brief grounding, the airline maintained its Concordes in full flying condition, with daily checks and regular engine runs. However, it soon became clear that Concorde would not be returning to the air for some time, and the fleet was mothballed in the maintenance area pending modifications. The grounding and rectification period lasted until 7 November 2001 – over nearly 15 months since services had been suspended.

passenger load of 92, eight fewer than the modified BA aircraft. With passengers now used to the idea of supersonic flight, it was felt to be right to underline Concorde's uniqueness and to reflect the aircraft's elegance and exclusivity in its interior. BA's stated aim with this £14 million programme (costing almost as much as the technical modifications that followed the Paris crash) was to "bring the excitement and elegance of the outside to the inside" and to "ensure that the interior of the aircraft is as elegant as the exterior".

Preparing for a short grounding

The airline initially cancelled all Concorde services only until early September 2000, and optimistically stated that it would be able to resume operations at 24 hours' notice should clearance be given before that. BA's engineers carefully maintained the airline's Concordes in airworthy condition, ready for a short-notice return to operations, checking them every day and testing the computer, electrical and hydraulic systems. The engines were also regularly run. Concorde flight crews, meanwhile, conducted regular training in the simulator. In the event, the solutions to Concorde's airworthiness issues were both time-consuming and expensive, and the aircraft's grounding lasted many months.

An Air France Concorde (F-BVFB) resumed flying in January 2001 after being fitted with hundreds of sensors, with the cabin interior stripped of its usual seating to accommodate the flight test equipment. The aircraft flew to the flight test centre at Istres in the south of France on 18 January 2001 for preliminary ground testing (including high-speed taxi tests) of the proposed modifications and for an investigation as to why two engines had failed in the original accident. Specially installed sprays and pipes were used to spray yellow-coloured water, simulating fuel leaks from different parts of the wing tanks, in order to determine how the aircraft's fuel had leaked from the tanks and caught fire during the original accident. The runway at Istres is claimed to be the longest in Europe, at 5 km (3.2 miles). The aircraft returned to Charles de Gaulle on 3 February 2001.

Another Air France Concorde (F-BTSD) returned to the air on 11 April 2001, carrying out a three-hour supersonic test flight from Charles de Gaulle that allowed all systems to be tested, before it flew to Istres for tyre tests on 17 April 2001. Michelin had been developing a new radial NZG (Near Zero Growth) tyre for Concorde – featuring improved resistance to foreign object damage and permitting substantially higher take-off weights – even before the Air France crash, and development of these tyres was immediately accelerated. During tests, the new tyre did not burst even when repeatedly run over a metal strip at speeds of up to 235 mph (378 km/h). It was expected that the new radial tyres would burst sideways in the event of a blow-out, breaking up into smaller fragments if they were catastrophically damaged. The tyres promised to avoid inflicting serious damage to the aircraft in the event of a blow-out. The aircraft flew from Istres to Orly Airport on 5 May 2001 to visit the Air France paint shop, before flying back to Charles de Gaulle on 30 May 2001.

Slow process

Keeping Concorde on the ground was expensive, and by early February it was estimated that maintaining BA's fleet of seven Concordes and keeping their crews as close to flight-ready as possible had already cost BA around £40 million. The airline had originally hoped to be able to modify at least three of its Concordes by 28 March, in order to be able to re-open services between Heathrow and JFK for the lucrative summer season, but progress was destined to be slow. Fitting the new Kevlar fuel tank liners to a British Airways Concorde (G-BOAF) for flight tests was not completed until 19 June, when the aircraft was ceremonially rolled out from its hangar prior to an exhaustive series of ground tests. This aircraft also had the armoured wiring around the undercarriage bay and was fitted with the new Michelin NZG tyres.

For these initial tests, heat sensors were mounted in key areas in the tanks to monitor fuel temperatures, and comprehensive test recording equipment was fitted in the rear of the passenger cabin. This equipment was required to validate the operational effect of the modifications on fuel capacity, fuel transfer rates and fuel gauge readings, and to confirm that the various flight safety modifications did not interfere with normal flight operations and had no implications for fuel cooling, fuel flow, heat distribution/dissipation or centre of gravity. Following three weeks of comprehensive ground tests to measure the effect of the new tank liners on the fuel transfer systems and gauges, G-BOAF finally undertook a taxi trial at Heathrow Airport on 4 July.

During the one-hour exercise covering 5 miles (8 km), the aircraft taxied around the airfield, checking the steering,

Right and below: The first British Airways Concorde to receive the modifications was G-BOAF, and it was rolled out of the Heathrow maintenance facility on 19 June 2001. G-BOAE followed it through the modification process, and was the aircraft used for the first service to New York on 7 November. G-BOAG had also been through modification by the time full service was resumed.

Return to the air

Getting the Concorde back into service was a long and painstaking process, involving fuel leak trials by F-BVFB in early 2001, and tyre trials by F-BTSD in April. Further trials were undertaken by BA's G-BOAF in July, including simulated Atlantic crossing cycles, thus becoming the first fully modified aircraft to return to the air. Exhaustive ground tests were needed to check the integrity of the new tank liners and tyres. The next step was refresher training for the aircrew, which began in August under a restricted CofA. With the modified CofA issued in September, full crew training flights could be undertaken, leading to two 'trial-run' services to New York on 22 October (BA) and 29 October (Air France). These final flights paved the way for full services to recommence on 7 November 2001.

braking and communications systems and the navigation computers, and reached a speed of 35 mph (56 km/h) before returning to the engineering base. Like many aircraft of its generation, Concorde is extremely reliable when regularly flown, but has a tendency to suffer trivial electrical problems, leaks, etc. when left standing idle for extended periods. Having been stripped down for the installation of the tank liners for an extended period, G-BOAF was perhaps bound to suffer such minor niggles, and hopes that a verification flight would be made on 9 July were frustrated.

BA back in the air

G-BOAF finally flew on 17 July 2001, leaving Heathrow for a technical verification flight designed to assess the operational impact of the modifications it had received, while simulating a normal Concorde Atlantic crossing as much as possible. The aircraft was able to fly at its normal 1,350-mph (2173-km/h) cruising speed and reach its normal operating altitude of 60,000 ft (18288 m). Under these conditions, Concorde operates in a unique environment: the outside air temperature is between -45°C and -70°C (-49°F and -94°F), but skin friction at supersonic speeds raises the airframe skin temperature to 127°C (260°F) on the nose and to approximately 100°C (212°F) at the wing. Such conditions cannot be replicated at lower speeds and altitudes, but were obviously an essential test of Concorde's new tank modifications.

The aircraft landed at RAF Brize Norton rather than returning to London's busy Heathrow Airport. Brize Norton was an ideal choice to host additional Concorde test flights, being relatively close to BA's maintenance base at Heathrow yet more isolated from media attention. BA was also able to avoid using scarce take-off and landing slots at Heathrow and simply to fly when the aircraft was ready, without having to wait for when slots had been pre-booked.

The aircraft remained at Brize Norton for several days, undergoing more ground tests, even deliberately running a modified tank dry and accurately recalibrating the fuel quantity indicators. The aircraft returned to the BA Concorde base at Heathrow on 20 July, making a second verification flight on the return journey.

Once the verification flights were complete, BA began refresher training for the first crews, flying missions on 7, 8 and 22 August 2001. This was undertaken at Shannon in Ireland, rather than at Prestwick or in Portugal where much of the airline's flight training is now regularly undertaken. The modified aircraft and its new Michelin tyres had not regained a full Certificate of Airworthiness, meaning these first training flights had to be carried out under a very limited special CAA flight certificate; this prohibited the carriage of passengers and even cabin crew, but did let pilots and flight engineers regain currency on the aircraft. The training flights included a brief foray over the Atlantic, sufficient to allow the crew to complete a full (if abbreviated) supersonic flight cycle, encompassing all the required checks and procedures.

Air France began its own programme of verification flights on 24 August, under which F-BVFB operated to and from Charles de Gaulle. Air France training flights began on 31 August 2001, using Vatry Airport for circuits, before training moved to Chateauroux-Deols Airport (Indre), a former US Air Force base with a 3.5-km (2.17-mile) runway.

On 5 September the British CAA and French DGAC issued a set of airworthiness directives for Concorde, making it clear that their implementation would lead to a restoration

Brize Norton, the RAF's principal strategic transport base, provided an excellent 'bolt-hole' for G-BOAF for its initial post-modification trials. It arrived at the Oxfordshire airfield on 17 July 2001 (left) after a Mach 2 verification flight. With trials largely completed, the aircraft returned to Heathrow before beginning flight crew training, using Shannon airport in Ireland.

F-BVFB (foreground) and F-BVFA are seen in Air France's maintenance hangar at Charles de Gaulle during modification work. Concorde maintenance schedules specify an A Check every 210 flying hours, B Check every 420 hours, C Check every 1,680 hours, IL Check every 6,000 hours and a D Check every 12,000 hours. The latter is a major overhaul which involves the aircraft being grounded for nearly a year, and in which it is completely dismantled and all paint removed. All parts are rigourously examined and a large number are systematically replaced.

A modified 'Fox Bravo' takes off for New York. During the long grounding, the dozen or so Air France flight crews maintained proficiency by using the simulator, 'flying' at least four hours per month with three take-off/landing cycles. When Concorde returned to the air Air France brought its service 30 minutes earlier – to 10:30 am. This arrives in New York at 8:25 am local time, easing the passage through customs and immigration and opening up more connecting flights. The return flight leaves New York at 8 am, arriving in Paris at 5:45 pm.

of the individual aircraft's Certificates of Airworthiness as soon as each surviving aircraft was modified. The directives included the use of the new Kevlar linings in certain key fuel tanks, the use of new Michelin NZG tyres on all eight main wheels, and the armouring of electrical wiring in the undercarriage bay. They also required the removal of the water deflector retention system, and the reprofiling of the deflectors to accommodate the new tyres. Operating procedures were changed so that the flat tyre detection and warning system had to be working on departure, and electrical power to the brake cooling fans had to be switched off before take-off and landing. Anti-skid system protocols were also changed to take account of the new tyres.

The modified G-BOAF's C of A was immediately restored, finally allowing it to carry passengers. This, in turn, allowed British Airways to begin the next stage of its programme to reintroduce the aircraft into full scheduled service. The airline conducted a series of operational assessment flights – three simple out-and-return flights over the Atlantic and a circuit of the Bay of Biscay – on 11 September, 5 October and 2 November, and one full 'stopping' service to New York's JFK Airport, with a return flight, on 22 October. The sorties were specifically designed to practise and refine all aspects of the British Airways Concorde experience, allowing cabin crews and ground handling staff to get back up to speed before fare-paying passengers were flown. For the operational assessment flights, passengers consisted of some of the BA engineers who had worked so hard to return the type to service and other BA staff who had entered a massively oversubscribed draw. Air France undertook a similar programme, with F-BVFB departing from Charles de Gaulle Airport for New York on 29 October. It night-stopped there before returning to Paris late on 30 October.

Return to service

Full-scale passenger services to New York restarted on Wednesday 7 November 2001, for which Air France and British Airways mounted near-simultaneous flights. Air France's F-BTSD left first, departing from Paris-Charles de Gaulle at 09:44 GMT and arriving at New York-JFK a little over three and a half hours later, at 13:20 GMT. The aircraft carried the President of Air France, Jean-Cyril Spinetta, and the French Minister for Transport, Jean-Claude Gayssot, together with a number of what were described as 'personalities of the aeronautical world'.

The first scheduled British Airways Concorde service to New York in nearly 16 months took off one hour after the Air France aircraft, with G-BOAE operating as 'Speedbird 001'. As the aircraft ignited its afterburners, a waiting American Airlines captain was heard to whoop over the radio, "Go Concorde! Go!" Although hailed as the first full passenger flight for paying customers, the British Airways Concorde carried some of the UK's top business leaders, hosted by the airline's chief executive Rod Eddington, as what he described as "a thank you for their support for Concorde over the years and to reaffirm our commitment to business travel between the UK and US". Also on board were a handful of representatives from the government, the aviation industry and the media. Both Concordes were greeted on arrival by New York's Mayor Rudolph Giuliani, who then hosted a joint press conference.

This was somewhat overshadowed by BA's second Concorde service – the type's first charter since the accident. In order to brief US President George W. Bush on his trip to the Middle East the previous week, and to discuss the progress of Operation Enduring Freedom (the US-led

British Airways refit

Despite the uncertainty of the post-Gonesse grounding, BA introduced a new interior with indigo-blue leather seats and a new, armoured cockpit door was installed in the aftermath of the 11 September attacks.

When British Airways adopted its 'One World' identity in 1997 – which employed a range of colour schemes inspired by art and craft from around the world – there was public outcry in the UK as no vestige of the national flag remained on the aircraft of what was the 'national flag-carrier'. Concorde, however, featured a representation of the Union Flag on the fin ('Chatham' scheme), in arguably the best-looking of the liveries applied to the type. Recognising the brewing storm, and in answer to arch-rival Virgin Atlantic's decision to add the national flag to its aircraft, BA subsequently back-tracked on its initial plans, with the airline's fleet now slated to receive the 'Chatham' scheme.

military campaign against the Taliban regime in Afghanistan), British Prime Minister Tony Blair chartered Concorde G-BOAF for his flight to Washington, leaving London-Heathrow at 16:36 GMT and arriving at Andrews Air Force Base at 20:11 GMT (15:11 EST), spending five hours in Washington before flying home.

British Airways recommenced its weekly Concorde service to Barbados on 1 December. G-BOAF opened the service, touching down at Grantley Adams International Airport some 15 minutes ahead of schedule at 09:30 local time. This marked the first of 21 return flights to the Barbados, undertaken every Saturday until 13 April 2002, many of which were rapidly sold out. Due to the level of demand, two services were flown on some Saturdays, including Christmas Eve.

Barbados was pleased to see the return of Concorde and accorded the first aircraft and its 76 slightly bemused passengers the full red carpet treatment. The Barbadian Minister of Tourism and International Transport, Noel Lynch, pointed out the value of Concorde's image in the branding of Barbados, and emphasised the pride he felt in Barbados being the only destination outside the United States to which BA's Concorde flew from Europe.

On the 'bread-and-butter' route to New York, load factors were consistently high (above 70 per cent) and the service quickly became extremely profitable. In an effort to further raise the aircraft's profile, and further stimulate demand, BA launched an offer under which a total of 205 return tickets to New York over the New Year period were offered at a knock-down £2,002 each – less than one-third of their normal price. They sold out within three minutes of the special phone line opening!

British Airways reinstated its Saturday service to New York in April, when the winter schedule to Barbados ended. Air France moved from five to seven services per week (recommencing flights on Tuesdays and Saturdays).

Charter flights resume

Air France relaunched its low-fare charter flights on Concorde (in association with French travel company Air Loisirs) to mop up its spare capacity on Saturdays, operating a one-hour 40-minute flight from Charles de Gaulle Airport that circled the Bay of Biscay and included a brief dash at Mach 2. The flights (which cost about £800 or 1220/FF8000) were the high point of an all-day experience that included breakfast, lunch and cocktails at the Hilton, VIP guided tours of the museum at Le Bourget and Charles de Gaulle Airport, and a champagne dinner on board the aircraft.

There had always been major differences between the British and French Concorde operators. Privatised British Airways enjoyed massive operating profits from its supersonic flagship, while Air France (a state-owned operator) experienced marginal economic success with its slightly smaller fleet of aircraft. (In its final quarter – April-June 2000 – Air France's Concorde division earned a profit of only 5 million euros, for example.) French morale was blighted by the fatal accident and Air France was gripped by caution, while BA sometimes seemed to be almost impatient to recommence Concorde operations. Many commentators believed that it would be inevitable that Concorde would re-enter service with the British airline first. In the event, politics and national pride intervened, and both airlines relaunched commercial services on the same day.

L'équipe Concorde – Team Concorde: pilots, flight engineers, flight attendants and mechanics pose in front of F-BVFB at its Roissy base. During the grounding Air France's Maintenance Division assigned a 25-member team to continue maintenance work on the stored fleet, including engine runs every 15 days. Over 100 mechanics were assigned during modification works, joined by around 30 sheet metal workers brought in from other divisions and from EADS. Other specialised teams handled the overhaul of engines (Air France Industrial Logistics Branch), avionics and components.

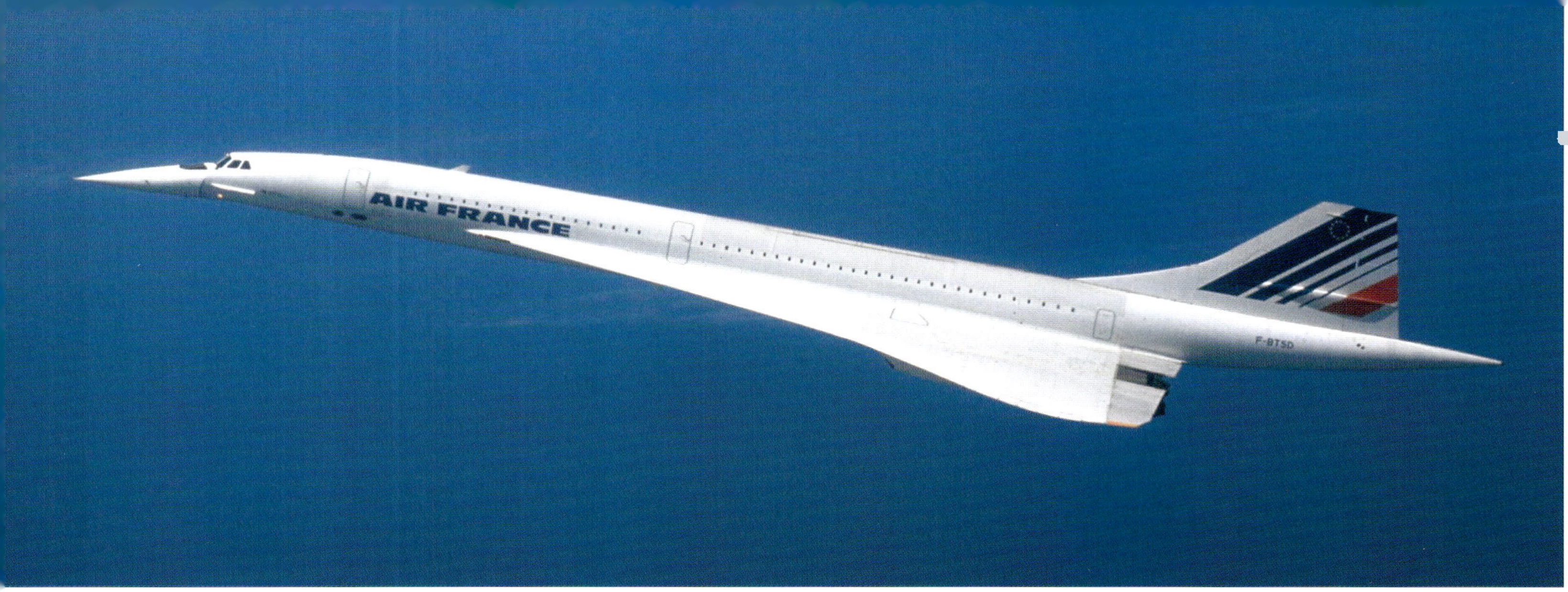

F-BTSD was the second Air France Concorde to fly again, returning to the air on 11 April 2001. Six days later it went to Istres for tests with EADS, principally concerned with the Michelin NZG tyres. These tests lasted until 5 May. The Near-Zero Growth tyres are wider than the earlier units, and required a redesign of the water/ FOD deflector bar fitted to the main undercarriage units. Following the success of these trials, 'TSD went back into the hangar for full modification, flying again on 15 October. The aircraft subsequently became the first to fly a full service to New York when Concorde operations resumed.

Even with the aircraft back in service, criticism of Air France continued, and there were sterile, unproven and unhelpful (but widely repeated) suggestions that the major causes of the accident had been traceable to uniquely French factors, and that this had been covered up by the official accident report. When the final report was published, it confirmed the theory that the disaster had been triggered by runway debris, but suggested that both Air France and America's Continental Airlines review their maintenance procedures. Controversially, Aéroports de Paris escaped censure, and the report failed to tackle the flight crew's lax adherence to proper procedures. The report did mention what it called 'several dysfunctions' in the airline's maintenance and operational procedures, though these were judged as being 'not directly related to the crash'.

Some experts had disagreed with some of the conclusions of the official French accident report, and some still believe that subtle double-standards were applied, grounding Concorde when other aircraft with equally significant design flaws (including the Boeing 737's well-publicised rudder difficulties) remained in service. International certification requirements for all commercial aircraft specify that a tyre explosion, such as happened to the Air France aircraft, should not on its own cause a catastrophic accident, but some experts challenge the finding that tyre failure alone led inexorably to the loss of the aircraft, pointing out that the accident was the result of a chain of events. These experts point to the part played by poor FOD (foreign object damage) control procedures at Charles de Gaulle Airport, and by the maintenance procedures that resulted in the aircraft taking off with an undercarriage spacer missing. There are suspicions that this missing spacer may have caused the aircraft to veer away from the centreline and into the rough ground beside the runway, where it ran over a runway light, debris from which may have caused one of the engines to fail, forcing the captain to rotate early and making it more difficult to reach safe flying speed.

Overweight take-off

Perhaps more significantly, the crew knowingly took off in an aircraft which was at least 1 tonne over its maximum structural weight – and perhaps as much as 6 tonnes above the weight required by the conditions actually encountered on the day, with an appreciable tailwind and a short runway. Not to have recalculated the weight in the light of the changed wind breached all proper procedures. It emerged that the aircraft was taking off with a centre of gravity that was behind its aft-most limit. It may also have been 'over-fuelled', with the over-full tanks perhaps contributing to the explosive nature with which hydrostatic shock caused the fuel tank to burst when hit by tyre debris.

A final contribution to the disaster was made by the aircraft's flight engineer, who shut down the number two engine at a height lower than specified in the operations manual – without being asked to do so by the captain. The engine itself was not on fire, and as the tank emptied and the fire burned itself out, it may have recovered. There are tightly delineated fixed drills for shutting down an engine, requiring the crew to wait until the aircraft is stable at 400 ft (122 m) or above, and then to initiate the shut-down only on the captain's command.

Finally, some analysts suggest that without an ignition source, the accident would have remained no more than a major fuel leak, rather than a catastrophic fire. The tyre failure and subsequent fuel leak and fire were undeniably the primary causes of the crash, but the crash might not have happened without some of the other contributory factors.

Former BA Concorde captain John Hutchison was quoted as saying, "The accident appalled me beyond belief... But it now seems that a single failing may not have caused the accident. In simple terms, if all the procedures and drills had been followed, if there had not been shortcuts and blind eyes, the crash might not have happened."

Some people still question whether the investigations properly served the aviation community, and still believe that Concorde was unnecessarily grounded, because a single failure was not ultimately responsible for the loss of the aircraft. Their concern remains that truth and justice were subordinated in favour of some dubious expediency, and that Concorde's designers took the blame for the accident rather than sharing it with Charles de Gaulle Airport, Air France's maintenance department and the aircraft's crew on the day.

This, they aver, is particularly unfair, since Concorde is actually an inherently safe design, thanks to the fact that its delta wing does not stall, and its phenomenal manoeuvre and gust margin. The absence of spoilers, flaps and slats is widely believed to enhance safety, as is the 'ground cushion' and almost automatic landing flare encountered on landing. Other safety features include the drooping nose, which gives better visibility of approach lights in poor visibility than is available from a subsonic aircraft.

Left and below: Using the callsign 'Concorde 002', G-BOAE arrives at Heathrow at the end of a routine return leg from New York-JFK. Before the Air France crash BA Concordes usually operated from Heathrow's south runway as it saved on taxiing times to the Terminal 4 gates. Since the accident, however, operations have switched to the north runway as it is slightly longer and has a marginally better surface.

Whatever the cause of the accident, it ensured that the aircraft has undergone in-depth inspection and examination, and has received a package of modifications that could only enhance its safety in the future.

Within a few months of the return to service, Concorde was fully back in business, apparently with undiminished passenger confidence, and on 4 June 2002 one of the BA aircraft formed the centrepiece of the Queen's Golden Jubilee Flypast, flying with the Red Arrows. BA were soon flying the company's traditional BA001 and BA002 services to New York seven days per week, initially using one aircraft, and then re-timing the service to a more popular 17:25 UK arrival time, by overnighting an aircraft in New York. The airline also reintroduced its Saturday-only flights to Barbados. Air France ran a New York service on five days of the week (not Tuesdays or Saturdays), plus occasional charters.

Five British Airways aircraft (G-BOAC, G-BOAD, G-BOAE, G-BOAF and G-BOAG) were modified and had their Certificates of Airworthiness returned, and modifications to the sixth aircraft (G-BOAB) had been expected to begin in mid-2003. The fourth aircraft, G-BOAD, carried out its first passenger flight on 10 February 2002 fitted with the new interior seating. The fifth (G-BOAC) flew again on 11 July 2002.

Before the 2003 retirement announcement, work had been expected to begin on G-BOAA, which was to be the first BA Concorde to be fitted with the full cabin upgrade, including the new washrooms and the new lighting effects (with a colour change at the point at which the speed of sound is reached). Other sources suggested that G-BOAA would have become a spares source and that the sixth and seventh Concordes, necessary to reopen a second daily New York service, would not be modified back to flight status..

Without a major engineering programme which would have added two years, or the proposed Concorde life-extension programme, known as 're-life2', which would allowed the aircraft to serve for an additional five or six years, Concorde's certification would have 'run out' in 2009, at which point the aircraft would have had to be retired from service. At the time Air France was scheduling to withdraw its Concordes in 2007, although this was known to be 'under review'.

Four-aircraft fleet

With Air France, four aircraft were modified and returned to service (F-BVFA, F-BVFB, F-BVFC and F-BTSD), F-BVFA being the first. Air France Concordes completed a taxi test and two flight tests (one reaching Mach 2) before being recertificated for passenger service. British Airways loaned a Rolls-Royce Olympus engine to Air France to expedite F-BVFA's return to service. The final Air France Concorde, F-BVFF, has fewer flying hours than the others (around 12,000) and acts as an in-use reserve, replacing other aircraft as they undergo maintenance. It was due to have replaced 'Fox Alpha' when that aircraft came to the end of its life, and Air France was due to complete the aircraft's D Check in November 2003.

Having survived the crisis that followed the loss of F-BTSC, the Concorde fleets of Air France and British Airways continued in operational service. It appeared that as long as there were sufficient passengers willing to pay the premium price charged for the Concorde experience, and for as long as the Concorde airframes had sufficient life remaining, the type would remain in service. Concorde continued to appeal to business people who were willing to pay for the ability to fly to New York or London or Paris and return the same day – an ability that was particularly highly prized in an age when face-to-face meetings were viewed as being of particular use and importance, despite the availability of alternatives like video-conferencing.

Just after the Air France crash, before they were grounded, BA's Concordes were flying half full and BA were bullish that such loads were normal and viable at that time. Since the return to service, similar loads have been cited as evidence that there has been a 'drop in demand', and as justification for an ongoing review. In fact the Saturday service to Barbados was running full (93 passengers and more) while most New York services carried more than 60 passengers, although this was the result of intensive marketing and price-cutting, and some sources suggest that aircraft were sometimes flying with only 20 fully-paid seats filled.

Long before the Air France crash, Concorde had suffered a succession of minor problems – many of them involving delamination or separation of rudders. These were never crit-

G-BOAF at rest: the elevons naturally droop on the ground without any hydraulic power. Concorde has no APU installed and relies on ground installations for power when at rest and for engine start.

G-BOAC takes off from Heathrow's north runway in August 2002. The aircraft had returned to the air the previous month after nearly two years on the ground. Throughout 2002 and early 2003 the possible retirement of Concorde was a recurring theme in the media. A series of minor engineering problems were widely reported, each time leading to another bout of media speculation. Finally, on 10 April 2003 the announcement came from British Airways that it would cease Concorde operations on 31 October. Up to that time, it stressed, it would continue in full service.

ical, but have continued, and interestingly have achieved some prominence in the media, leading some cynics to speculate that they were being highlighted and emphasised as excuses for the premature retirement of the aircraft.

During the spring of 2003, a down-beat spokesman for British Airways said that the long-term future of Concorde was kept under constant review, adding that: "It doesn't make much of a profit and BA is certainly reviewing its future. This is a prudent business planning process when one bears in mind the amount of work behind such a decision. We will continue to fly it so long as it is safe, reliable and commercially viable."

Another spokesman suggested that while "we are very pleased to be able to maintain the Concorde service at this present time.... Concorde is not deemed to be commercially viable, and we are currently reviewing ways of improving this, as we want to continue to provide this exceptional service in the future."

Concorde remained much more than a mere business tool, and continued to enjoy immense recognition and popularity among the public (including many who will never be able to afford to fly aboard the aircraft). For British Airways, in particular, the type remained an emblematic and glamorous flagship for the entire airline, and until the war with Iraq was continuing to generate a small but healthy operating profit. Spare Concorde capacity was still used for an astonishing array of *ad hoc* charters – some part of luxury holidays (perhaps flying home from a luxury cruise, or flying out and back to the 'holiday of a lifetime') and others aimed purely at offering enthusiastic passengers a brief sample of Concorde's unique flying experience.

However, it became increasingly clear that the pre-existing recession in air transport (already exacerbated by security fears after the World Trade Center attacks) was having severe effects on the world's airlines, and this only worsened with the March 2003 attack against Iraq. US carriers received an astonishing $5 billion of government aid and still suffered. Premium and business class-travel (especially to and from the Middle East and across the Atlantic) was particularly hard hit, with passenger numbers dropping in response to fears of terrorism, and with higher fuel prices dramatically increasing costs. Although some would expect that the high-profile, high-prestige Concorde might be specifically targeted by terrorists, and despite the massive cost-savings possible by travelling by other means (with full-price transatlantic Concorde tickets costing £8,293 – about 50 times the cheapest fare available on the route), Concorde's loss of passengers has been no more marked than that experienced by airlines offering subsonic First Class and Business Class seats.

Left: This model, in front of a Concorde nose section at Kemble, shows a potential configuration for British Aerospace's AST (Advanced Supersonic Transport). This naturally drew heavily on Concorde, and was later subsumed into a Europe-wide effort. Little meaningful progress has been made by any project.

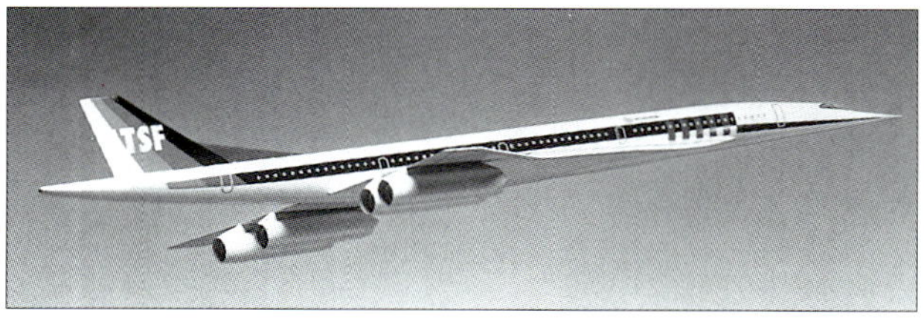

Right: Aérospatiale also continued with SST studies under various acronyms, this being the ATSF (Avion de Transport Supersonique du Futur). This was later refined into the Alliance project – in name at least a fitting successor to Concorde.

Concorde retirement

Speculation that Concorde's premature retirement might be impending was stimulated by the announcement by BA on 25 March that it was cancelling four return trips between London-Heathrow and New York-JFK between 31 March and 13 April. In fact, it transpired that these cancellations had nothing to do with flagging demand, but were a result of work needed to meet American Federal Aviation Administration security requirements, which required that any aircraft flying to or from the USA on or after 9 April must have a reinforced cockpit door. Installation of these doors on BA's Concordes began later than expected, and with only two aircraft available for service on some days, the airline cancelled services to ensure a 'robust operation' and prevent any risk of last minute cancellations.

Finally, on 10 April 2003, British Airways put an end to the speculation. Concorde would, indeed, be retired at the end of the summer season, that is on 31 October 2003, after which five of the airline's aircraft would be earmarked for museum preservation. Meanwhile, Air France announced that it would be suspending Concorde operations from 31 May, and would also completely retire its fleet no later than 1 November.

There is an outside chance that this is not the end of the road. The publicity- and PR-aware British carrier Virgin Atlantic has already expressed some interest in acquiring at least one Concorde from Air France and was said to be closely watching the BA decision. A Virgin spokesman said: "Concorde is an icon of world aviation. If British Airways calls time, we would certainly review the economics to see if we could make it work." Nothing could be better calculated to provoke a "Good old Virgin" reaction from many of the travelling public. Perhaps the canny carrier has realised that having Concorde as a flagship might bring huge goodwill, and that its presence in the Virgin fleet might actually attract passengers to services flown by other aircraft types.

Concorde successors

The US abandoned its full SST programme in 1971, and the NASA Supersonic Cruise Research Program (or Advanced Supersonic Technology Program) followed suit in 1980. NASA launched a High Speed Civil Transport programme in 1986 that aimed to ascertain whether it would be possible to develop an environmentally acceptable and acceptably economic SST. This was defined as being an aircraft that would have no significant effect on the ozone layer, while meeting then-current noise limitations and producing no perceptible sonic boom over populated areas. This study programme led to the High Speed Research Program in 1989, under which NASA eventually funded the conversion of a redundant Tu-144D into the Tu-144LL flying laboratory, with new 'Blackjack'-type NK-321 engines and extensive test equipment. The aircraft flew 19 research flights during June 1996 and February 1998, and seven more between September 1998 and April 1999.

It soon became apparent to both Boeing and McDonnell Douglas that the optimum high-speed aircraft would have a range of either 5,500 nm (10185 km) (McDonnell Douglas) or 5,000 nm (9260 km) (Boeing) and accepted that (in the absence of changes in regulations and improvements in technology) most overland flying would be at high subsonic speeds. Each company toyed with both high-speed and low-speed designs having maximum cruise speeds between Mach 1.6 and Mach 2.4. These studies were abandoned in 1998 and NASA brought its HSR programme to a premature halt in January 1999, with four planned Tu-144LL flights remaining unflown.

An International Supersonic Commercial Transport study group was formed in May 1990, including Aérospatiale, BAE and Deutsche Airbus, as well as Boeing, McDonnell Douglas, the Society of Japanese Aerospace Companies, Alenia and Tupolev. Meanwhile, several of the partners continued with their own independent SST studies, and Aérospatiale, BAE and Deutsche Airbus merged their individual programmes under a European Supersonic Research Programme in April 1994. Tupolev continued work on a second-generation SST under the designation Tu-244. Broad agreement was reached that any future SST should cruise at about the same speed as Concorde (Mach 2.05 being set as the limit) but have 40 per cent lower structural weight, 35 per cent better lift/drag ratio, and 10 per cent better specific fuel consumption at supersonic speed, and 20 per cent better lift/drag ratio and 10 per cent better specific fuel consumption at subsonic speeds. The aircraft would have to be able to operate acceptably from existing airports and have minimal environmental impact, with a ticket price surcharge of no more than 20 per cent.

Smaller supersonic business jet programmes were studied by Gulfstream, Sukhoi, Dassault and Nevada-based Reno Aeronautical, but all remain no more than paper studies. The US Defense Advanced Research Projects Agency has launched a Quiet Supersonic Platform programme, which could eventually have some civil applications, but it was not until Boeing launched its Sonic Cruiser in 2000 that any new-generation civilian supersonic aircraft looked like a serious possibility. Even then, it rapidly became clear that Boeing's new aircraft would not cruise at supersonic speeds, but would instead fly at close to the speed of sound. This represented a major about-face, since the US had hitherto regarded Mach 2.4 as a minimum speed (in order to guarantee two trips per day) and had felt that Europe's chosen speed of Mach 2.05 was inadequate.

While there was no immediate prospect of another airliner with Concorde's Mach 2 performance entering service, Boeing continued to press ahead with its Sonic Cruiser, which promised to offer a significantly lower operating speed than Concorde, albeit with a longer range and bigger payload. Boeing expected passengers to pay a premium price for the ability to cruise at only Mach 0.95, putting Concorde's performance in context.

In the battle of speed versus economy – personified by the Concorde and Boeing 747 – the airline industry chose the latter, relegating Concorde to the status of a novel luxury with little relevance to the global industry. However, BA and Air France managed for some years to sustain load factors on the New York run, and to operate their Concorde divisions at a profit, the figures topped up by special charters. By 2002 British Airways had flown over 2.5 million passengers. Their most loyal customer, an oil executive, chalked up around 70 return trips each year – one of a handful of individuals who saw Concorde as a vital business tool, rather than a lavish luxury. The 'war' between speed and economy loomed briefly again when Boeing announced the development of the Sonic Cruiser as a counter to the super-large Airbus A380. However, market forces dictated the shelving of a fast aircraft in favour of high efficiency.

Even more remarkably, Boeing discontinued the Sonic Cruiser at the end of 2002, replacing it with a new 'super efficient airplane' provisionally known as the Boeing 7E7. According to Boeing's hyperbole, the 'E' stands for several of the company's expectations for the aircraft – including 'efficiency, economics, extraordinary comfort and convenience, environmental performance, and e-enabled systems'. Some observers offered the more prosaic explanation that it stood for 'Eight', as in 787, the next number in Boeing's long-established sequence.

It remains a real possibility that people will one day be telling their disbelieving grandchildren of the days when it was possible to cross the Atlantic in only three and a half hours, and that this journey time may never be repeated once Concorde has retired.

Jon Lake

G-BOAF's first post-modification duty was to fly Prime Minister Tony Blair to Andrews AFB for a high-level meeting in Washington with President Bush. The charter was flown on the day that G-BOAE reinstated the New York service, although this first flight was for invited guests of British Airways, rather than fare-paying passengers.

Customers, operators and aircraft details

North American orders

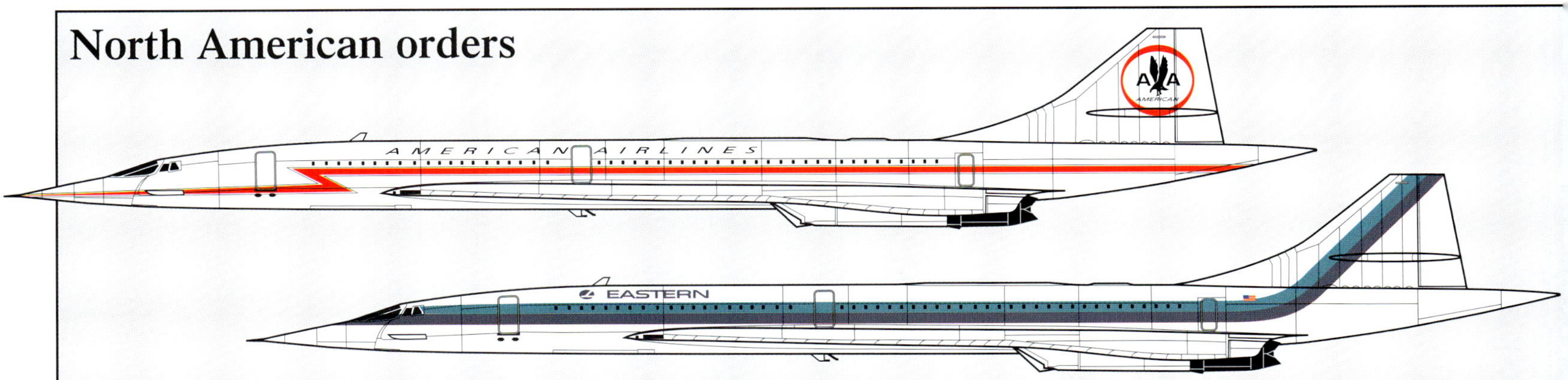

Of the 16 airlines which ordered Concordes, half were based in North America. As was the case with Air France and British Airways, the Atlantic was seen as the primary route, although overwater routes to South American destinations and even overland transcontinental services were considered. Leading the way in terms of numbers were American Airlines, which had 10 on order, Eastern Air Lines (eight), Pan American (eight) and TWA (10). Other orders were forthcoming from Air Canada (four), Braniff (three), Continental (three) and United (six).

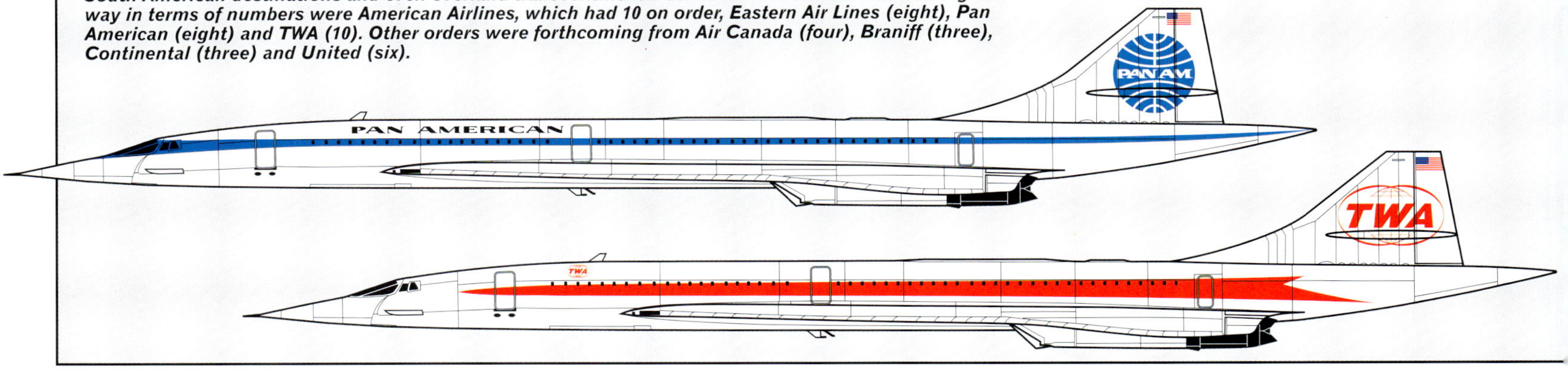

Production and operators

Shortly before 001 was retired in 1972, it joined 002 and 01 at Fairford for this unique family group. 01 in the centre had the new nose shape and visor.

BAC and Aérospatiale built only 20 Concordes between 1966 and 1979. The first two aircraft (001 and 002) were prototypes (one built in France and the second in England), while two more (01 and 02) were officially classed as pre-production aircraft, and were also used only by the manufacturers for test and trials duties. Although the remaining 16 aircraft (201-216) were officially classed as production aircraft, the first two aircraft (the first from each national production line) did not enter airline service but acted as production prototypes and for airline familiarisation, certification, training, publicity and route-proving.

This left only 14 aircraft (203-216) for the Concorde's two airline customers, British Airways and Air France, who initially purchased five and four aircraft, respectively. The five 'extra' aircraft were eventually given to the respective national airlines in 1980, on payment of a nominal one Franc each.

The two airlines operated seven-aircraft fleets for only the briefest period, British Airways withdrawing G-BOAG (214) from 1982 until 1984 due to spares shortages. Air France similarly retired F-BVFD (211) in 1982 when the Paris-Dakar-Rio route was closed down. F-BVFD had suffered significant damage during a heavy landing at Dakar in November 1977, and was used for spares recovery (allowing BA's G-BOAG to be returned to service) before eventually being broken up at Charles de Gaulle Airport, Paris, in 1994, its airframe severely corroded.

This left Air France with six aircraft, and British Airways with seven, and today (following the crash at Charles de Gaulle in July 2000) the airlines respectively have five and seven aircraft. The British Airways Concordes have been more heavily used, and have logged more than 150,000 hours of flight time so far, while Air France's aircraft have logged only about 100,000 flying hours. BA reportedly explored the possibility of bringing 202 to airline standards (which would have given the carrier an eight-strong fleet) but this proved prohibitively expensive.

Air France's first Concorde, F-BVFA, takes off, the vapour above the wings created by the immense low-pressure induced at high angles of attack.

Below: G-BOAC and G-BOAG share the Heathrow maintenance ramp in the early 1980s, when BA's livery removed the word 'Airways'.

Rest of the world orders

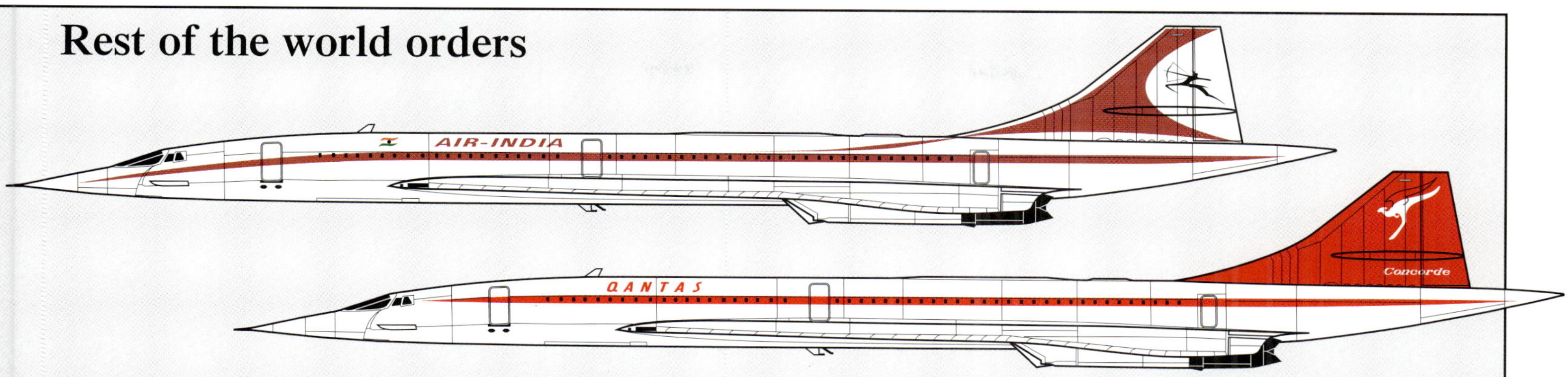

Around the world, major airlines debated the merits of purchasing the Concorde, not only to provide supersonic transport on important routes, but also to enhance the prestige of the carrier. Most orders outside the US were for small numbers, comprising Air India (two), Japan Air Lines (three), Lufthansa (three), Middle East Airlines (two) and SABENA (two). One exception was QANTAS, which saw the Concorde as a means of overcoming Australia's geographic isolation with rapid connections to the Far East and Europe. To fulfil its requirements QANTAS had eight on order. As well as the airlines which got as far as ordering the aircraft, China's CAC and Iran Air also submitted letters of intent to purchase.

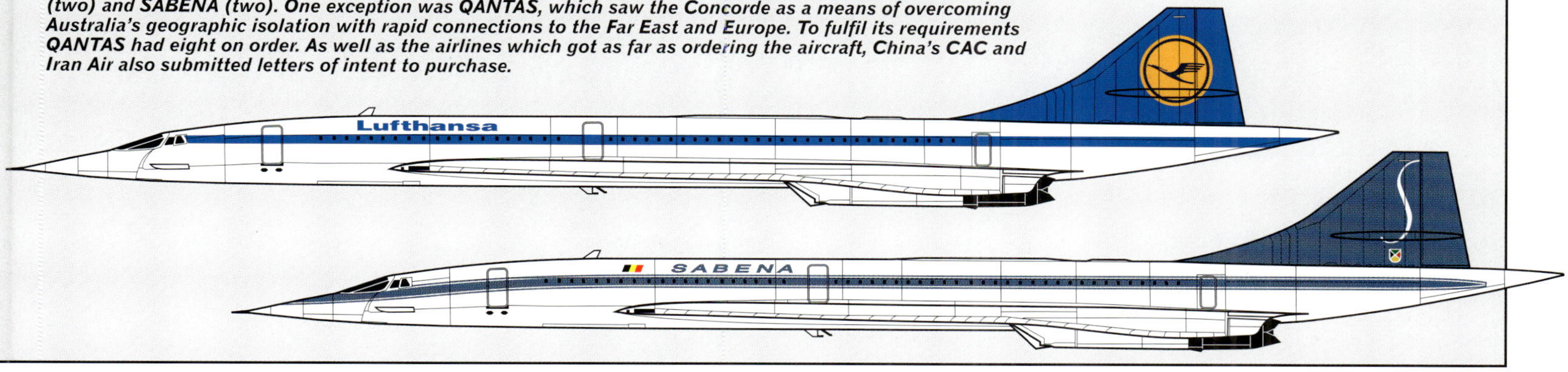

Individual aircraft

001 – F-WTSS

Final assembly of the first Concorde prototype began at Toulouse in April 1966, and resonance testing began there in August 1967. The aircraft was ceremonially rolled out on 11 December 1967, and began preliminary engine testing in March 1968. Taxi trials followed in August 1968 and the aircraft, registered to Aérospatiale as F-WTSS, made its maiden flight on 2 March 1969.

As the first Concorde prototype, 001 logged many of the programme's 'firsts', exceeding Mach 1 for the first time on 1 October 1969, during its 45th test flight. The aircraft achieved this milestone at an altitude of 36,000 ft (10973 m), some 75 miles (120 km) from Toulouse and sustained Mach 1.05 for nine minutes. Thereafter, both Concorde prototypes proceeded rapidly up the Mach scale in incremental steps during the flight test programme.

Concorde 001 made the type's first automatic landing on 13 May 1971, and on 25 May flew to Dakar, Senegal. In September 1971 the aircraft undertook a South American sales tour, but was retired to the French Musée de l'Air (Air Museum) at Le Bourget on 19 October 1972. The aircraft had completed 397 flights, logging 812 hours block time including 254 or 255 flying hours at supersonic speeds.

F-WTSS is seen (above, with Meteor NF.Mk 11 chase) on its second flight, during which the undercarriage was retracted for the first time, and below at le Bourget, where the aircraft is now on display in its own hangar.

002 – G-BSST

Final assembly of the first British Concorde began in August 1966, and the aircraft was ceremonially rolled out at Filton on 19 September 1967. The aircraft made its maiden flight on 9 April 1969 , landing at the Flight Test Centre established at nearby RAF Fairford.

Registered G-BSST to the UK Ministry of Technology on 6 May 1968, the first British Concorde made its first supersonic flight on 25 March 1970, and achieved a number of firsts during its career, which was rather longer than that of the first aircraft. G-BSST was re-registered to the Ministry of Aviation Supply on 19 February 1971, but was operated by the British Aircraft Corporation as a long-serving mainstay of the flight test effort. On 13 September 1970 G-BSST landed at London's Heathrow Airport for the first time, and later (fitted with the definitive production-type undercarriage from February 1972) undertook a sales tour of the Far East in June 1972, and carried out hot-and-high trials in South Africa in January 1973.

G-BSST was finally retired to the Fleet Air Arm Museum at Royal Naval Air Station Yeovilton (HMS *Heron*), making its final flight into Yeovilton on 4 March 1976. Among those present at the hand-over were test pilot Brian Trubshaw and Prime Minister Harold Wilson. Following its retirement, the aircraft was re-registered to its purchaser – the London Science Museum, on 26 July 1976. The aircraft had made 438 flights totalling 835 flying hours, with 173 supersonic hours logged during 196 supersonic sorties.

Above: G-BSST lands at Fairford at the end of its first flight. The prototypes had a tailskid in place of the later tailwheel.

Below: 'SST's final resting place is the Concorde Hall at the Fleet Air Arm Museum, Yeovilton. Here it is seen after arrival at the Somerset base.

01 – G-AXDN

During 1967 the design of the two planned pre-production aircraft (01 and 02) was revised in an effort to reduce drag. The aircraft were to receive a new nose (with a redesigned visor) and a lengthened rear fuselage. This took overall length from the original prototype's 184 ft 4.25 in (56.20 m) to 194 ft (59.13 m), (the definitive production aircraft would be even longer, at 203 ft 10 in/62.13 m). However, 01 was not fitted with the stretched, pointed tail sting like 02 and production Concordes.

Whereas the first prototype was French-built and the second English-built, that order was reversed for the pre-production machines. The first pre-production aircraft was thus the UK Pre-Production model, registered to the Ministry of Technology on 16 April 1969 as G-AXDN. The aircraft was rolled out on 20 September 1971, by which time it had been re-registered to the Ministry of Aviation Supply (this happening on 19 February 1971).

The aircraft made its maiden flight, from Filton to Fairford, on 17 December 1971, and went supersonic for the first time on 12 February 1972. Originally flown without an intake control system, G-AXDN was limited to Mach 1.5. The aircraft was returned to Filton on 10 August 1972 for modifications which brought it closer to the planned production standard, including the installation of a new digital intake control system and Olympus 593 Mk 602 engines. The aircraft returned from Filton to Fairford on 15 March 1973.

On 7 November 1974 G-AXDN made what was claimed as the the fastest ever civil crossing of the North Atlantic while en route to Bangor, Maine, on its way to carry out natural de-icing trials at Moses Lake. A highlight of the aircraft's next year was tropical icing trials at Nairobi, before it was retired to the Duxford Aviation Museum (part of the Imperial War Museum) where it flew in on 20 August 1975.

The aircraft had logged 633 flying hours (217 of them supersonic) during 269 flights (168 of them supersonic).

'XDN formates with BAC's other jetliner product, the prosaic (by comparison) One-Eleven, here represented by a Series 401AK.

Concorde 01 spent many years as an outdoor exhibit at the IWM at Duxford, but was moved inside in the late 1990s.

02 – F-WTSA

The French pre-production Concorde was registered to Aérospatiale as F-WTSA on 21 April 1971, and was structurally complete at Toulouse by February 1972. The aircraft had to wait until April 1972 for the first Olympus 593 Mk 602 engine to be delivered to Toulouse and the aircraft was not rolled out until 28 September 1972. When rolled out, Concorde 02 featured the revised nose with the new glazed visor, and also had a stretched rear fuselage tailcone, lacking the brake parachute fitted to earlier aircraft. This tail sting took overall length from 01's 193 feet, to 204 feet, like subsequent full production aircraft, and reduced drag at Mach 2. 02 was also the first Concorde (and one of the world's first airliners) to be fitted with carbon brakes.

The aircraft made its maiden flight on 10 January 1973. By the time it appeared at the 1973 Paris Air Salon the aircraft had a representative rear cabin, with sumptuous accommodation for VIP passengers and even a wall-mounted Machmeter.

On 20 September 1973 F-WTSA made Concorde's first visit to the USA for the opening of the new Dallas-Fort Worth airport, visiting Las Palmas and Caracas on the way. The aircraft broke the Washington-Paris speed record on its return flight on 26 September, completing the journey in three hours and 33 minutes. On 7 February 1974 F-WTSA flew to Fairbanks, Alaska, for 'cold soak' tests.

F-WTSA made its last flight on 29 January 1976 on delivery to the Musée Delta at Orly airport near Paris, where many systems (including the flight controls) were stripped and salvaged for use in other aircraft. On retirement (officially dated 20 May 1976), F-WTSA had completed 314 flights (including 189 supersonic sorties), totalling 656 flying hours of which 280 were at supersonic speed.

The aircraft has been described as 'semi-preserved' with suggestions of extensive corrosion. The aircraft tocay wears an Air France colour scheme, whereas for much of its active life it was painted up in British Airways colours to starboard and in Air France's 1970s livery to port (with its French registration on both sides). Its current owner is the Athis Aviation Museum.

A full-scale replica of F-WTSA is on display at the Luftfahrtausstellung in Hermeskeil, used as the museum's café.

F-WTSA starred at the 1973 Paris air show, its appearance being overshadowed by the loss of the rival Tu-144. CCCP-77102 fell to earth at Goussainville, killing eight on the ground – by coincidence almost within sight of the 2000 crash site at Gonesse.

Although it never flew with the airline, F-WTSA wore the original Air France scheme (above) on its port side, with BA scheme to starboard. Here its nose is adorned with special markings for the 1976 Olympics. That year the aircraft was retired from its test work, and was repainted in Air France's new scheme (right) prior to going on display at Paris-Orly, where it remains.

201 – F-WTSB

Officially allocated the Production Model Number 100, F-WTSB was registered to Aérospatiale, and made its maiden flight on 6 December 1973 at Toulouse, reaching Mach 1.57.

F-WTSB wore Air France colours, but never entered airline service. In June 1975 201 was used for 'endurance' testing flying to Bodø, Dakar, Keflavik, Shannon, and Tangier. On 19 October 1977 the aircraft gained the distinction of making the first Concorde landing in New York from Toulouse during a series of proving flights.

The aircraft logged 803 flying hours before being placed in storage at Toulouse, and on the 20th anniversary of Concorde was handed over to the Concorde museum, following a retirement ceremony for which it was painted in a gaudy colour scheme of red (nose and wing root leading edge), white (wing and centre fuselage) and blue (tail and rear fuselage). The aircraft is now displayed outside Aérospatiale's Clement Ader assembly building (now used by Airbus Industrie) at Toulouse.

Above: The first production Concorde was finished in the original Air France scheme, but with a calibration marking on the fin.

Right: F-WTSB now resides at Toulouse, in pride of place outside the main Airbus assembly (and former Concorde assembly) building. It wears this modified Air France scheme.

202 – G-BBDG

Like 201, G-BBDG – the first British production aircraft – was officially designated as a Model 100, and this imposed lower gross weights and made the possibility of modifying and refitting for airline service prohibitively costly.

The aircraft was first registered to the British Aircraft Corporation Ltd on 7 August 1973 and made its maiden flight from Filton to Fairford on 13 February 1974.

On 7 August the aircraft was used for a flight to Teheran, before then continuing on to Bahrain for hot weather trials. G-BBDG's world tour then continued with a demonstration tour of the Middle East, visiting Abu Dhabi, Dubai, Kuwait, Muscat, and Qatar.

The aircraft was then delivered on loan to British Airways for test, training and familiarisation purposes during 1975, but remained owned by the manufacturer, which became part of British Aerospace on 1 April 1977.

The aircraft was retired on 24 December 1983, after 803 flying hours, and was used for spares recovery. Finally, in 1985 it was placed in storage (minus its tailfin) in a purpose built hangar at Filton. The aircraft is

G-BBDG sits outside the Filton works, prior to becoming a spares 'Christmas tree'.

structurally sound, but has been used as a source of spare parts (not least to return G-BOAG to flightworthy status) and is now missing its landing gear, nose and tail.

203 – F-WTSC/F-BTSC

The second production aircraft from the Toulouse production line was a Model 100 originally registered to Aérospatiale as F-WTSC. This made its maiden flight on 31 January 1975, and was re-registered as F-BTSC on 28 May 1975, when it received a special category Certificate of Airworthiness for endurance testing.

Despite being a Model 100 (and thus almost a tonne heavier than subsequent production aircraft and with a smaller payload) F-BTSC did eventually find its way into airline service.

The aircraft was leased to Air France on 6 January 1976 and in November undertook a 30,000-mile demonstration tour of the Far East, visiting Bahrain, Singapore, Manila, Hong Kong, Djakarta, and Seoul before being returned to Aérospatiale on 8 December 1976. During 1978-79 F-BTSC was used in the film *Airport '79: The Concorde*, wearing a spurious colour scheme, with a large red speedbird on the fin and 'Concorde' titles.

Aircraft 203 was leased to Air France again on 11 June 1979, and was finally converted to Type 101 standards in June 1980.

F-BTSC was one of the unsold aircraft transferred to the British and French national airlines in 1980, and was officially purchased by Air France on 23 October 1980. The aircraft was used mainly as an in-use reserve by Air France, though on 2 May 1989 the aircraft carried Pope John Paul II.

In June 2000, F-BTSC completed a 12-month, 60,000-hour overhaul (D Check), after completing 12,000 hrs of flight (4,000 cycles). After three weeks of ground testing and two test flights, F-BTSC returned to service, but it crashed with the loss of everyone on board on 25 July 2000. The aircraft had logged 11,989 flying hours and 3,978 landings.

F-BTSC is seen on loan for the movie* Airport '79: the Concorde. *The aircraft was little used in its early career.

204 – G-BOAC/G-N81AC

The second aircraft from the Filton production line was the first Model 102, and was always expected to be the first in airline service, with what was then still the British Overseas Airways Corporation. As such the aircraft was registered to the British Aircraft Corporation Ltd as G-BOAC on 3rd April 1974. G-BOAC made its maiden flight on 27 February 1975 at Filton, landing at Fairford to join the flight test team. The aircraft was awarded a special category Certificate of Airworthiness on 30 June 1975.

On 1 September 1975, G-BOAC made two return flights from London to Gander, Newfoundland, thereby becoming the first aircraft to make four Atlantic crossings in the space of a single day.

The aircraft was delivered to British Airways on 13 February 1976, becoming its second Concorde, joining G-BOAA (206) which had been delivered on 14 January 1976.

G-BOAC was re-registered as G-N81AC/N81AC by British Airways and Braniff Airways on 5 January 1979, but reverted to its original registration on 11 August 1980.

G-BOAC suffered two significant inflight failures during 1998. On 24 May the aircraft lost its No. 3 Left Elevon in an incident which echoed the rudder section failures which had been experienced by Concorde during the late 1980s and early 1990s.

More worryingly, on 8 October 1998 G-BOAC suffered a failure of the lower rudder section during a routine flight to New York. Although Concorde had suffered fatigue-related rudder failures before, only original parts had been affected, while the 8 October failure was of a new part fitted to all seven BA aircraft only four years previously as part of the fix to the rudder failures.

Still in service with British Airways, G-BOAC is the oldest airworthy Concorde, and was the fifth aircraft to return to service with BA, flying again after modification on 11 July 2002.

G-BOAC had flown 21,959 hours by the end of August 1999.

205 – F-BVFA/N94FA

The third French production Concorde was the first built to Model 101 standards, and made its first flight on 27 October 1975, registered as F-BVFA to Air France, to whom it was delivered on 19 December 1975. It was the first aircraft flown from the start in Air France's new colour scheme, the first Air France Concorde, and was used for the airline's first Concorde operation, a Paris-Rio service, via Dakar, on 21 January 1976. British Airways flew its first service on the same day.

F-BVFA was re-registered as N94FA by Air France/Braniff Airways on 12 January 1979, but was re-registered to Air France alone on 1 June 1980.

F-BVFA was the Air France fleet leader, and was the first to undergo its 12,000-hour overhaul. The aircraft was stripped down to the bare metal at Orly, before being transferred to Roissy where it received a coat of khaki anti-corrosion primer. F-BVFA was then mounted on jacks and stripped and dismantled. Key parts then underwent non-destructive testing (many being X-rayed) before the aircraft was finally reassembled and rebuilt, emerging from its hangar at Roissy-Charles de Gaulle airport on 1 August 1990. By then F-BVFA had logged 11,650 flying hours and had covered an estimated 12,000,000 miles. By July 2000 flying time had reached 17,214 hours with 6,741 landings.

F-BVFA was the fourth Air France aircraft to return to service, flying again in February 2002.

206 – G-BOAA/G-N94AA

The third UK production Concorde was first registered to the British Aircraft Corporation Ltd on 3rd March 1974 as G-BOAA, and first flew on 5 November 1975, reaching Mach 2 on its maiden flight. The aircraft was delivered to British Airways on 14 January 1976, becoming the airline's first Concorde. G-BOAA flew BA's first Concorde service to Bahrain on 21 January (the day that Air France began services to Rio).

The aircraft flew to Dallas-Fort Worth on 10 December 1978 for route-proving flights to 16 US cities in association with Braniff's planned Concorde service. The aircraft was re-registered as G-N94AA/N94AA by British Airways and Braniff Airways on 12 January 1979 but was re-registered as G-BOAA by British Airways on 28 July 1980.

In April 1988 G-BOAA became the first Concorde to undergo a 12,000-flying hour D check, having made a record-breaking flight from New York to Heathrow in only two hours 55 minutes and 15 seconds on 7 February 1988.

On 6 June 1990 G-BOAA, captained by Captain W D Lowe, was used to commemorate the 50th anniversary of the Battle of Britain, flying over the White Cliffs of Dover in formation with a Spitfire.

The new upper rudder designed to cure a spate of rudder failures, and costing £1,000,000, was first fitted to G-BOAA on 19 November 1993. By mid-2000 G-BOAA had flown 22,769 hours and 7,394 landings, the highest of any Concorde.

G-BOAA was scheduled to be the seventh and final BA Concorde to be returned to service, but this was put on hold and subsequently cancelled.

BA's first Concorde should have been the last back in service, its modification programme being delayed in the schedule by essential maintenance required for the other aircraft.

207 – F-BVFB/N94FB

Like all subsequent Air France Concordes, 207 was officially designated as a Model 101, and was first registered to Air France on 12 January 1979 as F-BVFB. The aircraft made made its first flight from Toulouse on 6 March 1976, and became the third Concorde delivered to Air France on 18 April 1976.

The aircraft was re-registered as N94FB by Air France and Braniff Airways on 12 January 1979, but on 1 June 1980 was re-registered as F-BVFB for Air France. By July 2000 'VFB had amassed 13,745 hours and 4,984 landings.

F-BVFB was used for many of the tests and trials which followed the loss of F-BTSC, and on 26 January 2001 the aircraft was flown to the CEV at Istres for an exploration of fuel leak behaviour, flying back to Charles de Gaulle on 3 February.

Subsequently, F-BVFB became the first Air France Concorde to undergo 'return to flight' modifications, and on 24 August 2001 was used for Air France's first supersonic verification flight. The aircraft reached Concorde's normal cruising speed of around Mach 2.0 during a subsequent three and an half hour verification flight on 27 August. F-BVFB was then used for Air France's first operational assessment flight to New York on 29 October, the first Air France Concorde flight to depart to New York since the previous year's tragedy.

Compared with the elderly Boeing 707 behind it, 'VFB looks like a vision from the future, an image helped by Air France's vibrant new scheme. The year was 1976, when Concorde services began.

208 – G-BOAB/G-N94AB

G-BOAB was first registered as such on 3 April 1974 to the British Aircraft Corporation, and made its maiden flight on 18 May 1976, reaching Mach 2.05 at 63,000 ft during the flight. The aircraft was delivered to British Airways on 30 September 1976, as the airline's third Concorde. It was re-registered as G-N94AB/N94AB by British Airways/Braniff on 12 January 1979. The aircraft became G-BOAB again on 17 September 1980.

Highlights of G-BOAB's airline career included setting a distance record for the type of 4,563 miles (7342 km) during a flight from Washington to Nice on 11 September 1984. The aircraft was also used to inaugurate a charter service between London and Seattle (via New York) that November.

On 1 July 1998 G-BOAB was used to fly home the England World Cup 98 football team from Nantes. G-BOAB had flown 22,297 hours and 7,204 landings by July 2000.

The aircraft should have been the sixth BA aircraft to return to service before the programme was axed.

209 – F-BVFC/N94FC

The ninth production Concorde was registered to Air France as F-BVFC and made its maiden flight on 9 July 1976. The aircraft was the fourth Concorde for Air France when it was delivered on 3 August 1976. On 12 January 1979 the aircraft was re-registered as N94FC by Air France/Braniff Airways, but was re-registered as F-BVFC by Air France on 1 June 1980. The aircraft had flown 13,398 hours and 4,555 landings by July 2000.

F-BVFC was marooned in New York by the grounding of the Air France Concorde fleet following the fatal accident in July 2000, but was flown home on 21 September 2000. The aircraft subsequently became the third Air France Concorde to re-enter service, flying again after mods in October 2001.

***Below:* F-BVFC is seen with an unpainted upper rudder section, although the rudder actuator fairing retains the blue stripe.**

210 – G-BOAD/G-N94AD

The 10th production Concorde (and the fifth off the Filton line) was first registered to BAC as G-BOAD on 9 May 1975, and made its maiden flight on 25 August 1976 . The aircraft was the penultimate Concorde of BA's original five-aircraft order, and was delivered to the airline on 6 December 1976. The aircraft was re-registered to British Airways/Braniff Airways as G-N94AD/N94AD on 5 January 1979, but was re-registered as G-BOAD by British Airways on 19 June 1980 when the Braniff arrangement came to a premature end.

While artist's impressions and retouched photos were issued showing Concordes in Braniff livery, G-BOAD actually received Singapore Airlines colours on its port side during 1980, when BA and Singapore Airlines began a joint Concorde service. The service was flown by BA flight deck crews with cabin crews from both airlines.

G-BOAD had flown 22,300 hours by mid-2000 and had accomplished 7,195 landings. It was the fourth BA aircraft to return to service, its first post-modification flight occurring on 29 January 2002. On 4 June 2002 it accompanied the 'Red Arrows' over London in the Queen's Birthday Flypast.

G-BOAD lands at Heathrow (above), resplendent in the second major BA scheme (original colours but with 'British' titles). Previously the aircraft had worn SIA colours on the port side and a joint US/UK registration (below).

211 – F-BVFD/N94FD

F-BVFD made its maiden flight on 10 February 1977 and was delivered to Air France on 26 March 1977. The aircraft enjoyed a short period with the French flag carrier, before suffering a heavy landing at Dakar in November 1977. This landing (recorded at 14 ft/4.26 m per second compared to an airframe limit of 10 ft/3 m per second) led to the tail bumper being crushed, and required major repairs. After re-entering service F-BVFD was re-registered as N94FD by Air France/ Braniff Airways on 12 January 1979 then reverted to Air France on 1 June 1980.

The aircraft made its last flight (with 5,821 hours logged) on 27 May 1982 before being withdrawn from use and stored when the Paris-Dakar-Rio route was abandoned, leaving Air France with surplus aircraft. While stored the aircraft suffered major corrosion, and it was broken up at Charles de Gaulle in 1994, after 12 years out of service. It was however, used for spares recovery, and was instrumental in bringing British Airways' G-BOAG back into service.

F-BVFD is the only Concorde to have been retired from airline service. It was scrapped after parts salvage.

212 – G-BOAE/G-N94AE

Aircraft 212 was first registered as G-BOAE on 9 May 1975 to BAC, but did not fly until 17 March 1977. The aircraft was then delivered to British Airways on 20 July 1977, the last of BA's original five-aircraft order. The aircraft was re-registered to British Airways/Braniff Airways on 5 January 1979 as G-N94AE/N94AE, but reverted to its original registration on 1 July 1980.

By mid-2000 G-BOAE had logged 22,380 hours and 7,342 landings. On 23 July 2000, G-BOAE was temporarily grounded after small cracks were discovered in non-critical areas of the wings. All aircraft were inspected, and although cracks were only discovered in some aircraft, the entire Concorde fleet received a 'Spar 72' modification designed to rectify the problem and to prevent further cracking.

G-BOAE became the second BA Concorde to return to service, moving into the main Concorde hangar at Heathrow to start its modification programme on 20 June 2001. The aircraft made a three-hour supersonic verification flight on 28 September 2001, after the completion of its modifications. The aircraft was then used to re-launch BA's service to New York on 7 November 2001, with fare-paying passengers carried from the 9th.

213 – F-WJAM/F-BTSD

The 13th production Concorde was unsold when it was completed, and accordingly it was first registered to Aérospatiale as F-WJAM. The aircraft made its maiden flight on 26 June 1978, and remained on company charge even after it was re-registered as F-BTSD on 14 September 1978 (some sources give 4 September as the date of this change).

The aircraft was leased to Air France (becoming the airline's sixth Concorde) and was delivered on 18 September 1978. On 12 January 1979 the aircraft was re-registered as N94SD by Air France/Braniff Airways, reverting to its Air France registration on 12 March 1979, when the aircraft was returned to Aérospatiale.

F-BTSD was leased to Air France again on 9 May 1980, who finally bought the aircraft outright on 23 October 1980 (or 14 April 1980, according to some sources).

On 2 April 1996 F-BTSD was formally unveiled at Gatwick wearing the most unusual colour scheme ever applied to an airworthy Concorde. The aircraft had been painted in the new all-blue Pepsi livery to help a re-branding of the soft drink (whose can went from mainly white to a mainly dark blue finish), and remained in its new markings for some two weeks. The aircraft had logged 12,162 hours and 4,672 landings by mid-2000.

Following the July 2000 accident at Charles de Gaulle, F-BTSD became the second Concorde to return to the air. F-BVFB had undertaken the initial evaluation of leaking fuel behaviour at Istres in January 2001, while F-BTSD made a test flight (following its D check) on 11 April 2001. On 17 April the aircraft was flown to Istres for tests on the newly developed Michelin Near Zero Growth tyres returning to Orly for a respray on 5 May, and then to Charles de Gaulle on 30 May. Full modification followed, 'TSD flying again on 15 October 2001. The aircraft was then used to re-start Air France's Concorde service to New York on 7 November 2001.

214 – G-BFKW/G-BOAG

The penultimate Concorde built at Filton was initially registered to British Aerospace on 27 January 1978, as G-BFKW. The aircraft made its maiden flight on 21st April 1978, beating its French opposite number (213) into the air by two months.

With no customer, G-BFKW flew in an anonymous all-white colour scheme, and it was not until 1980 that it was sold to BA (for a nominal sum). The aircraft was then delivered to British Airways on 6 February 1980. On 26 April 1980, however, G-BFKW, suffered intake ramp failure at Mach 2, resulting in severe engine damage. This led to the aircraft being grounded awaiting repairs which would eventually cost more than a million pounds. The aircraft finally re-entered service, re-registered as G-BOAG, on 9 February 1981. The aircraft was soon grounded again to serve as a source of spares for BA's other Concordes and was not restored to flightworthy status until 1984, using parts from withdrawn Air France Concorde, F-BVFD, and from the newly-acquired G-BBDG. While parked at Heathrow as a spares source, G-BOAG carried no BA titles or markings, and rested on time-expired wheels, whose hubs were painted red.

The aircraft's return to service was marked by a ceremonial roll-out on 25 April 1985, since its refurbishing included a comprehensive refit with the new interior furnishings designed for the British Airways Concorde fleet, and a re-paint in the airline's new exterior 'Landor' livery. While other BA aircraft in the livery gained dark blue fuselage undersides and grey cabin tops, Concorde remained predominantly white, but did gain the new tailfin colours of the 'Landor' livery (a simple blue-for-red-for-blue reversal of the red and blue stylised flag used previously) as well as the new 'fag packet' crest and with a thin red speed line replacing the broad blue cheatline previously in use. The aircraft's facelift allowed it to be used for publicity in association with the privatisation of British Airways and its flotation on the Stock Exchange.

G-BOAG began another 'major' overhaul and refurbishment programme on 27 May 1996, but was soon back in service.

G-BOAG had flown 14,385 hours by the end of August 1999, making it BA's 'youngest' aircraft, though this was a higher figure than for any of Air France's

G-BOAG is seen on a return to its birthplace at Filton. The works is now used mainly for building Airbus wing components, before they are trucked for completion at Hawarden. The Brabazon hangar, in which the British Concordes were assembled, was used until 2002 for Airbus freighter conversions.

aircraft, with the exception of F-BVFA, the fleet leader, which had logged some 16,000 hours. By mid-2000 it had logged 15,088 hours and 4,976 landings. The aircraft became the last of BA's fleet to be re-painted in the new 'Chatham' colour scheme in December 1999.

On 19 October 2001 G-BOAG became the third British Airways Concorde to return to service after the completion of modifications.

215 – F-WJAN/F-BVFF

The last Concorde from the Toulouse production line was registered to Aérospatiale as F-WJAN and made its maiden flight on 26 December 1978. The aircraft was finally delivered to Air France on 23 October 1980, re-registered as F-BVFF. By July 2000 the aircraft had flown 12,327 hours and had performed 4,170 landings. It was due to be the last of the Air France Concordes to be returned to service.

Below: F-BVFF taxis while on a charter visit to the UK. The aircraft was to have been the fifth and last Air France Concorde to undergo modification.

Left: As an unsold 'white-tail', Concorde 215 sits somewhat forlornly on the Toulouse ramp shortly after its first flight.

216 – G-BFKX/G-N94AF/G-BOAF

The final Filton-built Concorde, registered as G-BFKX to British Aerospace on 27 January 1978, remained unsold when it made its maiden flight on 20 April 1979. The aircraft was re-registered as G-N94AF/G-BOAF by British Aerospace on 14 December 1979 in anticipation of its possible use by British Airways and Braniff. Concorde 216 (together with 214) was one of the two British manufactured Concordes that were built without a customer, and was sold to BA for the nominal sum of one French Franc. 216 was accordingly delivered to British Airways on 9 June 1980, who re-registered the aircraft as G-BOAF on 12 June 1980 (13 June, according to some sources).

G-BOAF is seen taking off from RAF Fairford during a 1997 charter to the Royal International Air Tattoo (below), and at Heathrow at its post-modification roll-out on 19 June 2001 (below right). It was the first aircraft to receive the 'Chatham' scheme.

On 1 April 1989 G-BOAF departed Heathrow on a supersonic charter intended to circumnavigate the globe (with a planned route covering 38,343 miles/61705 km). While flying between Christchurch, New Zealand, and Sydney, Australia on 12 April, G-BOAF lost a major section of its upper rudder as the aircraft accelerated to Mach 2, climbing through 43,000 ft (13105 m).

Similar rudder separation failures occurred to other aircraft several times, leading to a programme to fit new upper and lower rudders to all in-service Concordes.

G-BOAF was ceremonially rolled out on 21 May 1993 after receiving a £1,000,000 refurbishment of its interior, including the installation of new leather seats. G-BOAF had flown 16,517 hours by the end of August 1999.

G-BOAF was the first Concorde to receive a new colour scheme as part of the fleet-wide re-branding of the airline as a 'World carrier', under which all aircraft received a variety of 'ethnic' tailfins and had their red speed lines replaced by a more flowing curved red and blue marking (derisively referred to by some staff as the 'flying bogroll' or the 'AIDS ribbon'). This new colour scheme was officially known as the 'Utopia' livery.

While the allocation of tailfin colours across most of the BA fleet was arbitrary, it was decided that all seven Concordes would wear the same colour scheme, with a flowing, flag-like fin design based on an early Union Flag and officially known as the 'Chatham Historic Dockyard' scheme. Subsequently, the 'Utopia' livery was abandoned in favour of a fleetwide adoption of the fin design used by the Concorde fleet. The disparate and ethnic tailfin designs were found to have had a largely negative impact on passenger perceptions of the airline, and tended to undermine confidence and prestige, while diluting corporate identity.

Following the grounding of BA's Concordes after the Air France crash in July 2000, G-BOAF was chosen by British Airways to be the first aircraft in its Return to Flight programme in January 2001. The aircraft was the first to be fitted with new Kevlar-rubber fuel tank liners, armoured electrical wiring in and around the main undercarriage bays and later the new Michelin tyres.

Modifications to G-BOAF were completed on 19 June, by which time the aircraft had logged 17,265 flying hours and 5,615 landings. The aircraft began taxi trials on 4 July, prior to its first verification flight on 17 July. The aircraft was then used for a series of operational assessment flights between 11 September and 22 October, and flew British Prime Minister Blair to Washington on 7 November, the day that BA and Air France resumed services to New York.

BRITISH AIRWAYS

The three major engine manufacturers provide a range of engines to cover the spectrum of commercial aircraft requirements. This is part of the Rolls-Royce family, crowned by the massive Trent 800 which is matched to the Boeing 777.

Big fan engines

The engines of today's long-haul airliners are among the most powerful and most efficient sources of power ever created. Moreover, they are designed to get on with the job with minimum fuss. In the days of piston engines frantic servicing was needed after every flight, but today's jetliners can fly the Atlantic 1,000 times without even opening up the cowlings.

Fundamentally, today's impressive big fan engines work in exactly the same way as the original jet propulsion concept invented by young RAF pilot Frank Whittle in 1929. Air is taken in at the front – a process which in flight is assisted by the so-called ram effect – and compressed in a rapidly spinning compressor. The compressed air then enters a combustion chamber where fuel is sprayed in and burnt. This provides a flow of white-hot gas, which escapes between the rapidly spinning blades of a turbine, before thundering out of the aft-facing jetpipe to provide propulsive thrust. All that has to be done is to connect the turbine to the compressor.

Whittle soon saw that an excellent propulsion system for subsonic aircraft would be an intermediate species of engine. He called it a bypass jet, but today we call it a turbofan. Essentially, it is a turbojet with extra blades on the turbine to extract more power from the hot gas. This is then used to drive a large fan on the front which sucks in up to ten times as much air as before. Most of this enormous airflow is bypassed around the rest of the engine, which is called the core, and expelled as a relatively cool and quiet propulsive jet. Only the central part of the flow goes through the core.

Ideally, the big fan needs to rotate much slower than the slim core. Accordingly, the two portions are made separate. When the starter button is pressed, the starter motor drives only the core, which in principle is just a turbojet. This quickly runs up to speed, and gets air flowing through the engine. When the flow is sufficient, the fuel is turned on and ignited. This rapidly accelerates the core, and the flow soon starts to turn the larger multi-stage turbine at the back, which, via a separate central shaft, drives the fan.

Every modern turbofan has at least two main rotating parts. The relatively small core comprises the HP (high-pressure) turbine driving the HP compressor via a tubular shaft. Down the centre of this is a long slender shaft connecting the LP (low-pressure) turbine to the fan. Thus, such a turbofan is called a two-shaft engine. Rolls-Royce has gone even further and its big fan engines have three shafts. The air passes successively through the fan (driven by the LP turbine), the intermediate-pressure (IP) compressor (driven by the IP turbine) and finally the HP compressor (driven by the HP turbine).

Jet engines could hardly be more different from piston engines. In the latter the cylinders deal with the air in a rapid succession of what can be called 'parcels'. Each parcel of air is sucked in, compressed, burned and ejected all in the same enclosed space at the top of the cylinder, before being replaced by its successor. In the jet engine there is a continuous flow. At any place in the

ENGINE ALLIANCE GP7200

Traditional rivals General Electric and Pratt & Whitney announced in August 1996 that they were joining forces to develop an engine for the proposed 747-500/600. The 'stretch' 747 was subsequently shelved, although the GP7100 engine family is still nominally available should Boeing reconsider. Meanwhile, the GP7200 derivative has been developed as a competitor to the Trent 900 for the Airbus A380.

Three versions are currently planned, matched to the three planned A380 variants. The GP7268 is aimed at the 548-tonne aircraft, the GP7270 for the 560-tonne aircraft, and the GP7277 for the A380F freighter. As in other engine designations, the last two digits refer to the take-off thrust (x 1,000 lb).

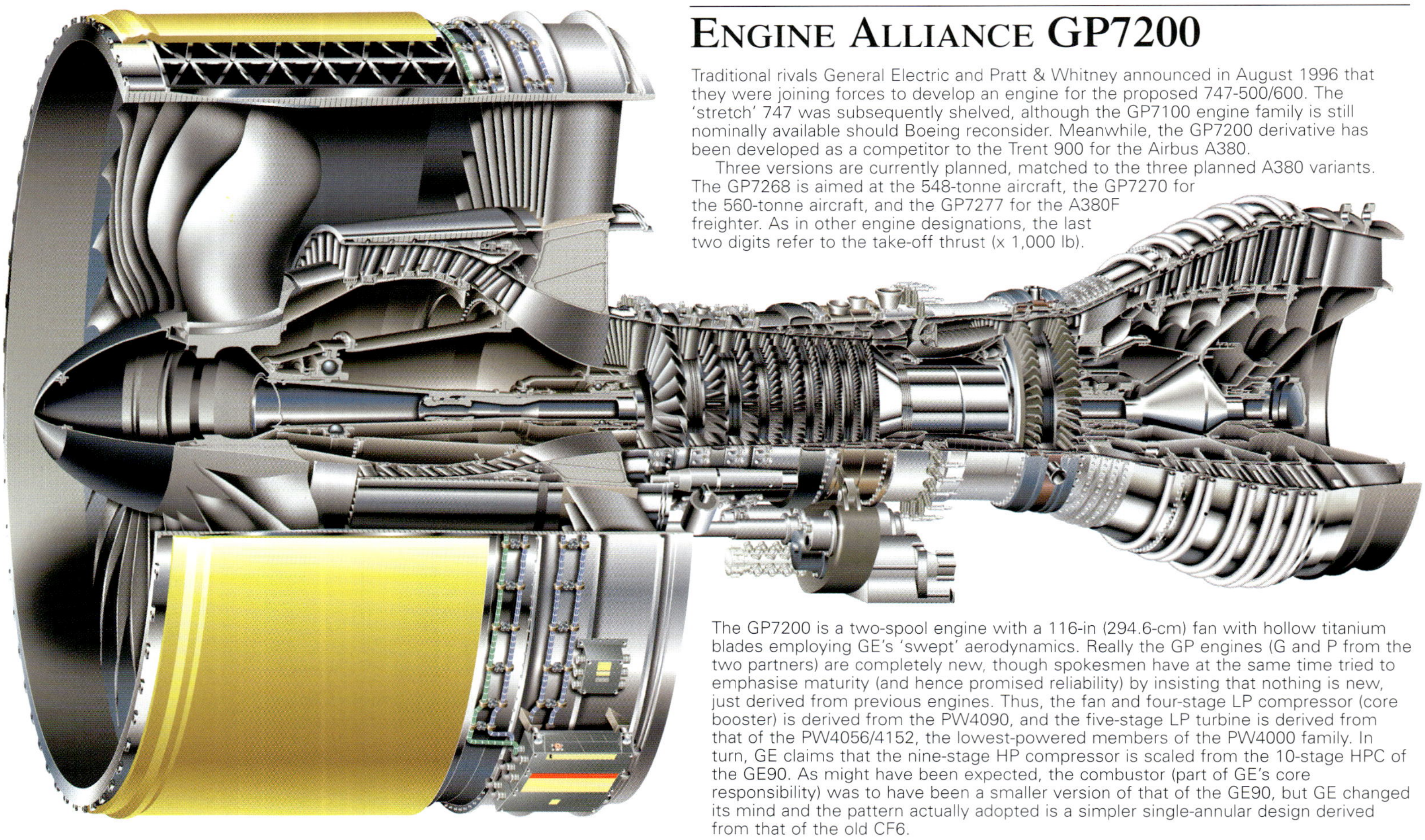

The GP7200 is a two-spool engine with a 116-in (294.6-cm) fan with hollow titanium blades employing GE's 'swept' aerodynamics. Really the GP engines (G and P from the two partners) are completely new, though spokesmen have at the same time tried to emphasise maturity (and hence promised reliability) by insisting that nothing is new, just derived from previous engines. Thus, the fan and four-stage LP compressor (core booster) is derived from the PW4090, and the five-stage LP turbine is derived from that of the PW4056/4152, the lowest-powered members of the PW4000 family. In turn, GE claims that the nine-stage HP compressor is scaled from the 10-stage HPC of the GE90. As might have been expected, the combustor (part of GE's core responsibility) was to have been a smaller version of that of the GE90, but GE changed its mind and the pattern actually adopted is a simpler single-annular design derived from that of the old CF6.

engine the flow velocity, pressure and temperature vary only when the pilot opens and closes the throttle, or (very gently) as the aircraft changes altitude. In normal cruising flight these values stay constant.

On the other hand, each small 'parcel' of air that enters the engine inlet individually undergoes extremely large and rapid changes as it passes through the engine. So far, all giant wide-body aircraft have the engines installed in close-fitting nacelles or pods hung under the wings (a few also have an engine mounted on the centreline of the aircraft at the tail). As far as possible, the inlet is designed to maintain pressure as high as possible. Relative to the aircraft, the speed of the incoming air usually falls slightly in the inlet in cruising flight, resulting in the pressure slightly increasing. In any airflow, if no heat or other energy is deliberately added or extracted, the flow's velocity and temperature are interchangeable: thus, reducing one will increase the other. It is the objective of the designer to convert as much as possible of the temperature energy into propulsive velocity. In a wide-body engine this is done by the LP turbine transferring jet energy to the fan.

The vital fan

In all older engines the air entering the engine first encountered a ring of inlet guide vanes. These were set radially round the inlet to the engine to guide the air into the compressor, and their angle could be adjusted. Today's engines have nothing in front of the fan, which reduces weight, improves efficiency and also dramatically reduces vulnerability to icing, though means must be provided for heating the front of the surrounding fan case.

As the air encounters the fan its pressure is significantly increased. Each of the enormous fan blades behaves as a miniature wing, set at a positive angle to the airflow. This has a profound effect on the airflow, greatly increasing its energy. The immediate effect is to multiply the pressure of the airflow by from 1.5 to 3. The lowest FPR (fan pressure ratio) is found in the General Electric GE90, because this increases propulsive efficiency and also means the fan needs a smaller core to drive it. One never gets anything for nothing, and the penalty is that the fan has to be larger and thus much heavier. The GE90, designed specifically for the Boeing 777, began with an enormous fan with a diameter of 123 in (312.4 cm) and has now been developed, in the GE90-115B, to a diameter of 128.2 in (325.6 cm). This is much greater than the ceiling height in an average house.

As the source of almost all the thrust, the fan blade has to be designed with the utmost care. Early blades were forged in titanium, and were slender rectangles. It was found that, despite the colossal centrifugal force tending to pull them out straight, the blades tended to flutter, vibrating dangerously in a way that could cause them to break off. The answer was to add a broad end-plate across the tip of the blade or, more often, a bluff projection on each side at about mid-span. Called a clapper, or snubber, or part-span shroud, these projections formed a complete ring when the fan was assembled. Each rubbed on its neighbours to damp out the flutter, but at the expense of extra weight and a serious reduction in aerodynamic efficiency because the airflow here is supersonic.

The concept of the turbofan, in which most of the thrust is generated by the fan, was (amazingly) ignored for almost 30 years after Whittle's arithmetic had shown the advantages. Then the US Air Force organised Project Forecast to look into the future, and one result was the Lockheed C-5 Galaxy strategic airlifter. US engine firms fought to produce the engines, and in October 1965 General Electric won, its contract for over $459 million for the TF39 engine being one of the biggest ever awarded up to that time. Only temporarily downcast, Pratt & Whitney won the propulsion of the Boeing 747 with its JT9D engine, and this proved to be even more important than the C-5. Both engines had fans with

Development of the 'big twins' – the Airbus A330 (illustrated) and Boeing 777 – was the spur for the dramatic upward surge in thrust ratings in the 1990s. At the same time, airlines were demanding ever greater fuel economy.

Battle of the big fans – P&W vs. R-R vs. GE

Airbus A330

The A330 engine market falls between the 747/767 and 777 thrust brackets, and is served by all three manufacturers. General Electric's GE90 is too powerful for the A330 requirement, and so the company offers an improved CF6 (the CF6-80E1) instead. It has secured significant sales in a market dominated by the PW4168 and Trent 772. One operator, TAM of Brazil, has R-R-, GE- and P&W-engined aircraft in its fleet.

Airline	Version	Engine
Aer Lingus	200, 300	CF6-80E1A2/A4
Air Canada	300(X)	Trent 772
Air France	200, 300	CF6-80E1A2/A3
Air Transat	200	Trent 772
Asiana	200	PW4168
	300	PW4164
Austrian AL	200	PW4168
BMI	200	Trent 772
Cathay Pacific	300, 300(X)	Trent 772
Cyprus Airways	200	Trent 772
Dragonair	300, 300(X)	Trent 772
Emirates	200	Trent 772
Eurofly	200	PW4168
Eva Air	200	CF6-80E1A3
Garuda Indonesia	300	Trent 768
Gulf Air	200	Trent 772
JMC Airlines	200	Trent 772
Korean Air	200, 300, 300(X)	PW4168
LTU Intl AW	200, 300	PW4168
Malaysia Airlines	300	PW4168
Monarch Airlines	200	Trent 772
MyTravel Airways	200, 300(X)	Trent 772
Northwest AL	300(X)	PW4168
Philippine Airlines	300	CF6-80E1A2
Qantas Airways	200, 300	CF6-80E1A2
Scandinavian AL	300(X)	Trent 772
Skyservice AL	300	PW4168
SN Brussels AL	300	CF6-80E1A2
SriLankan Airlines	200	Trent 772
Swiss Intl AL	200	PW4168
TAM	200	Trent 772, PW4168, CF6-80E1A3
Thai Airways	300, 300(X)	PW4164/4168
US Airways	300(X)	PW4168
VG Airlines	200	PW4168

Boeing 777

Arguably the most bitterly fought competition between the three engine manufacturers is the fight to power Boeing's big-seller. All three companies offer their current-generation engines, although for the latest 777-300ER only the monster 115,000-lb (511.7-kN) thrust GE90-115B is available. Rolls-Royce has achieved some significant sales in this market, notably the adoption of the Trent by two major US carriers (American and Delta), and by switching British Airways orders from GE90 to Trent power.

Aeroflot	200ER	GE90-92B
Air China	200	PW4084
Air France	200ER	GE90-92B/94B
	300ER	GE90-115B
Alitalia	200ER	GE90-94B
All Nippon AW	200	PW4084
	200ER, 300	PW4090
	300ER	GE90-115B
American AL	200ER	Trent 892
Asiana	200ER	PW4090
	300	PW4098
British Airways	200	GE90-76B
	200ER	GE90-90B/ Trent 895
Cathay Pacific	200	Trent 877
	300	Trent 892
China Southern	200	GE90-85B
	200ER	GE90-92B
Continental AL	200ER	GE90-92B
Delta Air Lines	200ER	Trent 892
Egyptair	200ER	PW4090
El Al	200ER	Trent 895
Emirates	200	Trent 877/892
	200ER, 300	Trent 892
Eva Air	200, 300ER	GE90-115B
Garuda Indonesia	200ER	GE90-92B
Japan Airlines	200	PW4084
	200ER	GE90-94B
	300	PW4090
	300ER	GE90-115B
Japan Air System	200	PW4084
Korean Air	200ER	PW4090
	300	PW4098
Kuwait Airways	200ER	GE90-92B
Lauda Air	200ER	GE90-92B
Malaysia Airlines	200ER	Trent 892
Saudia	200ER	GE90-92B
Singapore AL	200ER, 300	Trent 892
Thai Airways	200	Trent 875
	300	Trent 892
United Airlines	200	PW4077
	200ER	PW4090
Varig	200ER	GE90-92B
Vietnam Airlines	200ER	PW4084

Airbus A380

A380 customers face a simple choice, initially at least, between the Alliance GP7270 engine (produced jointly by GE and P&W) and the Rolls-Royce Trent 970. Both powerplants are rated at around 70,000 lb (311.5 kN) thrust. Rolls-Royce was stung by an announcement from A380 launch customer Emirates in February 2002 that it had gone for the Alliance engine (Emirates having been a staunch R-R supporter up to that point), but has subsequently gained significant orders such as those from Virgin, Qantas and Singapore Airlines.

Comparing the PW4000 (112-in version, left) with the GE90-115B (above), the most obvious difference is the shape of the fan blades. The GE90-115B introduced sophisticated blades of complicated profile (right) and graphite epoxy construction, offering enhanced aerodynamic performance, and reduced noise and fuel-burn. The titanium alloy leading edge is replaceable so that foreign object damage can be easily repaired.

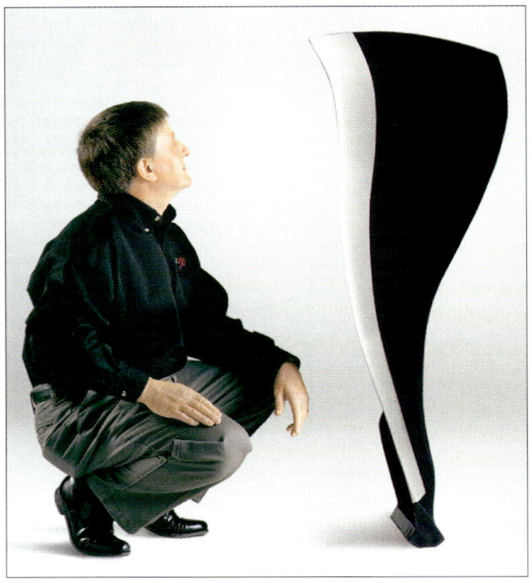

slender blades made of solid titanium with blunt part-span shrouds.

In order to try to compete, in the late 1960s Rolls-Royce designed the RB.211 with seemingly far superior blades made of the newly invented carbon-fibre composite (plastic). These needed no part-span shrouds, and were much lighter and more aerodynamically efficient. Tragically for the famous company, these shiny black blades could not withstand impacts from hail or erosion by sand. Failure of these blades delayed delivery of the first RB.211 engines, bringing about the financial collapse of the company in 1971. Because the firm is so important the UK government stepped in and re-formed it, but the first RB.211s had to fall back on heavy and less-efficient titanium blades like those of their US rivals.

The resurrected Rolls-Royce never gave up, and eventually found a way to make beautiful fan blades that were not only broader, so fewer were needed, but were also dynamically stable and flutter-free without requiring part-span shrouds. They are not made of fibre-reinforced composite but comprise two gracefully curved sheets of titanium alloy diffusion-bonded together round the edges and to a titanium honeycomb core. They entered service on the RB.211-535E4 in November 1983, making that engine absolutely dominant on the Boeing 757, having been selected by over 80 per cent of the customers. Subsequently, the engineers at Derby made similar blades for the bigger RB.211 engines, and while rivals Pratt and GE beavered away making improved fan blades of their own, Rolls-Royce came up with an even better blade for its own big engine.

This development led to an engine called the RB.211-524L, but it gradually became so different that it was given a name: Trent. One of the main differences was the completely new fan. Like that of the 535 engine, the Trent fan blade is based on two matching curved sheets of titanium alloy. The difference lies in the interior. Instead of a thin-foil honeycomb, the Trent fan blade has a core which starts as two quite thin sheets of titanium alloy forming a sandwich. These are then cunningly diffusion-bonded together along radial lines. The assembly is then heated and inflated by nitrogen under enormous pressure to convert it into what looks like a graceful piece of modern sculpture, curving in all directions. This goes between the convex and concave sheets and the whole assembly is then diffusion-bonded together.

Having the big advantage of being first on the 747, the Pratt & Whitney JT9D was developed in a quite relaxed way, until competition began to bite. The Connecticut company then redesigned the engine completely, among other things halving the number of parts, to produce the PW4000. First tested in 1984, this retained the traditional solid titanium fan blade with part-span shrouds, but in August 1992 Pratt & Whitney at last began testing a PW4000 with efficient broad blades of hollow titanium, basically like those of Rolls-Royce. The resulting PW4084 and PW4090 have done well on the Boeing 777, but the top-of-range PW4098 has been delayed by problems.

Meanwhile, General Electric was making so much money with its half share of the CFM56 for narrow-bodies (737 and A320 family) that it left the CF6 family with traditional fan blades. Instead, it boldly took the decision to start completely from scratch and design an engine for the 777 that would simply blow the competition away. This engine is the GE90.

From the start it has had a fan with blades superficially exactly like those Rolls-Royce tried to develop more than 30 years previously, moulded in graphite (carbon) epoxy. The difference is that this time GE has solved the problems. The basic blade has a thick coating of polyurethane on the convex face and an erosion-resistant leading edge made of titanium alloy. This leading edge is replaceable, and experience has shown that putting on new leading edges is no problem. The first GE90 went on test in April 1993, and soon racked up a thrust of 105,400 lb (469 kN), roughly double that of the CF6 family. There were plenty of problems, one of them involving birdstrikes in an echo of the original RB.211 weakness.

One of the most obvious features introduced by the GE90-115B is that the giant fan blades are not straight but curved. Such blades had been tested by Rolls-Royce years earlier, and were fitted to the Trent 8104 which was tested at over 114,500 lb (509.5 kN) thrust, then a world record, in December 1998. The GE90-115B fan, having the unprecedented diameter of 128 in (325.1 cm), handles a greater airflow than any other engine in history, and what GE calls a 'swept blade' increases flow still further and reduces fuel burn. A feature of all GE90 engines is a dual annular combustor. There are 60 fuel nozzles in concentric rings of 30 each. At take-off all are in use, but as a flight progresses and the aircraft gets lighter the inner burners are gradually shut down to reduce emissions.

Developing today's big fans is extremely expensive, requiring massive and hugely complex test rigs. This is the GE90-115B undergoing ground runs.

The future

When Boeing launched the 777 all three Western makers of giant turbofans said, "We can't afford not to be on it", but sharing the market caused furrowed brows, because the costs of developing such engines are astronomic. The upshot is that, in a massive deal with Boeing, GE obtained exclusive rights to put its GE90-115B engine on all future heavyweight 777s.

This has probably hit Pratt & Whitney hardest, because Rolls-Royce has made full use of the Trent's three-shaft layout to scale down particular parts to match the thrust requirements of other aircraft. As a result, the Trent 700 family (of 58,000-71,100 lb/258.1-316.4 kN thrust) is doing well on the A330, the Trent 500 family (53,000 or 56,000 lb/235.8 or 249.2 kN) is the exclusive engine of the stretched A340-500 and -600, and the Trent 900 (66,000-84,000 lb/293.7-373.8 kN) has so far won most of the orders to power the monster A380.

These Trents are hard to beat, because they combine brilliant performance and economy with the proven reliability of a mature engine. In order to compete, Pratt & Whitney has taken the unprecedented step of collaborating with its deadly rival GE; they have formed a company called Engine Alliance, which is developing an engine designated GP7200.

Bill Gunston; additional material by David Donald

General Electric GE90

Announced on 16 January 1990, the GE90 was a 'clean sheet' design launched to match the Boeing 777. GE shared risk with Snecma of France, FiatAvio of Italy and Japan's IHI. The aim of the GE90 is to provide engines to match thrust requirements from 75,000 lb upwards, the two-digit suffix in the engine's designation corresponding to the thrust rating. General Electric offers the CF6-80E1 family as its option for the A330, which has reduced thrust requirements compared to the 777.

The GE90 is a two-spool engine, with a single-stage fan and three-stage low-pressure compressor driven by a six-stage turbine. The high-pressure spool consists of a 10-stage compressor driven by a two-stage turbine.

British Airways was the launch customer for the GE90, installing GE90-76Bs in its first Boeing 777s, which entered service in November 1995.

GE90-76B: 76,400 lb/339.9 kN for 777-200
GE90-85B: 84,700 lb/376.8 kN for 777-200
GE90-90B: 90,000 lb/400.4 kN for 777-200(ER)
GE90-92B: 92,000 lb/409.4 kN for 777-200(ER)
GE90-94B: 94,000 lb/418.3 kN for 777-200(ER)
GE90-115B: 115,000 lb/511.7 kN for 777-200(ER)/300(ER)

GE90-115B for Boeing 777-300(ER)

Pratt & Whitney PW4000

The PW4000 family covers a thrust range from 50,000 to 98,000 lb, and is applicable to A300, A310, A330, 747, 767, 777 and MD-11. The first engine was flight-tested on an A300 in July 1985. The PW4000 is a two-spool engine with a single-stage fan and four-stage low-pressure compressor driven by a four-stage turbine. In the larger engines for the A330 and 777 the low-pressure spool has fifth stages added to both compressor and turbine. The high-pressure spool mounts an 11-stage compressor driven by a two-stage turbine.

Pratt & Whitney designations are based on a two-digit manufacturer identifier (40 = Boeing, 41 = Airbus, 44 = McDonnell Douglas), followed by two digits corresponding to take-off thrust. The family is split into three sub-families, known colloquially by the diameter of their fans. The '94-inch' (actual 93.6 in/237.7 cm) group powers the A300, A310, 747, 767 and MD-11. The '100-inch' (actual 99.8 in/253.5 cm) family is tailored to the A330, while the '112-inch' (actual 112.9 in/286.8 cm) engine is used in the 777.

'100-inch' fans
PW4164: 64,000 lb/284.8 kN for A330-200/300
PW4168: 68,600 lb/305.3 kN for A330-200/300

'112-inch' fans
PW4084: 84,600 lb/376.5 kN for 777-200/200(ER)
PW4090: 91,790 lb/408.5 kN for 777-200(ER)/300
PW4098: 98,000 lb/436.1 kN for 777-200(ER)/300

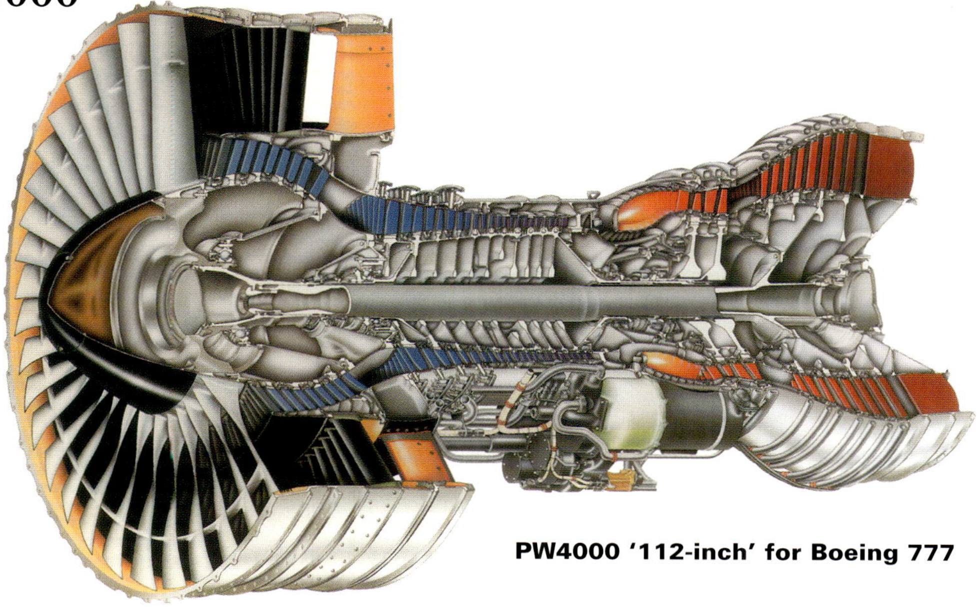

PW4000 '112-inch' for Boeing 777

Rolls-Royce Trent 700/800/900

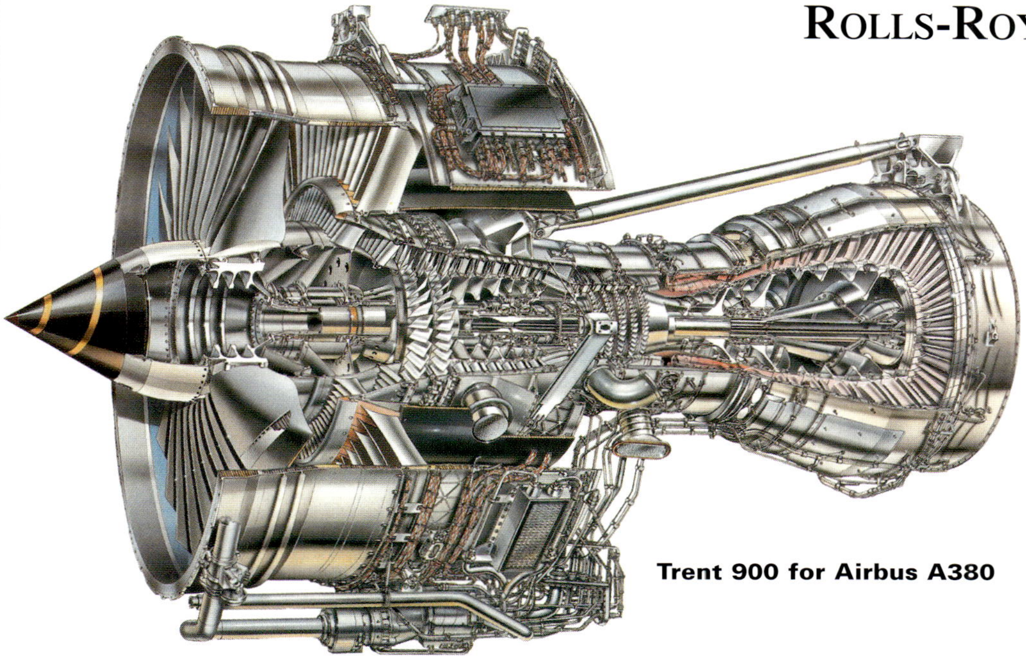

Trent 900 for Airbus A380

Like the PW4000, the Trent family covers a wide range of thrust requirements, from the 'small' Trent 500/600 engines for the A340, to the massive Trent 800s used in the 777, which have the development potential to considerably exceed 100,000 lb (445 kN) thrust, and have demonstrated around 115,000 lb (511.7 kN) during ground tests.

Unlike its two-shaft rivals, the Trent is a three-spool engine, consisting of a single-stage fan driven by a four-stage turbine (five-stage in Trent 800), an intermediate shaft mounting an eight-stage compressor and single-stage turbine, and a high-pressure spool with six-stage compressor and single-stage turbine.

The 'medium' Trent is the 700, with a 97.4-in (247.4-cm) fan for the A330. The Trent 800 for the 777 has a 110-in (279.4-cm) diameter fan and is available in a variety of thrust options. The Trent 900 family is offered for the Airbus A380, with the 70,000-lb (311.5-kN) Trent 970 being the initial engine option.

Trent 768: 67,500 lb/300.4 kN for A330-200/300
Trent 772: 71,100 lb/316.4 kN for A330-200/300

Trent 875: 77,900 lb/346.7 kN for 777-200
Trent 877: 80,080 lb/356.4 kN for 777-200
Trent 892: 91,300 lb/406.3 kN for 777-200/200(ER)/300
Trent 895: 95,500 lb/425.0 kN for 777-200(ER)

Erickson Air-Crane

Currently leased to Aeromaster in Canada, N6962R is one of the original S-64Es acquired by Erickson in the 1970s. Initially used in the timber harvesting role, the aircraft was converted to Helitanker status in the early 1990s and is seen here utilising its 'Sea Snorkel' water tank replenishment system.

'Flying Swiss Army knife'

Whether dousing fires, erecting powerlines, hauling heavy plant equipment or re-invigorating a devastated landscape, Erickson's bright orange Aircranes have become a familiar sight, not only in the USA, but at locations around the world. Re-manufactured and 'zero-lifed' by Erickson itself from ex-US Army CH-54 Tarhes, the Aircrane fleet has grown to some 18 examples and, with demand for its services increasing, these veteran aircraft, built over 30 years ago, look certain to continue their vital and largely unsung work for decades to come.

The fact that Erickson has become recognised as the world's leading specialist helicopter company is thanks to the vision of second-generation logger and entrepreneur Jack Erickson. In 1971 Erickson was looking at expanding the logging work undertaken by his own Erickson Lumber Company. Aware that in other parts of the world, and in particular in Russia, small companies were experimenting with helicopter logging operations, Erickson decided to pursue his interest in acquiring the most suitable aircraft for the task. While the foreign companies achieved little success, finding that the available helicopters either lacked sufficient lifting capabilities or were uneconomical to operate, Erickson wisely agreed to a short-term lease from Sikorsky helicopters for a single S-64E Skycrane to assess its suitability in the lumber harvesting role.

The S-64 was originally designed for use by the US military as a flying crane and, on entering service, was allocated the US Army designation CH-54 Tarhe. Although the aircraft had also been marketed for civilian sales by the Sikorsky company as the S-64, it was its sterling work during the Vietnam War that brought the aircraft to prominence. With a staggering lifting capability, the CH-54s, supporting the US Army's First Cavalry Division, retrieved over 380 damaged or downed aircraft, saving well over US$200 million of hardware that would otherwise have been abandoned.

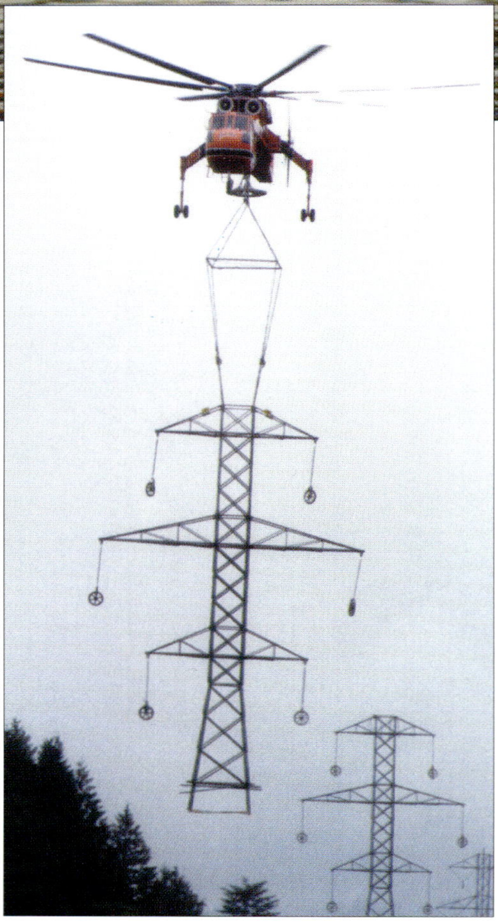

The Aircrane's hugely impressive lifting capability has been put to frequent use by America's utility companies. Erecting powerlines in remote locations or in difficult terrain, the aft-facing pilot is in total control of the Aircrane during load placement.

Above: ***Each of Erickson's Aircranes has been allocated a nickname, displayed on the nose of the aircraft, many of which were originally assigned during previous US Army service.*** **Elvis** ***was remanufactured as an S-64F Aircrane in 1994, and is seen here demonstrating its firefighting capabilities in Australia in 2001.***

Left: Often working within the proximity of inhabited dwellings, the 'Helitankers' can often reach conflagrations that fixed-wing assets are not capable of tackling due to the local terrain.

Anticipating that the aircraft could have commercial applications, Sikorsky had applied for and received Standard Transport Category certification for the type to carry loads of up to 20,000 lb (9072 kg) from the Federal Aviation Administration two years earlier. This enabled the logging work to start within days of delivery, and it quickly became apparent that the Skycrane was perfectly suited to the task. Within months, Erickson's expertise in applying the aircraft to only the tasks it was most suited had produced efficient and profitable results and led to the first outright purchase of an S-64 Skycrane in the spring of 1972. By this time Erickson had begun to receive requests for other uses of his Skycranes.

Acquiring Skycranes

Having designated the air operations subsidiary of his company Erickson Air-Crane, sub-contracting work on behalf of utilities such as the Bonneville Power Administration, Pacific Gas and Electric, and the Southern California Edison Company was undertaken commencing in 1972.

The primary role was power line construction. Bidding against land-based methods of power line construction over all types of terrain, the S-64 emerged as by far the most efficient tool for the project and was nominated as prime contractor. Over 1,000 miles (1600 km) of power lines were erected on time and on budget in a project that would become a launch-pad for the company's rapid expansion.

A further three S-64s were purchased in late 1972 as the success of the power line operations led to contracts in other areas of heavylift construction. From airlifting and installing ski lifts, to the construction of large buildings and the transport of heavy equipment to remote locations, the four S-64s were in increasing demand as they continued to fulfil their ongoing power line and logging commitments.

In 1975 the company received a further publicity boost as one of the S-64s was used in the final stages of the construction of what was then the world's tallest freestanding structure – the CN Tower in Ontario, Canada. The aircraft

Remanufacturing at Central Point

By 1992, with growing demands placed on Erickson's existing four-S-64 fleet, the company took the bold step of acquiring ex-US Army CH-54s and re-manufacturing the airframes, at its Central Point, Oregon facility, under a new designation – Erickson S-64 Aircrane. Since that time some 15 S-64Es and S-64Fs have undergone the 'zero-lifing' process from CH-54A and CH-54B airframes, respectively.

Once a decommissioned CH-54 has been selected for remanufacture, all existing avionics, wiring, hydraulic lines and accessories are removed and the airframe is subject to a chemical paint removal process down to a bare metal finish. At this point each individual fuselage section, spar and stringer is inspected for corrosion and is tested for integrity. Problems uncovered are repaired or remanufactured.

After passing the inspection procedure, the engines are installed along with the miles of wiring and modern communication and navigation equipment including GPS. The next stage is the installation of the aircraft's hydraulics and the Automatic Flight Control System (AFCS). Finally, the remaining components including wheels and rotors are added and the aircraft painted in the requisite scheme. The entire process takes 6-9 months from the receipt of the CH-54 to the granting of a certificate of airworthiness for the Erickson S-64E/F.

If intended for firefighting, the aircraft is additionally fitted with the 2,650-US gal (10030-litre) variable flow tank and snorkel devices. The water cannon is also available as an option.

Above: CH-54B 69-18480 is seen in a dismantled state as received by Erickson from the US Army. After a period in storage the aircraft is undergoing re-manufacture to S-64F Aircrane standard and has been allocated the civilian identity N213AC.

Left: S-64E N154AC **Georgia Peach***, already resplendent in the company's orange livery, approaches the end of a major overhaul in the main hangar at Central Point. Adjacent to* **Georgia Peach** ***a CH-54B undergoes remanufacture to Aircrane configuration. Spares from other aircraft may be used in the process, along with new parts manufactured at the facility. Erickson holds FAA repair, servicing and production certificates for the S-64 and, with many of the aircraft working abroad or in remote locations, has adopted digital web technology to support in-field repairs. When a problem occurs a mechanic takes high-resolution digital images of the affected area and sends them directly to Central Point, where Erickson engineers direct the correct repair procedure, or manufacture a replacement component. A computer-based information system ensures that all Aircranes have the same modifications, ensuring fleet-wide standardisation.***

transported and placed the 7-ton steel structures that formed the antenna and weather metering systems, bringing the two-year project to a close.

Throughout the remainder of the decade and the 1980s Erickson Air-Crane continued to diversify, receiving contracts from the oil and gas industry, including the transportation of drill rigs and platforms to remote locations. Its services were also in great demand for the lifting and placing of HVAC air conditioning units on large buildings.

In 1983 the S-64 was involved in more record-breaking achievements when US Borax contracted Erickson Air-Crane to facilitate the setting up of an assessment operation in the remote Quartz Hill mountain range in Alaska, where a large deposit of molybdenum had been located. In a four-day period the S-64 transported some 1,100 tons of large construction equipment used to build a 9-mile (14.4-km) access road through the harsh terrain in what was the world's largest civilian airlift operation.

By 1992 the company and the S-64 had firmly established itself in the USA as a reliable provider of a wide range of services for industry. It would be in this year, however, that three important events occurred, allowing Erickson Air-Crane to grow into the global air services provider it is today.

Firstly, the company purchased the S-64E and S-64F type certificates from Sikorsky, allowing the company not only to become the FAA's licensed major overhaul, repair and modification facility for the type but also allowing the remanufacture of ex-military CH-54s to zero-hour airframes under the designation Erickson S-64 Aircrane. This was facilitated by the second important event of 1992, the sudden availability of large numbers of ex-US Army CH-54As and CH-54Bs as the Army Air National Guard retired its final examples from service. In all, six airframes were purchased for remanufacture in 1992, followed by a further 15 in 1994-96. The third event was the unveiling of a new role for the aircraft as a firefighter following the development of a 2,500-US gal (9463-litre) tank attachment for the S-64, featuring a metered-flow drop system with microprocessor controlled tank doors, allowing for eight different coverage levels.

From 1992 the company's Aircrane fleet has grown to 17 aircraft, including examples leased to Canadian Air-Crane and Aeromaster in Canada. The company has sufficient airframes to complete at least a further eight examples and currently offers re-manufactured Aircranes for sale to civilian or governmental organisations. The first direct sale was to the South Korean government's Forest Service in 2001 for a firefighting-equipped S-64E Aircrane. Interest has also been expressed by the governments of Australia and Greece.

Today the company offers the services of its Aircranes in eight key areas:

Aerial timber harvesting

The first and still important area of employment for the Aircrane is year-round high-performance, low-impact timber harvesting.

Above: Both S-64E and S-64F Aircranes are available in construction or fire suppression (Helitanker) configuration. Here S-64E N189AC* Gypsy Lady *drops its load of water mixed with coloured fire retardant on a forest fire. The Korean Forest Service recently took delivery of the first exported S-64E Helitanker after taking up residence at the Central Point facility to observe and document the entire re-manufacturing process.

Inset left: Erickson's Aircranes have been called on to help with the final construction phases of many of America's tallest buildings. Here the tip of the spire is fitted to the 995-ft (303-m) Prudential Plaza, Chicago in 1990.

Below: For pinpoint firefighting, such as in burning high-rise buildings or crashed aircraft, Erickson developed the 'water cannon' spray nozzle attachment. Here N158AC* Goliath *demonstrates its abilities on a derelict Boeing KC-97.

Until 1993 there was no civilian equivalent to the US Army's ultimate Tarhe – the CH-54B. It was in February of that year that Erickson revealed its first conversion to S-64F standard. Erickson now offers both S-64E and S-64F Aircranes in either construction and fire suppression configuration (above and right). The first direct sale was an S-64E 'Helitanker', ordered by the Korean Forest Service in 2001. It is reported that following successful operations of Erickson-owned Aircranes, Australia, Italy and Greece have all expressed interest in acquiring examples. Erickson has around eight further S-64s in storage awaiting conversion for potential customers.

Since 1971 successful operations have been conducted in the Pacific northwestern USA, Canada, Indonesia and Malaysia, with an additional three Aircranes dedicated to the task, leased to subsidiary company Canadian Air-Crane.

Timber is lifted vertically and flown out rather than dragged through the forest floor, preventing damage to adjacent trees and soil. This is achieved using a grapple system powered by the aircraft's own hydraulic power source. The grapple can open and close its jaws within three seconds and exercise over 42,000 lb (19000 kg) of pressure, ensuring the security of the logs during a lift. In recent years the company has developed a new method of harvesting which involves the pulling out of standing trees out in-situ, preventing damage caused by ground felling. Suspending the grapple beneath the Aircrane horizontally, held in place by two welded shackles, the stem is snapped off at a pre-cut point and lifted to the drop zone. This method has been particularly valuable along the British Columbia, Canada, coastline where a high value is placed on the scenic quality of the landscape. Where this 'Standing Stem' harvesting method has been used it is almost impossible to tell that harvesting has occurred.

Heavy equipment lifting

Having already proved its worth in US military service as a 'flying crane' capable of lifting anything from large aircraft to large plant vehicles and drilling equipment, the Aircrane is available to industry around the world for the lifting and transportation of outsize items.

The most common use is in the construction of the final stages of large buildings and, with precise positioning required, the aircraft's unique rear-facing pilot station becomes invaluable. The Aircrane can guide its load to a tolerance measured in a few inches thanks to the patented anti-rotation system which prevents the suspended load from spinning. The powerful twin 4,800-hp (3580-kW) Pratt & Whitney JFTD12-5A turboshaft engines provide the aircraft with a lift capacity of 25,000 lb (11340 kg) at lower altitudes and 10,000 lb (4536 kg) at 10,000 ft (3048 m).

Oil and gas support

Aircranes have proved themselves vital tools in establishing drill rigs and platforms in remote locations around the world, where it has proved impossible to locate the necessary equipment by land. Transporting the aircraft either by ship or air, the latter by Antonov An-124, Aircranes

Above: The pilot peers out of the port side cockpit bubble of S-64F N223AC* Millie *while filling its tanks in the hover over an Australian swamp using the 'pond snorkel'. The lack of a rear-facing pilot, combined with the S-64's large rotor disc, makes the refilling process from small tree-lined ponds potentially dangerous, especially in windy conditions. The pond snorkel is capable of retrieving a full load from water as shallow as 18 in (45 cm) and can refill the tank in 50 seconds. Seen here during a demonstration of the type for government officials, the aircraft is also fitted with the water cannon on the port side of the forward fuselage.

Anti-rotation system

For powerline, ski lift and building construction, as well as precise placing of cumbersome and heavy objects (such as the CC-129 Dakota; right), the Aircrane is fitted with a patented anti-rotation device preventing the load from spinning independently of the Aircrane (below). In conjunction with the rear-facing pilot, the device also allows precision control during the lowering of the load. It consists of a 6-ft (1.82-m) spreader bar suspended by the 25,000-lb (11340-kg) capacity winch and a 'locking ring' able to anchor the load to face any major azimuth. The locking ring is secured to the Aircrane through four fuselage-mounted hardpoints.

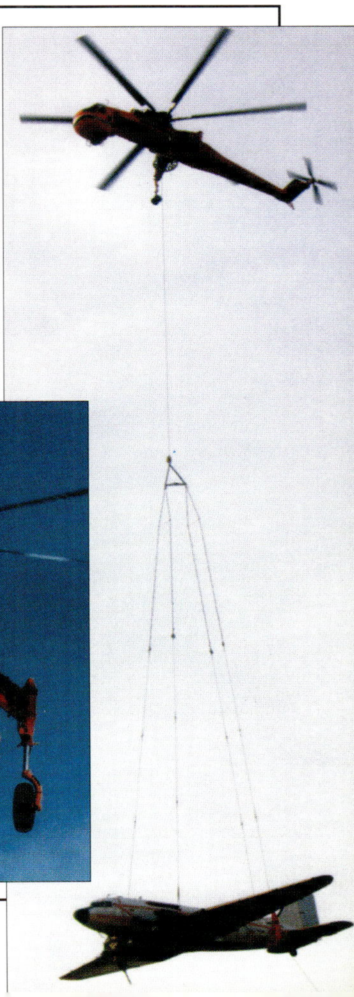

Above: Although the Aircrane's firefighting exploits receive the media attention, it is the 'bread and butter' construction and logging work that ensures Erickson maintains such a sizeable fleet. Here, a gigantic end section of a crane is carefully lowered into position by the aft-facing pilot in an Aircrane operated by Erickson's Malaysian subsidiary. In addition, the company has subsidiary Aircrane-operating companies in Canada (Canadian Air-Crane Ltd) and Peru (Erickson Air-Crane Selva).

An ability to harvest and transport timber from remote areas not easily accessible by road has led to increasing demand for the Aircrane's services. Operations are regularly conducted in the northern US states and Canada, as well as in the tropical forests of Malaysia and Indonesia. The long wire, combined with the aircraft's powerful winch, allows it to remain well clear of the forest canopy.

have fulfilled the requirements of petroleum companies in places as diverse as Ecuador, Peru, Indonesia, Papua New Guinea and Canada. To support its worldwide operations the company maintains permanent bases in Malaysia, Canada, Europe and Peru.

Firefighting

In recent years, and particularly in Australia and the west coast of the USA in 2002, Erickson's Aircranes have received massive media attention for their role in fighting wild bush or forest fires. The first Aircrane converted to the role began operations in 1993 and since that time the aircraft have seen service in Italy, Australia, Greece, Korea, Canada, Borneo, Turkey and Mexico, as well as in many states of the USA.

The large capacity 2,650-US gal (10030-litre) tank attaches to the airframe though eight hard-points on the fuselage and is removable, allowing for reconfiguration to other roles. With a fast

refill time of 45 seconds in water as shallow as 18 in (46 cm), the Aircrane is capable of delivering up to 30,000 US gal (113652 litres) of water, foam mix or retardant onto a fire per hour.

In addition, Erickson has developed a spray nozzle attachment for the Aircrane. Known as the 'water cannon', the nose-mounted nozzle is attached to the main tank and can direct 300 US gal (1136 litres) of water or foam mix directly at the point of a fire at ranges of up to 200 ft (61 m).

Powerline construction

Supporting utility companies since 1971, Erickson still regularly transports and places powerline transmission towers at locations around the USA. More than 7,000 miles (11265 km) of transmission lines have been laid in the past 30 years. The rear-facing pilot is crucial in the laying of towers, using his set of flight controls to manoeuvre the aircraft during hook-up and load placement. Using the anti-rotation device, the tower sections are aligned and held in position while they are bolted together. Up to 148 H-frame structures have been placed by an Aircrane in a single day.

Using the 'Sea Snorkel'

For refilling from open water sources the Aircrane's tank can be fitted with the special 'Sea Snorkel', designed to augment the freshwater hoverfill capabilities of the 'Pond Snorkel', by allowing refill from nearby saltwater sources. The tank can be fully replenished in an average of 40 seconds, or as little as 29 seconds, by skimming above the water surface at 35-45 kt (65-83 km/h) as the hydrofoil ram scoop forces the water up and into the tank. The 'Sea Snorkel' is the most efficient way of refilling the tanks as it dispenses with the need for the transitional lift period on entering or leaving the hover.

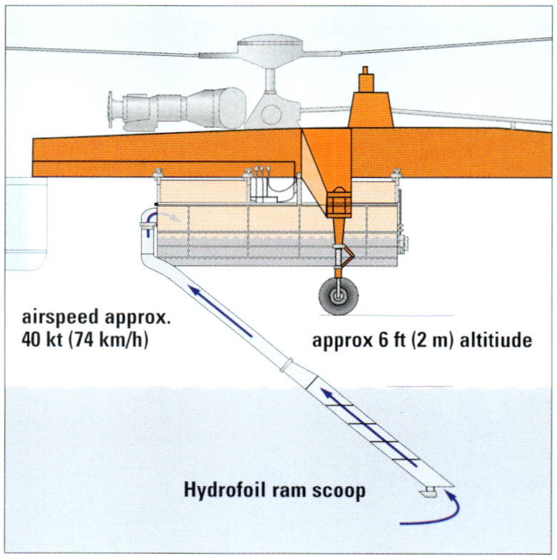

Open-water refill is the most efficient way to replenish the tank in coastal areas. However, environmental concerns over soil damage, caused by salt water, ensure freshwater drops are the preferred choice of most firefighting agencies.

Aircranes have been utilised in every region of the USA. N189AC (above) is one of several examples to operate from Van Nuys airport during the Californian fire season. If necessary, more than one firefighting Aircrane can be dispatched to work in harmony (right). Careful planning and co-ordination with ground-based services is vital to ensure the fire is prevented from reaching inhabited areas.

Heating and air conditioning

One of the major growth areas for the company and the use of the Aircrane has been in the placing of HVAC units on manufacturing plants and major building throughout the USA and Canada. Units in the weight range of 8,000-21,000 lb (3630-9500 kg) have been lifted into position. During a recent operation at the Toyota manufacturing plant, Indiana, over 1,700,000 lb (771100 kg) of HVAC components were placed in one day, including 134 HVAC units and seven exhaust stacks.

Ski lift construction

Since receiving its first S-64 in 1971, Erickson has been involved in the transportation and construction of ski lift towers throughout continental USA. With good lifting capacity at higher altitudes the aircraft is ideally suited to the task. The rear-facing pilot, using the anti-rotation device, is responsible for the accurate placing of the towers while ground engineers bolt-down the structure. The speed and efficiency offered by the Aircrane in locating ski towers in the most inaccessible areas is a major plus, as is the experience of Erickson's aircrew, which allows a complete assembly to be placed in a lift time as low as seven minutes.

Where topography of the land inhibits efficient ground-based hydroseeding for re-vegetation of barren ground, the Aircrane can be fitted with an advanced hydroseed tank. For lime delivery an onboard circulation system keeps the saturated lime and mulch in suspension during flight.

Aerial hydroseeding

In an environment that is excessively steep or contains a highly erodable soil type, the Aircrane is an efficient way of hydroseeding the area for rapid re-vegetation. A standard mixture of 2,650 US gal (10030 litres) of hydroseed can be accurately delivered, with as little as 3-4 minute turnaround times for each drop.

Additionally, lime pellets are another common load helping to reduce soil acidity and promote vegetation growth. A single Aircrane has delivered over 1,050 tons of lime pellets, covering some 235 acres (95 ha), in only five days during preparations for hydroseeding.

Future applications

Having established a reputation for innovation, Erickson, in November 2001, demonstrated its latest version of the Aircrane – the Erickson emergency rescue vehicle (ERV). The ERV is an alloy lattice frame pod suspended by a 200-ft (61-m) line beneath the Aircrane. Passengers can enter through sliding front doors or lowered side panels. Designed to facilitate large-scale evacuations from high-rise buildings, burning aircraft, floundering ships or wildfire situations, the ERV can lift up to 60 adults at a time.

Daniel J. March

Aircrane specification

Erickson S-64F Aircrane

Flight crew: 2/3
Powerplant: two Pratt & Whitney JFTD12-5A turboshafts, each rated at 4,800 shp (3581 kW)
Main rotor diameter: 72 ft 0 in (21.95 m)
Tail rotor diameter: 16 ft 0 in (4.88 m)
Main rotor disc area: 4,070 sq ft (378.1 m²)
Overall length: 88 ft 6 in (26.97 m)
Fuselage length: 70 ft 3 in (21.41 m)
Overall height: 25 ft 5 in (7.75 m)
Width (excluding blades): 21 ft 10 in (6.65 m)
Empty weight: 20,500 lb (9300 kg) or 23,000 lb (10433 kg) with tank
Maximum gross weight: 47,000 lb (21319 kg)
Maximum payload: 25,000 lb (11340 kg)
Maximum payload: 25,000 lb (11340 kg)
Water tank capacity: 2,650 US gal (10031 litres)
Foam capacity: 70 US gal (265 litres)
Standard fuel capacity: 1,356 US gal (5133 litres)
Extended fuel capacity: 2,356 US gal (8918 litres)
Fuel consumption: 550 US gal (2082 litres) per hour
Maximum cruising speed: 104 kt (119 mph; 192 km/h)
Endurance: standard 2 hours 28 mins; extended 4 hours 17 mins
Range: standard 292 miles (470 km); extended 509 miles (819 km)

Erickson Aircrane Fleet

Reg. No.	Type	c/n	previous ident.	FF	Del	Name	Status
N154AC	S-64E	64037	68-18435 (ex-CH-54A)	1967	Mar 92	*Georgia Peach*	Active
N158AC	S-64F	64081	HL9260 (ex-CH-54B)	1968	Jul 92	*Goliath*	Active
N159AC	S-64F	64084	69-18476 (ex-CH-54B)	1970	Aug 92	*Camille*	Active
N163AC	S-64F	64093	70-18485 (ex-CH-54B)	1970	Aug 92	*Bubba*	Active
N164AC	S-64E	64034D	C-FCRN	1968	Dec 81	*Incredible Hulk*	Active
N171AC	S-64F	64090	69-18482 (ex-CH-54B)	1970	Aug 92		Stored*
N173AC	S-64E	64015	66-18413 (ex-CH-54A)	1967	Apr 94	*Christine*	Active
N174AC	S-64F	64080	N7094X (ex-CH-54B)	1969	May 94		Stored*
N178AC	S-64F	64097	70-18489 (ex-CH-54B)	1970	May 94	*Isabelle*	Active
N179AC	S-64F	64091	C-GFAH	1970	Sept 94	*Elvis*	Active
N189AC	S-64E**	641001		1997	June 97	*Gypsy Lady*	Active
N194AC	S-64E	64017	C-GFLH (ex-CH-54A)	1967	May 96	*Delilah*	Active
N197AC	S-64F	64067	N7028U (ex-CH-54B)	1969	Dec 94		Stored*
N198AC	S-64F	64098	N70280 (ex-CH-54B)	1970	Dec 94		Stored*
N213AC	S-64F	64088	69-18480 (ex-CH-54B)	1970	Jul 95		Stored*
N217AC	S-64E	64064	N542SB (ex-CH-54A)	1968	June 00	*Malcolm*	Active
N218AC	S-64E	64033	N545SB (ex-CH-54A)	1967	June 00	*Elsie*	Active
N223AC	S-64F	64086	69-18478 (ex-CH-54B)	1970	Dec 94	*Millie*	Active
N227AC	S-64F	64078	69-18471 (ex-CH-54B)	1969	Dec 94		Stored*
N236AC	S-64F	64089	69-18481 (ex-CH-54B)	1970	Oct 95		Stored*
N237AC	S-64F	64095	70-18487 (ex-CH-54B)	1970	Oct 95		Stored*
N6962R	S-64E	64058	C-GFBH	1968	Mar 75		Leased Aeromaster
C-FCRN	S-64E	64061	N172AC	1968	Dec 94	*Mariah*	Leased Can A/c
C-FESG	S-64E	64065	N157AC	1968	Jul 92	*Ichabod*	Leased Can A/c
C-FJZK	S-64E	64003	N176AC	1962	Jun 83	*Lucille*	Leased Can A/c

*Aircraft undergoing/awaiting remanufacture by Erickson
**Composite aircraft re-built from two airframes

Inside the Aircrane – Technical description

Developed from Sikorsky's privately-funded piston-engined S-60, the S-64 emerged in 1962 as the world's first practical 'flying crane'. To enable the aircraft to lift bulky loads while still on the ground, the aircraft was fitted with a 'spider' undercarriage with a track of 19 ft 9 in (6.02 m), supporting the simple pod and boom structure of the main fuselage with a ground clearance of 9 ft 4 in (2.84 m).

Power for the Aircrane is provided by twin Pratt & Whitney JFTD12 turboshafts, mounted in an uncowled state above the centre of the fuselage boom, producing a total of 9,000 shp (6714 kW) for the JFTD12-4A-equipped S-64E and 9,600 shp (7162 kW) for the JFTD-12-5A-powered S-64F. The engines drive a 72-ft (21.95-m) diameter six-bladed fully-articulated main rotor and a 16-ft (4.88-m) diameter four-bladed tail rotor, the latter via an external drive-shaft mounted on the upper surface of the fuselage. Within the fuselage boom are the two main fuel cells and, if necessary, an auxiliary fuel cell.

Both the S-64E and S-64F model Aircranes are available in either 'construction configuration', with a fully operational aft-pilot station and a 20,000-lb (9072-kg) or 25,000-lb (11340-kg) capacity winch for the 'E' and 'F' respectively, cargo hook and the anti-rotation device, or in 'fire suppression configuration' with the underslung fire-fighting tank. Further accessories can include the wide-mouth hydroseeding manifold and an external 3,000-psi (211-kg/cm²) grapple for timber harvesting. The S-64F also benefits from a strengthened airframe and an increased chord rotor system.

Right: S-64E N217AC* Malcolm *demonstrates the water cannon attachment available for all firefighting-configured Aircranes. Fitted to the port side of the forward fuselage, the water cannon fires a concentrated stream of water or water/foam mix with great accuracy .

Left: Unlike conventional protocol for western helicopters, the CH-54/S-64 is flown from the left-hand seat.

Right: The centre console houses the comms and nav instruments. The water drop controls are incorporated into the bottom left portion of the panel.

Below: A primitive series of lights, controlled by the radar altimeter, is used as a 'heads-up' guide to the aircraft's altitude when sea snorkelling.

Erickson S-64F Aircrane
N223AC *Millie*
Essendon, Australia, 1998

Powerplant and rotors
Sikorsky's first 'flying crane' – the S-60 – suffered from limited lift capabilities due to the use of the drive and engine systems from the CH-37 Mojave. The introduction of twin Pratt & Whitney JFTD12 turboshafts and a six-bladed main rotor created a much more capable aircraft and the configuration was retained by Erickson during remanufacture. Modifications to the Aircranes include broader chord rotors (on the S-64Fs) and the removal of the engine intake filters fitted to the CH-54s.

Cockpit
The cockpit accommodates the pilot in the left- and co-pilot in the right-hand seat, along with a further aft-facing pilot's position in the rear of the cabin. In US military service the rear seat had 100 per cent authority during pick-up and placement of loads, however, the Aircranes have the 'twist grip' pedal control de-activated with the forward-facing pilot controlling the tail rotor at all times.

Left and below left: In fire suppression configuration the aircraft is controlled at all times by the pilot in the left-hand seat. The large bubble window on the cockpit side (left) provides the pilot with a good view of the accuracy of the drop. It is also invaluable for viewing underslung loads during timber/construction work. The aft-facing pilot's station (below left) is utilised in construction work allowing the accurate placement of equipment while the aircraft is in the hover.

Top and above: Two methods of refilling the firefighting tank during flight are available. On the starboard side of the tank is the 'Sea Snorkel', which incorporates a ram scoop design with two separate inlet valves, allowing the Aircrane to scoop up water from large salt or freshwater sources as the aircraft skims the water's surface at 35 kt (65 km/h). The pond snorkel on the port side uses an auxiliary hydraulic system to 'suck-up' water from smaller sources while in the hover.

The 2,650-US gal (10030-litre) main firefighting tank also incorporates a 70-US gal (265-litre) capacity foam injection system. The microprocessor-controlled doors allow for eight different coverage levels of between 1-8 US gal (3.7-30 litres) per 100 sq ft (9.3 m²). The water load is normally released at speeds between 40-60 kt (74-111 km/h), helping to prevent the break-up and dispersion of the retardant associated with fixed-wing firebombers. Care has to be taken, however, to prevent the aircraft's substantial rotor downwash from fanning the fire.

Using the 'Pond Snorkel' allows the Aircrane to utilise sources of water closer to the fire and therefore reduce transit time. A suitable water source can be as little as 18 in (45 cm) in depth, and the aircraft can completely replenish its main tank in as little as 50 seconds. Hydraulic lines run down the inside of the flexible 10-in (25-cm) diameter tube to power a large ducted brass propeller providing the suction. A mesh cover is fitted to the end of the tube to prevent unwanted debris from entering the tank.

Firefighting system
The firefighting tank system is attached to the Aircrane through eight hardpoints mounted on the underside of the boom fuselage. The aircraft's GPS (global positioning system) feeds airspeed information to a microprocessor controlling the tank doors and therefore the water flow. In high intensity situations, or to control hot spots, a salvo of 2,500 US gal (9463 litres) can be delivered in approximately three seconds.

Tail rotor
Controlling the tail rotor remains the responsibility of the forward-facing pilot even when the other control inputs are governed from the aft-facing cockpit. On firefighting sorties control of the aircraft remains with the forward-facing pilots at all times, the rear station often being used to house the crew chief as an extra pair of eyes and to reduce down time if technical problems are encountered.

Firefighting in Australia

Readers of Sydney newspapers in early January 2002 could have been forgiven for thinking that Elvis Presley was alive and well with headlines such as 'Elvis Seen Fighting NSW Bushfires' filling pages, and echoing from radios and televisions. Indeed, Elvis was alive and very well, but in the form of one of Erickson's S-64F Aircranes, brought up from Victoria to combat the bushfires ringing the harbour city. Named *Elvis* during its service with the US Army in Memphis, its effectiveness was such that a cult following among Sydneysiders soon developed.

For the reason that Erickson Aircranes have been regular visitors to Victoria, if not other parts of Australia, we must go back to 1997 and a particularly aggressive fire in eucalypt forest in Melbourne's Dandenong Ranges. This fire signalled to Victoria's Country Fire Authority and Department of Natural Resources and Environment, that a means of laying down large amounts of suppressant was required.

Until this time, Victoria had relied (and indeed, still does today) on a fleet of agricultural aircraft and medium helicopters, leased on a stand-by basis over the summer months. Despite the demonstration of types such as the DC-6, F27 and CL-215/415, no large aircraft had previously been adopted. The flexibility of the Aircrane, coupled with the large offload capability, impressed the Victorian Government and a deal was subsequently struck with Erickson to supply a machine for the next (1997/1998) fire season.

Accordingly, December 1997 saw an aircraft shipped to Perth, after completion of a logging contract in Malaysia. After re-assembly at Fremantle docks, it was flown across Australia on a marathon delivery flight to Melbourne's Essendon Airport, taking some 20 flying hours.

Because Erickson does not hold an Australian Air Operators Certificate, an arrangement with a local company (Helicorp) was struck, allowing operations under their AOC. This arrangement has been very satisfactory and is still in use today, with the Erickson crews sharing Helicorp's hangar and facilities during their stay.

The first year of operation was a bad year for bushfires, the El-Niño effect being strongly felt, and the Aircrane was soon in action. This has led to the contract being renewed every year since 1997, with a three-year contract (plus two-year option) beginning this year. The contract requires an S-64F, but Erickson crews consider that, for the fire-fighting role, there is not much to choose between the S-64E and F. The later model has a 5,000-lb greater lifting capacity, but

Top: **Isabelle** *sits on Essendon's ramp between sorties towards the end of the 2000 fire season. By this time the Aircrane had made a lasting impression on the Australian public earning the moniker 'Eric the Water Bomber'.*

Above: **S-64F** *Millie was the first of the Aircranes to operate in Australia and is seen here departing Essendon in February 1998, with its Pond Snorkel released for use. The cost of hiring an Aircrane was placed at around $250,000 for a 10-week period, plus operating costs of around $12,000 per hour.*

Left: Gaining notoriety in the Australian press, **Elvis** *operated from a forward operating base at Bankstown fighting devastating fires around Sydney in early 2002.*

Right: A total of three S-64s was committed to the 2002 firefighting effort, including **N164AC**, *seen here utilising its Pond Snorkel at a lake near Sydney.*

Operating at 100 ft (30 m) above the forest canopy, the Aircranes were credited with saving numerous isolated properties and villages from the ravages of the fires around Sydney in early 2002 (seen in the bottom right of the image above). Erickson claim that the aircraft's slower delivery speed and computer-controlled release mechanism ensure the dispensed liquid stays together as a single unit, allowing for more accurate drops (left).

the 'E is faster and has a lower fuel burn. Over a day's operations, what is gained by carrying a greater load by the 'F is almost made up by the faster transit times of the 'E. The 70-day contract runs until 12 March, with the helicopter being on 15-minute readiness between 1000 and 1600, with a less stringent response time required in daylight hours outside those hours. The Erickson crew comprises two pilots, a Crew Chief and an Assistant Crew Chief, working three-weeks on/three-weeks off.

Every year since 1997, an S-64F has been shipped to Australia as deck cargo, being reassembled dock-side (usually in Melbourne) and flown to Essendon in time for the contract to commence on 1 January. Re-assembly consists of the installation of main and tail rotor blades, and the fitment of the horizontal stabiliser. The only modifications for Australian operations are the fitment of DNRE 'trunking' radios and a HF set, in case of long transits over empty country.

The Aircrane is usually not the first to be called, but once summoned will deploy to a Forward Operating Location close to the fire front. This is usually an airfield (due to the absence of any wires), but can be any cleared area, such as a football field. The helicopter deploys with two pilots and a Crew Chief, the Assistant Crew Chief following in a support truck. Vital spares are carried aboard the helicopter, with a further supply being packed in the road transport. A more extensive spares holding (such as main gearbox, rotor blades etc) is cached at Essendon for the length of the stay in Australia.

Fire co-ordination

All airborne assets come under the control of the State Aircraft Unit, a joint operation between the DNRE and CFA, and due to initial unfamiliarity with the way the Americans operated, it was decided to dedicate a small command and control helicopter to the Aircrane. Currently a Bell LongRanger, known as a 'Firebird 10', though sometimes a Cessna 337 - 'Bird Dog 37', this aircraft carries the Air Attack Supervisor responsible for the co-ordination of aerial fire-fighting efforts. The practice of pairing these resources continues today, no longer because of mutual unfamiliarity, but to ensure that the Aircrane's high productivity is retained – clearing the way when necessary, and making routine 'ops normal' radio calls.

Because the Aircrane does not have an underslung bucket, it can get much closer to the rising column of heat and smoke than most types, and is therefore a highly prized tool when asset protection operations are required. A typical attack involves drops on the head of the fire with some forward speed (not exceeding 60 kt), and at an altitude of between 100 and 150 ft above the trees. This latter requirement varies with wind speed and direction, and the effect of rotor wash on the fire. Another plus is the turnaround time between drops – sucking a full tank of water from any dam or swimming pool in 45 seconds using the Snorkel, or using the Sea Snorkel to fill the tank from a fresh water lake or the sea in just 29 seconds. The latter method is preferred as it does not involve the transitional lift phase of flight when entering or leaving the hover. Major hazards when fire-fighting are the presence of wires and the risk of ingesting birds, feeding on the thousands of insects that flee any fire.

The outbreak of bushfires around NSW during Christmas 2001, saw 2002's Aircrane flown to Bankstown in Sydney, to assist the NSW Rural Bushfire Brigade. This was possible due to the un-seasonal cool weather in Victoria at the time, and gave *Elvis* the chance to establish his hero-like status over the following fortnight. During a fire at Sussex Inlet for example, the pilot shuttling to and from Sea Snorkelling operations recalls seeing the word 'ELVIS' written in the sand – the townsfolk had been evacuated to the beach and were displaying their appreciation in the only way possible!

This deployment bought the NSW Government time to urgently source a pair of S-64Es from Erickson, delivered by An-124, and may possibly result in a contract similar to that exercised by Victoria. Either way, *Elvis* and his mates look set to appear in Australian skies for some time to come!

Nigel Pittaway

Using the Pond Snorkel to refill from nearby freshwater sources, each Aircrane was averaging over 30,000 US gal (113562 litres) dropped per hour. The versatility of the aircraft and flight crew ensured that unlikely sources such as golf course ponds were utilised – causing much consternation to those on the 1st tee!

S-64F Aircranes operated in Australia

Year	Aircraft	Tanker	Name	Hours flown
1997/1998	N223AC	46	*Millie*	50 (including 20 hr ferry flight from WA)
1998/1999	N179AC	43	*Elvis*	6 (including 3 demo flights)
1999/2000	N178AC	43	*Isabelle*	12
2000/2001	N179AC	744	*Elvis*	14 (including display at Avalon Airshow)
20001/2002	N179AC	730	*Elvis*	86 (84 in NSW, incl. ferry to/from Sydney)
2002 (Sydney)	N154AC	733	*Georgia Peach*	n/a
2002 (Sydney)	N164AC	748	*Incredible Hulk*	n/a

SAN FRANCISCO AIRPORT

Serving the fourth largest metropolitan area in the United States, San Francisco International Airport is the fifth busiest airport in the United States in terms of passenger traffic and the ninth busiest in the world. Known since 1947 by its three-letter code, SFO, the airport is currently proposing an ambitious upgrade programme.

Above: Still more commonly referred to as Mills Field until after World War II, San Francisco airport underwent major expansion in the mid-1930s from capital raised by a successful bond issue. Some 300 acres (120 hectares) of land was reclaimed from San Francisco Bay, allowing runways of 3,000 ft (914 m) and 4,650 ft (1417 m) to be constructed. Note the 9,000-ft (2743-m) perimeter sea wall.

In 1938 United's Boeing 247s were replaced by Douglas DC-3s as the airline's main transport type operating from SFO. Named 'Mainliners', the aircraft offered new levels of comfort, including plush swivelling armchairs and folding tables.

Today, San Francisco International Airport (SFO) is by far the most active of the three international airports in the San Francisco Bay Area – the other two being Oakland (OAK) and San Jose (SJO). It offers extensive services into Asia and Europe as well as a large domestic network and growing cargo operations.

As with most airports associated with major world urban centres, SFO is located outside the 'city limits' of the city that it serves. It is 15 miles (24 km) south of the southern edge of the city and county of San Francisco; specifically, it is in San Mateo County adjacent to the suburban cities of San Bruno and Millbrae. It was founded on the shore of San Francisco Bay, and has been expanded into the bay over the decades through the use of landfill. Today, the airport is situated on 5,171 acres (2093 hectares), of which 2,383 acres (965 hectares) have been developed for aviation use.

San Francisco International Airport marked the turn of the century with the official opening of the largest international terminal in the United States on 7 December 2001. As of this milestone, San Francisco International Airport was served by 74 airlines, including 34 with international service.

As has been the case through most of the airport's history, the most active airline at SFO today is United Air Lines; at the turn of the century, the carrier accounted for 52 per cent of operations. For half a century, United has run one of its largest maintenance bases at the north end of San Francisco International Airport. American Airlines, the second place carrier at SFO, accounts for seven per cent of total operations and also has maintenance operations here.

The birth of SFO

The earliest aircraft to operate within San Francisco, around 1908, did so where they could find a level and unobstructed space; however, that was more easily said than done. San Francisco's topography is defined by its legendary hills and valleys, meaning level spaces are few, and the most suitable flying area seemed to be the strip of land adjacent to San Francisco Bay on the city's northern edge. This region, which is just inside the Golden Gate (the bridge of the same name was not completed until 1937), was a straight, level dune area inundated by marshy inlets. There, a landing strip was informally established on what is now the city park known as the Marina Green.

In 1915, the marshes were filled and the dunes in the Marina area were levelled for construction of the grounds for a world's fair celebrating San Francisco's recovery from the 1906 earthquake and the opening of the Panama Canal. The western portion of the dune area that fell within the US Army's Presidio of San Francisco became the fair's Grand Prix racetrack.

Flying exhibitions were an important part of the 1915 Panama Pacific International Exposition, and they featured the likes of the great Lincoln Beachy. Considered by many – including Orville Wright – to have been the greatest aerobat of the era, Beachy was killed in an accident at the fair.

Another highlight at the fair was the offering of airplane rides by a pair of brothers who had built their first aircraft in a loft at the corner of Polk Street and Pacific Avenue in San Francisco. After the fair, Al and Mal Loughead started an aircraft company that took as its name the phonetic pronunciation of their surname – Lockheed.

When the fair concluded, the US Army converted the Grand Prix racetrack into a military airfield, naming it for Army pilot Major Dana Crissy. For a few years starting in 1921, 5,000-ft (1524-m) Crissy Field became San Francisco's *de facto* airport, serving the Army as well as early air mail flights. It acted as a stopping point for the historic 1924 round-the-world flight of the Army's Douglas World Cruisers, but remained as a first-line field only until 1936. Although most of Crissy Field was turned back into marshland in the 1990s, there are still US Coast Guard helicopter operations there.

Meanwhile, many people within San Francisco had perceived the need for a perma-

Left: San Francisco airport as it looked circa 1940. A Lockheed Electra is about to pull up to the departure gate in front of the airport terminal for one of about 20 daily passenger services at that time. The US entry into World War II a year later would drastically reverse the airport's rapid expansion of services and passenger numbers.

Below: The Spanish Revival-style main terminal building was completed in October 1937 and would remain the airport's most prominent edifice until the opening of the radical new Central Terminal in 1954.

nent airport to serve the long-term needs of the city. Air travel grew in the 1920s the way the Internet grew in the 1990s – from an obscure novelty into an integral part of the way that people communicated. The tide of enthusiasm for making San Francisco a major airline hub was high. It must be noted that this civic pride arose against the backdrop of rival city Oakland's eager pursuit of airport development.

By 1926, with longer-range aircraft needing longer runways, San Francisco had outgrown the expansion potential of a civilian airport at that location. In November of that year, voters authorised the city government to find a suitable site outside the city limits. Most of the potential airport sites under consideration were located in northern San Mateo County. They were within 20 miles (32 km) of San Francisco, and most were within a 5-mile (8-km) radius of one another.

At last, a location was picked. It was a portion of the estate of California pioneer – and Gold Rush multi-millionaire – Darius Mills. Located between the Bayshore Highway and San Francisco Bay, the site was leased by the city for $US15,000 (10 times that in current dollars) annually.

Above: Typifying the rivalry between San Francisco and Oakland airports, Pacific Southwest Airlines commenced operations in May 1949 with a leased DC-3 flying from Oakland to San Diego. By the time this photograph was taken in 1952, the airline had been enticed to move its main operations to SFO and its fleet had grown to four DC-3s.

Right: By the early 1950s, United had established itself as the airport's dominant carrier and had replaced the majority of its DC-3s with DC-6s. The airline had also centralised its maintenance at the airport, having built a new high-tech 'push-button' facility, from which a DC-6 is seen emerging here.

Known as Mills Field, San Francisco's airport officially opened on 7 May 1927, just three weeks before Charles Lindbergh made the historic transatlantic flight that did so much to promote aviation in the United States. There were three runways, ranging from 1,850 to 5,770 ft (564 to 1759 m) in length. The airport's first superintendent, San Francisco native Frank Flynn, oversaw construction of the first hangar four months later, and in October 1927 a Boeing Model 40 – operated by Boeing Air Transport – began routine operations at the airport

The early years at SFO

Since the 19th century, relations between San Francisco and Oakland had been characterised by a rivalry – often congenial, occasionally nasty. During the late 1920s, this rivalry was most prominent with regard to the cities' respective airports. San Francisco Airport and its East Bay counterpart were like aggressive suitors in their attempts to woo the affections of the airlines of the day. In 1927, San Francisco became host not only to BAT but to the likes of Western Air Express (which eventually became Western Air Lines), only to lose them to Oakland – and, later, vice versa. San Francisco's airport was closest to the major centre of population, but Oakland's airport was less liable to be fogged in. As instrument flying became more advanced, this advantage at Oakland lessened in importance.

While the two cities flirted with his airline, Bill Boeing established his Boeing School of Aeronautics in Oakland. Although BAT abandoned San Francisco for a time, United Air Lines eventually returned to become San Francisco's largest tenant.

Another problem that dogged San Francisco Airport's ability to lure airline tenants in the early days was lack of space. Its proximity to San Francisco Bay's swamps and mudholes made expansion difficult. In 1928, a bond issue for airport improvements failed to get the required two-thirds majority, as did a similar bond issue in 1930.

Meanwhile, however, the city had concluded the deal with the Mills family for the outright purchase – for $US105,000 annually over a decade – of Mills Field. In 1931, the name officially was changed from Mills Field to San Francisco Airport, although 'Mills Field' was used informally until after World War II.

The Great Depression of the 1930s brought a slump in activity at San Francisco Airport. By 1932, the only airline still serving the airport was Century Pacific, a company that soon vanished into oblivion. A major player in saving the airport from a similar fate was Bernard Doolin,

Boeing Air Transport and United Air Lines

Boeing Air Transport was created as part of William Edward Boeing's desire to expand – from his base in aircraft manufacturing – into the airline business. In the 1920s, an integral part of operating airlines, especially in the American West, was to anchor them financially to lucrative air mail contracts. Bill Boeing's first order of business had been to create an aircraft that would allow him to win Contract Air Mail Route CAM-18, which connected San Francisco to Chicago.

Boeing's Model 40, the first Boeing aircraft mass produced as a commercial airliner, made its first flight on 20 May 1927, the month that San Francisco Airport opened. It was designed primarily for mail, but passenger seats were added in a section of the forward fuselage.

Having won the contract, Boeing created his airline. Boeing Air Transport (BAT) was to be a sister company to his aircraft manufacturing company. Eventually, BAT evolved into one the world's leading airlines, and the largest tenant at San Francisco Airport for most of its history – United Air Lines.

In 1928, Boeing acquired Pacific Air Transport (PAT), which had a north-south route between Seattle and Los Angeles via San Francisco. In October of that year, the Boeing Airplane & Transport Corporation (BATC) was incorporated as a holding company for BAT and PAT, as well as the Boeing Airplane Company.

Early in 1929, BATC became the United Aircraft & Transport Corporation (UATC) and acquired several new subsidiaries, including Pratt & Whitney, Hamilton Standard Propeller Company and the Chance Vought Corporation. In March 1930, UATC bought National Air Transport (NAT), an airline serving points from New York to Texas, whose route structure intersected BAT's at Chicago. A year later, United Air Lines was created as a management corporation to co-ordinate the operations of all of UATC's airline subsidiaries; it became an operating company in May 1934.

Meanwhile, industry irregularities had led President Franklin D. Roosevelt to cancel all commercial air mail contracts in February 1934 and have the air mail flown by the US Army Air Corps. The Air Corps proved to be ill-equipped for the task – especially in the dead of winter – and the experiment ended after just four months. Air mail contracts were put out to bid again in June, but big changes were afoot.

Passed on 12 June, the Air Mail Act of 1934 authorised bidding on new air mail contracts, but it forbade a single company from owning both airlines and/or aircraft manufacturing companies. As a result, UATC had to be dissolved. The airlines were spun off under the umbrella of the United Air Lines Transport Corporation (UALTC), doing business as United Air Lines. These entities were separated from the Boeing Airplane Company.

Displeased with this turn of events, company founder Bill Boeing permanently left the company that bore his name.

TransWorld Airline's flagship Constellations held a decisive speed advantage over United on the prestigious San Francisco-New York route until the introduction of the DC-6 (below over SFO) in 1947, which enabled coast to coast services in 10 hours.

Above: L-188C Electra N171PS was the first of the type to serve with PSA, entering scheduled service from San Francisco in June 1959. The aircraft was later converted into a freighter and now serves with UK-based Channel Express as G-CEXS.

Far right: There were other reasons for flying with PSA in the 1960s other than the cheap air fares. Attractive stewardesses were just part of the airline's 'glamour offensive'.

Below: N376PS was the last of the original six Electras to enter service with PSA. The aircraft is seen here at SFO with its outer starboard engine running as the last of the passengers dash up the steps.

Above: PSA's Electra 'Jets' offered rapid transport between west coast cities at low prices, as proclaimed by this roadside billboard.

Lockheed Electra – the 'PSA Jet'

In 1959 PSA introduced the Lockheed L-188 Electra into service, marketed as the 'PSA Jet'. Linking the west coast population centres of San Francisco, Los Angeles, San Diego and Oakland, the 98-seat Electra proved ideal for the airline's short-haul route network. The early 1960s saw PSA's fleet of L-188s grow to six and, as a forerunner to today's low-cost operators, fast turnaround times (particularly at SFO) combined with low fares produced healthy profits.

By the end of the decade PSA's Electras had disappeared from SFO's ramp, only to reappear again in the mid-1970s when the fuel crisis forced the airline to ground its Lockheed TriStars as a cost-saving measure. From 1978-79 the Electra was reinstated again to serve the SFO-Lake Tahoe route which was unsuitable for the Boeing 727.

who took over as airport superintendent in 1932.

In the depths of the Depression, Doolin managed to attract several important airlines to begin service into the airport. They included Transcontinental & Western Air (TWA), which later became TransWorld Airlines, as well as Walter Varney's Varney Speed Lines, which ultimately evolved into Continental Airlines. He also was responsible for getting United Air Lines back to stay.

During Doolin's 18-year tenure, San Francisco emerged as the West Coast's busiest airport, eclipsing not only rival Oakland, but Los Angeles as well. In addition to airline operations, he made space available at the airport for private pilots and related businesses. Aviation pioneer Lloyd Stearman even briefly operated a small aircraft factory on airport grounds.

In 1933, Doolin successfully convinced San Francisco voters to finally support a bond measure to expand and improve the airport. The work eventually included 300 acres (120 hectares) of bay fill, a 9,000-ft (2743-m) sea wall, and extension of the shorter runways to 3,000 ft (915 m) and the longer runway to 4,650 ft (1417 m). A new main terminal building for the airport was constructed, funded by the Works Progress Administration, an agency of the federal government that had been created during the Depression to achieve higher employment through public works projects. Designed in the Spanish Revival style that was fashionable in California during the period, the new building officially opened on 24 October 1937, and remained the centrepiece of the airport for nearly two decades.

At the same time that Doolin was expanding the Mills Field property, the airport boss was envisioning a second San Francisco Airport. Voters had approved a plan to create a 400-acre (162-hectare) man-made island in San Francisco Bay immediately north of Yerba Buena Island. The new island would be known by the fanciful name of Treasure Island, and would be the site of the 1939-40 San Francisco World's Fair, designated as the Golden Gate International Exposition. Yerba Buena, meanwhile, was used to anchor the mid-point of the San Francisco-Oakland Bay Bridge, which opened in 1936.

Treasure Island proved to be too small for a viable airport, but it did house – and still houses – San Francisco's first international airport terminal, the Pan American flying-boat terminal.

SFO airport in 1962 with the counter-clockwise roadway loop (and central parking lot) visible and the central terminal at its head. To the left is United's Concourse B including the unique 'spoke and pinwheel'. In the foreground, construction of the new south terminal is well under way, eventually opening in September 1963. Among the aircraft visible on the ramp are a Pan Am Boeing 707-321, two Constellations, an Electra, two Convair 340s, an F-27 Friendship and three DC-7s.

Above: Despite competing for custom for the majority of their histories, San Francisco and Oakland were linked by SF-O Helicopter Airlines in the 1960s, using passenger-equipped Sikorsky S-62s. Here a group of passengers at San Francisco airport transfer from their PSA Electra to an SF-O S-62 for the final short hop to their destination of Oakland.

Right: In the late 1950s and early 1960s an extensive runway lengthening programme was implemented. More and more of the bay was reclaimed, including the extension to Runway 10R/28L clearly visible here. The 10R/28L and 10L/28R would be extended again a decade later.

Pan American Airways was already flying the Pacific with its Martin M-130 and Sikorsky S-42 flying-boats, using Alameda, near Oakland, as its West Coast base. In 1937, Doolin managed to lure the airline to Treasure Island. Pan American built its imposing, sandstone-coloured terminal, added the huge Boeing Model 314 flying-boats to the fleet and made Treasure Island the jewel of its Pacific crown. Had it not been for World War II, this service might have continued indefinitely.

By 1940, it was beginning to seem that the American economy was pulling out of the Depression. There was a world war in Europe, but for most Americans this was a distant event. Originally envisioned to last just a year, the Golden Gate International Exposition continued into a second and turned out to be more successful than expected. So, too, was America's simultaneous second 1939 World's Fair in New York City. Leisure travel in the United States had increased to a greater level than could have been foreseen in the mid-1930s. Travel agents suggested that people take in "both fairs", and they did – many by air. Annual passenger traffic at San Francisco Airport was up to 127,000 in 1940, with nearly 50 take-offs or landings every day. United Air Lines began construction of its enormous maintenance base, which was to be located about a mile north of the terminal.

However, on 7 December 1941, the distant war came to the United States.

World War II led to a precipitous decline in commercial operations at all American airports – although military operations at civilian airports, primarily USAAF Air Transport Command flights, increased rapidly. Air defence fighter operations – mainly with Lockheed P-38s – were conducted at San Francisco Airport, although most USAAF interceptors were based at Hamilton Field, across the bay to the north of San Francisco in Marin County.

In 1941, the US Navy had taken over Treasure Island as a wartime emergency base. San Francisco still owned the island, so the Navy soon approached the city government about an outright purchase. The result of the negotiations was that, in exchange for the US Navy getting title to the island, the federal government would invest $US10 million ($US105 million in today's dollars) in San Francisco Airport.

The Navy got a seaplane base, Pan American moved its operations to the San Francisco Airport at Mills Field, and San Francisco became a one-airport city.

After World War II, Pan American expanded its operations and opened a large maintenance facility at San Francisco Airport. For nearly half a century, until its demise in 1991, Pan American was second only to United Air Lines as San Francisco International Airport's most important tenant.

The era of expansion

When the war ended, San Francisco Airport underwent another round of expansion. Voters approved a $US20 million airport bond measure in November 1945, and a $US10 million issue in

Left: As the 1950s came to an end San Francisco saw the operations of a wide range of aircraft as propliners were gradually replaced by turboprops and the new generation of jetliners. The contrast is well illustrated here with a Pan Am Boeing 707 sharing apron space with a DC-3. Other aircraft are two Convair 340s, an F-27 and a Constellation. The large building in the top right of the image is United's maintenance facility (see below).

Below: The Douglas DC-7's days in United Air Lines service were numbered at the time this photograph was taken in 1964. Two examples are seen here sharing ramp space outside United's maintenance/storage facility with three Boeing 727-22s (introduced a year earlier) and six Douglas DC-8s.

complete and scheduled within a year. As with BART, Air Train had been on the agenda for a 2001 beginning of service, but this was subsequently rescheduled for the latter half of 2002.

SFO airline operations in 2002

The New International Terminal that officially opened in December 2000 gave San Francisco International Airport a total of four terminals. This figure includes Terminal 2, the Central Terminal, which was taken out of service in 2000 pending its conversion from international to domestic airline use. With 11 gates grouped into what had been Boarding Area D, it remained closed and unused during 2002.

Today, Terminal 1, the South Terminal, contains 43 gates numbered between 1 and 48 that are grouped into Boarding Areas A, B and C. Although changes are ongoing, as of early 2002, Terminal 1 served America West, Continental Airlines, Delta Air Lines, Frontier Airlines, Hawaiian Airlines, US Airways, Vanguard and Air Canada, as well as the domestic operations of Alaska Airlines and Northwest Airlines.

Terminal 3, the North Terminal, has 31 gates grouped into Boarding Areas E and F. Gates 72 through 90 in Boarding Area F (most of them on the old Concourse 2) are the centrepiece of United Air Lines operations. American Airlines and its TransWorld Airlines (TWA) subsidiary use gates 60 through 71 in the Terminal E area.

The New International Terminal contains two boarding areas, International Area A and Area G. The former includes gates A1 though A12, and the latter has gates G91 through G102. In 2002, Boarding Area A serves such European carriers as Air France, British Airways, Virgin Atlantic, and the national flag carrier of the Netherlands, Koninklijke Luchtvaart Maatschappij (KLM, Royal Dutch Airlines). Also in Area A are the Mexico connections of Alaska Airlines and the international operations of Northwest Airlines, as well as those of the charter carrier Suntrips.

San Francisco International Airport is one of North America's key gateways to the Far East. Among the Asian carriers in Area A are Asiana, Cathay Pacific, China Air, Japan Airlines, Korean Air and Philippine Airlines. It is worth noting that Daly City, which is closer to SFO than San Francisco itself, is the largest ethnically Filipino city in the world outside the Philippines. Until 2002, when United States citizenship was mandated, a significant number of the security personnel at San Francisco International Airport were Philippine citizens.

In the New International Terminal's Boarding Area G are the international operations of United Air Lines, as well as Latin American carriers Mexicana and Transportes Aéreos Centroamericanos (TACA). Aeroflot and Lufthansa are the European airlines based in Boarding Area G, and the Asian carriers comprise Air China, All Nippon Airways, Eva Airways and Singapore Airlines.

Total passenger traffic at SFO was 40.1 million in 1998, 40.4 million in 1999, and 41.1 million in 2000. Because of the recession and the precipitous drop in airline operations after 11 September 2001, the number of passengers using the airport dropped to just 35 million in 2001.

In terms of cargo traffic, San Francisco International Airport ranks 13th among United States airports and 22nd in the world. However, in dollar value of imports and exports, SFO is the second largest American gateway after New York's John F. Kennedy International Airport.

Connections to and from Los Angeles area airports account for 14 percent of the passenger travel passing through San Francisco International Airport. This has been generally true for most of the airport's history. New York City connections are second, with a 10 percent share. As of the turn of the century, SFO boasted about 530 daily domestic non-stop flights and 87 daily international non-stops. Among the international flights, 40 percent were connections to Asia, 30 percent were to Europe and 11 per cent were to Mexico.

Bill Yenne

Accounting for some 47 per cent of the total market, United Airlines remains by far the most important carrier at SFO (the next biggest being American Airlines with 7.7 per cent). United's operations are conducted from Terminal 3, including United Shuttle – a low-cost domestic market division operating a fleet of Boeing 737-300s and -500s (above).

Airlines operating at SFO

New International Terminal

Gates A1-A12
Air France
Alaska Airlines (Mex. only)
Asiana
British Airways
Cathay Pacific
Japan Air Lines
KLM
Korean Air
Northwest (Int'l only)
Philippine Airlines
Suntrips (charter flights)
Virgin Atlantic

Gates G91-G102
Aeroflot
Air China
Alitalia
All Nippon Airways
Eva Air
LACSA
Lufthansa
Mexicana
Singapore Airlines
TACA
United Airlines (Int'l only)

Terminal 1

Gates 1-48
Air Canada
Alaska Airlines
America West Airlines
American Trans Air
Continental Airlines
Delta Airlines
Frontier Airlines
Hawaiian Airlines
Horizon Air
Midwest Express Airlines
National Airlines
Northwest (domestic only)
Sun Country Airlines
US Airways
Vanguard Airlines

Terminal 2

Gates 50-59
Taken out of service in 2000 pending conversion from international to domestic airline use

Terminal 3

Gates 60-90
American Airlines
United Airlines (domestic)
United Express
United Shuttle

Cargo operators

Air China Cargo
Atlas Air
Cargolux
China Airlines Cargo
DHL
Eva Air Cargo
Evergreen International
Federal Express
Gemini Air Cargo
Japan Air Lines Cargo
Korean Air Cargo
Lufthansa Cargo
Nippon Cargo Airlines
Northwest Cargo
Polar Air Cargo
Singapore Airlines Cargo
US Postal Service

A British Airways Boeing 747-436, Philippines Airlines A340-313(X) and a Virgin Atlantic Boeing 747-400 prepare to receive their next complement of passengers at the Boarding Area A of the new International Terminal in March 2002. A total of 28 airlines offers non-stop international services to 31 cities, the majority of which are to Asia (50 per cent) and Europe (35 per cent).

Regional Jet phenomenon

The RJ's climb to prominence

In the 1980s sales of commercial aircraft in the 20- to 75-seat class were dominated by well established turboprop aircraft. A decade later the market had been completely transformed by the arrival of a new generation of 'mini' jet airliners. Dubbed 'Regional Jets' by the company that started the revolution – Canadair – sales figures far exceeded the most optimistic predictions, and it remains today the fastest growing sector in commercial aircraft production.

*It was Canadian manufacturer **Canadair** (part of **Bombardier**) that began the **RJ** revolution in **1991** with the unveiling of its **CL-600-2B19 (CRJ100)**, based on its successful **Challenger** biz jet. Basing the aircraft on an existing design allowed design and development time to be kept to a minimum. By **1995 Embraer** was beginning to 'steal' **RJ** sales with its new **ERJ-145** and, to protect its position as market-leader, **Bombardier** released the improved **CRJ200** (above). This remains the highest-selling **RJ** variant to date, with sales approaching **700**.*

The definition of the term 'regional jet', or RJ, has proved difficult. Interviews with airlines and organisations involved in this sector of the airline industry have muddied the waters by widening the parameters rather than reducing them to a cohesive and understandable sector.

The definition in its simplest form is a jet-powered airliner with no more than 100 seats and a single aisle, operated on scheduled services. The aircraft's range does not seem relevant, nor does the number of engines that power it. The very word 'regional 'conjures up the image of a short-range aircraft, but today's aircraft can fly legs of up to 2,000 miles (3218 km). Operations within Europe are therefore international flights operated by medium-haul feeder-liners.

The early 50-seaters with a range of 1,000 miles (1610 km), as produced by Bombardier at the beginning of the 1990s, started the revolution. Today, the families of these original regional jets have grown to accommodate 70 to 110 passengers. The famous Bill Lear, upon seeing the fuselage diameter of the original Canadair 600 Challenger corporate jet, nicknamed it 'Fat Albert'. That large-diameter fuselage was the key to the future regional jet, because it could be extended to make a small airliner. It was predicted that the RJ could not only take a size-able percentage of the then healthy regional turboprop market, but also create new markets where none had existed before.

Currently, the regional jet market is the fastest growing sector in the entire airline industry. However, even this market has been reassessed in the post-11 September 2001 climate, with Fairchild Dornier becoming the first high-profile casualty of the downturn in orders.

*As revenue poured into both **Bombardier** and **Embraer** coffers from massive orders in the mid-1990s for their **50-seat RJs**, both companies looked to further expand the burgeoning **RJ** market into the **75-seat** aircraft class and beyond. **Bombardier** adopted the 'further stretch' option, allowing the relatively rapid and trouble-free development of its **CRJ700** (above), and ultimately, **CRJ900** variants, both of which are now in service.*

Brazilian manufacturer Embraer had achieved notable success in the lucrative US commuter airliner market in the 1970s and 1980s with its EMB-110 Bandeirante and EMB-120 Brasilia turboprops. With Bombardier beginning to transform the sector with its CRJ100 in the early 1990s, the company gambled on the RJ's continued growth and designed its own RJ – the ERJ-145 (above). Its success led to the development of the ERJ-135 'shrink' (left with ERJ-145) for the sub-40-seat market.

The term 'regional jet' was first coined in 1987 by Bombardier/Canadair with the announcement of the go-ahead for the design and development of what they termed 'a regional jetliner'. In August 1986 Bombardier Inc. had purchased the cash-starved Canadair company from the Canadian government (Canada Development Investment Corp.) for $120 million. In October of the same year, Aviation Planning Services (APS) of Montreal was contracted by Bombardier/Canadair to assess the potential for a 48/50-seat jet aircraft.

The results of the Bombardier/Canadair/APS survey indicated that there was probably a significant market for such a jet, provided it could match the turboprop economics for a similar-sized aircraft above approximately 250 miles (402 km), and have an initial range of about 1,000 miles (1610 km) with full payload. In-depth discussions with more than 130 airlines were completed by September 1987 and they forecasted that between 400 and 500 of these aircraft would be required by 2001, a prediction that turned out to be pessimistic. Encouraged by these predictions, the basic design configuration was frozen in 1988. Consequently, the CRJ100 was borne, and the first aircraft's maiden flight was made on 10 May 1991. This was to be the beginning of the modern regional jet saga.

Challenger origins

The proposed design was based on a lengthened version of the Canadair Challenger corporate jet (which first flew in 1978). This, according to the company, saved about 25 per cent of the projected $1 billion development costs of a totally new design. A lengthened fuselage derivative was a logical step; coupled with the new generation of economical turbofans, suddenly this size of 'mini' jet airliner made sense, despite the reservations of some aviation sceptics. It was designated the 'Regional Jet' programme.

Bombardier's designers then had to incorporate solutions for a much higher utilisation rate than that of the aircraft's corporate cousin, the Canadair Challenger. Corporate aircraft can log as little as a few hundred hours per year, whereas a short-haul RJ can accumulate the same hours in a month. (However, some early Challengers were operated – and still are – like regional jets in an 18-seat shuttle configuration by operators such as Xerox and Federal Express between their various company bases.) The RJ's undercarriage also had to be able to cope with the punishment of six or eight landings per day compared to a long-haul Challenger jet's possible one landing per day, followed by several non-flying days.

The maximum take-off weight of the original CRJ100 series was only 3,000 lb (1360 kg) more than the corporate Challenger 601-3A. The major change was in the exchange of fuel load in the Challenger for increased structural weight and payload in the RJ. Given that the aircraft was stretched nearly 20 ft (6 m), the weight increase was minimal. To meet FAA FAR25, Part 121 5,000-ft (1524-m) field lengths, significant changes were made to the basic wing. Flaps and ailerons were increased in chord and spoilerons were added, plus an additional ground spoiler.

Deregulation fires market

Deregulation of US airlines started in 1978, followed by Canadian operators in the mid-1980s and European liberalisation in the mid-1990s. The cumulative worldwide regional jet market expanded dramatically with demand from small enlightened setups and directives from the major airlines to their feeders. This resulted in a

Above: The success or failure of Bombardier's Regional Jet programme depended largely on orders from the lucrative US commuter market. Delta Air Lines subsidiary Comair took the plunge and eventually received 110 CRJ100s, becoming the largest operator of the first RJ variant.

Below: The 'small jet airliner' market had been in a state of stagnation before the emergence of the RJ. Companies such as BAe, with its 146/RJ series (background), had achieved some success with airlines such as Jersey European, although it too ordered CRJ200s (foreground) as RJ sales in Europe steadily rose.

In a scene typical across the US in the mid-1990s, Comair's CRJ100s share a ramp with turboprop commuter types (including EMB-120 Brasilias and Saab 340s). Within five years the turboprops had been largely and, in some inventories, completely replaced by regional jets. In a mirror image of the large airliner market, dominated by Boeing and Airbus, Bombardier and Embraer battle directly against each other for every RJ order.

Above: The RJ revolution really took hold in North America in the mid-1990s, with significant orders from Europe soon following. Sales in Asia have so far been less impressive, but are showing signs of increasing. Japanese carrier Fair initially took the first of two second-hand CRJ100s in 2000 (above) before receiving two further new CRJ200s in 2002/03. It is, however, in China where significant orders are most likely, although Embraer and Bombardier may soon be competing directly with the indigenously-designed ARJ21.

Right: The CRJ family is designed with a common modern 'glass' cockpit and avionics fit, allowing the aircraft to be operated in all-weathers and cross-operation of variants by pilots. The instrument panel is dominated by the Collins Pro Line 4 six-tube EFIS and a two-screen EICAS. Other avionics include dual attitude heading and reference systems (AHRS), TCASII traffic alert and collision avoidance system, and a Collins digital weather radar.

multitude of regional jet orders.

Bombardier believed from the outset (and rightly so) that with the advent of newer and faster computer reservation systems, code-sharing by major airlines with commuter/regional carriers and their partial or complete ownership of these carriers, the RJs could provide a jet-to-jet seamless passenger service. The RJs also offered the possibility of operations between smaller communities over longer distances, thereby bypassing congested hubs – although most current RJ operations are hub feeders rather than hub raiders.

Embraer entrance

It seems incredible now that it was only in 1995 that Embraer entered the fray and gave Bombardier serious competition for the first time, which it has maintained to this day. The innovative Brazilians revealed their regional jet plans in 1989, but it was not until October 1994 that assembly started on their 50-seat Embraer EMB-145 prototype. The first flight occurred in 1995 and first delivery was in December 1996. The aircraft is now offered in extended-range (ER), long-range (LR) and extra long-range (XR) versions, as well as spawning a family of sub-variants including the ERJ-140 for the scope clause-affected US market and the ERJ-135 'shrink'. By the time the ERJ-145 was entering service in 1996, Bombardier had already established itself as market leader, having delivered its first CRJ100 to Lufthansa CityLine in 1992, giving it a four-year lead over the Brazilians.

Turboprop tragedies

Further cementing the importance of regional jets versus regional turboprops, in 1993/94 there were a number of tragic US turboprop scheduled airliner accidents, culminating in the American Eagle ATR 72-212 at Roselawn, Indiana, on 31 October 1994 that killed all 68 aboard; the cause was determined to be icing. Two months later (on 13 December) an American Eagle BAe Jetstream crashed, killing 15; according to the NTSB, this was due to pilot error. More recently, on 9 January 1997, a Comair EMB-120RT crashed in Monroe, Missouri, killing 29; again, icing was held to be the cause.

The perception of the American public – and of some non-aviation media – was that turboprops were suddenly unsafe. The authorities found that in the pilot error cases, most pilots were either young and low-houred, and/or were asked to fly into airports without precision approaches. Despite these findings, regional turboprops picked up a reputation of not being as

Left: The similarity of the CL-600-2B19 (as the RJ100/200 is designated) to the CL-600 Challenger is clearly evident. The wide-diameter cabin, which was then a first for corporate aircraft of the Challenger's size, was perfectly suited for reconfiguration to a 2+2 passenger seating arrangement.

Customers of the CRJ200 include Salt Lake City-based Skywest Airlines, which operates services for both Delta Connection and United Express (below), and Adria Airways of Slovenia which operates four examples (below left) on European routes, alongside three Airbus A320s.

safe as jets, and as a result RJ sales boomed again. Also in the mid-1990s, regional jets were considered cheap by the growing major airlines. The product was definitely in the right place at the right time.

It must be remembered that the early twin-turboprop commuter aircraft featured improved speed and safety compared to their twin and multi piston-engined forebears. However, the replacement of turboprops by regional jets has been dramatic: in 1996 Continental Express operated an all-turboprop fleet, but by 2001 such aircraft accounted for just 16 per cent of the fleet. Bombardier has recently delivered its 700th CRJ100/200, and Embraer, which delivered its first ERJ-145 in 1996, has delivered more than 600 to date.

Despite the debate over RJs versus turboprops, the belief within the industry is that current/future turboprops will continue to hold their place, albeit with smaller fleets. Delta Connection President Fred Buttrell said recently, "We believe that an all (regional) jet fleet would be a mistake." The airline operates ATR 72s and Embraer EMB-120s, and Buttrell is convinced that when replacement falls due it will be with newer ATR 72-500s or Bombardier Q400 turboprops.

'Mini' regional jets

With Bombardier not having produced an RJ variant for the 20/39-seat market, competition for orders is currently between Embraer's 37-seat ERJ-135 and Fairchild Dornier's 328JET. The latter evolved from the twin-turboprop Dornier Do 328 which entered service with Air Engiadina in October 1993. In the late 1990s Fairchild Dornier planned a range of RJs encompassing all current and predicted capacities. The 32-seat 328JET was, however, destined to be the only model to enter service. The 40/43-seat 428JET was cancelled in 2000, incurring heavy financial penalties from customers which had ordered the variant. With costs of the 728/928 project mounting, the 55-seat 528JET was also put on the back-burner as development funds became scarce. The 728 family finally succumbed in 2002, leaving the 328JET as the sole revenue-earner. Entering production in 1998, and despite the worsening financial position at Fairchild Dornier, the 328JET has sold well and achieved a number of notable orders, including China's Hainan Airlines and Atlantic Coast Airlines in the USA. Unfortunately the company's 2002 insolvency affected a number of orders and options, with customers looking elsewhere as continued delivery could not be guaranteed. This played perfectly into the hands of Embraer, which had began production of its 37-seat ERJ-135 in 1999. Orders for the ERJ-135 now stand at over 120 with both American Eagle and Continental Express placing orders in large numbers.

Present and future RJs

Until around late 2000, regional jets carried up to 50 passengers. Now, 70-seaters are becoming more common on both sides of the Atlantic and 90-seaters are beginning to enter service.

Fairchild Dornier joined the battle for the large regional jet market on 21 March 2002 when its 728JET was rolled out. However, less than two weeks later, the Munich-based company, which had been actively trying to find a new strategic partner, filed for protection against its creditors. In a bid to keep Fairchild

'Regional Jets' of the past?

BAC One-Eleven
The BAC One-Eleven Series 475 could carry up to 89 passengers and had a range of 1,997 nm (3700 km). The Series 400/500 development aircraft was converted as a prototype and flew for the first time on 27 August 1970.

BAe 146
First flying on 3 September 1981, the BAe 146 was built in three versions; -100 seating 71/93 passengers, -200 seating 82/109 and the -300 seating up to 120. It boasted good short-field performance and low-noise, and is the only four-engined aircraft in the category.

Douglas DC-9
Douglas's DC-9 Series 11, Series 15 and DC-9 Series 20 were undoubtedly the predecessors of the modern RJ. Powered by two turbofan engines, the aircraft had maximum seating for 90 passengers and were utilised on thinner regional services.

Fokker 70/100
The Fokker 70 first flew on 2 April 1993 and was configured with 70-79 seats. It was a shortened version of the earlier Fokker 100 which could carry 97-109 passengers and entered service in 1987. Fokker went bankrupt in 1995.

Fokker F28 Fellowship
The prototype F28 Fellowship first flew on 9 May 1967. The Mk 1000/3000 version could be configured to carry from 50/65 passengers, while the Mk 2000/6000 extended-fuselage version could carry up to 79/85. Sales were reasonable and a number are still flying in airline service.

VFW-Fokker VFW 614
The first of three prototype VFW 614 twin jets was rolled out on 1 August 1968 but did not fly until July 1971. The 40-44 seat aircraft came within the category of a twin-turbofan short-haul transport before the term 'RJ' was thought of, and was powered by a pair of Rolls-Royce/Snecma M45H turbofans mounted above the wings.

Yakovlev Yak-40
The oldest and so far smallest regional jet produced is the tri-engined 27-seat Yak-40. It was the first of the true regional jets to enter service, following a first flight on 21 May 1966. 1,136 of these rugged mini-airliners were produced in the Soviet Union and it was the most successful RJ pre-1990.

***Right:* Continental Express is by far the most significant customer for Embraer's ERJ-145. The airline has firm orders for an incredible 245 examples, which is by far the largest inventory of an RJ variant operated by a single airline. The airline also operates 35 ERJ-135s .**

***Below:* Although entering the market some four years after Bombardier's CRJ100/200 series, the Embraer ERJ-145 family market share is close to parity with its Canadian rival. They are powered by versions of the Rolls-Royce AE3007 turbofan.**

Dornier operating, the German Federal Government and the Regional Government of Bavaria partly guaranteed payments by a group of German banks to keep the company viable until a buyer/strategic partner was found. However, despite approaches to Bombardier, a Russian consortium and various other interested parties, the future of the 75-seat Fairchild Dornier 728JET and its 95-seat 928JET big brother are increasingly in doubt. Ironically, the 728JET was likely to take the RJ revolution a stage further. With state-of-the-art construction techniques and a unique (among RJ manufacturers) 3+2 seating arrangement, the 728JET was regarded by many observers as the finest of the new-generation RJs. The cost of its development, however, combined with the global turndown, pushed the company well into the red. This apparently failed attempt to compete with Bombardier and Embraer may result in the 728JET being labelled as the only airliner designed and built in prototype form to airworthy condition, yet to never take to the air. At the time of Fairchild Dornier's collapse the 728JET had already received around 179 orders/options, many of which have now switched to alternate aircraft.

328JET survives

In contrast it appears that Fairchild Dornier's 32-seat 328JET RJ may well be saved. In March 2003 AvCraft Aviation, based in Leesburg, Virginia, acquired the rights and facilities to produce both the 328JET and its turboprop predecessor – the 328. Priced at $11.5 million in standard airline configuration, the company intends to resume full-scale production over the course of the next year, increasing to up to 50 aircraft per year by 2005.

With Fairchild Dornier having major financial problems, the market for 70/110-seaters is back in the hands of Bombardier and Embraer, offering, respectively, the CRJ700/900 and EMB-170/175/190/195 four-ship family. The lengthened-fuselage CRJ700 is already in service

***Left and below:* Embraer has been active in ensuring it tailors its product range to meet particular markets. The 37-seat ERJ-135 (left) filled a gap between Fairchild Dornier's 328JET and the 50-seat RJs, and has sold well in America where scope clause issues influence aircraft acquisition. Scope clause agreements were also directly responsible for the ERJ-140 (below), which had a seating arrangement for 44 passengers, placing it just below the clause's lower ceiling of 45 seats, thus allowing more airframes to be acquired.**

***Below:* Europe was behind the US in embracing the regional jet but, from 1996, has taken an increasing share of the total production. Embraer's 145 has, in particular, found a number of European customers including Luxair, which ordered nine of what it termed Eurojets. The aircraft are used on longer thin regional services, with Fokker 50s operating shorter routes.**

***Below:* This ERJ-145 was specially painted as the 100th example delivered to Continental Express. The airline is well on its way to becoming an all-jet fleet – a remarkable turnaround from a fleet of over 200 turboprops a decade earlier. The latest Continental deliveries are of the XR variant, allowing more distant USA city-pairs to be linked by non-stop services.**

Above: ***Like all new commercial aircraft designs, Bombardier's CRJ700 was subjected to numerous wind tunnel tests during the design stage. Along with a redesigned wing and stretched fuselage, the CRJ700 incorporated the 13,790-lb (61.3-kN) General Electric CF34-8C1 turbofan engine, replacing the 9,220-lb (41-kN) CF34-3B1 of the earlier CRJ200. Not only more powerful, Bombardier claims the new engines are some nine per cent more fuel-efficient.***

Above and below: ***Once the 50-seat Regional Jet market had been firmly established Bombardier sought to create a 70-seat regional jet to compete directly with the larger turboprop transports and traditional small jet airliners. Stretching the fuselage by 18 ft 10 in (5.74 m) allowed an extra five rows of seats to be incorporated. Lufthansa CityLine, the launch customer for the CRJ700, received the first of 20 examples in May 2001. Its aircraft are configured in a single-class 68-seat arrangement.***

in Europe and the USA, and the even longer 900 series is entering service with launch customer Mesa Airlines.

Embraer decided to start from a clean sheet design, opting for a twin underwing jet configuration, much the same as Fairchild Dornier's 728/928 series. The first EMB-170 flew on 19 February 2002 and the aircraft has successfully completed a large portion of its test programme prior to envisaged certification during 2003. Launch customer is the newly named Swiss airlines (formerly Crossair), which will receive the first four of 15 examples in August 2004. The 170/190 family has 138 orders and 229 options, including recent orders from India's Jet Airways and LOT Polish Airlines.

Airbus Industrie has also seen the potential for this higher end of the regional jet market and its offering, the A318, is the shortest-bodied Airbus derivative so far. In a two-class layout, the aircraft can carry 106 passengers; in single-class configuration, it can carry 117; and in a high-density seating layout, it will accommodate up to 129. Airbus forecasts that there is a requirement for 7,286 aircraft in the 125/175-seat category up to 2018, and 2,124 in the 70/100-seat market. The A318 flew for the first time in January 2002 and first deliveries are scheduled for the third quarter of 2003. Airbus holds around 161 orders plus 57 options for the type.

The Boeing 717-200, currently a 110/120-seater, could also be considered a regional jet. The proposed 717-100, a 90-seat 'shrink', appears to have been put on hold and there is speculation that the programme has been abandoned.

Second-generation RJs

The emerging 70/110-seater regional jets are the second generation of what started off as a battle to design and build an economical 50-seat jet airliner in the early 1990s. These aircraft had a maximum range of just under 1,000 nm (1852 km) but maximum range of the new generation of 70/110-seaters is creeping up to over 2,000 nm (3704 km). The term 'regional jet' may soon no longer be appropriate, as these new aircraft could be recategorised by their old title of 'short/medium-haul jet transport'.

The only realistic alternative to today's RJs is the new generation of Bombardier DHC-8 Q series turboprops, and ATR's 42-500 and 72-500 series. The Saab 2000, although no longer in production, is still very competitive, especially on block time.

Experts from within the industry believe that these modern turboprops are more economical on short-haul segments of up to 350 nm (648 km), while RJs come into their own on sectors longer than 400 nm (740 km). The Dash 8 Q, ATR 500s and Saab 2000 aircraft are virtually as fast as some of the older BAe 146 and BAe RJ series aircraft. With the Avro RJX programme being cancelled in November 2001 due to insufficient orders, we will never know if this aircraft would have been the world-beater that launch customer British European claimed. Perhaps if BAe had invested in its proposed rewinged, twin-engined RJ version, the aircraft might have had wider appeal.

Above: ***Fairchild Dornier achieved a major coup when it secured a deal for 19 328JETs with Chinese carrier Hainan Airlines. The first example entered service in late 1999 and, following the delivery of the subsequent 18, a further order for 21 examples was placed. Long lead items were ordered by the company before the Chinese government blocked the importation of all foreign regional jets. This situation did nothing to help the company's ailing finances and the orders were never fulfilled.***

Right: ***As one of the larger US commuter airlines, Bombardier and Embraer conducted hard-fought campaigns to win orders from American Eagle. The first round in the 70-seat category went to Bombardier with an order for 25 CRJ700s to be delivered between 2002-04.***

Airliners or Regional Jets?

Defining what is, and what is not, a regional jet has become increasingly difficult as the new generation of what their manufacturers define as regional jets impinges on the short/medium-haul jet airliner market dominated by Airbus with its A320 family and Boeing with its Model 737 family. In order to compete with the new 90/110-seat RJs from Embraer and Fairchild Dornier (before their financial collapse), Airbus developed a further 'shrink' of its successful A319, to produce the 106-seat A318 (below). It remains to be seen whether such a scaled-down aircraft can compete directly with the purpose-built RJs, but sales so far have indicated that this battleground between traditional airliner manufacturers Boeing and Airbus, and the RJ manufacturers, is likely to be hotly contested over the next two decades. The rise of the 'larger' RJs has directly affected the sales prospects of Boeing's 717 (above right), and other 'small airliners' such as Antonov's An 74-300 may find the operating economics of the higher-capacity RJs too much to compete with.

In the mid/late 1990s, Bombardier found itself competing with Embraer for RJ orders. From then, every major air show has been enlivened by press conferences from both camps announcing huge RJ orders. For instance, at the 1996 Farnborough air show, Embraer, which had brought its EMB-145 to the show for the first time, announced a $3 billion order from Continental Express for 25 firm orders and 175 options over 12 years. At the Paris air show in 1997, AMR Eagle placed orders with both Embraer and Bombardier for 137 RJs worth $2.4 billion. It ordered 42 EMB-145s plus options on 25, and became the launch customer for the CRJ700 with a firm order for 25 plus 25 options.

The battle for the 70/110-seat RJ market has been well and truly joined. The current regional airline market is split 55 per cent North America, 26 per cent Europe, 8 per cent Asia-Pacific, 6 per cent Latin America, 3 per cent Africa and Middle East, and 2 per cent China.

Regional aircraft sales and deliveries have slowed in the aftermath of 11 September 2001, but those RJs in service became busier because they temporarily replaced larger aircraft normally operated on some routes. Maersk Air in the UK, for instance, used its CRJ700s to the full and temporarily grounded two of its three Boeing 737-500s because of falling passenger figures. Business became tough for the manufacturers, as some regional airlines came close to collapse and did not need brand new aircraft. With other airlines, the decline of the regional turboprops was sometimes accelerated – or, in contrast, they were given a stay of execution, because either the airline could not afford to replace them or their economics were better suited to the present climate.

Long-range RJs

According to statistical analysis, the trend is for regional jets to be flown on longer stage lengths both in North America and Europe. To meet this demand, Embraer developed the ERJ-145XR. The prototype first flew in June 2001, and the first deliveries were made to Express Jet in November 2002. The aircraft differs from the standard ERJ-145 with the addition of winglets to improve longer-range econ-

Are the turboprop's days numbered?

The regional turboprop was the standard acquisition for commuter airlines in the 1980s and early 1990s. Aircraft such as the de Havilland Canada Dash 7 and Dash 8, ATR 42 and 72, Saab 2000, BAe ATP, BAe Jetstream 41 and Embraer EMB-120 Brasilia competed for massive orders, particularly in the USA, where orders could reach in excess of 100 units. The emergence of Canadair's CRJ100 in the early 1990s, combined with a spate of unfortunate accidents, dramatically affected the market, and sales towards the end of the decade declined to the point where many manufacturers considered pulling out of the market. Indeed, Embraer, Saab and BAe no longer produce regional turboprops. However, both ATR and Bombardier have persisted, and recent market research has shown that the new generation of turboprops such as ATR's 42-500 and 72-500 (above and right), along with Bombardier's Q400 development of the Dash 8 (above right), are economically superior to RJs on shorter routes, with both companies insisting that their products are complementary, rather than competitors, to the growing number of regional jets.

Bombardier's ultimate stretch of its CRJ family, the CRJ900, made its maiden flight in prototype form (above) on 21 February 2001. Following an extensive flight test programme the aircraft received Canadian, US FAA and European JAA certification in the second half of 2002, paving the way for the first deliveries in 2003. The CRJ900 retains 94 per cent commonality with the CRJ700 and will be produced in standard, extended-range (ER) and long-range (LR) versions. The CRJ900 has an additional pair of exits over the wings and an extra service door in the fuselage, allowing speedy cleaning and galley replenishment, thereby reducing turnaround times.

Scope clause agreements

Scope clauses exist principally in the USA, and are agreements entered into between pilot unions and major airlines. The clauses are in place with most of the top transcontinental airlines. They enable the unions to control the size of aircraft and the amount of seats that the airline's feeder operators are allowed to have. Scope clauses came into existence because senior pilots with the major airlines were concerned that their junior colleagues with the feeder operators will claim the same pay scales as themselves, if the regional jets they fly reach the size of those flown by some senior pilots of the major airlines.

Currently, feeder pilots are paid considerably less than main airline pilots, even though they may be members of the same union. This allows the pilot unions to dictate to the major employers how many aircraft and of what size their regional fleet will be. It also ensures that senior airline pilots can protect their own jobs and seniority ladder within the major airlines.

As an example, American Eagle's parent company American Airlines was forced to negotiate a delicate balancing act with its deliveries of three or four CRJ700s and ERJ-140s per month against scope clause agreements with the Allied Pilots Association (APA). So far, American Eagle has managed to offset the introduction of its new regional jets by cutting its turboprop fleet, removing seat rows and reducing operations. Unless the APA agrees a new deal with the main carrier, Eagle may be forced to sell some of its 56 ERJ-145s at the end of 2003. By that time, CRJ700 deliveries will have pushed the carrier over the 67-aircraft limit on the number of regional jets larger than the 44 seats allowed under its scope clause agreement. Scope clauses resulted in Embraer building its compromise EMB-140 44-seat regional jet and Bombardier creating the similar-capacity CRJ440 as a way to bypass the restrictions. The slower US sales of RJs with more than 70 seats is largely blamed on scope clause problems.

Scope clauses also operate in Europe between the main airlines and some of their franchise partners, but seem to be less stringent, allowing more 70-seaters to be operated. The upper limit seems to be around 100 seats. For instance, British European operates BAe 146-300s that could seat up to 120 passengers, but when operating these aircraft on behalf of Air France they can only operate them as 100-seaters under the existing scope clause agreement.

Bombardier CRJ900

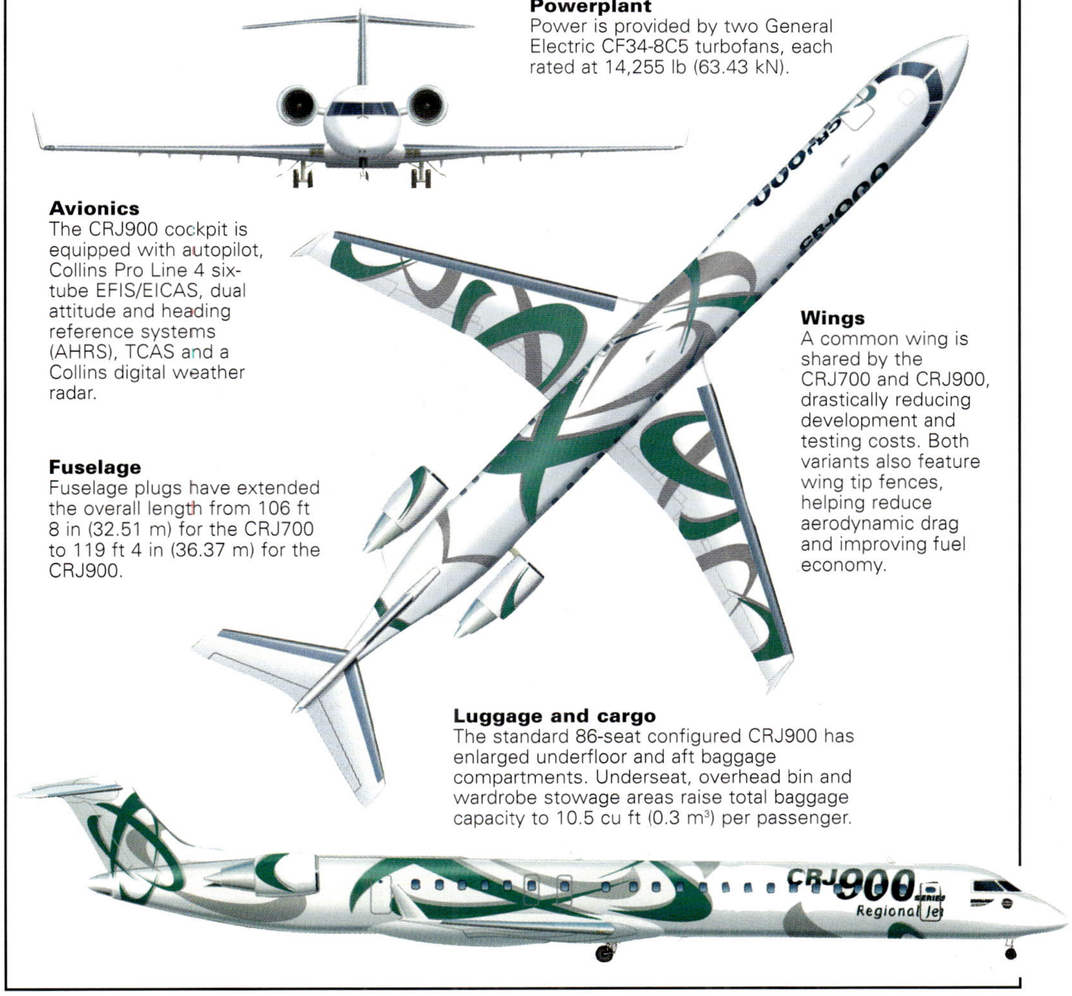

Powerplant
Power is provided by two General Electric CF34-8C5 turbofans, each rated at 14,255 lb (63.43 kN).

Avionics
The CRJ900 cockpit is equipped with autopilot, Collins Pro Line 4 six-tube EFIS/EICAS, dual attitude and heading reference systems (AHRS), TCAS and a Collins digital weather radar.

Wings
A common wing is shared by the CRJ700 and CRJ900, drastically reducing development and testing costs. Both variants also feature wing tip fences, helping reduce aerodynamic drag and improving fuel economy.

Fuselage
Fuselage plugs have extended the overall length from 106 ft 8 in (32.51 m) for the CRJ700 to 119 ft 4 in (36.37 m) for the CRJ900.

Luggage and cargo
The standard 86-seat configured CRJ900 has enlarged underfloor and aft baggage compartments. Underseat, overhead bin and wardrobe stowage areas raise total baggage capacity to 10.5 cu ft (0.3 m³) per passenger.

Embraer has gambled its future success in the regional jet market on its new family of high-capacity RJs. The first to take to the air was the ERJ-170 on 19 February 2002 (below). A total of six pre-series ERJ-170s is being utilised in the intense flight test and certification programme that, despite a number of setbacks, is due to be completed before the end of 2003. With four main doors and no overwing exits, the ERJ-170's configuration gives airlines maximum cabin flexibility, allowing dual-class, single-class or high-density arrangements. As is now vitally important in modern families of airliners, all new variants will be able to be flown on a common type rating, and Embraer also claims 90 per cent parts and systems commonality, helping operators to keep costs to a minimum.

omy, increased thrust 8,110-lb (36.09-kN) AE3007A1E turbofans and an auxiliary fuel tank, giving a maximum range of 2,000 nm (3704 km).

Bombardier, too, has been refining its options for its CRJ200 Series, and now offers a version certified for operations at airports as high as 13,000 ft (3962 m). Following a successful flight test programme at La Paz, Bolivia, the launch customer for this version was announced as China Yunnan Airlines. Modifications from standard include upgrades to the environmental control system, cabin pressurisation and the addition of a new Ground Proximity Warning System (GPWS).

Future markets

The success of the 50-seat regionals was in exploring the potential of new, long, thin routes and giving passengers greater flight frequency. The trend is now for larger regional aircraft to build on this success.

Despite the downturn from 2001 in aircraft orders in general, due to the prevailing economic situation in the airline industry and rising costs, the regional airline industry is anticipated to remain strong, although this is largely dependent on steady growth of the US economy over this period. The regional jet aircraft fleet is expected to double over the next two decades, with expected revenues for the 20/99-seat regional jet market likely to be in the region of $185 billion, with an increasing trend towards the higher-capacity 75/100-seat models. It is at this end of the market that both Bombardier, Embraer and, formerly, Fairchild Dornier, along with prospective Chinese and Russian-built RJs, are focusing their efforts. Bombardier has again managed to place its new CRJ900 in service before its Brazilian counterparts, but whether Embraer's decision to abandon the tried and trusted layout of rear-mounted engines in favour of a wing-mounted configuration for its new ERJ-170/190 family turns out to be decisive will not be known for a number of years. What is known is that the regional jet is here to stay, and the boundaries between the largest RJs on the one hand, and the Airbus/Boeing small airliners on the other, has yet to be fully defined.

Mike Vines

Production RJs seat capacity

Aircraft	Typical Seating	Entered production
Fairchild Dornier 328JET	32	1998
Embraer ERJ-135	37	1999
Bombardier CRJ440	44	2001
Embraer ERJ-140	44	2001
Bombardier CRJ100	50	1991
Bombardier CRJ200	50	1996
Embraer ERJ-145	50	1996
Bombardier CRJ700	70	2000
Embraer 170	70	2002
Fairchild Dornier 728	70	–
AVIC I ARJ21	85	2005
Bombardier CRJ900	86	2002
Embraer 175	86	2004*
Embraer 190	98	2005*
Tupolev Tu-334	100	2004*
Airbus A318	106	2002
Embraer 195	108	2004*

* Anticipated date for commencement of production

Russian and Chinese competitors

China Aviation Industry I (AVIC I) is planning to finalise the configuration of its 79/99-seat ARJ21 aircraft (left) in June 2003, with initial impressions showing a low-wing, twin-turbofan layout with the engines mounted on the rear fuselage. General Electric is developing the CF34-10A engine for the programme which will be tested using its Boeing 747 flying testbed prior to a proposed first flight in 2004. The aircraft will be produced at the company's Shanghai facility, with certification planned for 2005 and service entry in 2007.

With a ready market for the replacement of ageing Tu-134 and Yak-40 aircraft, Russia is actively seeking to develop new aircraft in the sub-110-seat aircraft class. A lack of funding produced lengthy delays in the much-needed 100-seat Tupolev Tu-334 (above). Designed in the 1980s, only a single example has flown and production is unlikely to commence until at least 2004. A revised Russian federal programme has targeted the development of aircraft in the 75/95-seat class. Facing competition from the 72-seat Tupolev Tu-414, and Myasishchev's M-60-70, the Sukhoi-led Russian Regional Jet (RRJ) – jointly proposed with Ilyushin, Yakovlev and Boeing – has been given the green light from the Russian government, to be produced in 55-, 75- and 95-seat versions.

Battle for supremacy – RJ sales

20/39-seat capacity

Fairchild Dornier 328-300JET

Air Namibia	Namibia	1
Air Vallee	Italy	2
Atlantic Coast Airlines	USA	32
Gandalf Airlines	Italy	7
Great Plains Airlines	USA	2
Grossman Air Service	Austria	1
Hainan Airlines	China	19
Skyway Airlines	USA	12
Tyrolean Jet Services	Austria	2
Wanair	Tahiti	1
Total		**79**

Embraer ERJ-135

American Eagle	USA	40
BMI Regional	United Kingdom	4
City Airline	Sweden	2
Continental Express	USA	30
Flandre Air	France	3
Pan Européenne Air Service	France	1
Proteus Airlines	France	3
Regional Airlines	France	3
Regional Air Lines	Morocco	1
Republic	USA	15
South African Airlink	South Africa	20
Total		**122**

40/59-seat capacity

Bombardier CRJ100

Air Canada	Canada	24
Air Littoral	France	19
Brit Air	France	20
Comair	USA	110
Lauda Air	Austria	8
Lufthansa CityLine	Germany	35
Skywest Airlines	USA	10
Total		**226**

Bombardier CRJ200

Adria Airways	Slovenia	4
Air Canada	France	2
Air Dolomiti	Italy	6
Air Nostrum	Spain	28
Air Wisconsin Airlines	Austria	64
Atlantic Coast Airlines	USA	121
Atlantic Southeast Airlines	USA	45
British European	United Kingdom	4
China Yunnan Airlines	China	6
Cimber Air	USA	2
DAC Air	USA	2
Delta Connection	USA	84
Fair	Japan	2
GECAS	USA	21
J-AIR	Japan	6
Kendell Airlines	Australia	12
Lufthansa CityLine	Germany	10
Eurowings	Germany	15
Maersk Air	Denmark	11
Malev Hungarian Airlines	Hungary	4
Mesa Airlines	USA	32
Midway Airlines	USA	24
Northwest Airlines	USA	54
Saeaga Airlines	Malaysia	1
Shandong Airlines	China	5
Shanghai Airlines	China	3
Skywest Airlines	USA	90
South African Express	South Africa	6
Southern Winds	Argentina	2
Tyrolean Airways	Austria	15
Total		**681**

Bombardier CRJ440

Northwest Airlines	USA	75
Total		**75**

Embraer ERJ-140

American Eagle	USA	139
Chautauqua Airlines	USA	15
Midwest	USA	20
Total		**174**

Embraer ERJ-145

Air Caraibes	Guadeloupe	2
Alitalia Express	Italy	14
American Eagle	USA	56
Axon Airlines	Greece	3
BMI Regional	United Kingdom	11
Brymon Airways	United Kingdom	7
Chautauqua Airlines	USA	38
Cirrus Airlines	Germany	1
Continental Express	USA	245
Flandre Air	France	7
GATX	USA	1
GECAS	USA	2
KLM exel	Netherlands	3
LOT Polish Airlines	Poland	16
Luxair	Luxembourg	9
Manx Airlines	United Kingdom	23
Mesa Airlines	USA	36
PGA Portugalia Airlines	Portugal	8
Proteus Airlines	France	11
Regional Airlines	France	17
Rheintalflug	Austria	4
Rio Sul	Brazil	16
Sichuan Airlines	China	5
Skyways Express	Sweden	4
Swiss	Switzerland	25
Republic	USA	7
Trans States Airlines	USA	12
Total		**583**

By the time the Fairchild Dornier 728 was unveiled to the press and public in early 2002, the company was already on the verge of insolvency. If no purchaser/investor can be found by the end of 2003 it seems certain the aircraft will end up an interesting but insignificant adjunct to the regional jet story.

60/79-seat capacity

Bombardier CRJ700

American Eagle	USA	25
Atlantic Southeast Airlines	USA	12
Brit Air	France	12
Cameroon Airlines	Cameroon	1
Comair	USA	20
Delta Connection	USA	26
GECAS	USA	20
Horizon Air	USA	30
Lufthansa CityLine	Germany	20
Maersk Air	Denmark	5
Mesa Airlines	USA	15
Shandong Airlines	China	2
Total		**188**

Embraer ERJ-170

Air Caraibes	Guadeloupe	2
Alitalia	Italy	6
GECAS	USA	50
LOT Polish Airlines	Poland	10
Swiss	Switzerland	15
Total		**83**

Fairchild Dornier 728

Eight customers including Lufthansa CityLine, GECAS, CSA Czech Airlines, SolAir, and Bavaria Leasing had placed orders when declared insolvent

Total **125**

80/99-seat capacity

Bombardier CRJ900

Mesa Airlines	USA	25
Total		**25**

Embraer ERJ-175

Jet Airways	India	10
Total		**83**

100/109-seat capacity

Embraer ERJ-195

Swiss	Switzerland	15
Total		**15**

Current and future cabin configurations

The original CRJ100 and all of Bombardier's subsequent aircraft have been based on the original 8-ft 4-in (2.54-m) passenger cabin diameter of the Challenger and are all arranged in a 2+2 single aisle configuration. The cabin length has grown from 48 ft 5 in (14.76 m) in the CRJ100/200 to 71 ft 11 in (21.92 m) for the CRJ900, allowing an additional nine rows of seats. Embraer adopted a much narrower 6-ft 11-in (2.10-m) cabin width for its original ERJ-145/135 series, allowing a 2+1 seating arrangement. During the design phase of the ERJ-170/190 family Embraer opted for a 2+2 cabin arrangement with a 9-ft (2.74-m) cabin width, allowing for slightly wider seats and aisle compared to Bombardier's CRJ700 and 900. Fairchild Dornier took the RJ to a new level by introducing a 3+2 seat configuration for its 728/928 family (right). The added capacity allowed by such an arrangement was a major marketing plus for the team and helped ensure the initial orders.

Pan Am's Clippers

The Pan American flying-boat story

During the decade before World War II, Pan American Airways became world-famous for its development of flying-boat services, which opened up new routes around the world. The vision of Pan Am's founder, Juan Trippe, and his adviser, the pioneering aviator Charles Lindbergh, ushered in a 'golden era' of air transport with a level of comfort and luxury that has seldom been equalled.

Entering service in 1939, the Boeing Model 314 represented the zenith of flying-boat development, though, by 1945, landplanes able to fly equivalent distances at higher speeds were making use of runways built during World War II, rendering these majestic craft obsolete. The practice of numbering the Pan Am Clipper fleet appears to have been shortlived; NC18604 was No. 20 and carried this number on its nose and middle tailfin.

Pan American Airways (PAA) began its first scheduled service on 28 October 1927, on a Key West, Florida, to Havana, Cuba, air mail route, using tri-motored Fokker F.VIIa landplanes. However, Juan Trippe, PAA's president and general manager, considered seaplanes more practical, as Key West was prone to wash-outs of its packed coral and sand runways. Trippe had already chartered a small Fairchild FC-2 seaplane to fly his 'proving' flight on the route on 19 October – hastily completed to comply with a Post Office requirement that the service begin on time.

A newly arrived B-314 follows a Pan Am launch to its mooring point. It was the general lack of suitable landing sites in destinations new to large passenger-carrying aircraft that spurred the development of the flying-boat by airlines like Pan Am and Imperial Airways.

From the start of service, mail loads were substantial and passenger traffic increased steadily during 1928, enabling Trippe to order more aircraft and extend the route. The lack of airfields in the Caribbean and South America remained a major concern and soon led to discussions with seaplane builder Igor Sikorsky. The purchase of a batch of eight-seater Sikorsky S-38 amphibians solved the problem for the moment, but larger seaplanes were soon required. In September 1928, seeking better rail connections in Florida, Trippe moved his base and terminus from Key West to Miami, where he built an airport; Miami also had an excellent harbour and potential as a seaplane base.

Trippe recruits Lindbergh

On 1 January 1929, Charles Lindbergh became Pan American's Technical Advisor. His tasks included the study of potential new routes,

Forerunner of the Clipper fleet and Pan Am's first flying-boat type was the Consolidated Commodore, acquired via Pan Am's take-over of NYRBA. NC669M was the penultimate of 14 delivered to the airline, entering service in October 1930.

The opening of the Dinner Key, Miami, terminal and maintenance base in March 1934, as depicted on this contemporary cigarette card, was an important event for the airline. It was the most impressive facility of its type anywhere in the world.

aircraft capabilities, and the preparation of specifications for new aircraft. Pan American then began a two-year period of expansion that extended its air mail routes from Miami to Buenos Aires, by way of South America's east coast, and from Texas through Central America to Panama, thence south to Chile and Argentina. This was accomplished by the purchase of several smaller airlines, and the award of new US air mail routes through South America, thus forming a cohesive network.

On the back of this route development Lindbergh and Pan Am's chief engineer André Priester began to prepare specifications for large, long-range flying-boats and, once again, entered discussions with Sikorsky. Their combined efforts resulted in the four-engined S-40 design, of which PAA ordered three in October 1929.

By mid-1930 the airline had extended its main route from Puerto Rico and Dutch Guiana, to Rio de Janeiro, using S-38 amphibians, which landed on water at most stations along the route. Pending the delivery of the first S-40s, Trippe and Lindbergh searched for a new aircraft to use as a stopgap.

First flying-boats

The highly successful Commodore flying-boat, built by the Consolidated Aircraft Company, was originally designed to a 1927 US Navy requirement, as the XPY-1 patrol aircraft. The Navy liked the twin-engined XPY-1, but chose a competing design from the Glenn L. Martin Company as it was offered at a lower price.

Reuben Fleet, president of Consolidated, was also a director on the board of NYRBA (New York, Rio, Buenos Aires), an airline formed in 1929 to provide a service between New York and the two South American cities. Fleet ordered a re-design of the XPY-1 as a passenger flying-boat for NYBRA. The reworked aircraft was named Commodore and 14 examples were ordered for the NYRBA line.

With its roomy cabin, the Commodore was attractive to Juan Trippe, who expressed interest in acquiring a number for PAA only to discover that the Commodore was being built exclusively for NYRBA. However, NYRBA was soon beset by financial difficulties; the airline's directors offered to sell its assets to Pan American and on 15 September 1930 the two companies merged. Included in the sale were NYBRA's highly-prized Commodores, some of which had yet to be delivered.

PAA received its final two Commodores (NC669M and 670M) in October 1930; these examples were fitted with extra fuel tanks and were earmarked for service on a new, more direct route between Miami and Cristobal, Panama. The new route was opened in December 1930, with stops at Cienfuegos, Cuba, and Kingston, Jamaica.

Navigation in those days was by bubble-sextant, using the sun, augmented by radio bearings. The thrice-weekly schedule left Cristobal at

Despite having won the contract to provide an air mail service between Florida and Cuba using a Fairchild FC-2 floatplane, Juan Trippe was forced to use landplanes for the service in the absence of a suitable seaplane design. Pan Am's first 'Fokker' was, in fact, an American-built ex-USAAC Atlantic C-2; two Fokker F.VIIA/3m aircraft, including the example pictured, were acquired later.

Entering service in 1928, the Sikorsky S-38 amphibian formed the backbone of the airline's Caribbean fleet during its early years. This example (above) carries the original PAA logo on its tail boom, while NC9776 (left), resting on its extended undercarriage, displays updated markings, including a new airline logo on its nose.

0515, stopped briefly at Kingston, and arrived at Cienfuegos (for a night stop-over) at 1715. Departing at 0815 the following day, the service arrived in Miami at 1045, thus reducing the elapsed time for the journey by nearly one day. The 662-mile (1065-km) Kingston-Cristobal sector was the longest over-water flight in any airline schedule at that time.

To Brazil by flying-boat

Commodores also replaced the Sikorsky S-38 amphibians on the long route to Rio de Janeiro and Buenos Aires, allowing the displaced amphibians to open a connecting service across South America's north coast from Trinidad to Panama.

In 1932 a flight from Miami to Rio de Janeiro by Pan American flying-boat was a thrilling adventure, and enjoyed considerable popularity. The 22-seat Commodores left Miami's Dinner Key base on Fridays at 0630, making 25 intermediate stops, including five overnight stays at San Pedro de Macoris, Port of Spain, Belém, Fortaleza and San Salvador. Passengers arrived in Rio at 1545 the following Wednesday. Those travelling on to Buenos Aires had two more days flying, with six stops en route.

Airborne radio communications – Pan American's early work

When Pan American's pilots requested that their aircraft be fitted with some type of airborne radio, to provide them with accurate weather information, the airline responded favourably and it became a major project. RCA (Radio Corporation of America) had been at the forefront of the development of such equipment, but had discontinued its efforts when it appeared that no market existed. In 1928, RCA engineer Hugo Leuteritz joined Pan American and began testing his radio sets on the Havana route. When voice communication proved to be unsatisfactory, radio-telegraph (CW or carrier wave transmission, using Morse code) was adopted.

During 1929, radio operators were added to all PAA crews, and work began on installing airborne and ground-based direction-finding equipment. All radio installations, with the exception of those at a few major cities, were built at Pan Am's expense.

Between March and July 1929, all Pan American aircraft were fitted with new lightweight radio transmitters and receivers, while ground radio transmitters were completed at all stations on the Miami-San Juan route and from Brownsville to the Canal Zone. By then, PAA had developed a dependable, standard radio installation for its growing fleet. The standard airborne units, capable of using many frequencies, weighed just 10½ lb (4.76 kg), with a total installed weight (wiring, antenna, racks etc.) of 42 lb (19.05 kg). The radio was powered by a dynamo powered by a 12-volt, 65-amp storage battery, its charge maintained by an air-driven generator.

The Commodores flew at lower altitudes, allowing excellent views of the tropical islands, and the South American coast, the latter with many large rivers flowing into the Atlantic. The Commodore's cabin was comfortable, the pursers attentive, and good meals, taken on daily at various stations, were provided. Transit time at the stations was usually 30 minutes.

Three time zones covered the route: Eastern Standard Time from Miami to Port au Prince, local island times to Puerto Rico, and 60th Meridian Time for the rest of the route to Buenos Aires. For the crew and aircraft, the trip took eight days southbound, but only seven days northbound, thanks to favourable trade winds and the fact that two hours were 'gained' crossing time zones.

In 1930, the one-way fare between Miami and Buenos Aires was US$737; by 1932, fares had dropped, with a $666 rate from Miami to Buenos Aires, or $536 to Rio.

In most Latin American countries, official entry and exit formalities were burdensome, causing numerous departure delays. Captains often had to sign or initial huge stacks of papers, then wait until these were stamped and acknowledged. Pan American began pressing governments for simpler clearance and documentation procedures for aircraft and passengers. By May 1933, the US and 31 Latin American countries had agreed to adopt a single clearance document. The 'Documento Unico' replaced the numerous entry or transit forms (bills of lading, consular invoices, etc.), while a Pan American way-bill sufficed for air express shipments.

A trans-oceanic vision

Trippe and Lindbergh always envisaged worldwide air services as a viable objective and, to this end, PAA's technical staff began to develop specifications for long-range aircraft capable of crossing oceans. Flying-boats were deemed necessary, as many routes would have to

Right: Pan Am associates Panair do Brazil, Pan American-Grace (Panagra) and CNAC (China) also operated Commodores; during World War II four were converted for use as navigation trainers, providing tuition for USAAF and RAF personnel.

Below: In the main the Commodore was employed on the Miami to Buenos Aires route, though it also saw some use on services to Panama and Havana. Here NC669M prepares to depart Panama for Miami, via Kingston, Jamaica and Cienfuegos, Cuba. Usually a 22-seater, the Commodore would carry 16 passengers on this route, to provide space for extra fuel tanks.

Below: The operation of the elevator at the Dinner Key maintenance base is demonstrated by this Commodore, fitted with beaching gear so that it can be wheeled into a hangar for attention.

terminate at coastal cities without airfields. The requirements included a range of 2,500 miles (4023 km) against a 30-mph (48-km/h) head wind, the ability to carry at least 300 lb (136 kg) of mail and 12 passengers, the use of variable-pitch propellers, and a wing loading of approximately 30 lb/sq ft (1.26 kg/m^2). Contemporary transport aircraft typically had wing loadings between 14-20 lb/sq ft (0.59-0.84 kg/m^2).

On 26 June 1931, Pan American wrote to six aircraft manufacturers asking them to submit designs for a high-speed, multi-engine flying-boat conforming to these specifications. The Glenn L. Martin Company and Sikorsky responded.

Meanwhile, beginning in July 1931, Charles and Anne Lindbergh made a survey flight from New York to Alaska, thence to Siberia and China. Their purpose was to evaluate a 'great circle route', which Lindbergh and Trippe believed was the most feasible route to Asia. Making thorough preparations, Lindbergh's Lockheed Sirius floatplane was fitted with standard Pan American radio and emergency gear (for both Arctic and over-water operation). Mrs Lindbergh was trained in the PAA radio school and became a proficient Morse code operator. The ensuing flight, completed successfully in early October, was convincing, though gaining landing rights in Siberia appeared unlikely.

Pan American's first Clippers

Later that month the first Sikorsky S-40 was ready for final testing by Pan Am. Basil Rowe, Chief Pilot, Seaplanes, reported it handled exceptionally well on the water and provided a comfortable ride for passengers. Visibility from the walnut-panelled cabin's large windows was described as excellent.

The First Lady, Mrs Hoover, was invited to christen the aircraft *American Clipper* and, shortly afterwards, Pan American's Board of Directors held a board meeting aloft for the first time, while flying over Manhattan. Juan Trippe adoption of the 'Clipper' name was inspired by the famous tea clipper sailing ships that sailed to the Far East during the mid-19th Century.

On 19 November 1931 *American Clipper* left Miami on its first scheduled flight, with Lindbergh at the controls, bound for Panama, via Cienfuegos, Cuba, Kingston, Jamaica, and Barranquilla, Colombia. A night stop at Cienfuegos was scheduled each way. The return flight was delayed at Barranquilla as repairs were necessary to a damaged pontoon. The next day Lindbergh left at dawn, made short stops at Kingston and Cienfuegos, and arrived at Miami after dark. Twenty-eight passengers and 15,000 pieces of mail were on board this record-breaking, one-day flight from South America to Miami.

Igor Sikorsky, the S-40's designer, accompanied Lindbergh on this trip, as work was in hand on the design of the company's next-generation aircraft. In October 1932, PAA ordered three new S-42 flying-boats from Sikorsky, with options for more. At the same time the airline ordered three Martin 130 flying-boats. (Glenn Martin, too, dreamed of air services across oceans and was prepared to lose money in the development of a new long-range aircraft if it resulted in a suitable machine.)

The S-42 was actually intended for Latin American routes, but was capable of undertaking transoceanic survey flights. The M-130 was

Pan American took delivery of three Sikorsky S-40s during 1931/32, including NC752V Southern Clipper. The aircraft offered a considerable increase in capacity on services in the Caribbean.

Right: Shortly after the airline's first S-40 was delivered and christened by the First Lady, a meeting of Pan American's board of directors was held aboard the aircraft – as it flew over Manhattan.

***Left:* Pan American's second S-40, NC81V Caribbean Clipper, set a world record on 30 December 1931, conveying 37 passengers between Miami and Havana, Cuba – then the largest passenger load ever carried on a scheduled flight.**

Ground staff attempt to manoeuvre an S-40 at its mooring at Nassau, Bahamas, as a second aircraft taxies past in particularly calm waters.

tentatively earmarked for transatlantic use, as Trippe believed operating rights to England and Europe might be more easily obtained than for the Asia route. These were the largest aircraft yet constructed in the US, and this was the largest commercial aircraft order ever placed in the US at the time.

The 1933 Atlantic Survey

On 9 July 1933, Charles and Anne Lindbergh left New York on a survey flight across the Atlantic. Again, the Lockheed Sirius floatplane (used on the 1931 flight to China) was equipped with new PAA long-range radio, with Mrs Lindbergh acting as radio officer, assistant navigator and co-pilot.

Flying by way of Newfoundland, Labrador, Greenland and Iceland, the aircraft visited England, Ireland and several cities in Europe. Lindbergh had planned to return via the Azores to Labrador, but in Horta he found the harbour too short to allow a fully loaded take-off and that the sea outside the harbour was too rough. Instead, they flew to Bathurst, in the Gambia, crossed the Atlantic to Brazil and flew back to Miami and New York. Lindbergh's detailed records of conditions on this trip and his study of the routes were a significant factor in Pan American's opening of Atlantic service.

On 25 March 1934, Pan American's new Dinner Key, Miami, terminal was completed. This was, for the next decade, the finest marine air terminal in the world. Passengers could board or disembark from the seaplanes directly, with all Government formalities being completed in a terminal building adjacent to the loading bays. A major attraction was the terminal's rotating globe, some 10 ft (3.05 m) in diameter and showing all the world's air routes. A large promenade on the terminal's roof allowed visitors to view seaplane operations.

The nearby maintenance area included a unique elevator, used to lift flying-boats out of the water. After a flying-boat was towed onto the lowered elevator, a wheeled cradle was placed under the hull. The elevator was then raised, taking the seaplane up to the service ramp; from there it could be towed into the hangar.

Sikorsky S-42

The first S-42 completed its certification tests on 4 August 1934, having set eight new world records for loads carried to altitudes, and for speeds over measured distances. The S-42 boasted a number of technically advanced features. The first three S-42s were built using 17ST aluminium alloy and flush riveting – the latter a first on a transport aircraft. The high-aspect ratio wing was attached to the fuselage using a cabane strut and two large lift-struts, extruded from a single piece of Duralumin alloy, saving weight and reducing drag.

The engines were faired into the wings, using the new NACA cowling. Variable-pitch propellers were used; these were equipped with brakes to stop 'windmilling'. A 68-ft (20.7-m) trailing-edge flap reduced take-off and landing distances considerably. The S-42's maximum take-off weight was 38,000 lb (17237 kg), and in PAA service its useful load was 16,000 lb (7258 kg).

The S-42s handled well, both in the air and on the water, and were well liked by pilots, though the type had a tendency to 'porpoise' on take-off and was sensitive to the descent angle on approach; flatter approaches were preferable.

Completed in 1935, four improved S-42A models were constructed using new, stronger 24ST alloy, and had an additional 20 sq ft (1.86 m^2) of wing area. Maximum take-off weight was 40,000 lb (18144 kg) and the wing loading 29.6 lb/sq ft (144.5 kg/m^2).

Delivered late in 1936, the three S-42B models had an improved wing flap, more

Lindbergh's survey flights

Between 27 July and 2 October 1931 Colonel and Mrs Charles Lindbergh flew Lockheed Sirius 8 NR-211 (below) on a survey flight over the 'great circle route' via Alaska to Japan and China. Though this route was to prove problematic, the Lindberghs' flight was the first step towards a Pan Am service across the Pacific. For the flight to China, Lindbergh had the aircraft re-engined with an uprated 575-hp (429-kW) P&W Wasp engine – in place of a 450-hp (336-kW) example – and equipped with a pair of Edo floats, each of which held 150 US gal (568 litres) of fuel. Upon its return to the US (having been damaged while being hoisted from a British aircraft-carrier into a flood-swollen Yangtze River) the Sirius was re-engined once again, this time with a 710-hp (529-kW) Wright Cyclone driving a Hamilton-Standard variable-pitch propeller.

The Lindberghs made one further Pan Am survey flight in the aircraft, around the North Atlantic between 9 July and 6 December 1933. This 30,000-mile (48280-km) journey yielded considerable useful data regarding possible landing areas, locations for radio stations, suitable routes and weather conditions. The 1933 flight paved the way for further surveys; Pan Am conducted joint survey flights with Imperial Airways in 1937; Pan Am's passenger service was inaugurated in 1939.

Sikorsky S-40

Pan American Airways System 1932

Sikorsky S-40 NC81V *Caribbean Clipper* was the second of three examples ordered in December 1929 and entered service in November 1931. All gave reliable service from their Dinner Key, Miami, base to Havana, Kingston, Barranquilla and Cristobal in Panama until scrapped during World War II. The S-40 fleet was limited to three aircraft as Pan Am shifted its efforts towards sponsoring the larger and faster S-42, which offered much improved range performance.

Load-carrying capacity
The S-40 was far ahead of its contemporaries in terms of its load-carrying capacity. Its maximum take-off weight was 34,000 lb (15422 kg), with an empty weight, including furnishings and equipment, of 21,000 lb (9526 kg), yielding a disposable load (fuel, passengers and cargo) of 13,000 lb (5897 kg).

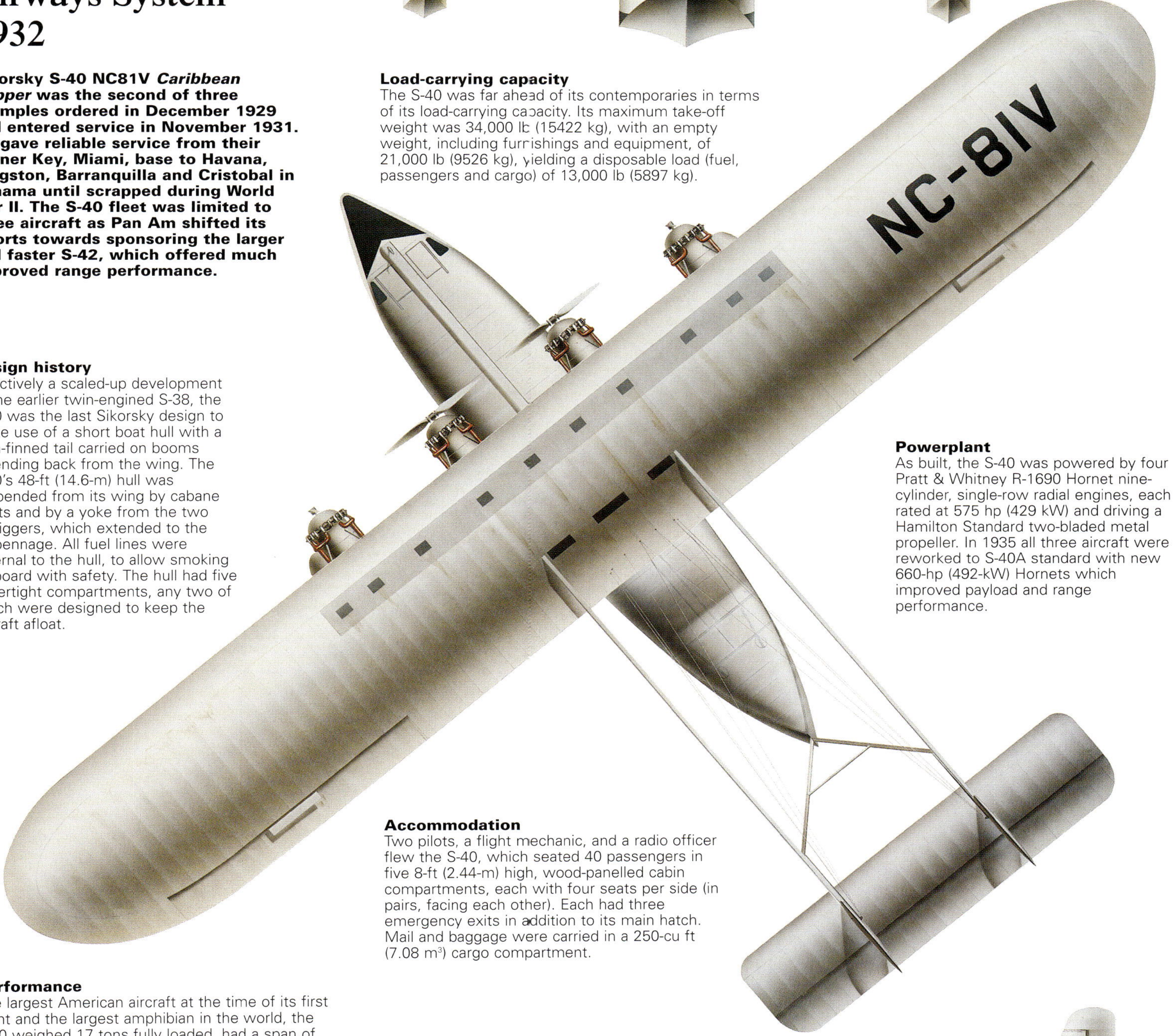

Design history
Effectively a scaled-up development of the earlier twin-engined S-38, the S-40 was the last Sikorsky design to make use of a short boat hull with a twin-finned tail carried on booms extending back from the wing. The S-40's 48-ft (14.6-m) hull was suspended from its wing by cabane struts and by a yoke from the two outriggers, which extended to the empennage. All fuel lines were external to the hull, to allow smoking on board with safety. The hull had five watertight compartments, any two of which were designed to keep the aircraft afloat.

Powerplant
As built, the S-40 was powered by four Pratt & Whitney R-1690 Hornet nine-cylinder, single-row radial engines, each rated at 575 hp (429 kW) and driving a Hamilton Standard two-bladed metal propeller. In 1935 all three aircraft were reworked to S-40A standard with new 660-hp (492-kW) Hornets which improved payload and range performance.

Accommodation
Two pilots, a flight mechanic, and a radio officer flew the S-40, which seated 40 passengers in five 8-ft (2.44-m) high, wood-panelled cabin compartments, each with four seats per side (in pairs, facing each other). Each had three emergency exits in addition to its main hatch. Mail and baggage were carried in a 250-cu ft (7.08 m³) cargo compartment.

Performance
The largest American aircraft at the time of its first flight and the largest amphibian in the world, the S-40 weighed 17 tons fully loaded, had a span of 114 ft (34.7 m) and was some 77 ft (23.5 m) in length. With 38 passengers aboard it was able to fly 500-600 miles (805-966 km) at a cruising speed of over 100 mph (161 km/h).

The Sikorsky S-42 (above) was an advanced aircraft for its time, employing a number of structural and aerodynamic features to reduce weight and drag, while maintaining airframe strength.

Below: The second S-42, with 'restricted' registration NR-823M and extra fuel tanks fitted, departs Dinner Key on 27 March 1935 at the beginning of its flight to Alameda for a series of Pacific survey flights.

Above: Comfortable wood-panelled compartments (above) were separated by watertight doors. S-42s were generally configured to carry 32 passengers in four compartments.

advanced instrumentation and 750-hp (559-kW) engines. Maximum take-off weight was increased still further, to 42,000 lb (19051 kg); wing loading was 31.1 lb/sq ft (151.8 kg/m²).

The S-42 entered service on 16 August 1934, initially between Miami and Puerto Rico, the Commodores continuing to serve on the route from San Juan to Buenos Aires. Delivered between November 1935 and June 1936, the four S-42As were placed on the Buenos Aires route and on routes to Colombia and Panama. The S-42 schedule made stops only at the major cities (with PAA's new twin-engined Sikorsky S-43 amphibians providing faster local services). Rio de Janeiro was then just five days from Miami, as Fred Astaire and Ginger Rogers showed the world in the film *Flying Down to Rio*.

Across the Pacific

During 1934, difficulties had arisen in negotiations for operating rights to England and France, so Trippe shifted his priority to the mid-Pacific, where key staging locations were under US control. Thus, early in 1935, PAA made ready to thrust its wings across the Pacific Ocean by way of Honolulu, Hawaii, the islands of Midway, Wake, and Guam, to Manila, Philippines, and later to Hong Kong (assuming British approval was obtained). The Pacific Division's base was at Alameda airport, across the bay from San Francisco. New base installations were also constructed at Midway, Wake and on Guam.

The second S-42, NC823M (named *Pan American Clipper*), was fitted with nine additional 170-US gal (643-litre) fuselage fuel tanks to extend its range. A newly developed automatic carburettor was installed to improve fuel consumption and a new device, a fuel flowmeter, provided continuous indication of the precise amount of fuel being consumed by each engine. An additional 68-US gal (257-litre) oil tank was also installed in the fuselage.

In January 1935, PAA Captain Ed Musick began a series of 30 long-range test flights from Miami to test fuel consumption, navigation techniques and new equipment, including instrumentation, sextants, an autopilot and radios. *Pan American Clipper* was relicensed by the Department of Commerce as NR823M, the 'R' in the registration indicating restricted operation at weights above previously approved passenger flight limits. A weight limit of 41,500 lb (18824 kg) was approved for the survey flights.

As no sextants suitable for aerial use were available, PAA asked the Pioneer Instrument Company to make a special 'bubble' type octant for them. (While surface ship navigators could use the natural horizon for levelling their sextants, aerial navigators often found it obscured by cloud or haze. Thus a bubble was added to provide a levelling reference for the aviation octant.) Radio bearings were provided by NR823M's improved direction-finder loop antenna, and also by long-range radio direction-finders at Alameda and Honolulu.

At 1550 on 16 April 1935, Captain Musick and his crew left Alameda on the first survey flight, carrying 17,000 lb (7711 kg) of fuel, sufficient to fly 800 miles (1287 km) beyond Honolulu. They landed at Pearl Harbor next morning, after a flight of 18 hours, 39 minutes, with 5,000 lb (2268 kg) of fuel remaining. The navigation went well, using radio bearings, four fixes by stars, a line of position from the sun, and a latitude line from Polaris (the North Star).

The Clipper returned to Alameda on 23 April, the navigation again working well, but winds were adverse, and flight time was some 21 hours, cutting deeply into fuel reserves. Musick then requested the installation of an additional 170-US gal (643-litre) tank. Along with flight-testing for evaluation of fuel consumption rates, and navigation practice, return survey flights were made to Midway and Wake Islands. In October, following a survey flight to Guam and return, all the new stations and the route were declared ready for service.

Nicknamed the 'Baby Clipper', the Sikorsky S-43 replaced the Consolidated Commodore on the Miami-Buenos Aires route from June 1936, serving locations not served by the larger S-42 Clippers plying the same route. Other S-43s served with Pan Am's associate airlines; this example, the second delivered, entered service with Panagra in 1936 and served on the Cristobal (Panama) to Guayaquil (Colombia) sector of the airline's 'La Diagonal' route to Buenos Aires.

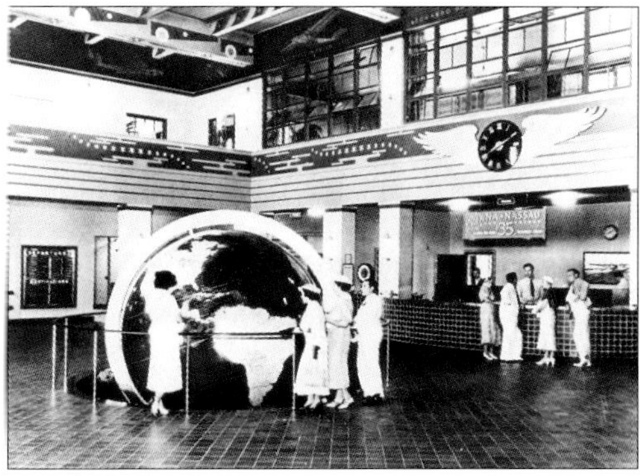

Pan Am's Dinner Key terminal and maintenance base (above) was opened on 25 March 1934, replacing a smaller terminal built on a barge. Covered walkways linked the new terminal with each of the docking jetties, Government immigration formalities taking place in the ground floor of the building. Also on the ground floor were a ticket sales desk and Pan Am's famous rotating globe (left). Maintenance took place in two hangars adjacent to the US Coast Guard facility on the same site. An elevator was provided (to the right of the terminal building) for lifting flying-boats into and out of the water; amphibians could use the nearby ramp.

In the meantime, the first Martin 130, NC14716 (named *China Clipper*) completed its licensing tests and was delivered to Pan American. This flying-boat was revolutionary in many ways, with all-aluminium construction, except for the wing skin aft of the main spar. Single sponsons (or seawings) on each side held the 'X'-shaped struts to the wing. The sponsons provided stability on the water, reduced spray during take-off, and their aerodynamic shape contributed to lift. There were dual hydraulic and electrical systems, but wing flaps were dispensed with to save weight – the M-130 alighted at only 65-70 mph (105-113 km/h). Pilots were happy with the M-130, it handled well in the air and on the water.

Martin 130 described

The M-130 was the first transport to use two-row radial engines, and the first to have adjustable cowl flaps for better in-flight engine temperature control. It could fly on only two of its four engines and maintain an altitude of 6,000 ft (1829 m). The pitch of the constant-speed Hamilton Standard propellers was controllable in flight, and their rotation could be arrested by a brake if necessary. The M-130 was also the first transport aircraft to employ integral fuel tanks. An important achievement of the M-130 was its empty weight of 25,363 lb (11505 kg), leaving 26,637 lb (12082 kg) for furnishings and a useful payload. The 45-ft (13.7-m) cabin was divided into three compartments and the passenger seating could be converted into berths during overnight, overwater hops. There were two lavatories, and a galley equipped to prepare hot food.

On 22 November 1935, *China Clipper* departed from Alameda on the first airline flight across the Pacific. At 1546 the aircraft lifted from the water, and was joined by an escort of military aircraft – a spectacular sight as they passed under the incomplete structure of the new Cross-Bay Bridge. The first leg of the flight was routine, arriving next morning in Honolulu.

The next day, *China Clipper* continued on, making overnight stops at the islands of Midway, Wake, and Guam, arriving in Manila with the first trans-Pacific air mail consignment on 29 November. It had covered the 8,210 miles (13212 km) after an elapsed time in the air of 59 hours 48 minutes.

The return flight progressed without incident, arriving back in San Francisco on 6 December. These flights carried no passengers until October 1936, when passenger-carrying flights were finally approved. In September 1936, Pan American was authorised to serve both Macau and Hong Kong, making connections there with a new Imperial Airways landplane service to London, and with a CNAC service to Shanghai.

In April 1937, a new Sikorsky S-42B, NC16734, was despatched to survey a route from Hawaii to New Zealand. (The S-42 NR823M had been returned to Miami for Latin American service.) The Department of

Such was the fascination with the activities at Dinner Key that a typical Sunday afternoon would see crowds gather to watch 'comings and goings' at the airport. This wintertime scene from 1937/38 includes an S-42B (NC16735), on the ramp awaiting departure, an S-40 and a visiting British-registered Grumman G.21A Goose.

At the beginning of its first round trip air mail flight across the Pacific, M-130* China Clipper *passes over San Francisco's as yet incomplete Golden Gate Bridge on 22 November 1935 (above) en route to Honolulu, where the aircraft is seen arriving the following day (above right).

Commerce had approved a special takeoff weight of 45,500 lb (20639 kg) for this S-42B, with a maximum landing weight of 41,000 lb (19598 kg), with all engines operating, or 36,600 lb (16602 kg) with fewer than four engines running. All S-42s had a fuel jettisoning system for use in meeting landing weight limits with inoperative engines.

From Honolulu, the route went via Kingman Reef, and Pago Pago, Samoa, to Auckland. There was no docking facility at Kingman Reef, so the SS *North Wind* was fitted to serve as a mobile station, with the necessary radio gear, weather observation devices, fuel and other supplies. Pago Pago's harbour would provide for the flying boat's overnight and operational needs in Samoa. On 23 March 1937, at 0650, Captain Musick left Pearl Harbor for Kingman Reef, 1,075 miles (1730 km) to the south. After a flight of 7 hours 55 minutes, the flight landed beside *North Wind,* anchored in the small sand-covered reef. Next morning, Musick departed on the 1,600-mile (2575-km) leg to Samoa, crossed the equator and landed in Pago Pago's cup-shaped harbour at 1714 (0414 GMT). Here the flight was delayed for four days because of a typhoon near the route to Auckland. On the 29th the

Martin M-130 *China Clipper*

NC14716 was the first of three M-130s and inaugurated Pan American's transpacific service to Manila in November 1935. *China Clipper* was the longest-lived of the three aircraft, finally sinking in Trinidad in January 1945. Of the other aircraft, *Hawaii Clipper* was lost over the Pacific in 1938 and *Philippine Clipper* crashed in 1943.

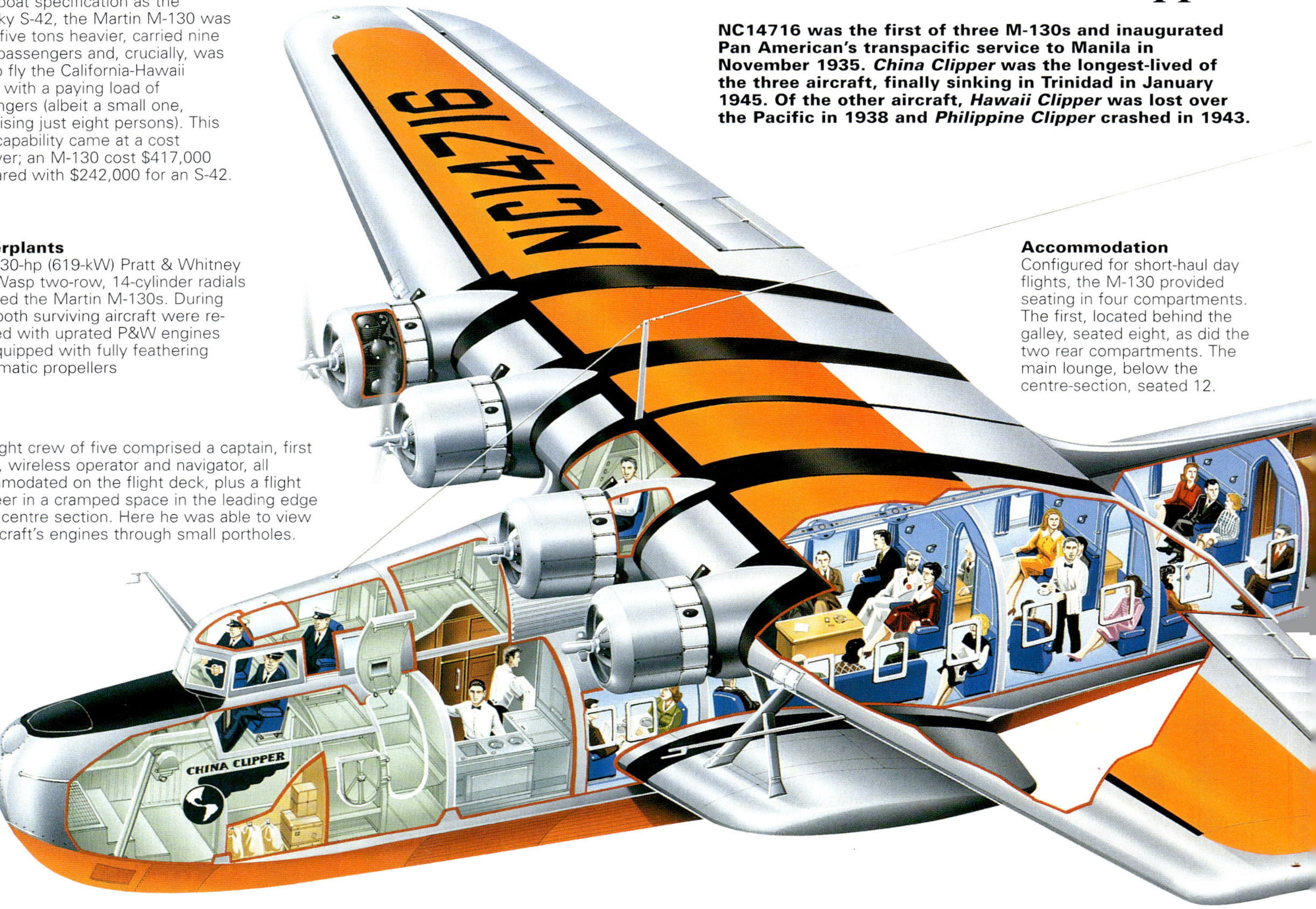

S-42 rival
Designed to the same long-range flying-boat specification as the Sikorsky S-42, the Martin M-130 was some five tons heavier, carried nine more passengers and, crucially, was able to fly the California-Hawaii sector with a paying load of passengers (albeit a small one, comprising just eight persons). This extra capability came at a cost however; an M-130 cost $417,000 compared with $242,000 for an S-42.

Powerplants
Four 830-hp (619-kW) Pratt & Whitney Twin Wasp two-row, 14-cylinder radials powered the Martin M-130s. During 1939 both surviving aircraft were re-engined with uprated P&W engines and equipped with fully feathering Hydromatic propellers

Crew
The flight crew of five comprised a captain, first officer, wireless operator and navigator, all accommodated on the flight deck, plus a flight engineer in a cramped space in the leading edge of the centre section. Here he was able to view the aircraft's engines through small portholes.

Accommodation
Configured for short-haul day flights, the M-130 provided seating in four compartments. The first, located behind the galley, seated eight, as did the two rear compartments. The main lounge, below the centre-section, seated 12.

China Clipper ***cruises over San Francisco (with Alcatraz Island and its notorious prison in the background) on 6 December 1935, at the end of the inaugural trans-Pacific service. Passenger services on the route began during October 1936.***

flight continued on to Auckland, crossing the international date line and alighting at 1700 hours, after a flight of 11 hours, 57 minutes.

On 3 April the S-42B left Auckland and returned to Honolulu by the same route. *North Wind* also returned to Hawaii; further flights would have to await the delivery of new aircraft. Meanwhile, NC16734 was refitted as a 28-seat aircraft and renamed *Hong Kong Clipper* before being sent to Hong Kong to operate the schedule between there and Manila.

The Boeing B-314

In 1936, responding to Pan American's request for a still larger, long-range flying-boat, four manufacturers offered new designs. Trippe's specifications included a range of 4,000 miles (6437 km) against a 30-mph (48-km/h) headwind. Of the four responses (from Boeing, Douglas, Martin, and Sikorsky), only Boeing promised delivery by the end of 1937. The wing and empennage of its Model 314 design were adapted from Boeing's XB-15 bomber, a 70,000-lb (31752-kg) landplane. The flying-boat's empty weight was to be 40,000 lb (18144 kg) with a maximum all-up weight of 82,500 lb (37422 kg).

Douglas proposed a 62,000-lb (28123-kg) flying-boat using the wing from its planned DC-4E landplane. The DC-4E had not yet been built, though Pan American and four other airlines had, in March 1936, agreed to share in its development costs.

On trans-Pacific flights one of three overnight stops was made at Midway Island, where M-130 NC14715 **Philippine Clipper** ***is seen taxiing towards the island's dock.*** **Philippine Clipper** ***made the second flight over this route in December and undertook a special passenger service, with Juan Trippe and invited guests from the publishing world, to Hong Kong on 14 October 1936, seven days before the trans-Pacific was inaugurated.***

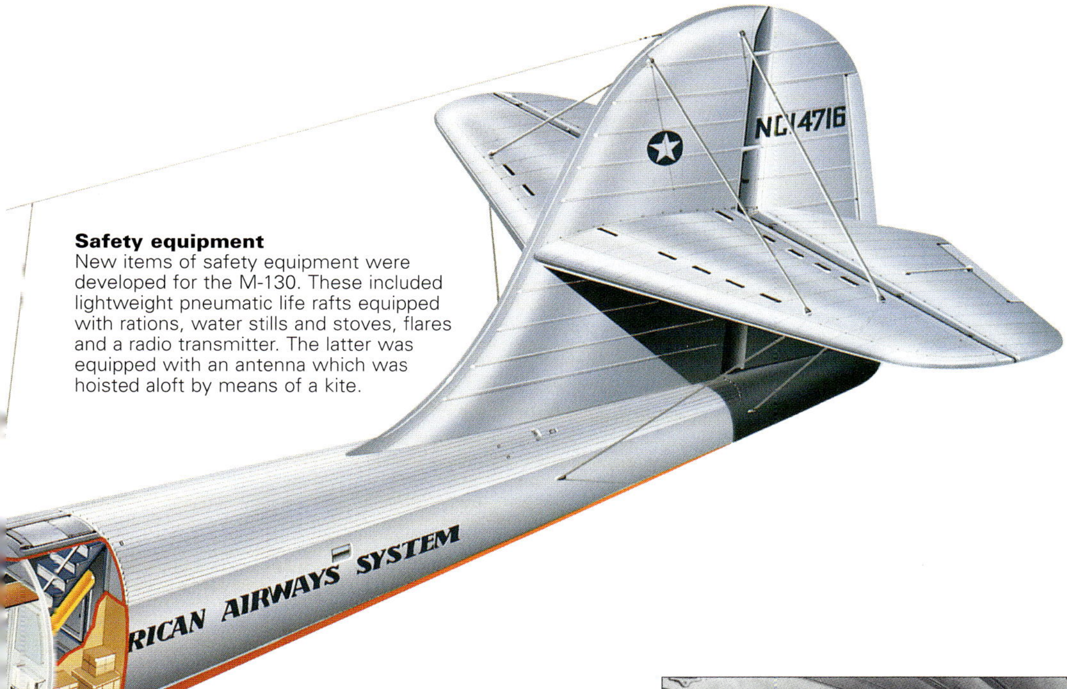

Safety equipment
New items of safety equipment were developed for the M-130. These included lightweight pneumatic life rafts equipped with rations, water stills and stoves, flares and a radio transmitter. The latter was equipped with an antenna which was hoisted aloft by means of a kite.

Aft hatch
The rear entrance to the passenger cabin was located on the top surface of the rear fuselage, above a stairway between two baggage compartments.

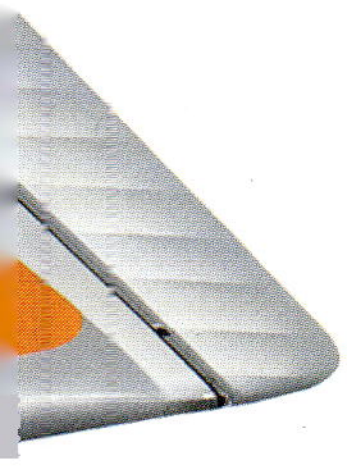

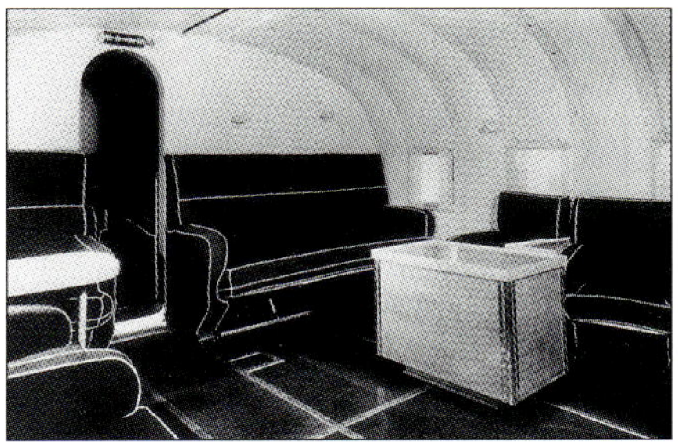

A lounge area (left), situated beneath the M-130's wing centre-section, was used for dining (above). On longer flights passenger compartments (top right) could be converted to provide bunk-type sleeping berths (right).

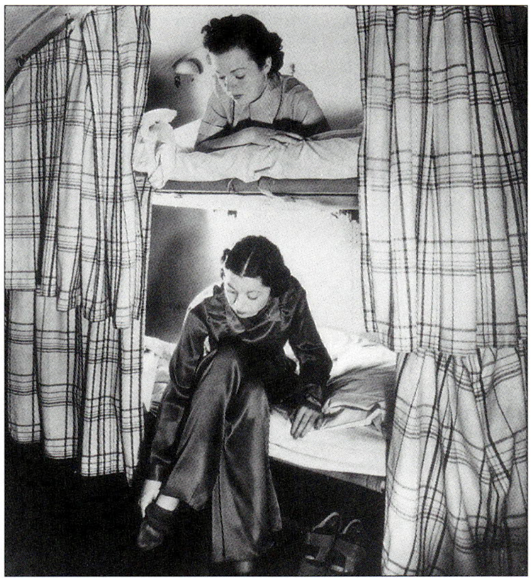

As a harbour ferry steams by, Pan Am's survey flight from San Francisco arrives in Auckland, New Zealand, on the afternoon of 30 March 1937. S-42B* Pan American Clipper II *and its crew, led by Captain Edwin Musick, was greeted by 30,000 Aucklanders on this momentous occasion. Air mail services began on the Auckland route the following December, but only a single round trip was completed before NC16734, refitted as* Samoan Clipper*, crashed at Pago Pago on 11 January 1938, killing Musick and his crew. Services to Auckland did not resume until 22 August 1939.

Martin responded by designing the M-156, a larger, 65,000-lb (29484-kg) version of the M-130, with increased range and load-carrying capacity. Sikorsky's 87,000-lb (39463-kg) S-45 design would have a 34,930-lb (15844-kg) empty weight, and allow 52,000 lb (23587 kg) for optional items and useful load. Its projected delivery date was early in 1939.

Early delivery was critical to Pan American and, as Boeing offered delivery almost two years earlier than Sikorsky, a contract was duly signed on 21 July 1936, calling for delivery of the first B-314 by 21 December 1937.

In May 1937, Pan American formed an Atlantic Division, and opened a flying-boat base at Long Island's Port Washington, in New York. By agreement, both PAA and Imperial Airways flying boats would begin services between New York and Bermuda, using the new base.

On 25 May, PAA's S-42B NC16735 flew from Port Washington to Bermuda, alighting at Darrell's Island after taking 4 hours 45 minutes to cover the 773 miles (1244 km) between the two centres. Simultaneously, Imperial Airways' Short S.23 *Cavalier* flew from Bermuda to Port Washington.

After two more proving flights, both airlines opened scheduled services between New York and Bermuda, passenger service beginning on 12 June. The PAA flights left Port Washington on Thursdays at 0900 and arrived at Bermuda at 1430, returning the following day. Imperial Airways flights left Port Washington on Saturdays. Fares for both companies were $100 one-way, or $180 for the round trip.

To aid navigation PAA had installed radio and weather stations at Bermuda and New York, but crews found that navigation and weather forecasting on this route more difficult than in the Pacific. Water temperature dramatically affected frontal systems moving from the coast, and wind direction and velocity seemed to change almost hourly.

North Atlantic survey flights

Under a 1936 agreement, airlines of four nations – the US, Great Britain, France and Germany – were able to freely conduct survey flights across the Atlantic during 1937 and 1938. The designated airlines involved in these surveys were Pan American, Imperial Airways, Air France and Lufthansa.

In preparation for these flights PAA installed intermediate stations at Shediac (New Brunswick), Botwood (Newfoundland), and Foynes (Ireland), while Sikorsky installed extra fuel tanks and other equipment in a new S-42B, NC16736 *Pan American Clipper III.*

On 3 July 1937, Chief Pilot Gray and his crew flew the S-42B to Shediac and Botwood, where they waited for two days, then departed for Foynes. At the same time Imperial Airways' S.23 *Caledonia* departed from Foynes, crossing the Atlantic in the opposite direction. Gray ascended to an 8,000-ft (2438-m) cruising altitude, where tailwinds were forecast. A cold front stretched across the track, moving toward Foynes, which reported a ceiling of 500 ft (152 m) and visibility of 1½ miles (2.4 km) in light rain and fog. About one hour from Foynes Gray descended, crossed the mouth of the Shannon River in heavy rain, and alighted at Foynes, just six minutes late according to their flight plan. The flight had taken just 12 hours, and the aircraft had sufficient fuel remaining to fly another 1,500 miles (2414 km).

The next day Gray and his crew flew to Southampton, bringing the total flight time from New York to 22 hours 32 minutes. On the return flight, they arrived in New York with a total westbound time of 28 hours 26 minutes. On 28 July Gray made another survey flight to Southampton and return, and then prepared to cross the mid-Atlantic.

On 16 August *Pan American Clipper III* flew to Bermuda, on a rhumb-line track approximately along the 40th parallel, to the 40th meridian (a point known to sailors as 'Jones Corner'), thence to Horta. Flight time for the 2,067-mile (3327-km) Bermuda to Horta segment was 15 hours 24 minutes.

On 20 August, the Clipper flew to Lisbon, making the 1,056 miles (1699 km) in 7 hours

Pan American's Clipper fleet

c/n	registration	delivery date	name(s)/disposition
Sikorsky S-40			
2000	NC80V	12 Oct 1931	*American Clipper* scrapped, 1946
2001	NC81V	16 Nov 1931	*Caribbean Clipper* scrapped, 1946
2002	NC752V	30 Aug 1932	*Southern Clipper* scrapped, 1946
Sikorsky S-42			
4200X	NC822M	4 Aug 1934	*Brazilian Clipper/Colombian Clipper* scrapped, July 1946
4201	NC823M	19 Dec 1934	*Pan American Clipper/West Indies Clipper*; destroyed in crash, Antilla, Cuba, 7 Aug 1944
4202	NC824M	1 Jul 1935	destroyed in crash, Port of Spain, Trinidad, 20 Dec 1935
Sikorsky S-42A			
4203	NC15373	26 Nov 1935	*Jamaican Clipper* scrapped, 1946
4204	NC15374	1 Jan 1936	*Puerto Rican Clipper* scrapped, 1946
4205	NC15375	1 Feb 1936	*Brazilian Clipper* scrapped, July 1946
4206	NC15376	10 June 1936	*Dominican Clipper* destroyed in crash, San Juan, 3 Oct 1941
Sikorsky S-42B			
4207	NC16734	26 Nov 1936	*Pan American Clipper II/Hong Kong Clipper/Samoan Clipper* destroyed in crash, Samoa, 11 Jan 1938
4208	NC16735	2 Jan 1937	*Bermuda Clipper/Hong Kong Clipper* destroyed by Japanese bombing, Hong Kong, 8 Dec 1941
4209	NC16736	Mar 1937	*Pan American Clipper III/Alaska Clipper/Amazon Clipper* destroyed by fire at Manaus, Brazil, 27 Jul 1943
Martin 130			
556	NC14714	30 Mar 1936	*Hawaii Clipper* disappeared without a trace, between Guam and Manila, 28 Jul 1938
557	NC14715	14 Nov 1935	*Philippine Clipper* destroyed in crash Booneville, California, 21 Jan 1943, on USN mission
558	NC14716	9 Oct 1935	*China Clipper* destroyed in crash, Port of Spain, Trinidad, 8 Jan 1945

Boeing's Model 314 was the largest production aircraft in service with any airline at the time of its introduction. The prototype (NX18601, right) made its first flight on 7 June 1938; the second aircraft (NC18602, above) was the first to enter service, in the Pacific, in March 1939; two months later the type was in use over the Atlantic.

22 minutes, and alighted on the Tagus River, just upstream from the Torre de Belém.

The next day Gray flew to Marseille, by way of the Bay of Biscay, and across southern France, being sure to avoid Spain, then in the midst of civil war. The 1,203 miles (1936 km) to Marseille was covered in 8 hours 22 minutes. On 25 August, *Pan American Clipper III* flew on to Southampton, a distance of 702 miles (1130 km) covered in 4 hours 45 minutes. Gray departed from England on the 29th, crossing the Atlantic again via Marseille, Lisbon, Horta and Bermuda, arriving in New York on 3 September. The round trip had been uneventful and almost routine, Pan American subsequently declaring its survey flights complete. NC16736 then entered service on the Bermuda run, for both carriers had added another weekly flight.

During the autumn of 1937 it was decided that, given the possibility of ice forming in Port Washington harbour during the winter months, it would be sensible to move operations further south. Thus, from 1 November services to Bermuda, by both Imperial Airways and PAA, originated from PAA's new Baltimore terminal, situated in Baltimore Harbor, adjacent to Logan Field, Baltimore's municipal airport.

Pan American's activities on the Atlantic route during 1938, other than the Bermuda service, were devoted to preparation for the delivery of

Across the Pacific

Juan Trippe was able to achieve the first stage of his ambitious plan to create a round-the-world air service without the need for sensitive international negotiations for access to foreign territories. At the time of *China Clipper*'s pioneering first scheduled flight, Hawaii, Guam and the Philippines were US territories, Midway was an outpost of the Hawaiian Islands group and Wake had not been claimed by any nation. From September 1936 Pan Am was authorised to serve Macau and Hong Kong, allowing connections with Imperial Airways' landplane service to London.

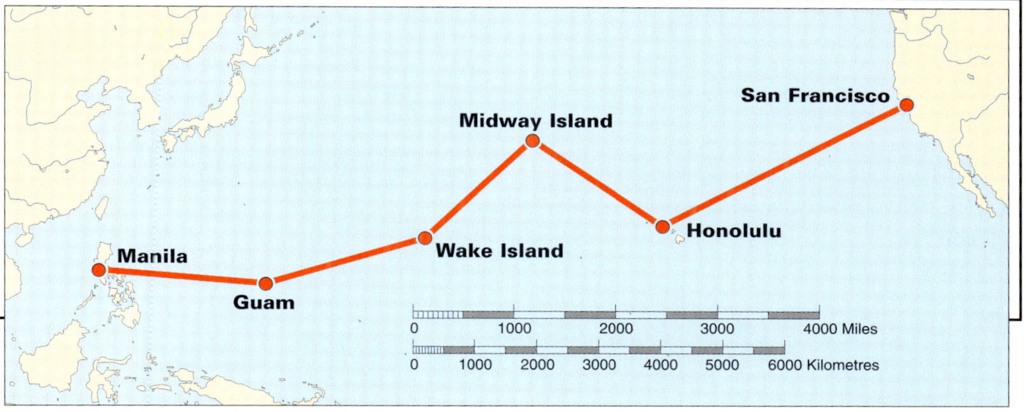

The first B-314 to enter Pacific service – NC18602, later named* California Clipper *– arrives at Manila on 3 March 1939. In August '602 opened the route to Auckland, via Honolulu, Canton Island and Fiji.

28 June 1939 saw the first passenger-carrying commercial crossing of the Atlantic depart Port Washington, New York (left),* Dixie Clipper *taking the southerly route via the Azores and Lisbon (where passengers are pictured disembarking, above) to Marseilles. The aircraft carried 22 passengers and 12 crew.

the first Boeing Model 314. Imperial Airways, Air France and Lufthansa continued their survey flights into 1938, some employing new aircraft.

B-314 delayed

During June 1938, flight testing of the B-314 had begun and immediately threw up a problem with directional control, which was found to be inadequate. The prototype's single tail was replaced with twin fins and then with three tail-fins, the latter modification solving the problem. The angle of the aircraft's hydrostabiliser, or 'seawing', was also reduced to improve control on the water. These changes further delayed delivery of the first aircraft to PAA but, finally, on 27 January 1939, NC18602 *California Clipper* was delivered to San Francisco, and on 29 March made its first flight over the route to Manila and Hong Kong.

The B-314 had a cantilevered wing attached to the top of its large fuselage. The aircraft's mainplane was quite thick at its centre, with sufficient room for flight engineers to crawl out to the rear of the engine nacelles to make minor adjustments. To provide stability on the water, the aforementioned hydrostabiliser was attached at the bottom of the hull.

On 23 February 1939 Captain Gray flew the first Atlantic Division B-314, NC18603, from San Francisco to Baltimore. A few days later, the First Lady, Mrs Eleanor Roosevelt, christened this aircraft *Yankee Clipper.*

On 26 March, Gray left Baltimore in *Yankee Clipper*, bound for Southampton via the mid-Atlantic route. Flight time to Horta, the first stop, was 17 hours 30 minutes, at an average speed of 160 mph (257 km/h). The flight continued to Lisbon on 30 March, docking at the Cabo Ruivo float; due to the Tagus River's fast current, it was best to moor the B-314s and disembark passengers by small boats. The Clipper then continued on to Marseille, Southampton, and Foynes, returning to Baltimore via Lisbon, Horta and Bermuda. The Horta-Bermuda leg took 16 hours 3 minutes to complete, against a 44-mph (71-km/h) headwind. Total flight time was 83 hours for this 22-day, 11,017-mile (17730 km) 'shake-down' trip.

Transatlantic flights begin

On 18 May 1939, the US Civil Aeronautics Board granted Pan American permission to fly a northern route via Newfoundland and Foynes to Southampton, and a southern route via Horta, Lisbon and Marseille to Southampton. At this time, Baltimore was still used as the airline's base and continued to have a terminal alongside New York harbour, though flights between the two were not permitted to carry local traffic. Scheduled service started over the mid-Atlantic route, via Lisbon and Marseille, on 20 May, the first five round-trips carrying mail only. On 24 June, service was opened on the Newfoundland and Foynes route to Southampton, and passenger operations began on 28 June.

In May 1939, PAA began construction of a hangar and terminal at the new North Beach (La Guardia) Airport, which had just been completed. This was the first step toward moving the airline's Atlantic base from Baltimore to New York.

When services commenced the one-way fare from New York to Marseille or Southampton was $375, to Lisbon, $309, and between New York and Bermuda, $70. These were standard fares though the service was closer to 'first class'.

The 'Super Clippers' – Boeing's Model 314

c/n	registration	delivery date	name(s) and Division/disposition
Model 314			
1988	NC18601	1 Apr 1939	*Honolulu Clipper* (Pacific Division) to US Navy as BuNo. 48227; damaged during ditching in Pacific after two engines failed, 4 Nov 1945; sunk by gun fire
1989	NC18602	27 Jan 1939	*California Clipper/Pacific Clipper/California Clipper* (Pacific Division) to USAAF as C-98 42-88632, 18 Dec 1941; to US Navy as BuNo. 99084, 1 Oct 1943; sold to Universal Airways, 1946 (sold to American International, 1947; sold to World Airways, 1948; scrapped, 1950
1990	NC18603	27 Jan 1939	*Yankee Clipper* (Atlantic Division) to US Navy as BuNo. 48224, 1941; sank attempting to land on River Tagus, Lisbon, 22 Feb 1943
1991	NC18604	18 Mar 1939	*Atlantic Clipper* (Atlantic Division) to US Navy as BuNo. 48225; sold to Universal Airways, 1946 (sold to American International, 1947 and broken up for spares)
1992	NC18605	April 1939	*Dixie Clipper* (Atlantic Division) to US Navy as BuNo. 48226; sold to Universal Airways, 1946 (sold to American International, 1947; sold to World Airways, 1948; withdrawn, 1949 and scrapped, 1950)
1993	NC18606	June 1939	*American Clipper* (Atlantic Division) to USAAF as C-98 42-88631, 18 Dec 1941; to US Navy as BuNo. 99083, 17 Aug 1943; sold to Universal Airways, 1946 (sold to American International, 1947; sold to World Airways, 1948; withdrawn, 1949 and scrapped, 1950)
Model 314A			
2081	NC18607	8 Apr 1941	delivered to BOAC as G-AGBZ *Bristol*, 13 Apr 1941; sold to World Airways, 1948 (withdrawn 1949; sank in gale Baltimore Harbor, 1951/52)
2082	NC18608	8 Apr 1941	delivered to BOAC as G-AGCA *Berwick*, 15 Apr 1941; sold to Baltimore Lumber Company, 1949 and scrapped
2083	NC18609	May 1941	*Pacific Clipper/California Clipper/Pacific Clipper* to US Navy as BuNo. 48228; sold to Universal Airways, 1946 (destroyed in storm, Gibraltar, 3 Feb 1947)
2084	NC18610	May 1941	delivered to BOAC as G-AGCB *Bangor*, 15 Jun 1941; sold to Baltimore Lumber Company, 1950 and scrapped
2085	NC18611	June 1941	*Anzac Clipper* to USAAF as C-98 42-88630, 18 Dec 1941; to US Navy as BuNo. 99082; sold to Universal Airways, 1946 (sold to American International, 1947; sold to World Airways, 1948; withdrawn, 1949 and scrapped, 1951)
2086	NC18612	July 1941	*Capetown Clipper* to USAAF as C-98 42-88622, 18 Dec 1941; to US Navy as BuNo. 99081, 17 Aug 1943; sold to Universal Airlines, 1946 (sold to American International, 1947 as *Bermuda Sky Queen*; ran out of fuel over Atlantic, landing near weather ship; crew and passengers taken off and aircraft sunk by gun fire, 8 Oct 1947)

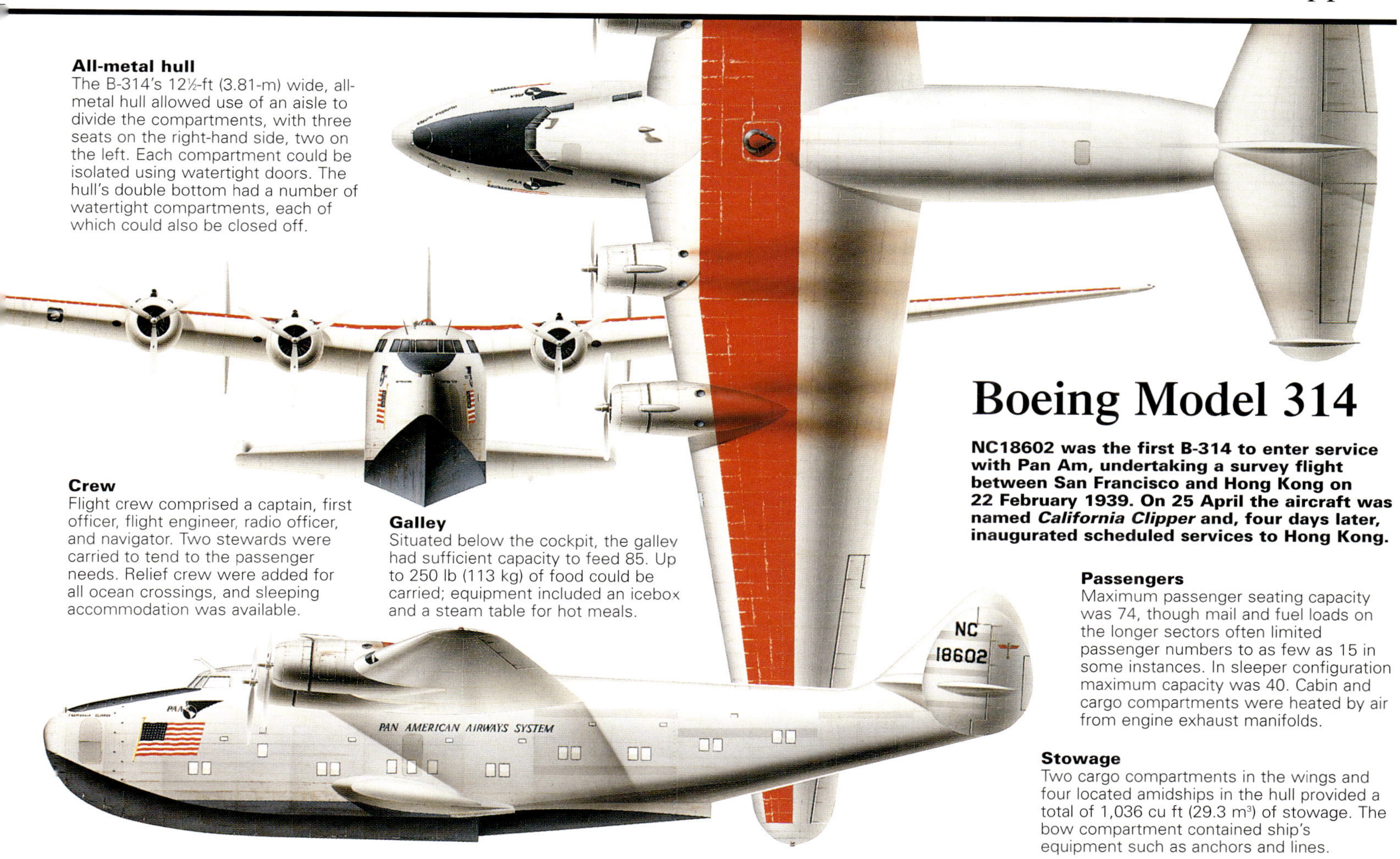

All-metal hull
The B-314's 12½-ft (3.81-m) wide, all-metal hull allowed use of an aisle to divide the compartments, with three seats on the right-hand side, two on the left. Each compartment could be isolated using watertight doors. The hull's double bottom had a number of watertight compartments, each of which could also be closed off.

Crew
Flight crew comprised a captain, first officer, flight engineer, radio officer, and navigator. Two stewards were carried to tend to the passenger needs. Relief crew were added for all ocean crossings, and sleeping accommodation was available.

Galley
Situated below the cockpit, the galley had sufficient capacity to feed 85. Up to 250 lb (113 kg) of food could be carried; equipment included an icebox and a steam table for hot meals.

Boeing Model 314

NC18602 was the first B-314 to enter service with Pan Am, undertaking a survey flight between San Francisco and Hong Kong on 22 February 1939. On 25 April the aircraft was named *California Clipper* and, four days later, inaugurated scheduled services to Hong Kong.

Passengers
Maximum passenger seating capacity was 74, though mail and fuel loads on the longer sectors often limited passenger numbers to as few as 15 in some instances. In sleeper configuration maximum capacity was 40. Cabin and cargo compartments were heated by air from engine exhaust manifolds.

Stowage
Two cargo compartments in the wings and four located amidships in the hull provided a total of 1,036 cu ft (29.3 m³) of stowage. The bow compartment contained ship's equipment such as anchors and lines.

The B-314 flying boats offered the most luxurious air travel yet seen, with standards of privacy and comfort that would not be seen again in commercial airliners.

Operational experience

Pilots liked the B-314, as it handled quite well, though it was heavy on the controls, and had a good autopilot for use en route. On the water, however, the B-314 was difficult to turn in cross-wind conditions, as the hydrostabilisers could not keep the aircraft from heeling.

Landings and take-offs were adversely affected by moderate swells, which could impose severe strain on the aircraft's structure. This condition occurred mostly at Horta, where the tiny harbour forced the use of the open sea for take-offs and landings. In 1940, Captain Gray requested an engineering study of the problem; an incident during a take-off in March had caused the left hydrostabiliser of a B-314 to break loose.

Soon after this, another B-314 alighting at Horta struck an unusually heavy swell, which caused severe damage to its hull. Engineer Borger, sent to Horta to oversee repairs, devised a method for temporary repair by reinforcing the affected area with concrete moulded round the breaks. (This method of quick repair soon became quite common in seaplane operations.)

Thereafter, PAA imposed a rule restricting take-off and landing to a maximum swell-height of 3 ft (0.91 m). This restriction caused numerous delays, especially during the winter months.

Further analysis and testing by Boeing later resulted in a 20-in (50.8-cm) extension of the hull's step, which solved the landing problem and improved handling. All B-314s were modified during 1940, and henceforth drew much praise from their pilots.

The elevators (balanced statically, but not aerodynamically) were operated through control servo tabs, but at high-angle displacement became directly operated through the control column. The rudders also had this spring and tab arrangement. The wing flaps were the 'split' type (fitted under the wing's trailing edge). Usually a setting of 10° to 20° was used for takeoff, and the full 60° was used for landing.

Following the step modification, the B-314 was landed easily, but a problem of crosswinds tipping a wing tip into the water remained; sometimes crewmen were sent into the wings to add weight on the upwind side.

Transatlantic routes

Operations in the Atlantic presented Pan American with a new set of challenges (largely meteorological), the airline's experience thus far having been confined to the warm waters of the Caribbean and Central America. Survey flights during 1937 covered a northerly route (via Shediac, New Brunswick, Botwood, Newfoundland and Foynes) to Southampton and a southerly alternative (via Bermuda, the Azores, Lisbon and Marseilles). The British government insisted that Imperial Airways be able to operate a reciprocal service, but lacked a suitable aircraft; once Pan American introduced the Boeing 314 (which had sufficient range to bypass Bermuda) and secured landing rights in Marseilles the British relented. Pan American was authorised by the Civil Aeronautics Board to operate over both routes in May 1939. With the outbreak of World War II flights over the southerly route terminated in neutral Lisbon.

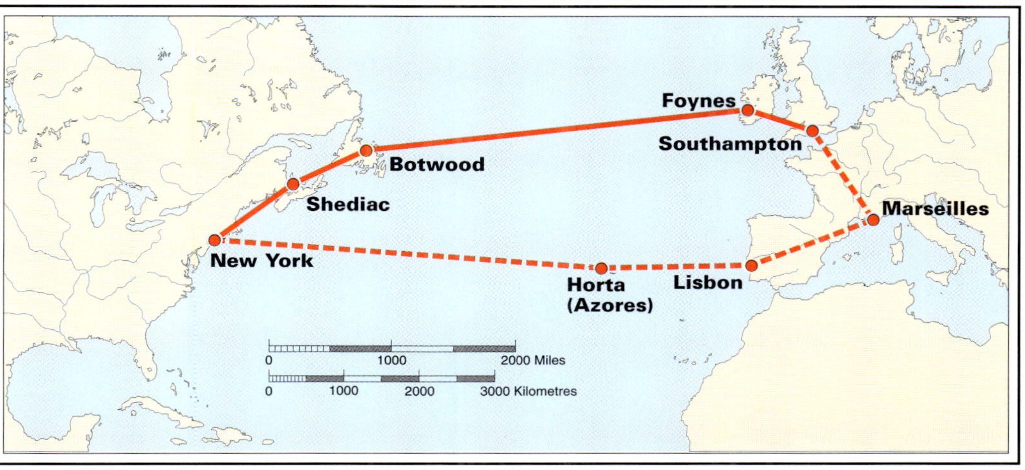

The famous 'Horta swell' often stranded aircraft in the Azores, on the southern route across the North Atlantic; it was not unknown for as many as three B-314s to be caught at the same time. The markings carried by the aircraft (including NC18603 and NC18606) suggest that they were probably photographed in Horta's harbour during the winter of 1939/40.

Left: Four of the B-314s turned over to the military in 1941 were loaned back to Pan Am for their own services (though government personnel had priority over other passengers, as they did with all US airlines in wartime). These aircraft were NC18601, 18603, 18609 and 18611. Here passengers are disembarking from NC18611 **Anzac Clipper*****, at Pan Am's North Beach Marine Terminal in New York, possibly during 1943.***

When the war in Europe began, tremendous demands were placed on the scheduled service, as loads increased rapidly. Delays caused by heavy seas in the Azores, the so-called 'Horta swell', led to a decision to omit the Horta stop on some flights to improve schedule reliability, even though this reduced the permitted payload.

By autumn 1940, the B-314 turnaround and servicing times had been reduced from six days to 48 hours. This was achieved by the standardisation of all six of the B-314s flying in both Atlantic and Pacific Divisions, thus streamlining servicing procedures. A new beaching technique, used to haul a B-314 from the water and into the hangar, required little more than an hour to complete, compared to the usual five hours. New electric winches were employed in place of the tractors previously employed.

Early in 1940, a new route was opened from Lisbon to Bolama, Portuguese Guinea, thence across the South Atlantic to Brazil and Trinidad

Pan Am at war

With the outbreak of war much of Pan Am's equipment was immediately devoted to the war effort. Boeing 314s and Martin 130s were transferred to the USAAF or US Navy, which also acquired title to the airline's Treasure Island, San Francisco base. Pan Am gained a number of contracts to operate services for the Naval Air Transport Service (NATS), the largest of these being in the Pacific, flying supply missions as far west as Australia. Crewed by Pan Am Pacific Division personnel, US Navy PBY Catalinas, PBM Mariners and PB2Y Coronados were employed. The latter included PB2Y-3s, converted as PB2Y-3R freighters (below).

Concurrently, the Atlantic Division had a smaller contract to crew Coronados on services to Port Lyautey, Morocco and Lough Neagh, Northern Ireland. The Alaska Division operated a daily NATS transport landplane service from Seattle, Washington, to the Aleutian Island chain.

Above: Wartime service has taken its toll on M-130 NC14716 **China Clipper*****. This historic aircraft, which had flown the first trans-Pacific service in 1935, was the last surviving M-130 when destroyed in a crash in Trinidad in early 1945.***

Opened on 31 March 1940, the hangar and terminal building at Pan Am's North Beach Terminal (below) were built by the City of New York, at a cost of $40 million, on land leased by the airline. Expanded in later years, North Beach became what is now La Guardia Airport. At the time of the opening the hangar and ramp were still under construction. The latter incorporated an electric winch for hauling the heavy B-314s from the water for maintenance (right).

to New York. This route was intended for winter operation in order to avoid strong winds and the reduced payloads on westerly crossings via the Horta route. However, by early 1941, the US needed to provide more service to West Africa to carry war supplies to British forces in the Middle East. B-314s then began shuttling back and forth between Natal, Brazil (where cargo was flown in from Florida by landplanes) and West Africa. An 18-day schedule was developed for the B-314s, originating in New York from where the aircraft would fly to Natal, make five round trips between Natal and Africa, and return to New York, after 197 flight hours – just in time for the aircraft's required 200-hour maintenance check.

Six new B-314A aircraft were delivered to PAA between April and August 1941. Three of these were relinquished to British Overseas Airways Corporation (BOAC, formed in 1940 by the merger of British Airways and Imperial Airways) and used to maintain essential lines of communication throughout the British Empire.

American Clipper (NC18606) is pictured at Pan Am's Treasure Island, San Francisco base, opened in late 1939. The date is believed to late 1943/early 1944, when Pacific division B-314s were being returned to commercial service on the Hawaii route. Note that the aircraft has been stripped of its camouflage paint (which reduced the flying-boat's weight by 400 lb/181 kg) and has highly polished propeller blades.

The remaining three aircraft were assigned to the Pacific Division, allowing all six B-314s to operate on Atlantic routes, further streamlining aircraft servicing. The B-314s were later brought up to -314A standard.

Pacific services

In the Pacific, meanwhile, B-314s and a pair of M-130s were operating the Manila and Hong Kong service, and a new schedule to New Zealand. Delay in the expansion of the Pacific service was the result of late B-314 delivery and the loss, on 28 August 1938, of the M-130 *Hawaii Clipper*, which disappeared without a trace between Guam and Manila.

S-42B NC16734 had originally inaugurated the scheduled service to Auckland in December 1937, but was lost on 11 January 1938. The flight had left Pago Pago for Auckland, but shortly after departure was forced to shut down no. 4 engine after it lost all its oil. While jettisoning fuel to reduce weight for landing, fire broke out in the aircraft, and it plunged into the sea. All aboard perished. The Auckland service was then suspended until 22 August 1939, when it was re-opened with B-314s over a shorter route, via Honolulu, Canton Island, Nouméa, New Caledonia, and Suva, Fiji.

When Japan attacked the United States on 7 December 1941, two Pan American flights were aloft beyond Hawaii. One, an M-130, was en route between Wake Island and Guam. Returning to Wake Island, it survived a Japanese attack, then made its way back to the US. The other, a B-314 en route from Nouméa to Auckland, returned to the US by way of Australia, Ceylon, Africa, and Brazil. It arrived in New York on 6 January 1942. The flying-boat flew 31,500 miles (50693 km) – 6,026 miles (9698 km) over desert and jungle – crossed the Equator six times, visited five continents, and made the longest non-stop flight in Pan American's history – 3,583 miles (5766 km). It flew 209½ hours in all, with only minor delays – surely one of the greatest feats in airline history.

Hong Kong Clipper (S-42B NC16735), making a night stop at Hong Kong before returning to Manila, was destroyed at the dock in a surprise attack by Japanese bombers on 8 December.

As part of the war effort, all divisions of the Pan American began carrying military supplies and personnel, and all the B-314s and M-130s were requisitioned by the military, Pan American crews operating them under military direction. A limited number of commercial services were also flown.

As the war drew to a close in 1945, it was clear that the days of the flying-boat were numbered. Thanks to the war effort the world now had plenty of land airports and, sure enough, from early 1946 PAA began replacing its flying-boats with Douglas DC-4s and Lockheed Constellations with the equivalent range but better speed performance. The final Pan American B-314 flight arrived in San Francisco from Honolulu on 9 April 1946. There was no fanfare and no celebration, though tears were shed by the staff and others present, as they realised that a romantic and wonderful era had come to an end.

Gene Banning

Sharjah airport, located within the Emirate of the same name on the shores of the Persian Gulf, is a mecca for cargo carriers, plying their trade with freedom from the designated ' international free-trade zone'. The 'maintenance area' or 'northern apron' is home to the vast array of prop-driven freighters tasked with transporting a bewildering array of goods to destinations in the Middle East, Africa, Asia, Russia and the CIS states. The mainstay of these carriers is the Antonov An-12 of which as many as 20 are present at the airport on any one day. Nestled among the numerous An-12s are a handful of its predecessor, the An-8, in various states of repair. Approaching the end of their careers, only one is in a near-airworthy state (EL-AKZ; above). With the type no longer having operator's certificates to many destinations, including Russia, it is unlikely that two other examples present (EL-AKY; left and 3C-QQE) will ever return to commercial service.

Antonovs in the desert

An-8s and An-12s at Sharjah

Photographed by Daniel J. March and David Donald

Above: *Believed to be operated by Aerocom of Moldova, immaculately-finished* ***ER-ACJ*** *is one of a growing number of Moldovan-registered An-12s regularly seen at Sharjah. With plenty of available airframes at relatively low cost, the An-12 has proved the ideal acquisition for the growing number of cargo airlines based at the airport.*

Right: *Sharjah's Sky Aviation maintenance, repair and overhaul facility boasts the ability to cater for the needs of both western and Soviet commercial types. Refurbishment and painting of at least four An-12s was underway in the spring of 2002, with another example undergoing heavy maintenance.*

Below: *Sharjah's northern apron teems with Antonovs in the spring of 2002 either undergoing routine maintenance or awaiting their next tasking. An-8* ***3C-QQE*** *on the left of the image is currently in a non-airworthy state, although some work does appear to be continuing. In the right of the image, Sharjah-based Lotus Airways's sole An-12B is loaded with crated goods prior to another charter cargo flight. In the foreground, an unidentified Mil Mi-8 is typical of the wide range of Soviet-built types operating from Sharjah.*

Above: ***Formed in 1998, Lotus Airways is one of a number of Sharjah-based carriers to have registered its aircraft in Equatorial Guinea (3C-ZZD). One of the An-12's drawbacks as a freighter is the lack of a rear loading ramp. Here cargo is loaded with the aid of a flat-bed vehicle. In the background are two of the four Air Bas (formerly Air Cess) Ilyushin Il-18s resident at Sharjah. These too have adopted Equatorial Guinea registrations.***

Right: 3C-QRN was one of the few An-12s seen at Sharjah that retained the rear gun turret, albeit without guns. The registration was applied with black tape, indicating that this may be a temporary registration. Other types, mainly of Soviet origin, are usually present awaiting maintenance or overhaul. Seen here is Moldova-based Aerocom's sole Tu-154B-2 ER-TAI.

Below: Work was underway on An-8 3C-QQE in early 2002, however, the aircraft had not flown for several months and may well have been being stripped of useful components before scrapping.

Above: ***Owned by Cambodian-based President Airlines, An-12BP XU-355 was acquired from Bulgarian cargo carrier Inter Trans Air in September 2000. Cargo flights to Asian countries constitute an important percentage of Sharjah's movements.***

Left: ***Baking in the 38°C (100°F) midday temperature on Sharjah's northern ramp is Flying Dolphin/Santa Cruz Imperial An-12BP EL-ALJ. Based at Sharjah, the airline is currently moving its aircraft from the Liberian register (as seen here) to the UAE register.***

Above: ***With operators and individual aircraft registrations often changing by the month, keeping track of Sharjah's regular An-12 visitors is never easy. This ex-Aeroflot example, like numerous other examples, carries no operator markings and is believed to be used for ad hoc charter flights to former CIS states and Russia.***

It is believed that only five nominally airworthy Antonov An-8s are left in the hands of commercial operators. Three of these five were present at Sharjah in 2002 including two (EL-AKY; left and EL-AKX; above) which last saw service with Santa Cruz Imperial Airlines. EL-AKY is in a poor state of repair and is very unlikely to fly commercially again. EL-AKZ is in much better condition, and although not currently listed on Flying Dolphin's airworthy inventory, may well see further service. Equatorial Guinea seems to be the favourite 'registration of convenience' for a number of Sharjah-resident cargo companies. The third An-8 (opposite right) is registered in that country to an unknown operator after serving with Bangladesh-based Bismillah Airlines in 2000-01 as 3C-ZZO. The two other An-8s were based at Fujairah, United Arab Emirates in mid-2002.

Boeing 767

Everett's wide-bodied twin family

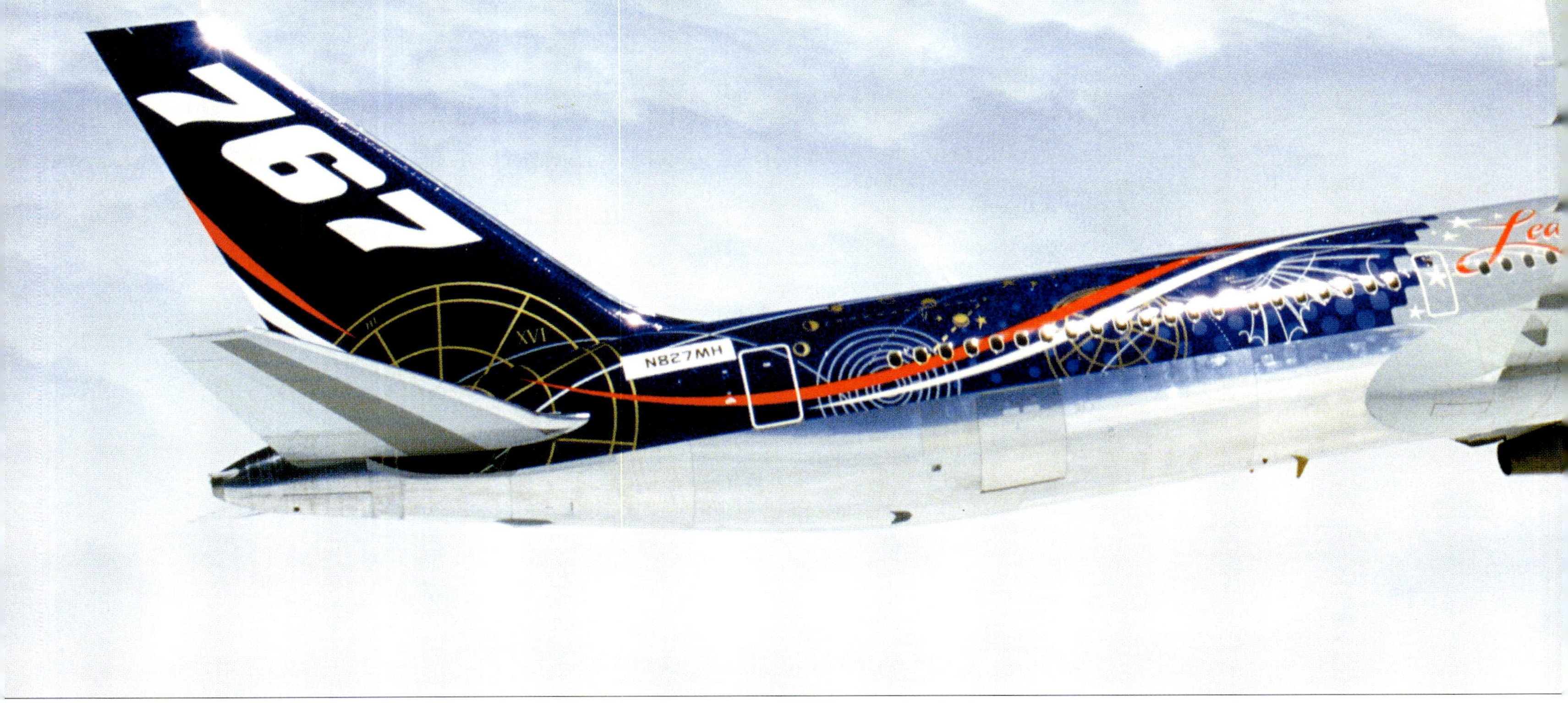

A product of the ambitious 7X7/7N7 programme of the 1970s, the 767 was launched in 1978 as a 175/190-seat, twin-jet, semi-wide body with a 2,000-nm (3704-km) range. In the 22 years since its first flight the 767 has notched up sales exceeding 930 and, in its latest 767-400ER guise, is able to carry 300 passengers over distances exceeding 5,700 nm (10555 km).

Following a protracted evolution commencing when the project was first revealed in August 1971, and working through a number of derivative and new projects, the 767 was announced by Boeing in mid-February 1978. In January 1978, Boeing had already committed to extending the manufacturing facility at Everett to produce a new family of airliners with the designations of 757, 767 and 777 and aimed for a product launch around mid year.

The new projects included the 767-100 – an all new semi-wide body with a seven-abreast seating layout to satisfy an American Airlines requirement for carrying 175 passengers over 2,000 nm (2,301 miles; 3704 km). There was also the 767-200, two seat rows longer to match a United requirement for 190 passengers over the same range; and a pair of 777 tri-jet variants for transcontinental and intercontinental services.

The wings, tail, flight deck and cabin cross-section were to be common to all members of the 767/777 family. To share the economic risks of starting a multiple programme, international collaboration was sought, with Aeritalia transferring its support on earlier projects to the 767/777, and investment from Japan was encouraged. The choice was still to be made between three proven engines and the 767 was beginning to emerge as a shorter-range twin-engined aircraft, but the common wing policy with the 777 provided a greater wing area than optimum to cope with higher gross weights.

By May 1978 the 767-200 was given priority due to firm interest by United Airlines. Design was progressing on wing aerodynamics with some 67 different wind tunnel models being tested, and the cabin would seat up to 250 passengers without the fuselage being structurally too long, or

Boeing 767 prototype N767BA, seen here over Mount Rainier, Washington, flew for the first time on 26 September 1981. With the exception of Australian flag-carrier Qantas, which bowed to trade union pressure to operate its first 767-200s, at least initially, with three-person crews, all 767s are equipped with a two-crew flight deck.

Picture acknowledgments

Front cover: British Airways/John M. Dibbs. **4:** Boeing (two), Bombardier. **5:** Boeing, Sergey Popsuyevich. **6:** Airbus, Boeing, Bombardier. **7:** Bombardier, Airbus, Boeing (two). **8:** Boeing (four), David Fraser, Nigel Pittaway (two), LOT Polish Airlines. **9:** Boeing, Airbus, Bombardier (two). **10:** Steve Kinder (two), Alvaro Romero (three). **11:** Shlomo Aloni, Airbus, Steve Kinder. **12:** Steve Kinder (two), David Fraser (two), David Donald. **14-16:** Boeing. **17:** Bombardier via Terry Panopalis, Santiago Rivas (two). **18-19:** Santiago Rivas. **20:** Mike Vines, Airbus. **21:** Airbus. **22:** Werner Münzenmaier, Airbus (two), Airbus via Mike Jerram (MJ). **23:** Airbus via MJ, Airbus (two). **24:** Airbus, Mike Vines, Airbus via MJ. **25:** Airbus (two), Mike Vines. **26:** Airbus, David Willis, Gerhard Wilhelmer. **27:** Mike Vines, Airbus (two). **28:** Airbus (three), David Fraser. **29:** Gerhard Wilhelmer, Airbus, Nigel Pittaway, Mark Munzel. **30-31:** LOT Polish Airlines. **32:** LOT (two), Günter Endres. **33:** LOT (four). **34:** Günter Endres, Aerospace Publishing, LOT (two). **35:** LOT (five). **36:** LOT (two). **37:** Günter Endres (two). **38:** Günter Endres (two). **39:** LOT, Peter R. March, Günter Endres. **40:** LOT (two), Daniel J. March. **41:** Günter Endres (two), LOT. **42:** Günter Endres, LOT, David Fraser, Daniel J. March. **43:** Günter Endres, LOT, Aerospace Publishing. **44:** AV Photos, LOT. **45:** AV Photos (two), LOT (three). **46:** Boeing via Mike Stroud, AV Photos (two), Daniel J. March, LOT (two). **47:** Günter Endres, LOT (two). **48:** David Willis, Moritz Herrman. **49:** A. Laws (two), Igor Salinger. **50:** Chris Knott/API (two), Steve Kinder (two), David Willis. **51:** David Willis (two), Daniel J. March, Chris Knott/API (two), Marcus Fülber. **52:** Dmitriy Pereslavtsev, Günter Endres (two), David Willis, Steve Kinder. **53:** Chris Knott/API (two), Peter R. March, Daniel J. March, Dmitriy Pereslavtsev, Steve Kinder. **54:** Chris Knott/API, David Willis, Steve Kinder (three), Peter R. March. **55:** Chris Knott/API, Marcus Fülber, A. Laws, David Willis (two), Eugene Gadet. **56-57:** British Airways/John M. Dibbs. **58:** British Airways. **59:** Air France, British Airways/Newscast. **60:** Aerospace Publishing (two), Aerospace Imaging, Bristol Siddeley via Terry Panopalis (TP). **61:** RAE via TP (two), Rolls-Royce via TP, Fairey. **62:** Sud-Aviation, BAC (seven). **63:** Aerospace Imaging (two), Sud-Aviation. **64:** BAC (two), Aerospace Imaging. **65:** Peter R. March, BAC, Rolls-Royce via TP, Aerospace Imaging. **66:** Aerospace Imaging (four). **67:** Aerospace Imaging (three). **68:** Chris Knott/API, Aerospace Imaging (two), BAE Systems. **69:** A&AEE via TP, BAE Systems, Arthur Gibson Collection, EADS. **70:** BAC, Peter R. March, Arthur Gibson Collection (two). **71:** Arthur Gibson Collection (three). **72:** Arthur Gibson Collection (four). **73:** Aérospatiale (two), Chris Knott/API, Arthur Gibson Collection. **74:** BAC, Aerospace Publishing (three), Aerospace Imaging. **75:** Arthur Gibson Collection (two), Aerospace Publishing. **76:** Arthur Gibson Collection (two), via Peter R. March. **77:** Chris Knott/API, EADS, Aerospace Publishing, British Airways. **78:** Chris Knott/API, BAC. **79:** GIFAS, Chris Knott/API, via Peter R. March. **80:** Air France (two), Chris Knott/API. **81:** BAC (two), Arthur Gibson Collection. **82:** SNECMA via TP, Rolls-Royce (two), Aerospace Imaging, Arthur Gibson Collection (two). **83:** Sud-Aviation, British Airways, Arthur Gibson Collection (two). **84:** BAC, Air France, British Airways, Arthur Gibson Collection. **89:** Aerospace Imaging, David Donald, Peter R. March. **90:** Air France, Chris Knott/API, Aerospace Publishing. **91:** Peter R. March, Air France, Braniff International. **92:** Chris Knott/API, AeroTransport Data Bank (ATDB), Terry Panopalis. **93:** Chris Knott/API (four). **94:** Peter R. March (two), Air France. **95:** Air France, Peter R. March, British Airways. **96:** Peter R. March, ATDB (two). **97:** Air France, British Airways (two), Jim Winchester. **98:** Jim Winchester, British Airways (two). **99:** British Airways (two), Air France. **100:** Air France, British Airways/Newscast (two). **101:** British Airways, Air France. **102:** Air France (two). **103:** Peter J. Cooper (two), Peter R. March. **104:** Peter J. Cooper, David Willis, GIFAS. **105:** British Airways (two). **106:** Aérospatiale, Air France, Aerospace Publishing. **107:** Sud-Aviation, Chris Knott/API. **108:** Aerospace Imaging, Peter R. March (two), Arthur Gibson Collection. **109:** Peter R. March, ATDB (four). **110:** Peter R. March, ATDB (two), Peter R. March, David Donald. **111:** British Airways, Peter R. March (two), ATDB, David Donald. **112:** ATDB (three), Chris Knott/API, Terry Panopalis. **113:** Peter R. March (two), Terry Panopalis, British Airways. **114:** Peter R. March, GIFAS, Andrew P. March, Daniel J. March, Jim Winchester. **115:** British Airways/John M. Dibbs. **116:** Rolls-Royce, Pratt & Whitney. **117:** Rolls-Royce. **118:** Pratt & Whitney, General Electric (three). **119:** General Electric, Pratt & Whitney, Rolls-Royce. **120:** Erickson. **121:** Peter R. March, Erickson (three). **122:** Erickson (three). **123:** Ted Carlson, Erickson (four). **124:** Erickson (four). **125:** Werner Münzenmaier, Erickson (two). **126:** Erickson, Nigel Pittaway (three). **127:** Nigel Pittaway (six). **128:** Nigel Pittaway (two), Erickson (three). **129:** Australian DNRE (two), Erickson (two). **130:** Arthur Gibson Collection. **131:** via Bill Yenne (four). **132:** Robert F. Dorr, via Bill Yenne (two). **133:** Robert F. Dorr (four), via Bill Yenne. **134:** Robert F. Dorr, via Bill Yenne (three). **135:** via Bill Yenne (two). **137-138:** Space Imaging. **139-140:** via Bill Yenne. **141:** Marcus Fülber, Bill Yenne. **142:** Bombardier (two). **143:** Mike Vines (two), Embraer via Mike Vines, via Terry Panopalis (two). **144:** Bombardier (two), via Terry Panopalis, Marko Malec, Ted Carlson. **145:** Aerospace Publishing (four), Mike Vines (three). **146:** Peter R. March (two), Daniel J. March (two), Embraer (two). **147:** Bombardier (two), via Terry Panopalis, Moritz Hermann, Mike Vines. **148:** Boeing, Daniel J. March, Mike Vines, EADS (two), Bombardier. **149:** Bombardier (three). **150:** Embraer (three), Mike Vines (two). **151:** Mike Vines (two). **152:** Aerospace Publishing, Gene Banning. **153:** Gene Banning (two), Pan Am. **154:** Gene Banning (two). **155:** Gene Banning (four), Aerospace Publishing. **156:** Aerospace Publishing (two), Gene Banning. **158:** Pan Am (two), Gene Banning (two). **159-162:** Gene Banning. **163:** Aerospace Publishing, Pan Am, Gene Banning. **164:** via Mike Stroud (two). **166:** Pan Am (two), Gene Banning (two). **167:** Gene Banning (two), Aerospace Publishing. **168-171:** Daniel J. March and David Donald. **172-173:** Boeing. **174:** Boeing via Phillip Birtles, Boeing (two). **175:** Boeing. **176:** Boeing (three), Phillip Birtles. **177-181:** Boeing. **182:** Boeing, Phillip Birtles. **183:** Daniel J. March, Boeing. **184-185:** Boeing.

INDEX

Page numbers in **bold** refer to illustration captions.

Left: Over long sectors Boeing claims that the raked wing tip fitted to the -400ER can bring a 4-5 per cent fuel saving. Removable in 30 minutes, the wing tip can be easily replaced with a conventional tip if required.

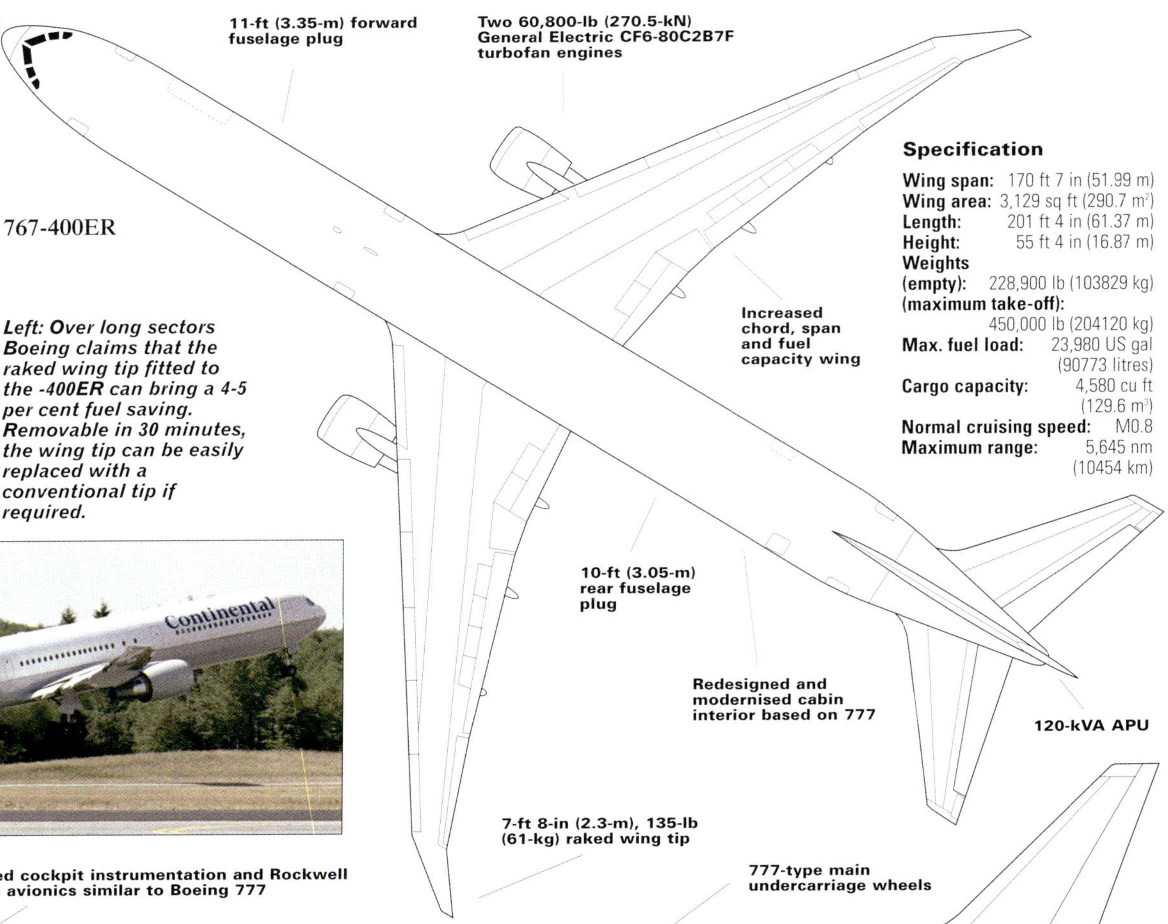

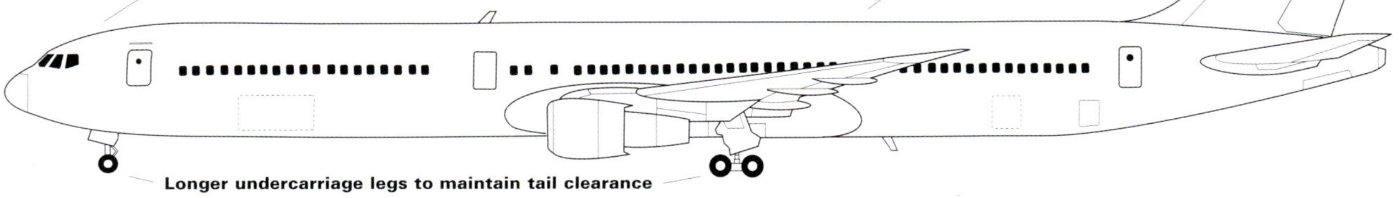

Specification

Wing span: 170 ft 7 in (51.99 m)
Wing area: 3,129 sq ft (290.7 m^2)
Length: 201 ft 4 in (61.37 m)
Height: 55 ft 4 in (16.87 m)
Weights
(empty): 228,900 lb (103829 kg)
(maximum take-off): 450,000 lb (204120 kg)
Max. fuel load: 23,980 US gal (90773 litres)
Cargo capacity: 4,580 cu ft (129.6 m^3)
Normal cruising speed: M0.8
Maximum range: 5,645 nm (10454 km)

Above: Introduced to plug a capacity gap between its 767-200s and 777-200s, Continental uses 767-400ERs on transatlantic, Caribbean and South American routes.

Below: The 767-400ER test programme involved four aircraft, including N76400 (c/n 29703), first flown on 9 October 1999.

767-400ERX

By 1999 Boeing was studying a further extended range version, reviving the 767-400ERX designation for a proposed American Airlines requirement with a further 600-nm (1110-km) range. American was interested in the possible use of a new type for routes from the USA to Europe and South America replacing earlier 767s, but service entry had been delayed until at least 2003. The take off weight was to be increased to 465,000 lb (210924 kg) with the addition of 2,000 US gal (7570 litres) of fuel in the horizontal stabiliser, and the aircraft would require a 68,000-lb (303-kN) thrust powerplant. Lufthansa was also evaluating the 767-400ERX for transpacific routes. By mid-1999 Boeing was also considering a shrink of the Series 400ER as an alternative way to meet the long range requirement. A possible layout would be with a 767-300 fuselage with the -400 wing, or just a shrink of the -400 fuselage.

The first airline interest in the 767-400ERX was an order for three from Kenya Airways, with interest being shown by Lauda Air for up to eight aircraft, with a launch of the new variant planned when the market justified it. However, the downturn in the commercial aircraft market from late 1999 ensured a dearth of real interest and the project was abandoned in 2001.

767-400 MC²A

Boeing announced in March 2002 a proposal of the 767-400 airframe being used for a multi-role command & control aircraft (MC²A), combining airborne and ground surveillance with electronic intelligence (ELINT) in one platform. The 767-400 would have a dorsal mounted Wedgetail-type electronically scanned airborne early warning (AEW) antenna, and a ground surveillance array in the underside of the forward fuselage. The major challenge will be to determine whether it will be practical to install multiple sensors in one platform. The aircraft would be a common replacement for the USAF E-3s, EC-135 Rivet Joint ELINT and Northrop Grumman E-8Cs JSTARS. Boeing is proposing a phased introduction of the MC²A aircraft, with a ground surveillance-capable aircraft entering service in about 2010; ELINT and AEW capabilities would be added later. If the USAF decides to opt for single sensor platforms, Boeing intends to propose the use of the 767-300 or -400 as the basis for such an aircraft. Engine and cockpit commonality between the new sensor platform and the proposed lease of 767-200 tankers is being stressed by Boeing.

main-deck power cargo handling system, no fire suppression system for live or perishable loads and reduced galley and toilet compartments.

Construction of the first UPS aircraft commenced in January 1995 with a roll-out in May and a first flight on 20 June. Following certification, the first 767-300F was delivered to UPS on 12 October with proving flights from the Louisville, Kentucky, base completed by the end of the month. The FAA gave tentative approval for 180-minute ETOPS with full approval to follow when UPS maintenance, operations and support systems had been reviewed. Two of the 30 options have been converted into firm orders, bringing total 767-300F sales to 40 aircraft.

The first full-specification 767-300F General Market Freighter was delivered to Asiana in August 1996 fitted with a main deck power freight handling system, full fire suppression for live and perishable loads and enhanced galley and toilet facilities. LAN Chile has also taken delivery of six -316F Freighters, the last in September 2001. In addition, All Nippon Airways (ANA) has ordered a single example.

***Above:* The 767-300F's fuselage is completely windowless to save weight, unlike many other freighters which have 'plugged' window spaces. LAN Chile cargo operates six examples.**

***Left:* Freight is loaded into the 767-300F via an upward-opening door on the port side of the forward cabin.**

***Below:* As it had been for the earlier 757PF, UPS was launch customer for the 767-300 Freighter; here N301UP, the first 767-34AF of 30 ordered by the parcel carrier, shares Everett's tarmac with an example of the largest member of the Boeing freighter family, the 747-400F.**

767-300ER tanker conversion

In February 1999 the UK's Ministry of Defence (MoD) issued a request for information to industry for a Future Strategic Tanker Aircraft (FSTA) for the RAF to replace its ageing VC10 and TriStar tanker fleets. This was anticipated to be the largest Private Finance Initiative (PFI) run by MoD and the requirement included a secondary transport role. Companies were asked to put forward proposals covering supply, management, funding and operation of the aircraft that could be chartered-out for civilian passenger use when not required.

By early 2000 three of the original four teams bidding were offering converted surplus British Airways 767-300ERs. By mid-2001 two teams remained in the bidding process with the Tanker & Transport Service Company (TTSC) offering surplus British Airways 767s. TTSC is a joint venture between BAE Systems, Boeing and Strategic Support Management, the latter itself a Spectrum Capital/Serco joint venture. The winner is expected to provide a flight refuelling service for some 27 years with a guaranteed provision of 10 tankers; a surge requirement of around 20 to meet operational needs also exists.

MoD was expected to make a decision by the end of 2002, with contract signature in 2003 and service commencement before 2007. However, in July 2002 MoD announced that service entry would begin in early 2008 citing "delays in contract negotiations" and the decision was delayed.

The aircraft will be role-equipped with hose-and-drogue units; these will need to be removed to satisfy CAA requirements when the aircraft are used for third-party work. The aircraft will be certificated to European Joint Aviation Authority (JAA) standards.

767-300X

In 2001 a Boeing product development document described the proposed 767-300X as the "the perfect solution for Asia", aiming the variant squarely at the short- and medium-range market, where it would replace A310s, A300s and early production 767s. Essentially an updated 767-300, the -300X featured the new flight deck, updated 777-style cabin and raked wing tips of the 767-400ER. It also retained the ability to be converted to 'extended range' standard, should the operator so desire, at a later date. With no firm interest the project is currently on-hold.

767-400ER

Probably the ultimate stretch of the Boeing 767, the -400ER has seating for up to 375 passengers in a single-class high-density configuration. Studies of the 767ERY were first revealed by Boeing in April 1993 as a new long-range version to compete with the Airbus A340, increasing the range from 6,048 nm (11200 km) to 7,181 nm (13300 km). The principle focus for changes was the wing with overall area and fuel capacity increased by a chord extension and greater span. Additional structural strengthening was required in the stretched cabin over the wing centre-section, the rear pressure bulkhead and tail assembly.

The fuselage is lengthened by 21 ft (6.40 m) to 201 ft 4 in (61.37 m) by inserting two plugs either side of the centre section, and the maximum take off weight has increased to 450,000 lb (204120 kg). The wing span has increased to 170 ft 7 in (51.99 m), including new raked wingtips, giving significant improvements in aerodynamic efficiency. The canted winglets offset the weight increase, enabling the -400ER to be flown on the same routes as the -300ER without additional fuel. An all-new main landing gear with 777 wheels was fitted to cope with the increased weight and to maintain adequate ground clearance during take-off rotation. The flight deck has been updated along similar lines to the Boeing 777, featuring six large liquid crystal displays (LCDs). The cabin was also updated to incorporate many of the proven 777 features.

Following a range of detailed internal studies, Boeing announced the 767-400ER on 6 January 1997. The new derivative was expected to be capable of operating all US domestic services, as well as flying transatlantic routes from Atlanta to London, New York to Rome and Chicago to Frankfurt.

In March 1997 Delta Air Lines and Boeing came to a controversial agreement covering a 20-year exclusive fleet renewal programme for the purchase of up to 644 aircraft. This included the launch order for 21 767-400ERs with options on a further 24, powered by 60,800-lb (270.5-kN) GE CF6-80C2B7F turbofans. After roll-out on 26 August, the first aircraft flew on 9 October 1999, starting an 850-hour flight test programme, with FAA certification achieved in July 2000. The only other firm order for the 767-400ER is from Continental for 30 (later reduced to 16) aircraft within another sole supplier deal in June 1997. Delta placed the aircraft into service on 1 May 2001, the last of its 21 aircraft being delivered in early 2002. Continental had 16 767-400ERs in service in spring 2003.

Boeing also studied a freighter derivative of the -400ER in 2001; the so-called 767-400XF was aimed the DC-10-30F replacement market.

The 767-400ER was designed to replace ageing Lockheed TriStars and McDonnell Douglas DC-10s, as well as older Airbus A300 and A310s.

fleet by 51 767-300ERs over a period of time, and United eventually added 33 of this version. In North America, Air Canada ordered 10 767-300ERs to add to earlier 767-200/-200ERs.

The 767-300ER proved to be popular with a number of European charter airlines with Spanair taking two, Air Europe eight, Condor nine, Leisure International two, and Airtours three. Britannia Airways added a total of 10 767-300ERs for long-haul charters for both its UK-based operations, and those of its German subsidiary, which was subsequently absorbed into LTU. Other European charter operators of 767-300ERs include the now defunct City Bird, Sobelair (four), Balair (two) and Eurofly (one).

China has been buying western produced airliners for some years, and 767-300ERs are in operation with China Southern, Air China, Shanghai, and China Yunnan. With the opening up of the former Soviet Union, there has been a need to replace the older, less efficient airliners, and Aeroflot has six 767-300ERs on lease with additional aircraft operated by Transaero and four PW4000-powered 767-300ERs with Uzbekistan. One VIP Series 300ER has been delivered to the UAE Amiri Flight, and one was delivered to the Chinese Air Force in September 2001, with another added in 2002. Nine -300ERs have been delivered to Royal Brunei, linking the Kingdom with Europe and the USA. Amongst the European operators are Alitalia with eight aircraft, Iberia with two and KLM with 11.

767-300ER orders account for over 50 per cent of 767 sales, with the current figure standing at 506.

At the behest of British Airways, the 767-300ER was offered with a Rolls-Royce RB.211 option. BA and Qantas, which operates seven ex-BA examples, are the only Rolls-engined 767 operators. 767-336ER G-BZHC is pictured on approach to London-Heathrow in April 2002.

767-300ERX

767-300ERX was the subject of a study initiated in 1998, with a view to extending the range of the -300ER still further, providing what Boeing described as "-300ER capacity at -200ER range". This would have been accomplished by adding a tailplane fuel tank with a capacity of 2,000 US gal (1,665 Imp gal; 7571 litres). An increase in range of some 6,695 nm (7,704 miles; 12398 km) was envisaged. Raked wing tips, as fitted to the 767-400ER also appeared to have been an option. Boeing also looked at a '767-400ER Shrink' variant to fill the same requirement.

767-300F Freighter

Boeing studied specialist cargo versions of the 767 to provide an intermediate capacity between the 757PF (Package Freighter) and the larger 747. In January 1993 the long awaited freighter version was launched following an initial order from UPS (United Parcel Service) for 30 aircraft plus options on 30 more. The new aircraft was based on the 767-300ER and was expected to replace earlier models of the DC-8 with UPS. Despite stiff competition from McDonnell Douglas with the MD-11C and Airbus with the A300-600C, the selection process was helped by the fleet commonality with the earlier 757PF, which was launched by UPS in 1987.

To adapt the 767-300 airframe to the freighter role, Boeing added local strengthening to the main undercarriage and the internal wing structure. A new 8.8 x 11 ft (2.67 x 3.35 m) upward opening cargo door was fitted on the port side of the forward fuselage, and the main deck floor structure was strengthened to take a load of up to 24 cargo containers. Because the order was of a reasonable size no window cut-outs were fitted during production allowing stringers to be deleted, saving weight. The initial maximum take-off weight was 408,510 lb (185300 kg) with a planned growth to 424,383 lb (192500 kg). The maximum revenue payload varies from 101,411 lb (46000 kg) over a 4,000-nm (7407-km) range to 125,667 lb (57000 kg) over 2,997 nm (5550 km).

The competition for engine supplier was intense with Rolls-Royce hoping to gain a second 767 application for the RB211-524H turbofans following its success with the RB211-535E4 with the earlier 757PFs. However, the winner was GE with CF6-80C2 engines, which were selected in mid-1993 due to the ability to deliver a new low-emission engine in time for the first delivery, a deadline which Rolls-Royce and Pratt & Whitney could not meet. The terms of the agreement included the modified 62,100 lb (276.34 kN) thrust CF6-80C2B7F with a 40 per cent reduction in hydrocarbon, carbon monoxide and nitrogen emissions, and included 68 engines for the 30 aircraft on firm order. The engine/airframe combination was to be certificated with full ETOPS capability.

The Freighter development programme lasted only 31 months from go ahead to delivery of the first aircraft. The UPS version differed in a number of ways from the proposed Boeing generic freighter including the deletion of the

Asiana's -300 General Market Freighter is equipped with a powered cargo-handling system. Here the airline's sole example receives a 'representative' load, including a spare CF6-80 engine and a 1969 Corvette sports car.

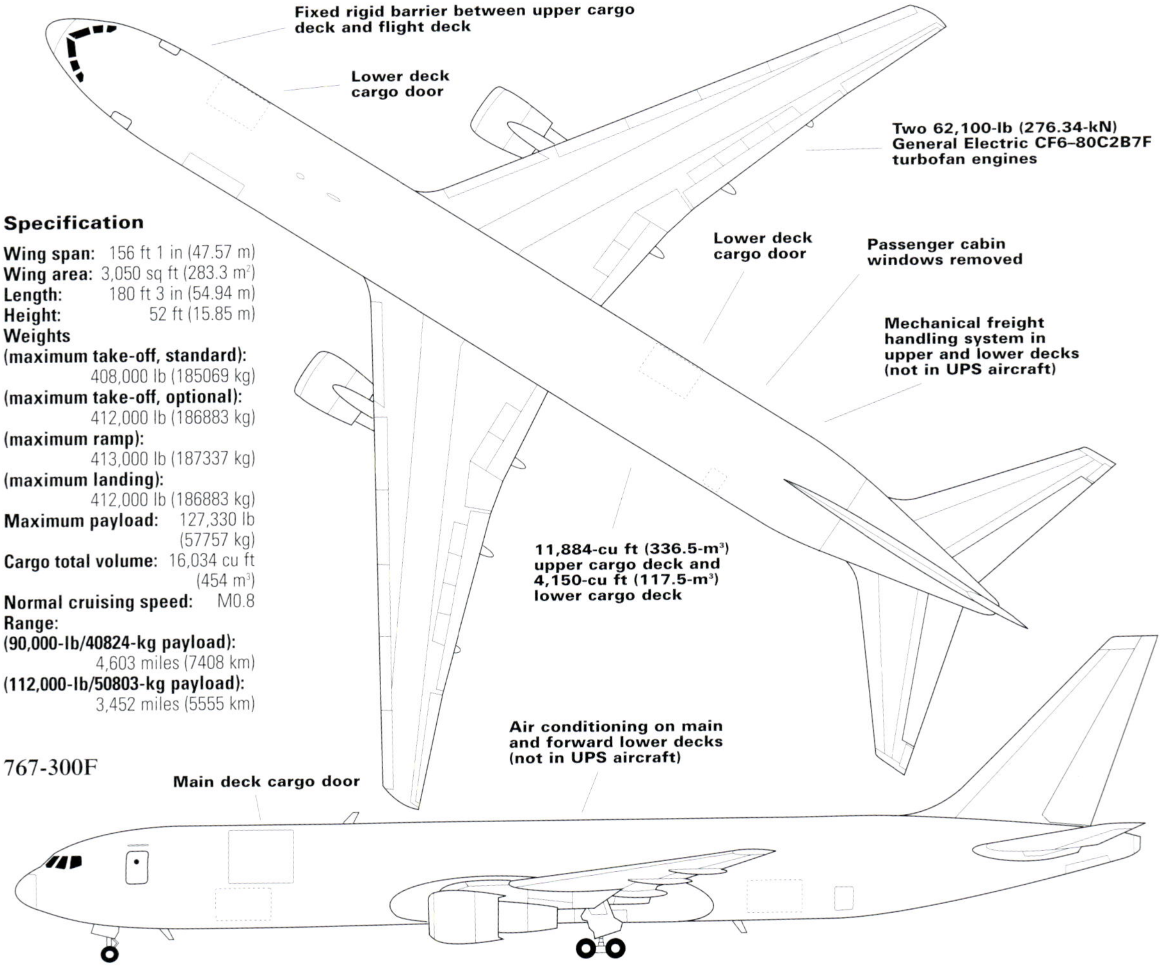

Specification

Wing span: 156 ft 1 in (47.57 m)
Wing area: 3,050 sq ft (283.3 m^2)
Length: 180 ft 3 in (54.94 m)
Height: 52 ft (15.85 m)
Weights
(maximum take-off, standard): 408,000 lb (185069 kg)
(maximum take-off, optional): 412,000 lb (186883 kg)
(maximum ramp): 413,000 lb (187337 kg)
(maximum landing): 412,000 lb (186883 kg)
Maximum payload: 127,330 lb (57757 kg)
Cargo total volume: 16,034 cu ft (454 m^3)
Normal cruising speed: M0.8
Range:
(90,000-lb/40824-kg payload): 4,603 miles (7408 km)
(112,000-lb/50803-kg payload): 3,452 miles (5555 km)

767-300

The first major 767 development was the -300 with a 10-ft 1-in (3.07-m) fuselage plug in the forward cabin and an 11-ft (3.35-m) plug aft, increasing the maximum seating capacity to 351 passengers. This simple development was made possible by the original generous wing area. The 767-300 was revealed in September 1983 when Japan Airlines placed a launch order for six aircraft for high-density domestic services in Japan. The stretched 767-300 combined the structural features of the 767-200ER, including strengthened undercarriage, thicker wing and fuselage skins and increased all-up weight.

Powered by JT9D engines, the first 767-300 made its maiden flight from Boeing's Paine Field on 30 January 1986, with deliveries commencing to JAL on 9 September 1986. JAL eventually increased its fleet of high-capacity 767-300s to a total of 19 aircraft, and All Nippon Airways had a fleet of 30 of this version. Delta Air Lines is a major user of the 767-300 on US domestic services, ordering a fleet of 23 aircraft, while others were ordered by Asiana and Varig, bringing total production of this variant to 77.

Like the 767-200, the 767-300 sold in relatively modest numbers, the longer-range -300ER proving more popular with operators. The fuselage stretch was a straightforward one, as it used the existing -200ER's wing.

767-300ER

The most popular 767 development is the 767-300ER, which combined the high-capacity stretched cabin of the 767-300 with additional fuel in the wings as well as the centre-section. The initial gross weight was 380,000 lb (172368 kg) giving a similar range to the 767-200ER, but with a further weight increase to 400,000 lb (181440 kg) an additional range of 500 miles (805 km) was achieved. To provide sufficient power for this heavier weight aircraft the newer generation Pratt & Whitney PW4056 and General Electric CF6-80C2 turbofans, developing up to 63,300 lb (281.7 kN), were fitted in nacelles similar to the 747-400. As a result of a British Airways order, the Rolls-Royce RB.211-524H was added as a powerplant option.

The first 767-300ER was delivered to American Airlines on 19 February 1988 and remains as one of the options in today's Boeing 767 catalogue. Following the initial American order for 30 767-200s, all subsequent orders by the airline were for 767-300ERs , eventually totalling 49 aircraft. Transbrasil was an early customer with three 737-300ERs, followed by Lauda Air, which eventually bought nine aircraft, although one was lost on 27 May 1991 after take-off from Bangkok when control was lost after an uncommanded deflection of the port engine reverse thrust during the climb. Transbrasil ceased operations in November 2001. Other early major orders came from Canadian Airlines for an eventual total of 14 Series 300ERs, and Qantas, which now has 22 in service, in addition to some passed on by British Airways.

For charter operations LTU had a fleet of five -300ERs and Martinair of Holland bought a fleet of six. Also in Europe SAS operates a fleet of 13 767-300ERs as far apart as Hong Kong and Seattle, and Air France ordered a total of six. As already mentioned, the BA order, which eventually grew to 28 aircraft, launched the Rolls-Royce RB.211 turbofan-engined version. BA initially used its aircraft on European services until experience had built up for transatlantic ETOPS routes. They are now flown regularly on longer thin routes, taking full advantage of the range and economics of a smaller twin-engined aircraft, replacing larger Boeing 747s.

Already a major operator of earlier 767s, ANA ordered a total of 12 767-300ERs for its longer range regional routes and in the Middle East the Gulf Air fleet grew to a total of 18 767-300ERs, while Egyptair added two. Delta had already had in operation 767-200s and -300s and increased its

American Airlines took delivery of the first -300ERs in 1988 and has amassed a fleet of 49 examples. Most seat 190 passengers in three classes, though a handful are 228-seaters with first and economy class seating only.

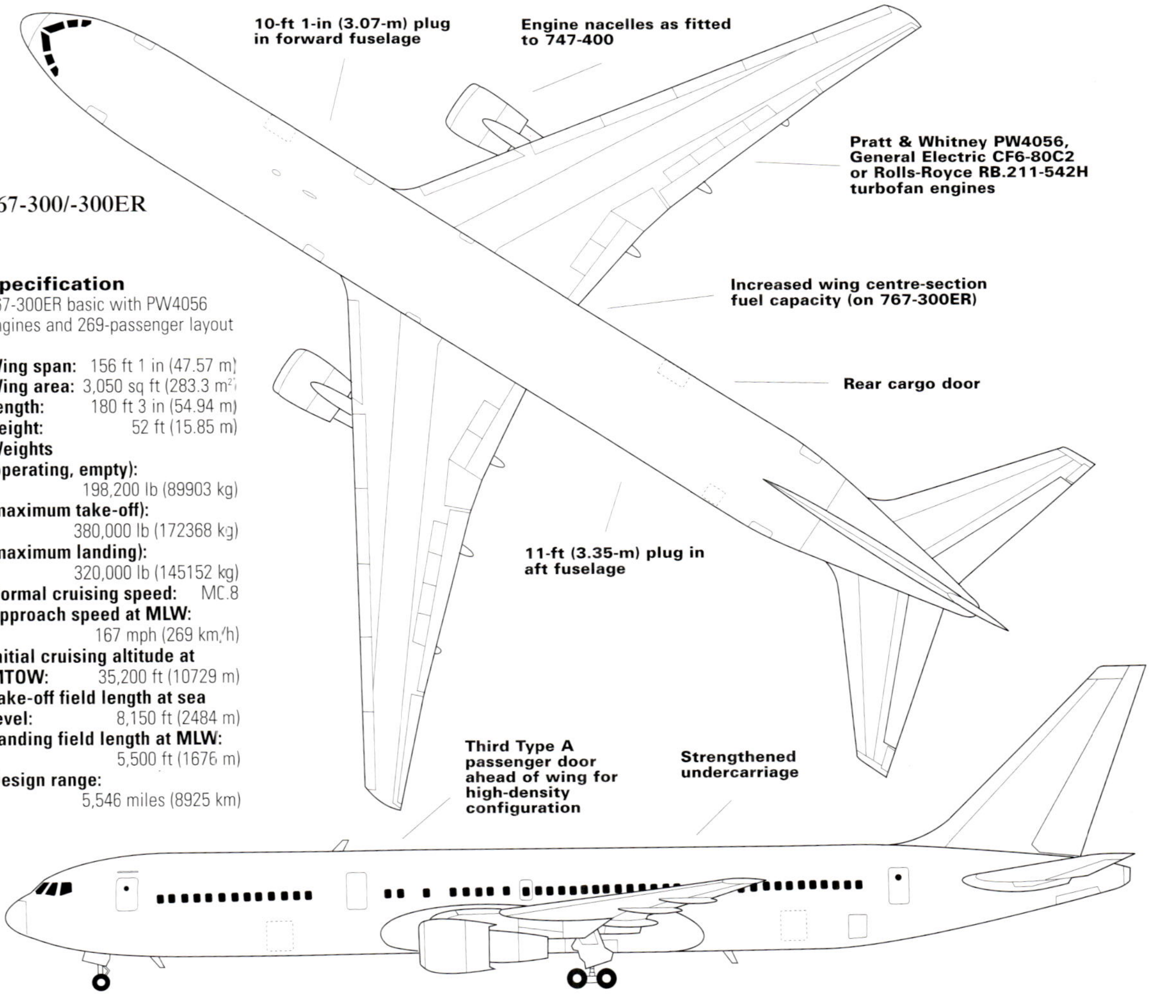

767-300/-300ER

Specification
767-300ER basic with PW4056 engines and 269-passenger layout

Wing span: 156 ft 1 in (47.57 m)
Wing area: 3,050 sq ft (283.3 m²)
Length: 180 ft 3 in (54.94 m)
Height: 52 ft (15.85 m)
Weights
(operating, empty): 198,200 lb (89903 kg)
(maximum take-off): 380,000 lb (172368 kg)
(maximum landing): 320,000 lb (145152 kg)
Normal cruising speed: MO.8
Approach speed at MLW: 167 mph (269 km/h)
Initial cruising altitude at MTOW: 35,200 ft (10729 m)
Take-off field length at sea level: 8,150 ft (2484 m)
Landing field length at MLW: 5,500 ft (1676 m)
Design range: 5,546 miles (8925 km)

767 final assembly takes place at Boeing's massive Everett plant, originally built for 747 production and extended to accommodate the 767. Here -400ER fuselage sub-assemblies, manufactured in Japan by Mitsubishi and Kawasaki, are being lowered onto jigs as the complete aircraft begins to take shape.

The Boeing-owned first 767 (N767BA), powered by P&W JT9D-7R4 engines, was rolled out at Everett on 4 August 1981, followed by preparations for the maiden flight which was made by Tom Edmunds, the project pilot, on 26 September 1981. This start to a very demanding flight development programme was three days earlier than scheduled when the overall programme had been planned three years previously. The aircraft took off on its first flight at a gross weight of 240,000 lb (108864 kg) and handling characteristics from the stall buffet boundary at 102 kt to 225 kt (117 mph; 189 km/h to 259 mph; 417 km/h) were checked during the 2-hour, 4-minute flight. Flap operation in the landing configuration of 30° was checked prior to landing, and the undercarriage and speed brake operation were checked with flaps retracted and lowered. The aircraft behaved exactly as predicted, and the digital flight instruments were praised by the crew for clarity and ability to provide precise orientation.

Following initial testing at Paine Field, where the wide body facility was located, the bulk of the flight test programme was undertaken at the Flight Development Centre at Boeing Field just south of Seattle. The first aircraft was allocated to airworthiness testing including control and stability, and aerodynamic performance with flutter testing completed in the first 15 flying hours. Early flight trials covered longitudinal stability and control, buffet boundaries, dynamic damping and the approach to the stall in a variety of configurations. The 767 achieved a speed of Mach 0.91 and an altitude of 43,100 ft (13137 m) during the early part of the flight testing. In December the first aircraft was based at Palmdale near Los Angeles to give access to the long runways at Edwards AFB, where minimum unstick velocity testing and other critical trials such as maximum energy brake tests could be carried out.

Second aircraft joins programme

On 4 November, the second 767 joined the flight development programme and was allocated to control testing, plus digital avionics, engines and electrical systems. The third aircraft flew on 28 December and was used to check flight loads, test pneumatic and automatic flight controls, and examine in more detail the stall and buffet characteristics. The fourth aircraft flew on 30 December and was used for aerodynamic measurements and noise investigations. The first four P&W-powered 767s flew 1,445 hours in 1,251 sorties up to the end of June 1982 and the second aircraft was allocated to FAA evaluation starting on 10 December.

Following United, Delta had placed orders for 767s powered by two General Electric CF6-80C2 turbofans, developing 56,430 lb (251 kN) thrust. Its first aircraft, the fifth off the production line, flew on 19 February 1982 and was used for engine performance measurement in 230 sorties over 239 flight hours. Certification flying started in March with approval achieved in six months.

The original flight deck had been configured for three crew, but the advances in the displays and systems allowed the aircraft to be operated by a crew of two. This added some 185 hours to the development programme out of a total of 1,600, which was completed, over a period of 10 months, on 30 July 1982, a deadline set in December 1978. Following the findings of a US Presidential task force confirming the safety of two-crew operations, 16 of the first 17 customers changed to a two-crew layout, 30 of the earlier aircraft being converted by Boeing before delivery. The sixth 767 was allocated to testing this configuration and flew again on 27 May 1982, ready for a demanding 15-day 29,000-mile (53708-km) FAA monitored functional and reliability tour starting on 6 July. During this operation, seven countries were visited in Europe and the Middle East, where testing was combined

Above: In response to demands from airlines for a variant with great range, Boeing produced the 767-200ER. As well as finding favour on transatlantic, intra-Asian and African routes, this variant was popular with South American carriers. Brazilian airline Varig (above) ordered six with other customers including TACA, Lan Chile, Transbrasil and Avianca.

The definitive 767 in terms of sales is the 767-300ER. Lauda Air was an early customer, placing an initial order in 1987 and eventually taking nine examples.

earlier than anticipated and specified a 198-in (5-m) wide twin-lobe cabin capable of carrying up to 197 passengers. The low fuselage-mounted tailplane configuration was settled at the last minute before placing the order, having previously been of a T-tail layout. The underfloor hold was configured to accommodate 22 LD-2 containers with additional room for bulk cargo. Power was from a pair of Pratt & Whitney JT9D-7R turbofans developing 44,300-lb (197-kN) thrust, similar to the power of the airline's 747s. The 2,200-nm (4074-km) range was ideal for United's transcontinental routes. Meanwhile, the 777 project was quietly shelved to re-emerge later as a larger long-haul twin-engined airliner, and all the extended range requirements were achieved by developments of the basic 767 airframe.

The 767 is built using mainly traditional structural techniques, but advances were made in the use of new materials. These included the latest aluminium alloys giving improved strength and corrosion resistance, and composites were used in a number of secondary and non-load bearing structures, saving weight of around 1,000 lb (454 kg) compared with the use of light alloys, increasing the payload accordingly. The main components incorporating composites were ailerons, elevators, rudder, spoilers, undercarriage doors, wing fixed leading- and trailing-edge fairings, engine cowling skins, wing to fuselage fairings and cabin floor panels.

For the most cost effective operations the 767 used supercritical wing technology with a 22 per cent thicker aft-loaded section developing more lift for less drag. This offered a lighter and simpler wing structure with less sweep back, and more fuel volume for longer range. A complex range of devices mounted on the main wing box provided control, including hydraulically operated outboard low-speed and inboard high-speed ailerons, leading-edge slats and trailing-edge flaps, and electrically operated flight and ground lift dump spoilers. The inboard ailerons droop with the flaps to keep the nose lower on the approach for a better view. The leading-edge slats are built in six sections and can be set in various configurations for optimum performance during take-off and landing. The single-slotted flaps occupy the wing trailing edge not covered by the ailerons. The swept tail surfaces are fitted with conventional rudder and elevators. The demands for greater efficiency required careful refinement of the design to achieve competitive performance.

Structural testing

Structural testing was an important element of the overall design programme, a complete static airframe being tested in three phases. The first phase was to ensure the 767 could carry the normal design loads, phase two was to determine whether the airframe would achieve the anticipated growth development with adequate margins, and the final phase was a test to destruction as a final proof loading. From April 1982 testing began on a fatigue test specimen and a year later had achieved the equivalent of 20 years operation, which was the equivalent to 50,000 flight profiles and well ahead of normal flying. The fatigue test airframe eventually completed 100,000 flight cycles – equivalent to some 40 years of airline operation, and structural modifications were found to be minimal proving the use of the new materials and processes in manufacture.

With a 21-in (6.4-m) fuselage stretch, the 767-300 accommodates an extra 50 passengers at the same gross weight as the 767-200ER. The 767-300ER followed and served as the basis for the first new-build cargo variant – the 767-300F. Launch customer for this version was UPS, ordering 30 examples in January 1993. The latest customer is All Nippon Airways, which received a single example (left) in 2002, to add to its 10 -200s, 34 -300s and 26 -300ERs.

Not only is the -400ER a further stretch of the 767, but it also ushers in a raft of major upgrades which effectively add up to a 'second-generation' 767. Along with the raked mainplane wing tips, intended to improve fuel economy, the -400ER has an upgraded flight deck, a new cabin interior and new landing gear.

aerodynamically too short. The cabin was wide enough for a twin-aisle layout, but the underfloor cargo hold only had room for one standard LD-3 container, not two across as with the wider body Airbus. Boeing therefore proposed the smaller LD-3A container to fit alongside the LD-3.

The vast Everett facility, which had been built for 747 production, was being expanded to accommodate the new aircraft assembly with a capability of producing a total of 200 wide-bodied aircraft annually and employing 12,000 people over the seven-year build up. The combined 767/777 line was expected to start at two aircraft a month over the first two years, and a market was seen for 1,500 767s and 777-100s worth $32 billion, with another 300 to 400 intercontinental 777-200s worth another $10 billion. The total investment in the programme by Boeing and its collaborative partners was estimated to reach $1.5 billion by 1986.

Finally, on 14 July 1978 the long awaited launch order was placed by United for 30 767-200s worth $1.2 billion for service entry in mid-1982, some 12 years after the original studies were made. United made the decision six weeks

Below: At the time of their launch much was made of fact that the 767 (foreground) and narrow-body 757 (rear) shared a common two-person flight deck, enabling crews to be licensed to operate both types without additional conversion training.